THE CREATION OF
THE ROCOCO
DECORATIVE STYLE

BY

FISKE KIMBALL

DOVER PUBLICATIONS, INC., NEW YORK

Published in Canada by General Publishing Company, Ltd., 30 Lesmill Road, Don Mills, Toronto, Ontario.

Published in the United Kingdom by Constable and Company, Ltd., 10 Orange Street, London WC2H 7EG.

This Dover edition, first published in 1980, is an unabridged, unaltered republication of the work originally published by the Philadelphia Museum of Art in 1943 under the title *The Creation of the Rococo*.

International Standard Book Number: 0-486-23989-6
Library of Congress Catalog Card Number: 79-55748

Manufactured in the United States of America
Dover Publications, Inc.
180 Varick Street
New York, N.Y. 10014

Preface

MY chief obligation is to the officials of the French archives and libraries in the period 1932-1938: at the Archives Nationales to M. H. Courteault, Director, and M. G. Bourgin, Secretary, among many others there; at the Bibliothèque Nationale to MM. P.-A. Lemoisne, Adhémar, Prinet and the other officials of the Cabinet des Estampes, particularly to M. Alfred M.-E. Marie, as well of the Département des Manuscrits; at the Louvre, to the staff of the Cabinet des Dessins; at the Bibliothèque des Arts Décoratifs; at the Bibliothèque de l'École des Beaux-Arts; at the Bibliothèque d'Art et Archéologie; at the Musée Carnavalet; at the Musée de Versailles; in the Archives Départementales, especially at Versailles and at Nancy, where M. Pierre Marot was particularly helpful; at Strasbourg, especially to M. Hans Haug, then Conservateur des Musées de la Ville.

Equally friendly have been the authorities in institutions outside of France: in Berlin at the Staatliche Kunstbibliothek; in Bonn at the Denkmalrat der Rheinprovinz; in Stockholm at the Royal Museum (where Professor Johnny Roosval and Dr. Arvid Baeckström also undertook researches for me), also at the Cooper Union and the Metropolitan Museum of Art in New York, and at the Philadelphia Museum of Art. Here the librarian, Paul Vanderbilt, the photographer, Charles Whitenack, and my secretary, Miss Elizabeth B. Kunkel have been of unwearied assistance. There are few of the major libraries of America to which I am not under obligation for the loan of rare volumes.

Among many private individuals not less kind, I feel particularly indebted to M. l'abbé Chagny at Lyon for making available to me his precious volume of drawings by Oppenord and to Madame la Duchesse de la Trémoïlle and Miss Belle da Costa Greene for assisting me to secure photographs of rooms otherwise inaccessible.

My gratitude is still deeper to several personal friends in France: to André Carlhian for constant assistance from his immense fund of knowledge of the French interior; to Ogden Codman for the freedom of his remarkable dossiers on the châteaux of France; to Marcel Aubert for valuable suggestions and introductions.

After the manuscript was completed, my friends Erwin Panofsky and Lionello Venturi, with both of whom I had previously had more than one stimulating discussion, were kind enough to read it, and to make several trenchant and welcome suggestions which it was not too late to turn to advantage.

Preface

The editors of the *Gazette des Beaux-Arts*, of *Metropolitan Museum Studies*, of the *Art Bulletin*, of *Art in America*, and of the *Journal of the Warburg and Courtauld Institutes*, have indulgently permitted the inclusion of material I first published in their pages, as papers which are here revised and brought into relation, along with much else.

I should be remiss indeed if I did not gratefully acknowledge the financial assistance, for travel, photography and publication, of the Philadelphia Museum of Art, of the American Council of Learned Societies, and of the Carl Schurz Memorial Foundation.

In all these researches I have never failed to encounter a uniform courtesy from the owners and custodians of old buildings, to all of whom it is a delight once more to render thanks.

The work, pursued in Paris and elsewhere in Europe in 1932, 1935, and 1938, has since suffered from the threat and the vicissitudes of war, which twice involved packing up the volumes at the Cabinet des Estampes and have since made them, and certain documents elsewhere, unavailable for further examination and photography. Fortunately the greater part of the relevant manuscript designs had previously been photographed for me. For photographs of existing works, however, it has been necessary to have recourse mainly to previous publications, reproductions from which have been held to the minimum requisite to make the text intelligible. For these I can only express here, to the authors and publishers, now inaccessible to correspondence, my deepest sense of appreciation and obligation.

FISKE KIMBALL

Philadelphia, September 8, 1942.

Contents

Contents

Illustrations

[ix]

Illustrations

Illustrations

Illustrations

Illustrations

Illustrations

Illustrations

Illustrations

Illustrations

Introduction

WE seek in this book to establish more precisely the origin and development of that phase of decorative art which, emerging in France about 1700 and characteristic of the reign of Louis XV, dominated Europe until the advent of classicism in the latter years of the century.

The same general artistic movement had, inevitably, manifestations not only in ornament, but in painting and sculpture, as well as in architecture. In architecture these included novel treatments of the spatial and plastic form of buildings. Brilliant as were some of these manifestations, supremely so in the painting of Watteau, the primary sphere of the movement was, to a degree almost unique in artistic history, in the realm of decoration: in the interior, whether domestic or religious, and in ornament, chiefly the ornament of surface. Thus it is not merely an arbitrary limitation when we devote our discussion to this sphere. We do not undertake to cover, on the one hand, the major arts, or, on the other, the individual crafts except when their practitioners assume a leading rôle in the field of decorative design generally. It is in the interior and its enrichment that we shall find the essential creative works here discussed.

The art with which we are concerned presents first of all a problem of nomenclature. We deal with things, which we hope better to understand, but also with words, to which without violence to historic or current usage, we hope to give greater precision. We realize that by adopting the word rococo, in a book published in English and dealing primarily with France, we expose ourselves to a belief, still widespread, that any art called by that name can only be trivial and "debased." A study of the history of its usage, however, should convince the reader that no other term so fully corresponds in scope with the art we are discussing, or applies so properly to its central as well as to its extreme or provincial manifestations—indeed that we are fortunate to have a term where the correspondence is of such exactness.

The contemporaries of this art, like those of many other creative movements, called it merely "modern." We find the expression "le goût moderne" applied in 1713[1] to work of 1704. This is precisely such work as we consider belongs to the genesis of the movement. By 1738,[2] Jacques-François Blondel speaks generally of such work as in "le goût de ce siècle," "le goût du siècle." By that time an extreme phase, characterized by asymmetry, was still more modern. Blondel writes of various designs for the crowns of panels:[3] "une partie est tenue symmétrisée & l'autré dans le goût du temps." Obviously these contemporary designations, rendered obsolete by the passage of time, will not help us with our problem of choosing a general name for this work.

For subordinate aspects and elements, indeed, early usage is more helpful to us. To the limited phase characterized by asymmetry was applied the term "le genre pittoresque," which we shall adopt in that meaning. In the titles of certain compositions in this phase, from about 1734, we find the word "rocaille," both as a noun and as an adjective, acquiring gradually, by comparison with its older meaning of rock-work and shellwork for the incrustation of

[1] Germain Brice: *Description de Paris*, 1713 ed., II, 31.
[2] *De la distribution des maisons de plaisance*, II, 1738, iv, 95.
[3] *Ibid.*, 149, discussing his Plate 92.

grottoes and fountains,[4] a new and wider sense as a designation of style. Thus Jacques-François Blondel wrote in 1772: "Il y a plusieurs années qu'il sembloit que nôtre siècle étoit celui des Rocailles."[5] Although the word was sometimes extended to cover the work of the whole movement,[6] we shall find it wiser to restrict its application, as at first, to the later and more extravagant phase.

Among modern writers, the French—favoured by the approximate coincidence of artistic movements with their reigns—tend to employ the name of Louis XV. The relation of artistic and dynastic events is at best a superficial one, whether in causation or in time. We shall see that the movement associated with Louis XV had well begun before he came to the throne; the neo-classic reaction which succeeded it was felt in France some years before his death.

A word still earlier applied, and from the beginning specifically equated with the art we discuss, is the word rococo. Like so many designations of artistic styles—like Gothic, like baroque—it was coined in contempt, doubtless as a derivative of *rocaille* on the analogy of *barocco*. Rarely can one fix so exactly the origin of a word. Delécluze wrote, late in life, of a brilliant and short-lived fellow-student in the atelier of David: "Ces expressions: *Pompadour*, *rococo*, à peu près admises aujourd'hui dans la conversation, pour désigner le goût à la mode pendant le règne de Louis XV, ont été employées pour la première fois par Maurice Quaï en 1796-97. Alors ces locutions (on pourrait dire cet argot) n'étaient usitées et comprises que dans les ateliers de peinture."[7] We find the word rococo in literature, still close to its origin but more loosely and broadly used, in Stendhal's *Promenades dans Rome*, 1828 (I, 244): "Me permettra-t-on un mot bas? Le Bernin fut le père de ce mauvais goût designé dans les ateliers sous le non un peu vulgaire de rococo." Victor Hugo in 1839 applies it to the architecture of Nancy, a Louis XV town beyond all others, and also to that of Lisbon, rebuilt after the earthquake of 1755 and thus predominantly of the same moment. We see too, in what he writes, a first glimmering of aesthetic appreciation: "Les clochers de la cathédrale sont des poivrières Pompadour. Cependant je me suis reconcilié avec Nancy . . . la place de l'Hôtel-de-Ville est une des places rococo les plus jolies, les plus gaies et les plus complètes, que j'aie vues. . . . C'est une place marquise . . . [de] cette ville toute dans la style Louis XV. L'architecture du XVIIIᵉ siècle, quand elle est riche, finit par racheter son mauvais goût. Sa fantaisie végète et s'épanouit au sommet des édifices en buissons de fleurs si extravagants et si touffus que toute colère s'en va et qu'on s'y acoquine . . . La partie inférieure des edifices Pompadour est nue, morose et lugubre. Le rococo à de vilains pieds."[8]

The word did not appear in the 1835 edition of the dictionary of the French Academy, but was first defined in the supplement of 1842: "Rococo se dit trivialement du genre d'orne-ment, de style et de dessin qui appartient à l'école du regne de Louis XV et du commencement

---

[4] The Abbé Bouillet: 'Contribution à l'histoire des rocailleurs," in *Réunion de la société des beaux-arts des dé-partements*, XVII, 1893, 322-336, deals with this older meaning from 1540 onwards. The Abbé Lacombe in his *Dictionnaire portatif des beaux-arts* still gives the word in this sense only, even in the second edition of 1759.

[5] *Cours d'architecture*, III, 1772, lviii.

[6] E.g. by Victor Hugo: "Franckfort et Mayence sont des cités gothiques déjà plongées dans la renaissance, et même, par beaucoup de côtés, dans le style rocaille et chinois." *Le Rhin*, letter XXIII, 1839.

[7] M.-E.-J. Delécluze: *Louis David, son école et son temps*, 1855, 82n, kindly called to my attention by Walter Friedlaender. Cf. his *Hauptströmungen der fransözischen Malerei von David bis Cézanne*, I, 1930, 32, 53ff.

[8] *Le Rhin*, 1842, Letter XXIX, 1839, cited from the edition of 1855, II, 171.

Introduction

de Louis XVI. Le genre rococo a suivi et précédé le Pompadour, qui n'est de même qu'une nuance du rococo. Le rococo de l'architecte Opdenord. Il se dit en général de tout ce qui est vieux et hors de mode dans les arts, la littérature, le costume, les manières, etc. Aimer le rococo. Tomber dans le rococo. Cela est bien rococo." In spite of the addition of a general meaning, we see the word crystallized here as applying specifically to the characteristic work of the reign of Louis XV. So it was used by the Goncourts in 1860, when they spoke of Madame de Pompadour as "une patronne de luxe et de la rocaille . . . la marraine et la reine du *Rococo.*"[9] In the latest edition of the dictionary of the Academy, 1935, it is defined as "un genre . . . à la mode au dixhuitième siècle . . . caracterisé par la profusion des ornements contournés."

Among art historians, the Germans were first to take up and fix the word as a formal designation of the general period and style of Louis XV, both in France and elsewhere under French influence. The earliest such use there of which we know, in 1840, applying to Meissonnier,[10] is already in the sense now prevailing. Jacob Burckhardt, to be sure, employed it in 1843[11] for what he himself later called baroque. The artistic equation rococo-Louis XV, then already adopted by French men of letters, was, however, soon permanently established also in Germany,[12] where for the past generation no disparagement of the style has been implied by this name, in spite of occasional survivals of a derogatory overtone in general parlance.

French scholars, in view of the connotation of ridicule which the word originally carried, have been loath to apply it to one of their most genial creations.[13] As late as 1894 one might still say that only in Germany was the name rococo used formally in the history of art.[14] French art-historians today are apt to employ it only for the later and more extravagant manifestations of the style, particularly those abroad, for which, with greater historical exactitude, they also use the expression *style rocaille.* Nevertheless with the gradual aesthetic acceptance of the work itself, the broader usage of rococo is gaining ground in other languages beside German.

English use of the term began by 1836, when we read: "There are two especial new *mots d'argot, rococo* and *décousu.*"[15] The *Oxford Dictionary* in 1909 defined it, applying to furniture or architecture, as "Having the characteristics of Louis Quatorze or Louis Quinze workmanship, such as conventional shell- and scrollwork and meaningless decoration, excessively or tastelessly florid or ornate." In common English parlance the word is still loosely applied in a derogatory sense. Its use by art-historians, however, has tended to follow developments in Germany.

[9] *Les mâitresses de Louis XV,* 1860, II, 110.

[10] Nagler's *Künstler-Lexikon,* article Meissonnier.

[11] "Uber die vorgotischen Kirchen am Niederrhein," in *Lerschs Niederreinisches Jahrbuch,* 1843.

[12] A. Springer: "Der Rococostil," in *Bildern aus den neueren Kunstgeschichte;* A. von Zahn: "Barock, Rococo und Zopf," in *Zeitschrift für bildende Kunst,* VIII, 1873. The history of usage in Germany is best summarized by H. Tietze: *Die Methode der Kunstgeschichte,* 1913, 85-87.

[13] H. von Geymüller discusses French usage in *Die Baukunst der Renaissance in Frankreich,* 1898, I, 265 ff. Himself a nephew of the Comte de Laborde, he cites with special respect the judgment of Henri Destailleur (1822-1893) of whom he writes: "Den Ausdruck *Style rocaille* or *rococo* hat er (so weit ich mich errinere) niemals gebraucht."

[14] P. Jessen: *Das Ornament des Rococo,* 1894.

[15] *Fraser's Magazine,* XIII, 214.

The Creation of the Rococo

The rococo has ordinarily been interpreted[16] as a specific last, extreme phase of the baroque —somewhat as the Flamboyant is of the Gothic—taking form to be sure, on French soil, but under Italian influence. Our text will be largely concerned with the relation of the baroque and rococo, and with the question of Italian influence as a factor in the genesis of the rococo in France. In our present consideration of nomenclature, we need only remark one aberrant usage, which, by exception, equates the rococo with late baroque as a whole, and thus automatically makes its whole origin Italian. This equation appears, to my knowledge, only in the writings of Marcel Reymond,[17] which give the word a meaning wholly foreign to other current usage. He sees in Italy from the time of Innocent XII (i.e. from 1691) "se créer et se developper l'art du rococo avec tous ses raffinements," incorporated first by Sardi at Sta. Maria Madellena at Rome, and in Santa Maria dell' Orto, the Palazzo Doria and the Palazzo del Grillo. Obviously such a usage would beg the whole question of the genesis of the rococo. The character of this indigenous late Italian baroque to which Reymond applies the word is essentially different from that of the rococo as generally understood, which, as no one doubts, reached Italy from France.

There has been a tendency in Germany to apply the term rococo to the character of later phases of artistic styles generally. This first appeared with Burckhardt, then using the word as equivalent to baroque, when he wrote, "Rokoko entsteht immer da, wo die eigentliche Bedeutung der Formen vergessen worden ist, die Formen selbst aber um die Effectes willen fortwährend und zwar mit Misverstand benutzt werden. Es gibt sonach einen römischen, gotischen u.s.w. Rokoko."[18] This usage is linked with the effort to find a rhythmic periodicity in artistic development, pursued by such disciples of Burckhardt as Wölfflin and Schmarsow,[19] and involves a conceptual definition of the formal artistic characteristics of the rococo which must be forcibly imposed, with a vicious intellectualism, on the endless variety of individual creative works. We recognize, as others have done,[20] that such use of well-established designations of a single movement to apply to tendencies present in all periods of art is apt to destroy the meaning of words which, just because they are external, cover all such variety in that movement, and thus do no violence to the complexity of artistic phenomena.

As in any broad study of artistic creation and evolution, the questions to be answered are: what? how? when? where? and who? As to the "why," we follow Goethe's sage advice, and do not ask. It is possible to point out certain relationships with political, social and economic movements, certain analogies with trends in criticism and the other arts, certain influences and derivations, but not causalities. Essentially, we shall find, the development is immanent, the miracle of creation is wrapped in the mystery of personal artistic individuality.

The question "how"—regarding the formal and aesthetic nature of works of the rococo— has received various answers. We cannot escape the conviction that many recent attempts at

[16] E.g. among many others by Andreas Lindblom: "Rokokons uppkomst" (The Origin of the Rococo), in *Ord och Bild*, 1924, 561-577.

[17] In A. Michel: *Histoire de l'art*, VI, i, 155 ff., Hermann Voss, in his *Malerei des Barock in Rom*, 1924, 614, adopts the name "Roman rococo" for late baroque painting of the eighteenth century in Rome, but fully appreciates the "Entwicklung des Franzosentums."

[18] *Loc. cit.*

[19] A. Schmarsow: *Barock und Rokoko*, 1897, e.g. page 359.

[20] E.g. Tietze, *op. cit.*, 98-99.

Introduction

...nesis have been premature. Scholars—particularly scholars in Germany, where inventory and monographic study of their own art have indeed approached exhaustiveness—have proceeded on the assumption that the philological groundwork in the fields here concerned has likewise previously been completed, and that the time has been ripe for drawing conclusions as to the sum of artistic, sociological, and national characteristics. I believe it will be appreciated, after what is presented here, that many fine-spun deductions as to these matters have rested on inadequate factual premises, that much of the imposing edifice of historical and aesthetic theorizing, too hastily run up, has been built upon sand. We shall leave discussion of these, as well as any new attempt at characterization, until after determination of what actually happened.

This is accordingly, in many regards, a consciously old-fashioned book, devoted in the first instance to establishing with exactness the sequence of events, the identity and rôle of personalities individually concerned with them, in the genesis of the rococo and in its successive transformations. The questions regarding these have remained without adequate or convincing answers. The remoter converging lines of influence have been recognized, the chronology of certain individual monuments has been well established, but as the moment of synthesis approaches the existing studies become unsatisfactory, above all in matters of sequence and of personal responsibility. To these matters, at the decisive moments, earlier scholars have given little serious study.

We here attempt to investigate more fully who were the truly creative forces, what were their real initiatives and contributions, and when these were made. It is essential, for instance, especially in the royal works, to know who were in control at any particular moment, who were their subordinates, and what were their respective shares in the making of important designs. To establish the initiative it is equally necessary to know the sequence of different works, and thus to give certain parts of the book the form of annals. We trust it will not be thought pedantry that we undertake, in some instances, a most minute dating, at moments of intense creative activity such as the great year 1699 or the lustrum 1730 to 1735.

Our problem does indeed offer difficulties, from whatever side it is attacked. The engraved models of the ornementalists,[21] from which certain scholars have hoped to reach a solution, cannot alone furnish the necessary basis. The larger number of their plates are undated; where they are dated their execution usually lagged some years after the creation of the designs, the varying delay introducing a new element of confusion. To work from the engraved models, moreover, is to run the known danger of drawing from imaginary compositions conclusions as to current practise. Similar dangers beset any attempt to infer the course of evolution merely from the systematic handbooks published in successive editions at short intervals during the period in question. They do not lead but follow the course of events.

Of the monuments themselves, many of the most important have been lost through remodelling or destruction. Saint-Cloud, Clagny, Marly, Meudon, Choisy, Bellevue, and La Muette are gone, as in the Palais-Royal of the Regent. Versailles was constantly remodelled

[21] Cf. H. Destailleur: *Notices sur quelques artistes français*, 1863, and *Recueil d'estampes relatives à l'ornementation des appartements*, 1863; D. Guilmard: *Les Maîtres ornemenistes*, 1880; P. Jessen: *Der Ornamentstich*, 1920, *Rococo Engravings*, 1922; R. Berliner: *Ornamentale Vorlage-Blätter*, 1925; and *Katalog der Ornamentstich-Sammlung der Staatlichen Kunstbibliothek*, Berlin, 1936-1939.

even in the eighteenth century, and all but the royal apartments have been swept away. The private hôtels have fared little better. The churches have been denuded of their commemorative monuments and their woodwork. An extensive critique of modification and of restoration is necessary before conclusions can be drawn from the monuments.

The greatest difficulty, inherent in the artistic organization of the time, attends the effort to distribute personal creative responsibility. Under Mansart, in the Bâtiments du Roi, was developed the first great modern architectural office in which the functions of director, comptroller, inspector, architect and draughtsman were specialized. Its uniform official façade was a mask of anonymity for all but the Premier Architecte, who received all public credit. Hitherto little attempt has been made to penetrate this mask, to distinguish the creative contribution of individual designers.

As materials for the solution of our problems, to surmount these difficulties, the most important are the original drawings of designers of the period. They show the initial form of works modified or destroyed; indeed, in successive studies, they may even show the process of creative gestation. In many instances they bear a date or can be dated by accompanying memoirs. Most important of all, they show the technique, often also the handwriting, of the actual designer. Rarely, to be sure, is there a signature, unless it be that of the official endorsement: "Bon à exécuter, Mansart." But comparison with known specimens of the handwriting of the men employed in the Bâtiments at the time, even the coincidence of appearance and disappearance of certain techniques and handwritings with the dates and duration of the employment of certain artists, will often suffice to establish the authorship of the designs beyond doubt. Thus a key to the solution of our problems is the study and identification of the manuscript designs.

By far the most considerable body of them is the mass of drawings of Bâtiments du Roi, preserved integrally in the series o¹ of the Archives Nationales.[22] Here are nearly two thousand cartons, including, beside written documents, manuscript drawings to the number of many thousands, covering every royal construction of the old régime. It is not unfair to say that they have slept in their cartons little disturbed by scholars. Dussieux, Nolhac, Magnien, Deshairs, Marquet de Vasselot, the Comte de Fels and others have utilized the drawings in the study of particular works, with not much critical discrimination as to their authorship. But in general this vast body of designs has been little exploited, and it has remained neglected for the study of our problem.

Other drawings of the royal works are dispersed in the Bibliothèque de l'Institut, the Archives des Bâtiments Civils, and the Cabinet des Dessins of the Louvre, which has the papers of Le Brun.

Second only in importance to the archives of the Bâtiments are the papers of the De Cotte collection at the Cabinet des Estampes.[23] Here are more than two thousand drawings, for both public and private works, from the period crucial for us. Many which have been uncritically published as drawn by De Cotte himself may now be recognized as from the hands of his collaborators.

[22] Cf. H. de Curzon: *Répertoire numérique des Archives de la Maison du Roi* (Série o¹), 1903.
[23] Cf. P. Marcel: *Inventaire des papiers . . . de Robert de Cotte . . .* 1906.

Introduction

Drawings of the principal private designers are scattered far and wide: those of Oppenord in Berlin, Stockholm, Lyons, Paris and New York, those of Nicolas Pineau (admirably published by Deshairs)[24] chiefly in Paris and Leningrad.

Of written documents the chief body is again those of the Bâtiments du Roi, with their immense wealth of memoranda and accounts. Jules Guiffrey, by publishing[25] the volumes of accounts for 1664 to 1715 (o¹2129-2215), with his exhaustive indices, provided the engine for all subsequent study of the buildings of Louis XIV, which previous writers are far from having exhausted. The accounts for the reign of Louis XV (o¹2216-2278) remain unpublished and unindexed. Fortunately those on Versailles have been systematically exploited by Nolhac, and those on several other royal châteaux have been embodied in documented monographs.

Rich mines of further documents have been made available by the publication of the *Archives de l'art français*, of the *Procès-verbaux* of the Academies, of the correspondence of the directors of the French Academy in Rome. They are supplemented by the unexampled wealth of diaries and memoirs, from which much that has been hitherto unobserved may be brought to bear on the monuments.

In the vast field of Parisian topography only a few buildings have received really adequate documentary study. The series *Les Vieux hôtels de Paris*,[26] which offers so much, nevertheless leaves the dates and authorship of interior features very uncertain. Here the successive editions of published Paris guides and descriptions, extending at a few years' interval throughout the eighteenth century, offer many opportunities for following the construction and transformation of buildings.

All these resources and many others we shall lay under contribution.

The study of French art of the period at the hands of Frenchmen has been embodied, with few exceptions, in monographs, whether on individual artists or individual monuments. What is needed, after verification and completion of such studies, is to combine the many individual works in a single series, which alone can bring out the priority and sequence of truly creative acts. In the few instances where efforts have recently been made to combine chronologically the studies of individual monuments and artists,[27] it is obvious that the attempt has been unsuccessful, and that the task is still to be accomplished.

Whatever one's devotion to scholarship in the abstract, one obviously does not devote years of study to a body of works of art without having or gaining a keen delight in them, a deep aesthetic enjoyment. The contempt and contumely of the nineteenth century for the rococo has reserved this enjoyment as an experience for our generation. To partake in it, we must lay aside the prejudices of our grandfathers and our fathers, even many of our own: the moral prejudices which confounded artistic qualities with presumed moral qualities of the period, as "corrupt" and "frivolous"; the older artistic prejudices in favour of purity of self-contained elements, as against dynamic unity of ensembles, the newer artistic prejudices in favour of plastic form and of spatial form as against form in line and surface; the architectural prejudices, older and newer, that confine all merit in buildings to the expression of structure

[24] *Nicolas et Dominique Pineau* (*Dessins originaux des maîtres décorateurs*), n.d.
[25] *Les Comptes des Bâtiments du Roi sous le règne de Louis XIV*, 5 vols., 1881-1901.
[26] Edited by J. Vacquier and others, 21 vols., 1908-1919.
[27] E.g., in M.-J. Ballot: *Le Décor intérieur au XVIIIe siècle*, 1930.

The Creation of the Rococo

and of "function" in a narrow sense, seeking vainly to exclude from art all free play of form, whether spatial, plastic, or linear. Finally one must overcome the historical prejudices which find an absolute "religious character," for instance, only in the buildings of the Middle Ages, forgetting that the baroque had its own intense religious experience in a Saint Ignatius Loyola, a Saint Teresa, a Saint Francis de Sales, that Louis XIV must have had more than a false bigotry or a passion for worldly fame to raise, in moments of deepest defeat, the dome of the Invalides, the chapel of Versailles, the mantle of the choir of Notre Dame, and that even the eighteenth century must have had its own passionate devotion, to bring into being the great churches—so different from those of the Gothic—of Saint-Sulpice or of Vierzehnheiligen.

This book is obviously addressed primarily to that elite of scholars whose reception of its conclusions will influence the writing of art history generally. Nevertheless we are not without hope that some cultivated laymen may enjoy gaining an insight into the process of artistic creation in a period of the greatest brilliance.

We have previously studied several of the crucial problems, in published discussions here embodied in their place. Many other such problems remain to be attacked here, particularly in the earlier and later phases. Above all, the solution of all these problems must be brought into relationship, if we are to understand the genesis and evolution of the rococo.

Background

THE background for the creation of the rococo in France was the architecture and ornament of the reign of Louis XIV down to the end of the seventeenth century, which we shall have first to analyse. It is vital for us to have a clear understanding of this art, its sources, its character and its evolution, to appreciate the degree of originality in the work which followed, to gauge the extent and even the nature of the creative achievement, and to determine the moment and the agents of its genesis.

The remoter background of the early years of Louis XIV, during his minority (1643-1678) and during his early personal rule (1661-1678), may be sketched summarily, to bring out the major forces in play. We must presume the reader has some general knowledge of baroque art in Italy and in France, so that we may confine ourselves to a brief statement of those factors relevant to our subject. The central period of the art of the reign (1678-1699) must be discussed more fully, not only to define the character of its work but to establish the contributions of individuals, who remained upon the scene during the creative epoch of the King's last years, the first years of the new century. Even that immediate background of the central period we have naturally to discuss not for itself, not as its own end and goal, but as means and approach to the artistic movement which forms our subject proper.

Remoter Background:
Early Years of Louis XIV, 1643-1678

In the earlier periods of the reign of Louis XIV, French art, which had previously felt the influence of mannerism and of the early baroque, was coming to terms with the newly created Roman high baroque. The time of greatest baroque influence, which had begun with Rubens' work in Paris in 1625, was in the early years of Mazarin. The calling of Bernini to France in 1665 represented the culmination of Italian prestige. His visit, however, actually marked the downfall of Italian baroque supremacy; its failure was the beginning of the end of French artistic subjection.

It is essential for us to study the infiltration of high-baroque elements into France, not to demonstrate that their adoption was the differentia or stimulus of the rococo, for we shall find that this was not the case, but because it will demonstrate that most of them had already been domesticated long prior to the genesis of the rococo, without having brought it into being.

Vouet, founder of the French school of painting, who had led the way to Rome in 1612, had returned with many assistants in 1627. Poussin had gone in 1624, Errard, with Claude Lorrain, in 1627. Their style rests primarily on the eclectic mannerism of the Bolognese, as embodied, for instance, in the decoration of the Farnese gallery by the Carracci, 1597-1609.

The real impact of the high baroque came in a new wave, about 1640. From 1639 to 1650 Stefano della Bella, greatest of the Italian engravers of baroque ornament, was in Paris. In 1640 Roland Fréart de Chambray, with his brother, was sent to Italy to bring to France "the greatest virtuosi,"[1] and to induce Poussin to return with them. Among their train was Adam

---

[1] Fréart de Chambray: *Parallèle de l'architecture antique et de la moderne*, 1651, *Epître dédicatoire.*

The Creation of the Rococo

Philippon. While Chambray was moulding the reliefs of Trajan's columns, Philippon was drawing the "beaux morceaux d'ornéments," modern as well as antique, which he was afterwards to publish. Mignard was in Italy from 1636 to 1656; Puget, from 1641 to 1643, again, working with Pietro da Cortona, from 1646 to 1649; Le Brun, from 1642 to 1646; Michel Anguier from 1642 to 1652; Girardon, for a few months, in 1649 to 1650. From 1644 to 1648 Romanelli, who had worked first for Pietro da Cortona, then for Bernini, was in Paris in the employ of Mazarin; he returned for the years 1655 to 1658 in the service of the Crown.

The decisive works of the high baroque were already dazzlingly visible to French students in the Rome of the 'forties. Bernini's celebrity was fully established. His tabernacle of Saint-Peter's had been executed in 1624-1633, the baldachino in 1631-1632. The Palazzo Barberini, on which Borromini had worked under Maderna and under Bernini, had been built in 1626-1632. Borromini's own San Carlo alle Quattro Fontane, as yet without its façade, was constructed in 1634-1641; his San Filippo Neri, in 1637-1650; his Palazzo Falconieri, in 1640-1643; his Sant' Ivo della Sapienza was begun in 1642. In sculpture, Bernini's groups for Scipio Borghese, completed by 1622, had first established his fame; his Saint Theresa, undertaken in 1644, marked its apogee. In painting, the school of the Carracci had yielded to new tendencies, among which the classical rationalism of Poussin was less influential than the bravura of Pietro da Cortona. He decorated the great hall of the Palazzo Barberini in 1633-1639, the first of his rooms of the Pitti Palace at Florence in 1637, the others in 1641-1647.

We should be greatly mistaken if we assumed that the eyes of the French in Rome were turned at this period solely to works of antiquity and of the time of Raphael. Philippon's drawings of ornament, engraved by the young Jean Lepautre and issued in 1645,[2] are one concrete evidence to the contrary; more than half are baroque elements: herms and masks, trophies of arms, friezes of foliage with grotesque sphinxes, fountains with dragons. In the sculpture of Puget and, to a less degree, of Girardon, the Italian baroque influence is too obvious to require specification. We shall cite instances in the decorative treatment of interiors which establish how keenly Le Brun had observed works in contemporary Italy.

Of the three dominant artists of the high baroque in Rome it was Pietro da Cortona, at once painter and architect, whose influence in France was most immediate, direct, and traceable. While he himself was still working on the decorations of the Stanze dei Planeti, his assistant Romanelli was already at work in Paris. Before the Sala di Apollo was completed from Cortona's designs by Ciro Ferri (1659-1660), Le Brun was working in a similar manner at Vaux; the last of the series, the Sala di Saturno (1663-1665),[3] was scarcely executed before Le Brun was engaged on the Appartement du Roi at Versailles.

We stress these relationships particularly to establish that French decoration had by no means to wait, as some have supposed, until the advent of Oppenord in Rome (1692) for an observation of high-baroque forms, nor for his return to Paris (1699) for their influence to be felt in France.

Cortona's work was not only the fullest expression of historical painting in high-baroque

[2] *Curieuse recherches de plusieurs beaux morceaux d'ornement antiques et modernes, tant dans la ville de Rome que autres villes, & lieux d'Italie, dessinés par moi Adam Philippon* . . . Paris, 1645.

[3] For the dating, see H. P. Geisenheimer: *Pietro da Cortona e gli affreschi del Palazzo Pitti*, Florence, 1909.

Background

Rome, but was a repertory of baroque motifs of decoration scarcely less varied and advanced than we find in the architecture of Borromini. In the corner supports of the Barberini ceiling —candelabra-like in composition, with pairs of supporting figures in violent action—broken pediments, volutes, masks, cartouches, vases and garlands disguise all structural lines. Here all this is a painted simulation of plastic stucco; at the Pitti Palace the decorative elements are modelled in actual relief, with unexampled splendour of development:

> The individual members, the profiling are handled with the most extreme subtlety. The old classical rules seem forgotten. The profiles are doubled and tripled, as well as overspread at pleasure with an ever changing dynamic ornament, that enlivens with dazzling lights and deep shadows surfaces already curved in themselves. Fluttering banderoles, draperies, and garlands of stucco overspread otherwise vacant surfaces, unite abutting elements. Figures, shellwork, cartouches and masks hide the points of intersection. Every hard even line is consciously avoided. A veritable vibration is achieved. Round arches rise against gable-segments, only to be immediately interrupted by a projection. The cartouches and shields turn and bend, curved lines predominate. Nowhere does one encounter a uniform circle or square, for its place has been taken by the more exciting forms, suggesting movement and depth, of the oval and rectangle.[4]

Obviously men who knew such work were familiar with baroque principles and with the baroque vocabulary.

In French architecture also it was in the time of Mazarin that baroque influence was at its height, notably in the work of Louis Le Vau, born in 1612. Even though, so far as we know, he had never been in Italy, his Hôtel Lambert, begun before 1642, his château of Vaux-le-Vicomte, constructed for Fouquet in 1657-1661, are rich in characteristic high-baroque spatial forms such as the concave approach, the oval room. His new constructions at the Louvre included the projecting circular Rotonde de Mars and Rotonde d'Apollon, built in 1655-1658. This sway of the baroque extended until Bernini's visit of 1665, which did not fail to leave one typically Italian work in France, the altar of the Val-de-Grace, as executed in modified form from his design by Mattia Rossi and Le Duc,[5] with its six twisted columns, its great horizontal chaplet of palm and rose, its arcs rising to support the canopy.

The common error has been to suppose that the severely academic, anti-baroque attitude, which characterized French art after 1665, prevailed already in the 'forties and 'fifties. The founding of the Academy of Painting and Sculpture in 1648 has been carelessly regarded as a major illustration. Actually the Academy of Painting and Sculpture, as is well known, was founded for different motives—to support the royal artists against the *maîtrise*. The artists active with Le Brun in its foundation included such men as Guillain, with his occasional earthy realism, and Van Obstal, a Fleming strongly under the influence of Rubens. Discussions of doctrine, such as those later so typical of the Academy of Architecture, formed no part of the early deliberations of the Academy of Painting. True, its statutes from the beginning called

---

[4] Translated from H. Posse in *Jahrbuch der preuszischen Kunstsammlungen*, XL, 1919, 161. In certain of the ceilings at the Pitti, to be sure, lunettes and central panels remain unbroken semicircles and rectangles.

[5] Cf. Marcel Reymond: "L'autel du Val-de-Grace," in *Gazette des beaux-arts*, IVe pér., V, 1911, 367-394. The altar of the Abbaye du Bec (now at Bernay), dating from 1685, is a provincial version of the design. Cf. also Reymond: "Autels berninesque en France," *ibid.*, IX, 1913, 207-218.

for the holding of "résonnements des arts de peinture et de sculpture," but not until 1653 did the Academy remind itself of this function[6] and once more, after solemn preparations, the matter seems to have been neglected in the midst of pressing practical exigencies.

It took the insistence of Colbert to force the actual inauguration of such conferences in 1666, and the authoritative registration of their conclusions. It was then that the academic doctrine took official form, elevating to dogmas the *grand goût*, the drawing of Raphael and Poussin, the Roman precepts and practice of Le Brun. Even then their victory was not without a struggle. The partisans of color, of the Venetians, and of Rubens, led by Philippe de Champaigne, took up the cudgels in the *querelle du dessin et de la couleur*, of Poussinistes and Rubénistes, in 1671-1672, in which Le Brun had for the moment the deciding word.[7]

This was the moment of Colbert's foundation, in 1666, of the Academy in Rome, to regularize the Italian studies which had so long been customary for ambitious French artists. Here it was indeed desired, from the very beginning, to cultivate "le bon goût et la manière des Anciens."[8] The admiration of the Academy—inaugurated under the directorship of Errard, whose own Roman studies had antedated the high-baroque—was given in sculpture to the antique, in painting to Raphael and the Carracci, in decoration to the Loggie of the Vatican and the Farnese gallery. Its regimen, in copying Raphael and the antique, in measuring ancient buildings, had little relation to the contemporary art of Italy, then at the very culmination of the baroque. This insulation of the pensioners from the artistic life of Rome, often remarked,[9] was in the most striking contrast with the intimate commerce which had prevailed a generation earlier.

Similar motives of academic purism dominated in the founding of the Academy of Architecture in 1671, "pour conférer sur l'art et les règles de l'architecture."[10] Its principal occupation, from its first séance onward, was to read and comment the ancient authorities of Rome and of the Renaissance who had codified the orders and discussed ancient buildings: Vitruvius, Palladio, Alberti, Serlio, Delorme and Bullant. The same motives led Claude Perrault, who assisted sometimes at the sessions, to publish his translation of Vitruvius in 1673. Much has been made of his contention[11] that the proportions of the orders rest, not on immutable laws like musical harmony, but on custom and consent. But it is a far cry from this philosophic conclusion to its modern interpretations,[12] which would make of Perrault the spiritual destroyer of the academism he in fact so actively promoted.

The academic victory over the baroque reflected the new political prestige of France, which no longer willingly accepted the leading-strings of contemporary Italy even in artistic matters. It reflected the discipline which Colbert, like the King, now wished to impose in artistic

---

[6] *Procès-verbaux de l'Académie Royale de Peinture et de Sculpture*, ed. A. de Montaiglon, I, 1875, 72, 74, 76-77.

[7] A. Fontaine: *Conférences inédites de l'Académie Royale de Peinture et de Sculpture*, n.d. (1903); *Les doctrines d'art en France*, 1909.

[8] Letter of Charles Perrault, on behalf of Colbert, to Poussin, written about 1665 but not sent, in *Correspondance des directeurs de l'Académie de France à Rome*, ed. by A. de Montaiglon, Paris, 1887, I, 1.

[9] E.g., by A. E. Brinckmann: *Barockskulptur*, 1919, II, 328.

[10] *Procès-verbaux de l'Académie Royale d'Architecture*, ed. by H. Lemonnier, I, 1911, 3.

[11] *Vitruvius*, 100, 102n; *Ordonnance des cinq espèces de colonnes*, 1683. Preface.

[12] E.g., C. Gurlitt: *Geschichte des Barockstils...*, II, 156: "Dieser Gedanke ... macht Perrault geistig zum Begründer des Rococo."

as well as political affairs—a discipline which in art was thought to be found only in academic grammar and rules—rules which had been flouted by the extravagances of the baroque, the licences of Borromini. More than all, however, the change reflected a purely artistic reaction against the height of baroque influence and baroque tendency which had so lately been reached in French design and French decoration themselves. While in the field of theory there was a triumph of academism; in actual practise there followed a progressive enfranchisement of French creative effort, soon to dominate all Europe.

By contrast with the acceptability of Le Vau's rotundas of the Louvre under Mazarin, we may note the criticism of Colbert in 1669 on similar forms proposed by Le Vau for the Château Neuf at Versailles: "les figures rondes qu'il affecte aux vestibules et salons . . . ne sont point du bon goût en architecture, particulièrement pour les dehors."[13]

We may illustrate the change of view by a less hackneyed example than Bernini's designs for the Louvre. In 1662 Guarini, on the eve of his great success in Turin, had been brought to Paris to design the church of his order, the Théatins. Of this Germain Brice wrote, a score of years afterwards:

> On ne doit guère regretter si l'ouvrage de leur Église n'est pas dans son entière perfection. La Bizarrerie du dessein dont elle est commencée ne fait rien esperer du beau. Cependant dans l'opinion ridicule que l'on ne trouveroit point d'Architecte en France assez habile pour donner des desseins de cet édifice, on fit venir exprès d'Italie le Pere Camille qui fit bien voir la forfanterie de sa Nation, & le peu de goût & d'experience qu'il avoit dans la belle Architecture. Ce Pere se voulant distinguer en s'éloignant des regles ordinaires, enterprit de suivre les extravagances du Cavalier François Boromini Romain, qui s'étoit fait une manière tout particulière, en renversant ce que l'usage & la raison avoient autorisé avant lui par mille exemples: où l'on voit des édifices de son dessein, dans laquelle la singularité produit des effets assez supportables; Mais ici le Pere Camille n'a imité que le plus ridicule & le plus extravagant . . . poussé sans doute par la présomption ridicule de vouloir passer pour Auteur & pour Maître.[14]

The reign of Louis XIV, five years of age at his succession, had opened with a long and troubled minority; it was no time for great artistic enterprises. Mazarin, favorite as well as minister, was a passionate collector of works of art. Like the Queen-mother, he loved opulence and gilding, but, except through his patronage of his fellow-countrymen such as Romanelli and Vigarini, had little influence on the evolution of creative art.

The post of authority at the head of the royal works was that of the Surintendant des Bâtiments,[15] which Mazarin had not disdained briefly to occupy. Since 1648 it had been filled successively by minor figures, Le Camus and Ratabon, who continued until 1664.

From the death in 1654 of Lemercier, the Premier Architecte, the leading post in the royal works had been taken by Louis Le Vau. In 1656 he was receiving 3000 livres, the highest stipend, as "architecte du roi."[16] By 1664 when the main surviving series of the *Comptes des*

---

[13] *Lettres, instructions et mémoires de Colbert*, ed. P. Clément, V, 1868, 286.

[14] We quote from the edition of 1698, II, 302-303, the editions of 1684 and 1687 being inaccessible to us in America. Chantelou and other Frenchmen had already condemned Borromini from the later '60s onward. Paul Fréart de Chantelou: *Journal du voyage en France du Cavalier Bernin*, 1930 ed., 289-290, October 20, 1665.

[15] Cf. R. Guillemet: *La surintendance des Bâtiments du Roi . . . 1662-1715*. 1912.

[16] *Nouvelles archives de l'art français*, 1872, i, 37.

Bâtiments du Roi[17] opens, he was listed as Premier Architecte at 6000 livres, a charge he had already long fulfilled in fact.

Poussin had been named by Louis XIII his "peintre ordinaire" in 1639, but, after his brief stay in Paris, 1640-1642, had returned to Rome where he was to remain until his death in 1665. Errard was named Peintre du Roy in 1643. His real aptitude, like that of Le Brun after him, was in decoration: "Il donnoit," says Guillet de Saint-Georges, ". . . quantité des dessins d'architecture et d'ornements aux meilleurs ouvriers de Paris . . . enfin c'étoit lui qui donnait tous les dessins qui se faisoient chez le roi pour la sculpture, la menuiserie, la serrurerie, et généralement pour tout le travail qui dépend du dessin."[18]

As in most minorities, that of Louis was a time when undertakings for the Crown were relatively minor. At the Palais Cardinal—left to the Crown by Richelieu and thus henceforth Palais-Royal—Anne of Austria created the Appartement des Bains in 1643. From 1653, following the interval of the Fronde (1648-1652), apartments were fitted up at the Louvre both for the Queen-mother and for the young King; in 1655-1658 an enlargement of the palace toward the west was undertaken, and the rooms below the Petite Galerie were decorated as a summer apartment for the Queen-mother; in 1660 an apartment was created for the new queen, Marie-Thérèse.[19] At Vincennes, in 1754, Levau began for Mazarin, already actively seconded by Colbert, the Pavillon du Roi, soon followed by other structures.[20]

Paris remained also the center of activity in private building, notably so as compared both with the time of the Valois and with the later years of Louis XIV. New hôtels multiplied, from the hands of Le Muet, François Mansart, Le Vau, and others. The engraved sections of Jean Marot show us the interiors of several of these, now destroyed. In the country around, the greatest enterprise was the château of Fouquet, Surintendant des Finances, at Vaux-le-Vicomte, begun in 1657, where for the first time we find Le Vau, Le Brun, and the great gardener, Le Nôtre, working together, as later for the Crown at Versailles.

With the King's assumption of personal rule in 1661, the major artistic personalities began to serve directly the will of the monarch, expressed first through instinctive preferences, but increasingly by conscious initiative.

In the direction of art from this time, indeed, we must give first place to the King himself. The idea of Louis XIV propagated by Saint-Simon, as merely a pompous figurehead or as an artistic blunderer—insisting obstinately on ill-chosen sites, overriding Colbert's superior wisdom, hoodwinked by his architects into costly and frivolous enterprises—is little in accord with the picture we shall derive from our study of events, and of documents annotated by the King's own hand.

Colbert, his minister in artistic as well as financial affairs, became Intendant des Finances in 1661. He lost no time in reaching out for power over the Bâtiments. Already by 1662 he was organizing his "petit conseil," of which Charles Perrault, as his clerk, kept the proceed-

[17] Ed. by J. Guiffrey, 1881-1901.

[18] In *Mémoires inédites de l'Académie Royale de Peinture et de Sculpture*, ed. L. Dussieux, etc., 1854, I, 76, 79.

[19] L. Hautecoeur: *Le Louvre et les Tuileries sous Louis XIV*, Paris, 1927.

[20] J. Cordey: "Colbert, Le Vau, et la construction du château de Vincennes," in *Gazette des beaux-arts*, VIe pér., IX, 1933, 273-293; Col. de Fossa: *Le Château Historique de Vincennes*, 1909; Pradel de Lamase, *Le Château de Vincennes*, 1932. Pavillon du Roy, 1654-1658; Pavillon de la Reine, 1658-1660. Of the decorations we have only one minor drawing (o¹ 1899).

ings. January 1, 1664, he acquired the charge of Ratabon and received his appointment as Surintendant des Bâtiments, which he was to hold until his death in 1683. His reform and aggrandizement of the institution are well known;[21] we need enlarge on them only as they concerned trends in style and responsibility for design. While power was centralized in the person of the Surintendant, he was far from delegating such centralized power to the Premier Architecte, on the contrary he circumscribed the existing powers of that functionary with whose designs he evidently soon became dissatisfied.

Colbert's failure to support Le Vau may indeed have been due partly, as has been alleged, to personal rancour, but a more fundamental cause, felt rather than analysed, lay doubtless in Le Vau's pronounced baroque trend. This was the deeper reason why, both at the Louvre and at Versailles, Colbert subjected Le Vau to the humiliation of inviting designs from other architects. In calling Bernini, Colbert may well have thought of him less as the designer of the baldachino of Saint-Peter's than of its colonnades. When the idea of a colonnade at the Louvre was adopted, even though it had been first embodied in a design by Le Vau,[22] Colbert's mistrust continued, and he charged the study of its form to a commission including also Le Brun and Claude Perrault. Its final form, from 1668, due to Perrault, had a cool classical monumentality which realized the hopes of Colbert, and made it the manifesto of the new academism. At Versailles, to salvage his control, Le Vau had again to sacrifice his proposals as to form. In the end it was not only by this sacrifice, but also by his greater respect for considerations of economy[23]—even stronger with Colbert than academic predilections—that the Premier Architecte was able to triumph over his rivals, and thus indemnify himself for his mortifications at the Louvre.

Long before this Charles Le Brun had been raised to a position of power in the Bâtiments rivalling and exceeding that of Le Vau. Entrusted in 1661, in preference to Errard, with the decoration of the Galerie d'Apollon at the Louvre, he had been ennobled in December, 1662. The patent already alluded to him as Premier Peintre, although his formal appointment to this office is dated July 1, 1664. From 1663 he was also director of the Manufacture Royale des Meubles de la Couronne established at the Gobelins, comprising not only tapestry weavers but painters, sculptors, silversmiths, cabinet makers—"les ouvriers les plus excellents dans toutes sorte de manufacture."[24] His regular appointments rose to 12,000 livres per annum. A finished courtier, he knew how to satisfy both Colbert and the King by progressively tempering any baroque extreme, as well as by magical facility and promptitude of execution. Through his underlying tendencies, nevertheless, baroque influence continued to be felt in the royal interiors throughout the early personal rule of Louis XIV, and, with diminishing intensity, even down to the death of Colbert and to the completion of the enterprises then in progress.

While, in view of the great number of his surviving sketches, we cannot doubt Le Brun's personal responsibility for the motifs of decorative designs, as well as of paintings and sculp-

[21] Cf. Guillemet, *op. cit.*

[22] L. Hautecoeur in *Gazette des beaux-arts*, V^e pér., IX, 1924, 151-168; and *op. cit.*, 166-173.

[23] "Il conserve ce qui est fait," wrote Colbert, in the first line of his comment on Le Vau's design of June, 1669. *Lettres . . . de Colbert*, V, 286.

[24] Documents in H. Jouin: *Charles Le Brun*, 1889, 690-697.

ture, he was not without assistants in this field. From 1666 we find the painter François Francart paid "pour avoir mis au net les desseins et autres ouvrages faits par M. Le Brun;"[25] and Baudrin Yvart, as well as Francart, was paid for such work at the Gobelins from 1664.[26]

As early as 1661[27] we find Le Vau making use of his son-in-law François Dorbay, in the draughting of his projects. From 1666 Dorbay's name appears in the accounts of the Bâtiments; he was paid in July, 1669, "pour les plans et élévations des bastimens qu'il a faits ... pendant l'année dernière." A week after Le Vau's death in 1670 he received 1200 livres "par gratification, en considération des plans et desseins qu'il a faits pour les bastimens du Roy pendant la présente année." A similar gratuity was accorded in 1671. Henceforth he was carried regularly on the staff of the Bâtiments as Architecte, with the highest compensation, but never attained the coveted post of Premier Architecte, which remained vacant from 1670 until 1683.

Dorbay himself, on assuming the leadership, had the assistance of draughtsmen. Thus we find Antoine Desgodetz occasionally employed, from 1671, when he was but eighteen, to 1674, when he went to study in Rome. In the first entry of all it was "pour plusieurs dessins et plans mis au net;" by June, 1671, it was "pour plans et eslévations de plusieurs maisons royalles," by 1674, "pour plusieurs dessins des maisons royalles"—at small but rapidly increasing rates of pay. There were also certain payments to Vigneux, likewise qualified as "dessignateur," for similar services in these years.

It was not until after the death of Louis Le Vau that Colbert, as we have seen, brought into being the Academy of Architecture, complementing those already existing for literature and for painting. The original members were François Blondel, as Professor, Liberal Bruand, François Dorbay, Daniel Gittard, Antoine Lepautre, François Le Vau, and Pierre Mignard as other members, with André Félibien as Secretary. The members had right to the title of "architecte du Roi"—henceforth denied to contractors[28]—and received 500 livres per annum for their attendance at the sessions, where their opinion was occasionally asked on matters of design and, especially, of construction. Their position as academicians, however, did not necessarily secure them employment in the royal works, and most of them had to look primarily to other patronage. Of them all, only Blondel and Mignard had been in Italy, and most were men of the second flight. While their deliberations took a direction of classical purism, as against baroque freedom, this tendency was already well inaugurated, so that we cannot feel they exercised at this period any decisive initiative in the evolution of French design.

Their instruction, exercised by François Blondel (1618-1686) did doubtless intensify this tendency. It was he who was to codify the doctrine in his published *Cours d'architecture*, which appeared in five parts from 1675 to 1683.[29] As he wrote of the book in his preface "il regarde purement la pratique," almost the only theoretical discussion being that in which he sustains,

---

[25] *Comptes*, I, 126 ff.

[26] *Ibid.*, 54 ff.

[27] Dorbay's handwriting appears in that year on a plan for the apartment of Colbert at the Louvre, reproduced by Marquet de Vasselot in *Gazette des beaux-arts*, V^e pér., IX, 1924, 151-168.

[28] *Procès-verbaux de l'Académie Royale d'Architecture*, March, 1676, I, 109.

[29] This and other publications are discussed, somewhat superficially, in K. Cassirer's *Die ästhetischen Hauptbegriffe der französischen Architektur-Theoretiker von 1650-1780*, Berlin dessertation, 1909. Cf. also Mauclaire and Vigoreux: *N.-F. de Blondel*, n.d.

against Perrault, the value of integral proportions. He assumes the merit of the antique, and of the formulation of the classical orders by Vitruvius, Palladio, Scamozzi and Vignola; while his Porte Saint-Denis, designed in collaboration with Le Brun, was intended as a classic triumphal arch, it was itself not free from the baroque tinge which still prevailed.

Among the artists with the official sanction of membership in the Academy of Painting and Sculpture there are figures more significant for the future evolution. Not to speak further of Le Brun or Errard we find there many other ornamentalists. Thus the painters Nicolas Loir and Georges Charmeton, members from 1663 and 1665 respectively, engraved designs of arabesques in the style of Le Brun, beside doing much decorative painting in the royal châteaux. Most important was the engraver Jean Lepautre (1618-1682). His first plate dates from 1643. Among his earliest works was the series of baroque motifs we have mentioned, sketched in Rome by his master Adam Philippon. After some years of engraving for painters, he produced a vast body of ornamental designs and motifs. The dated suites of these range from 1657 to 1667.[30] We are personally of the opinion that the bulk of the undated ones, closely related in style, were made before 1670, at which time he first appears in the employ of the Crown. The *Comptes* show him more and more actively engaged there from then until 1680. In 1677 he was elected to the Academy as "Designateur and Graveur." His style rests directly on that of Le Brun; like that, it shows, within an academic framework, a rich assemblage of high-baroque motifs.

From the King's majority the royal works at once took the leading place in magnitude and importance. The time before the Peace of Nimwegen embraces the extension of the Louvre and the work at Versailles through the completion of the Château Neuf.

Colbert's first solicitude was for the completion of the Louvre. Le Vau had taken up the work on the great unfinished court already under Mazarin in 1660, and was rapidly pressing the north and south sides. The Petite Galerie, burned out internally in 1661, was magnificently rebuilt from designs by Le Brun, as the Galerie d'Apollon (Figure 2). In 1663, Le Vau made a second project for the east front; it did not satisfy Colbert, nor did those of other French architects, called in next year, nor did some solicited from Italy. This was the occasion for the invitation to Bernini, who came in 1665, with the result which all the world knows. With the Louvre certain to continue overrun with workmen, Colbert had begun in 1664 to fit up apartments for the Court at the Tuileries, where, he said, the King could remain seven or eight years, and their decoration was still being actively prosecuted after 1670.

Meanwhile, from 1661, the King had taken an initiative of his own in the embellishment of his father's hunting lodge, Versailles. It has scarcely been remarked how exclusively the splendours of the first Versailles of Louis XIV were splendours of the garden, in which Louis called on Le Nôtre to surpass his own first triumph for Fouquet at Vaux. While the dependencies about the forecourt at Versailles were enlarged by Le Vau, all work on the château proper was confined within the existing walls, where Errard, assisted by Coypel and Claude

[30] Particularly relevant to our subject, as offering a welcome addition to the executed works of this time, are the *Lambris à la romaine*, 1661, the *Cheminées à la romaine*, 1661, the *Grandes cheminées à la romaine*, 1663, the *Cheminées à l'italienne*, 1667, and the *Grandes alcôves à la romaine*, 1667. For the dates, many of which were omitted in the later collected edition of Jombert, see H. Destailleur: *Notices sur quelques artistes français*, Paris, 1863, 84-87. The *Grandes alcôves*, not listed by Destailleur, is preserved in a dated example at the Metropolitan Museum.

Audran, enriched the rooms by painted ornaments,[31] and where the "Chambre aux miroirs" and the "Chambre aux filigranes," executed in 1664-1665,[32] dazzled by the richness of their materials and their contents. It is too often forgotten that Colbert's supplication to the King in 1663: "Quelle pitié que le plus grand Roi . . . fût mésuré a l'aune de Versailles," had reference merely to the Petit Château, as it existed at this date.

The great and decisive royal enterprise of the time, which was to remove this reproach, was the construction of the Château Neuf, begun in 1668. Again the work was begun by Le Vau, again other architects were called in; the design received its final form, this time from Le Vau himself, the next year.[33] Following the death of Le Vau in 1670, the general character of the interior treatment was first established by Dorbay in 1671. The Appartement des Bains was executed from designs chiefly by him, with some ornaments by Le Brun, in 1671-1677. The Appartement du Roi, with its magnificent ceilings by Le Brun and others, was executed in 1671-1681. The Escalier du Roi, begun on a plan by Dorbay, was completed, with decorations entirely from designs by Le Brun, in 1674-1679 (Figure 4). Wholly surrounded by building masses, it was the first of all rooms to be illuminated by a glass skylight.

The Trianon de Porcelaine, first of the French garden casinos, must also have been from a plan by Le Vau, rather than by Dorbay, as mirrors for the interior were already paid for in 1670.

Private works of the time were secondary in importance to those of the Crown. Saint-Cloud was built in 1660 for Monsieur, brother of the King, and wings designed by Antoine Lepautre were added by 1677. One of them was devoted to a gallery then decorated by Mignard with subjects like Le Brun's at the Louvre, chosen from the cycle of Apollo.[34] A salon at either end preceded and followed this, foreshadowing, in a measure, the relation to be adopted at Versailles. The great ministers housed themselves handsomely: Colbert by rebuilding Sceaux in 1673-1674, Louvois, who acquired the old château of Meudon, by building also, in 1669, a vast hôtel in Paris. All these buildings have been swept away, and we have little knowledge of the artistic form of their interiors. In Paris generally, aside from the Hôtel de Louvois, few indeed were the important hôtels built at this time.

The nature of French interior treatment in the period before 1678 may now be briefly analysed, with particular reference to its relation to baroque Italy and to future developments in France.

With few exceptions the French rooms were rectangular, and, characteristically, with sides approximately equal. Oval and circular rooms were the rarest exceptions, even before 1660, as well as after. Thus even in Antoine Lepautre's Hôtel de Beauvais (1656), with its plan of dazzling baroque virtuosity, most of the individual rooms preserve rectangularity.

[31] P. de Nolhac: *La Création de Versailles*, 1901, revised ed. 1925. Guillet de Saint-Georges in *Mémoires . . . de l'Académie*, I, 12, 81.

[32] *Comptes*, I, 20, 22, 79. Nolhac quotes other documents, *op. cit.*, 122 note. The rooms were described by Mlle. de Scudéry, as they were in the summer of 1668, in *La Promenade de Versailles*, 1669.

[33] Kimball: "The Genesis of the Château Neuf de Versailles" (awaiting publication abroad).

[34] A view of the gallery in the seventeenth century and others before the destruction of Saint-Cloud in 1870 are reproduced by le Comte Fleury: *Le palais de Saint-Cloud*, Paris (1901), on pp. 62, 161, 232. Cf. Combes: *Explication historique de . . . Saint-Cloud*, 1681. The fête inaugurating the decorations of the gallery took place October 10-15, 1677. Thus it preceded the undertaking of the Grande Galerie at Versailles, instead of following it as writers on Saint-Cloud have supposed.

Background

François Mansart made the side vestibules at Maisons oval internally. Le Vau, and Le Vau only, gave curved forms a large place. At the Hôtel Lambert, Le Vau used oval vestibules in each story; at Saint-Fargeau (1654-1657) he made a circular vestibule; in remodelling Meudon (from 1655), an oval salon through two stories; at Raincy, another. At Vaux he gave the place of honour to a great oval salon, projecting toward the garden, within a generation after Bernini had placed his oval hall, within rectangular walls, in the center of the garden front of the Palazzo Barberini. At the Louvre Le Vau introduced the Rotondas, with similar projection. We have noted Colbert's later reprobation of such baroque forms for Versailles. In the Château Neuf as built, the rooms of the Grands Appartements were all rectangular, most of them square or nearly square, with few of greater or less length than the rest. The height was uniform—in the main story about two-thirds of the width; the ceilings there were uniformly coved. Essentially the Grands Appartements were thus sequences of approximately equal units, without spatial differentiation or climax.

Unlike the Italian interior, whether mannerist or baroque, in which the walls were normally of plaster, decorated in fresco or covered with stuff, the French interior, where damask or tapestry was also not unusual, was characteristically panelled in wood. Romanelli indeed used fresco in the apartment under the Petit Galerie at the Louvre, but already by 1663 it was discredited on account of its scaling as a result of dampness.[35] At the least, rooms had a panelled dado. In the early period of Louis XIV this was often of substantial height—the *lambris à l'hauteur du bras levé*—perhaps with panels in more than one tier, decorated with landscapes, or with arabesques, as in the Cabinet de l'Amour of the Hôtel Lambert. With the high chimney pieces and low doors then still in vogue, the top of the panelling often lined with these. This was the case in the Pavillon du Roy of the Louvre under Louis XIII, as well as in the Hôtel d'Aumont, both shown by sections in Jean Marot's *Architecture françoise*.

Such treatment was gradually abandoned in favor of panelling the whole height of the room, which had long been employed in many instances. Notable early examples survive at the Arsenal, as well as at the Hôtel Lauzun, the latter under construction in 1657.[36] Here between dado and entablature we find panels, dominantly rectangular, in several tiers, richly sculptured, painted and gilded. At Vaux-le-Vicomte, 1657-1661, where Le Vau and Le Brun collaborated, dignity and largeness of scale were attained by the clear ordering of the panels, large central fields dominating over narrower pilaster-like tiers (Figure 1).

It was very characteristic for the panelling of the principal rooms to include an order. Such treatment appears already both in the chapel of the main story and in the great attic of the Pavillon d'Horloge at the Louvre, built by Lemercier under Louis XIII, as they are shown in Jean Marot's plates. The Hôtel de Sully preserves an early example, also from the last years of Louis XIII, with carved pilasters, small single-valve doors and oval overdoor panels. Among many others, we may mention the Chambre du Roi at Maisons, after 1658, still surviving, and the salons of the Hôtel de Jars, as shown by Marot, both works of François Mansart. At Vaux several rooms have such pilaster treatment, the Galerie d'Apollon of the Louvre (Figure 2) has it at the ends only.

---

[35] Letter of the ambassador of Modena quoted by Hautecoeur, *op. cit.*, 49, from *Archivio storico dell' arte*, 1888, I, 279.

[36] As we have remarked in previous studies, and shall develop later, the chimney pieces and pier glasses at the Hôtel Lauzun are modifications of a later date.

The Creation of the Rococo

In the Château Neuf at Versailles, to be sure, the Grands Appartements, as first built, had plain walls entirely without any ordonnance. Even the Escalier du Roi as first proposed by Dorbay was to have not an order but large herms. As redesigned by Le Brun in 1674 it had coupled pilasters of the Ionic order.

Where there was an order, there was usually a full entablature, or at least there were fragments of entablature over the pilasters. It was by no means uncommon, however, for the cornices of rooms at this time to consist of less than a full entablature, a large bed moulding replacing the frieze. This is true of many of the rooms at Vaux, and again of the Salle de Mercure, the Salle de Diane and other rooms at Versailles. The treatment which was ultimately to be most characteristic in France, with consoles in the frieze—based on Cortona's in the Pitti Palace—was first adopted by Le Brun in the Galerie d'Apollon of the Louvre, and was used at Versailles in the Cabinet des Bains, the Salle d'Apollon and the Salle de Mars.

Paintings on canvas were often incorporated as chief features in the design of the walls. Large figure compositions filled the whole wall above the high dado in the Cabinet d'Amour of the Hôtel Lambert, from 1645. In the gallery there, painted panels by Le Brun alternated with piers ornamented with plastic motifs by Van Obstal. A painting frequently occupied the panel of an overmantel, as well as the pier opposite. In numerous instances panelling was painted throughout with arabesques, in which, as well as on the mouldings, gilding played a large part. The patterns of the arabesques themselves, of great importance for the future, we shall later consider more at length.

In the Italy of the high baroque a magnificent incrustation of colored marbles frequently enlivened the architectural membering and dissolved the unity of every surface by its flaming veins. In French decoration marble was a rarity before the majority of Louis XIV,[37] employed sparingly for pavements and for certain mantels. Not before the building of the Château Neuf at Versailles was it more extensively used.[38] Even Dorbay's general design of 1671 for the northern files of apartments at Versailles[39] shows, aside from marble columns in the ground story, only window casings of marble, of which were also the door frames. It was in the Cabinet des Bains there, begun in 1672, that we first find a complete marble revetment (Figure 3)[40] leading to the name of Appartement de Marbre sometimes applied to the Appartement des Bains. While such incrustation was later widely adopted in the royal works, to which it added a splendour truly regal, the King's monopoly on the output of such quarries as those of Campan[41] prevented any wide imitation by private individuals.

Beside marble, mirrors began to add their lustre to walls of the French interior, at a date much earlier than has generally been realized. Entries for "glaces de Venise" abound in the

[37] One exceptional instance of early marble incrustation was the Salle des Antiques at the Louvre under Henri IV, as described by Sauval. Cf. Hautecoeur, *Louvre*, 46.

[38] The Magazin des Marbres du Roi, rue Saint-Nicaise, was established in 1669 (*Comptes*, I, 310) and from that year the purchases of marble became immense.

[39] Bibliothèque de l'Institut, MS. 1307. The photographs were kindly secured for me by M. Alfred M.-E. Marie.

[40] The designs, which we believe may well be from the hand of Desgodetz, are preserved at the Archives Nationale, o¹ 1768, and reproduced by P. Francastel: "Quelques intérieurs disparus de Versailles," *Gazette des beaux-arts*, VIᵉ pér., I, 1929, 285-294. Such revetments in the main story of the château were not to be added until later as we shall see.

[41] C. Imbert: "Les marbres de Campan," in *L'architecture*, XL, 1928, 89-96.

royal accounts even from the first years for which these are preserved. The cabinets executed at Versailles in 1664-1665 were largely incrusted with mirrors, to a cost of 5770 livres.[42] Mlle. de Scudéry speaks of "pilastres de miroirs entremêlés d'autres pilastres de feuillages dorés sur un fond de lapis." Such cabinets became the height of fashion: in 1668, "144 glaces," to the value of 1440 livres, were furnished for the grand cabinet of Mme. la duchesse de la Vallière (*Comptes* I, 259); in 1669, mirrors to the value of 19,207 livres for the apartments of the Tuileries and for the Grotto of Versailles (I, 366); in 1670, for the apartments of Monseigneur and of Mme. de Montespan (I, 471), and for the Trianon de Porcelaine with its ten large mirrors (I, 421);[43] in 1671, to the value of 11,373 livres, for the apartment of the King at Saint-Germain (I, 533).

Although Venetian glass was still imported on occasion as late as 1685 (II, 778), the demand had led in 1665 to the founding of a royal glass factory, which received large grants from 1668 (I, 286). At this time the mirrors were still made of blown glass; the invention, at the royal works, of the pouring of plate glass did not occur until 1688-1691, and was a result, not a cause, of the great use of mirrors.

August Schmarsow stressed the quality of lustre (*der Glanz*) as a chief characteristic of the rococo,[44] emphasizing the profusion of mirrors and gilding under Louis XV. We see that this idea involves a misconception both chronological and stylistic: A wealth of polished marble, of mirrors, and of gilding was already typical of the work of Louis XIV, even before the central period of his reign.

The doors of rooms under Louis XIII were typically ones with a single valve, and were not of great height, sometimes with cornices of free profile, sometimes with panels above having little integral relation to the doors. We still find many single doors at the Hôtel Lauzun, after 1657, but also some double-valve doors—both with richly plastic frames. Double doors were uniformly employed at Vaux, 1657-1661, and in all other works with which Le Brun was concerned, such as the Galerie d'Apollon, from 1661. Henceforth they were universal, except for very minor openings. Le Brun commonly subsumed doorway and overdoor within a single outer architrave rising to the cornice. In the Château Neuf at Versailles, in the interior work begun by Dorbay in 1671, these tall door casings, as we have seen, were of marble.

Here the doors themselves offered almost the only woodwork which can give us an idea of the style of carved ornament. Those of the Escalier du Roi (Figure 4) carved for Le Brun in 1678 by Philippe Caffieri, led to the provision of similar doors by his atelier in the Appartement du Roi, in 1679-1681. The rails were broken in arches which gave a concave form, at top and bottom, to the major panels. Within these was a second border, broken at the cardinal points by paired scrolls, framing a field with circular medallions. A similar border had already been used in the shutters of the Appartement des Bains in 1672.

As always in the North, the chimney piece was the focus of the room, the principal feature of the decorative treatment of the wall. The Renaissance chimney piece both in Italy and in France had taken its departure from the overhanging chimney piece of the Gothic, with

---

[42] *Comptes*, I, 21, 22, 79. The reports to Colbert cited by Nolhac, *Création de Versailles*, 1925 ed., 122 note, make apparent that the mirrors in these rooms were quite numerous, if indeed they did not cover the walls.

[43] These were to be supplemented in 1680 by "vingt-quatre glaces de 26 pouces" (I, 1318). The *Mercure* of November, 1686, remarked "le murailles . . . toutes couvertes de glaces."

[44] *Barock und Rokoko*, 355-356.

hood or breast rising to the ceiling. The overhanging members were at first transformed into an entablature resting on consoles and pilasters. In Italy after 1500, in France after 1600, this entablature retreated to the plane of the supports. In the hands of the mannerists the fireplace opening was surrounded by an architrave of classical or free profile, often flanked by herms or consoles.

In the French Renaissance it was typical for the chimney breast to be carried up vertically to the ceiling, creating an overmantel, which, like the mantel itself, was framed with the elements of the orders. Such a projecting chimney breast was long retained in France, and gave rise to the distinction cited by François Blondel in his *Cours d'architecture*, 1683:

> Scamozzi dit qu'il y a de trois espèces de Cheminées sçavoir *à la Romaine, à la Lombarde, & à la Françoise*. Les Cheminées à la Romaine sont prises entierement dans l'épaisseur du mur; celle qui sont à la Lombarde ont la moitié de leur enforcement au dedans du mur, & l'autre moitié en dehors; Mais à la Françoise, elles sont, dit-il, entierement hors du mur.

Already under Louis XIII, however, we find certain French chimney breasts flush with the wall,[45] thus making possible simple cubic spaces.

At the same period orders tended to be abandoned on the overmantel, where was placed a panel for painting or sculpture, often round, oval, or octagonal. The chimney piece itself, following Italian baroque models, frequently suggested the recession of the flue by a receding frieze, or by some receding moulding or pedestal with bust or vase above the cornice. Both types were given rich baroque treatment, often with broken or scrolled pediments and figural supports. During the minority of Louis XIV, the receding form persisted: fine examples of it survive at Sucy-en-Brie by Le Vau, built 1641-1643. The receding mouldings, however, tended to be replaced by a vertical frieze or attic with a bas relief or painted arabesque, as at Maisons by François Mansart, 1642-1651.

The use of marble for the *chambranle de cheminée* or mantelpiece proper, adopted at the Tuileries in 1666 (*Comptes* I, 124) and at Versailles after 1668, gradually became general, and tended to distinguish it from the overmantel, which became rather a feature of the wall treatment.

While suspended ceilings of Italian type, coffered and carved, had been occasionally executed earlier, as that of Henri IV in the Antichambre du Roi at the Louvre,[46] ceilings in which the joists rested on heavy beams remained common until the middle of the century, when Le Muet is credited with the initiative of unifying the surface.[47]

More characteristic, in major rooms, was the adoption of vaults ornamented by paintings and stuccos. Already under Francis I such a treatment, of mannerist character, had been given by Niccolo dell' Abbate to the room at Fontainebleau now housing the Escalier du Roi. In the upper story of buildings the use of coved ceilings became general, while in the ground story there were flat ceilings, even in the Château Neuf at Versailles. For the vault of the Grande Galerie du Louvre, Poussin proposed in 1640 an incrustation including casts of antique orna-

---

[45] H. Sauval in his *Histoire et antiquités de la ville de Paris*, written in the 1650's and '60's but published in 1724, states (III, 6) that this innovation was made by Le Muet in the Hôtel Tuboeuf, which is illustrated in the second edition of Le Muet's *Manière de bien bastir*, 1647, but there were earlier examples, as in the Hôtel de Sully.

[46] Cf. the view of the room (Salle Henri II) by Silvestre, reproduced in Hautecoeur, *Louvre*, Pl. XIII.

[47] Sauval, *loc. cit.*

Background

ments.[48] Feeling himself little at home in the rôle of decorator, he seems to have merely reflected ideas of an earlier time in this field.

It was Romanelli who introduced in France the decoration of vaulted ceilings in the manner of Pietro da Cortona, though with a more restrained, less extreme baroque character. Mazarin employed him to adorn his gallery, newly built by François Mansart in 1644, surviving as part of the Bibliothèque Nationale. It appears in Nanteuil's engraving of the Cardinal seated among his collections, and has lately been restored. As in the Farnese gallery, the vault was a cloister vault, henceforth characteristic in France. Here the ceiling was painted, with panels of geometrical outline—circles, and rectangles cut or crowned by circular arcs—as yet with little inter-penetration.

The first of the great ceiling decorations of Le Brun were those of the Galerie d'Hercule of the Hôtel Lambert, begun about 1650. Again the architecture was simulated, but here it was freely overflowed by floating figures in the manner of Cortona in the Barberini ceiling. In 1655 to 1658, Romanelli, following his return to France, executed the vaulted ceilings of the Appartement d'Été de la Reine-Mère at the Louvre,[49] now, as at the Pitti Palace, with bold stucco frames, executed by Michel Anguier. The first room to be attacked was the Grand Cabinet (Salle de Sevère). The outlines of the major panels are geometrical and little broken. In the corners, as in those of the Barberini ceiling of Romanelli's master, are pairs of figures supporting medallions, here in relief. Although these motifs with central candelabrum, scrolled pedestal and cartouche, and fragments of curved pediment at the base are here, by contrast with their wild overflow in the Palazzo Barberini, confined almost wholly within the major architectural lines, they are derivative throughout from the Italian models, which thus became generally familiar in France.

In other rooms of the apartment the character is similar. Subjected to clear geometric disposition of the major lines are large fluted shells, or cartouches with masks, uniting the borders, pairs of volutes filling the concave corners at the head of panels with segmental arches—a multitude of characteristic high-baroque motifs.

At the Hôtel Lauzun, immediately afterwards, the vaults have similar treatment, but with simulated architecture and sculpture.

At Vaux, completed in 1661, the vaulted ceilings of Le Brun follow the Louvre in having a sculptural framework. In their design Le Brun depends partly on Romanelli, partly on the ultimate Italian models. The vault of the royal chamber has its lunettes flanked by stucco figures supporting the central panel, here an unbroken circle. Shells which unite this with the lunettes are less pronounced in the French example, the great cartouches of the Pitti are lacking in it. The vast volutes at the base of the lunettes at Vaux, however, perhaps suggested by Romanelli's in the Antichambre de la Reine-Mère, have a baroque swing almost as pronounced as that of the Tritons and dolphins on the Pitti cornice. The design of the cove in the corresponding room in the opposite apartment is suggested, like that of Romanelli's Antichambre, by that of the Palazzo Barberini, with its standing motifs in the corners, though

---

[48] Fréart de Chambray, *op. cit.* The other documents regarding Poussin and the Grande Galerie are best assembled in E. Magne: *Nicolas Poussin*, Paris, 1914, 123-124. No drawing survives to show the form of this decorative treatment, which J. F. Blondel speaks of in 1756 as ruinous. Cf. *Bulletin de la Société de l'histoire de l'art français*, 1925, 210, 1931, 40-44.

[49] Cf. L. Hautecoeur: *Louvre*, 36-49.

again the central panel is simpler in outline and the whole movement is much less violent than in the Italian example.

In the Galerie d'Apollon of the Louvre (Figure 2), Le Brun's barrel-vaulted ceiling, from 1663, again is membered by stuccoes in bold relief. The disposition of the panels, for all their variety, is of ordered clarity, but again the multiplied elements offer a rich repertory of baroque plastic forms. We need, perhaps, no longer labor the point of their familiarity, which was only reinforced by Le Brun's ceilings at Versailles, from 1671 onward, which ring the changes on the types already established. We may note a diminution of baroque character, in order of execution, from the Salle d'Apollon to the Salle de Mars and beyond, as well as in the Appartement de la Reine.[50] The painted compartments of Mignard's gallery at Saint-Cloud, more conservative in their major outlines, did not differ in essence from those of Le Brun.[51]

In these early years of the reign of Louis XIV, floors received an elaboration comparable with that of walls and ceilings. While the earliest reference in the first years of the royal accounts, 1664, is to "parquets de chêne" at Fontainebleau, we soon find "parquets de bois de rapport" and, frequently, "parquets de marqueterie"—many, toward the end of the period, of ebony with pewter, copper, and latten, particularly for the Louvre, with some for the Cabinets at Versailles. None of this type, to my knowledge, is preserved in France. In the vestibules at the Hôtel Lambert, and in a number of the inhabited rooms at Vaux, there was a pavement of marble, mostly in alternating squares of light and dark, laid diagonally. Marble was adopted at first for the Grands Appartements of the Château Neuf at Versailles, where the floor was at this time in "riches compartiments." The true decoration of the floors, in harmony with the treatment elsewhere, was by the Savonnerie carpets, no longer "façon de Turquie," but from patterns in the style of Le Brun, from cartoons by Francart and Yvart.[52] Those for the galleries of the Louvre, woven in 1664-1683, are in compartments of baroque outline, closely related to the design of the ceilings, with rich acanthus foliage.[53]

Three motifs of ornament of particular importance for the future rococo call for special discussion: the cartouche, the trophy, and the arabesque.

The cartouche, essentially a shield with its field surrounded by a border or frame, while corresponding in use to the antique medallion or tablet, was essentially a modern invention of the Italian mannerists. The very derivation of its name, *cartoccio*, from *carta*, paper, suggests its original and characteristic form, with a frame of rollwork: paper, card, or carton, its scrolls pushing forward. The baroque cartouche, heavily plastic, was already domesticated in France under Henry IV, as we may see in the vestibule and tribune of the chapel at Fontainebleau, and under Louis XIII, as in Barbet's *Livre . . . d'autels et de cheminées*, 1632. The high-baroque forms, at the apogee of their fire and complexity, were embodied in Stefano della Bella's *Raccolta di varii capricii*, and his *Nouvelles inventions de cartouches*, published in Paris in

[50] In the Galerie des Tuileries were installed in 1670-1671 copies of the paintings of the Farnese gallery executed by the pensioners of the Academy in Rome, but we have no knowledge of the form of the borders and other ornaments.

[51] Fleury, *loc. cit.*

[52] *Comptes*, I, 386, 446, 1110.

[53] J. Prentice: "A Savonnerie Carpet from the Grande Galerie du Louvre," *Burlington Magazine*, LXXIX, 1941, 25-27.

1646 and 1647. His cartouches offer every variety of border, including even the rim of shell which was ultimately to have such a great fortune at the height of the rococo.

Compared with these last engraved models the executed examples in the work of Romanelli and of Le Brun were far from representing any advance in style; indeed, as generally in their work, these artists were apt to return to more classical forms of the medallion, itself found, like the cartouche, in the protean vocabulary of Pietro da Cortona. Henceforth under Louis XIV the cartouche was rarely employed except in its basic usage as a shield for arms, cyphers, or devices. A form frequently used for such purposes was the winged cartouche, which goes back at least to Borromini,[54] as over the main doorway of the nave of Saint John Lateran. Le Brun adopted it in the borders of his tapestry suite *L'Histoire du Roi*, 1668; it appears in the overdoors of the Salles de Vénus and de Diane, also, for instance, in a manuscript design for interior doors for Versailles (o¹ 1768, No. 45), with the date 1681. These, characteristic of Le Brun, have oval medallions for their central fields, instead of the bulbous forms of the many Italian baroque examples.

French ornament, like the Italian, from the early Renaissance onward, had made use of the trophy, usually in its classical type of the trophy of arms, but also occasionally in types of the "trophy of peace"—with instruments of music, of the chase, and—more rarely—of husbandry and of the arts. Under Le Brun such trophies became a major motif of ornamental sculpture, and they replaced arabesque motifs in the borders of many of his tapestries. He not only used suspended and standing trophies, but heaped similar elements at the base and in the lower borders, choosing always such elements as comported with the subject.

François Blondel, after discussing the antique type of trophy of arms, codified the practice of Le Brun in giving greater appositeness and variety of subject to the trophy:[55] "Il s'en fait en diverses autre manières à cette imitation. Il y a dans le Livre d'Albert Dürer des desseins de Trophées faits de pieces de ménage rustique & d'instruments servans au labourage arangez avec grand art. . . . L'on en fait en maniere de pantes ou de festons, non seulement sous la figure de Trophées d'armes ou de guerre, mais même sous celle des Trophées de Paix: comme des Sciences, des Arts, des divertissemens &c, arrangeant par exemple divers instrumens de musique: ce qui sert aux Sciences, comme Livres, Sphere, Globes, instrumens de Mathematique: Les principaux ornemens du Bal & de la Comedie: des Equipages de Chasse ou de Pêche, & mille autres de cette nature, dont la beauté consiste principalement dans le choix & la disposition, & dans le rapport, que ces ornements doivent avoir au dessein general de l'édifice."

Conspicuous early examples of sculptured trophies at this period were those of scientific instruments on Perrault's Observatoire, 1667, and the military ones of the Porte Saint-Denis, begun in 1672, on which Le Brun and Michel Anguier collaborated with François Blondel. In interiors we find many examples both painted and in relief, such as those of Lesueur in the vestibules at the Hôtel Lambert, and in the gallery of François Mansart's Hôtel de la Vrillière, decorated by François Perrier. Jean Lepautre engraved several suites, including his

---

[54] We find winged circular cartouches or medallions as early as the decoration of the dome of San Pietro in Montorio.

[55] *Cours d'architecture*, 1683, 2ᵐᵉ partie, 173-175.

The Creation of the Rococo

Montans de trophées d'armes à l'antique, 1659. The culmination of the use of the trophy at this period came in Le Brun's decorations of the Escalier du Roi at Versailles, with heaped trophies of gilded metal in the four niches, painted standing trophies at the corners of the ceiling. While in all such compositions there was freedom in the collocation of individual elements, the major units at this time remained generally symmetrical.

The most characteristic form of surface decoration was the grotesque—from the later seventeenth century in France called arabesque,[56] in spite of its classical origin—that playful, transitory, dreamlike ornament which permitted the most fanciful union of varied elements, its very essence lying in its irreality. The arabesque in France was gradually to take a characteristic national turn, and was ultimately to play a role of decisive importance in the genesis of the rococo. Although this turn still lay in the future, it is important for us to observe with particular attention the arabesque from the time of Mazarin onward, and to note its transformations.

Prior to the mid-seventeenth century there had already been three chief successive phases in the evolution of the arabesque. Following classical suggestions, the early Renaissance, both in Italy and elsewhere, had used it as a carved ornament, in narrow vertical panels such as those of pilasters, basing its form primarily on a central stem or candelabra, with branching scrolls of light foliage. Raphael in the Loggie of the Vatican, gave the classic expression to a new initiative,[57] stimulated more directly by the painted and modelled ornament of buried Roman buildings, the "grottoes," which gave the name of *grotteschi* or grotesques. Raphael's arabesques were chiefly painted, although they incorporated stucco medallions in relief; they preserved the character of narrow panels and bands. In the hands of the Roman mannerists the painted arabesques were transformed by application to broad surfaces, sometimes with three-dimensional central scenes, light baldachinos framing mythological figures, the surrounding surface patterns being often of the greatest attenuation. There was frequent employment of flat bars or bands, often disjointed, parallel to the borders or in step-like angles, reflected in France in Ducerceau's grotesque suite of 1566. In stuccoes at the Villa di Papa Guilio we even find, by exception, such bands combined with opposite scrolls. In Rome also, as a frame for the central composition, appeared the cartouche, at first modelled in relief, with a frame of rollwork, its scrolls curling forward.

In northern Europe the carved arabesques of the Early Renaissance had been followed immediately by the mannerist forms. In the School of Fontainebleau they acquired a distinctive character, with broad central fields, often painted, surrounded by borders of varied ornaments of plastic character, including much rollwork as well as interlaces of continuous flat bands in geometrical patterns. In the engraved arabesques of Flemings and Dutchmen such as Cornelis Floris and Vredeman de Vries (the activity of the latter extending into the seventeenth century) there was a great development of the rollwork as pierced strapwork, sometimes with C-scrolls united by short straight bars—characteristically, but not without excep-

[56] The Italians of the sixteenth century already used "rabeschi" to describe the pilaster ornaments of acanthus foliage. In France we find in 1684 "Rabesques d'après Raphaël" used in the present sense.

[57] Regarding its origins cf. Schmarsow: "Der Eintritt der Groteske in die Dekoration der italienischen Renaissaince," in *Jahrbuch der preuszischen Kunstsammlungen,* 1881, II, 131, and later discussions well summarized by W. K. Zülch: *Enstehung des Ohrmuschelstiles,* 1932, 12 ff.

tion, curling forward. None of the forms of bandwork so far mentioned has any close analogy with that which we shall find in the later French arabesque.

Independent of all these were the continuous bands appearing in the veritable "moresques" of Islamic derivation. The title *Passements de moresques*, of an anonymous work of 1563,[58] shows the analogy to the braids and galloons of embroiderers, who were in fact some of the chief users of such patterns, and who found bandwork patterns specially adapted to the technique of appliqué. While the *passements de moresques* of 1563 are in interlaces of continuous bands, in lozenge, trefoil and other patterns, we find numerous actual embroideries of the later sixteenth century with passements, fillets or braids in opposite C-scrolls, united by short straight bars.[59] While it is difficult to date these executed specimens exactly, we have manuscript designs and sketches by Georges Boissonet of Rheims,[60] dated as early as 1610 (Figure 6), of embroideries which include similar forms approaching those characteristic of the future development in France. This is fortunate, for it is at just this moment that the publication of model-books, which had propagated Renaissance designs of lace, basically Italian, comes to an end with the passage of the vogue of such designs,[61] so that none of such model-books includes bandwork of the sort we are discussing. Moreover the chief engraved French designs of the century for embroideries and woven stuffs, those of Paul Androuet Ducerceau (1630-1710), while they contain such scrolled bands in connection with acanthus foliage, were published too late to bear on the date of adoption of these forms. Clearly, however, the forms were in common use by French embroiderers early in the seventeenth century.[62]

Such forms were adopted also in French garden design under Henry IV and Louis XIII, with a name which indicates their relation to embroidery. From earlier times there had been occasional use in parterres of armorial bearings and of cyphers. Claude Mollet, Premier Jardinier under these kings, lays claim, very circumstantially, to the invention of "parterres et compartmens en broderie," of which numerous designs, prepared by his sons during his lifetime, are included in his *Theatre des plans et Jardinages*,[63] issued posthumously in 1652. Substantially identical in style with these are the parterres of Jacques Boyceau—who as Indendant des Jardins of Louis XIII, laid out the first gardens of Versailles—appearing in his posthumous *Traité de Jardinage*, 1638 (Figure 5). Both include bandwork as well as foliage. Indeed it is in their garden designs, among all the engraved surface patterns of whatever sort known to me, that we first find bandwork combined with acanthus foliage in the general manner which was to be characteristic of the later French arabesque—that is to say, with C-scrolls connected by short straight bars, with palmettes of foliage radiating from the junction of opposite scrolls. A minor feature already found here was the leaf of acanthus diverging from the termination of the scroll—a feature which, in the sequel, was to become universally char-

[58] Reproduced, Berliner, *op. cit.*, pl. 95. There are also such patterns in French bookbindings of the period.

[59] L. de Farcy: *La Broderie du XIe siècle jusqu'à nos jours, d'après des specimens authentiques et les anciens inventaires*, 1890, e.g., II, pls. 83, 91.

[60] *Ibid.*, II, pl. 100.

[61] Cf. Arthur Lotz: *Bibliographie der Modellbücher ... 16. und 17. Jahrhunderts*, 1933, esp. p. 29.

[62] We find related patterns in marquetry furniture, such as the bureau with the arms of the Maréchal de Créqui (d. 1638) at the Musée de Cluny.

[63] The relevant passages in the text are on pp. 191-192, 199, 201. They point to a date of writing about 1622-1632, or earlier. I cannot find authority for the statement that Mollet wrote "in 1613, towards the end of his life," made by M. L. Gothein: *History of Garden Art*, 1928, I, 420.

acteristic.[64] We can scarcely doubt that these novel garden designs, so conspicuously used and so much admired, were not without influence on the subsequent development of the French arabesque, in which these forms were subsequently to appear.

A new vogue of painted arabesques in France was inaugurated by Vouet, under the influence of Italian mannerism to which he had been subjected. Vouet painted the panels of the Appartement des Bains de la Reine-Mère at the Palais-Royal in 1643.[65] The central medallions are of geometrical form—mostly oval and octagonal, rarely with rollwork—buttressed by pairs of supporting figures, with acanthus foliage and other motifs. Similar compositions of large scale occur at the Arsenal.[66] At the Hôtel Lambert minor arabesques abound in the rooms decorated by Lesueur, 1645-1649,[67] and by Le Brun, after 1650, as also at the Hôtel Lauzun, after 1657, and elsewhere.[68] In contrast with these, which follow mannerist tradition, were those of Errard, leader of the academic trend, which reverted more directly to the arabesques of Raphael. His decorations at the Louvre, from 1654 onward have largely perished, but a series of panels from the Appartement de la Reine, 1657, were incorporated in 1817 in the Chambre du Livre d'Or at the Luxembourg.[69] Other fine arabesques of Errard, closely similar, survive in the Chambre d'Anne d'Autriche at Fontainebleau, 1664. In none of the painted compositions so far mentioned do we encounter any of the bandwork which was afterwards to play such a significant part in the development of French arabesques.

Meanwhile in baroque Italy we do find such bandwork, related to what we have observed in embroidery and in French parterres, appearing in the marble intarsia of floors and incrustations which then became popular.[70] Where in the sixteenth century there had been acanthus scrollwork, in the mid-seventeenth century scrolled bands were often used. Though occasionally a plastic effect was sought, the nature of the material favored flat bands, even to approximate the frame of a cartouche. Thus a pairing of opposite scrolled bands was characteristic. In some instances there were borders of moresques or other scrolled bandwork in repeating

[64] H. von Geymüller, in *Baukunst der Renaissance in Frankreich*, 1901, called such a scroll a bec-de-corbin (bill-hook, or hawk's-bill), and German writers have followed him. Although Geymüller had the advice of Destailleur in matters of usage, I do not find in French parlance, either of the eighteenth century or today, just such a use of the term, which was applied to a somewhat different foliate element—a *feuille de refend* ending in a very delicate scroll turning backwards. Cf. the key to diagrams of parterres in an engraved suite issued by Nicolas Langlois (Print Department, Metropolitan Museum of Art). In the absence of any term better grounded historically we are constrained to adopt this one.

[65] V. Champier and R. Sandoz: *Le Palais-Royal*, Paris, 1900, 114. Fourteen panels were engraved by Dorigny in 1647.

[66] In the so-called "Cabinet de Sully," actually decorated for the Maréchal Duc de la Meilleraye, Grand Maître de l'Artillerie, 1634-1648. His capture of Hesdin, June 29, 1639, which appears in one of the panels, gives a *terminus post quem*, later than usually assumed. The decorations may have been executed any time before 1648.

[67] In the dado of the Cabinet des Muses a few of these early panels remain in place; some from the Cabinet de l'Amour, including circular cartouches framed by palm, are preserved at the Château de La Grange in Berri. Cf. L. Dimier: *La Peinture française ... 1627-1690*, Paris, II, 1927, pls. 10, 11.

[68] Both at the Hôtel Lambert (Cabinet des Muses) and the Hôtel Lauzun (Ancienne Salle à Manger) certain arabesques date from remodellings of the eighteenth century, and may readily be distinguished from those of the seventeenth.

[69] Dimier, *op. cit.*, 16, pls. 14, 15, and *Bulletin de la Société de histoire de l'art français*, 1927, 37-39, following A. de Champeaux: *L'art décoratif dans le vieux Paris*, 1898, 74-77, an identification resting on the engraved suite *Ornemens des Appartemens de la Reine au Vieux Louvre par le sieur Errard*.

[70] W. Kern and P. Schubring: *Italienische Marmor-Intarsien*, 1921.

patterns (Figure 7). In others there were panels with an inner border or band ending semicircularly at top and bottom with paired scrolls. Among notable examples of such marble intarsia in Rome were panels of Bernini's sepulchre of Santa Francesca Romana at Santa Maria Nuova, about 1648. Here in the pavement we find even a hint of the French developments, in borders with scrolled crossettes set off by a leaf.[71] Beside its architectural uses, such intarsia was incorporated in marble table-tops which formed an article of export, notably to the Court of France. Some of these tables combined bandwork and foliate elements in much the same way as did the French parterres, which appear to antedate them.

The decorative repertory of Charles Le Brun was so vast that his arabesques have attracted little attention, yet they are of much importance. His personal concern with their design we know from his manuscript drawings at the Louvre[72] (e.g., Figure 8), although their execution was doubtless left to assistants. Rather than analyse these drawings, which cannot be dated, we shall discuss datable examples carried out under his direction, which in fact show a similar character.

In the interiors at Vaux, completed in 1661, Le Brun gave arabesques a large place.[72a] They decorate the woodwork in several rooms of the Grand Appartement. In general they continue the French tradition of Vouet, with figural elements on a large scale, acanthus foliage, and oval medallions here placed against a background of drapery, hanging sometimes from a valanced baldaquin. This traditional Italian element, adopted by Ducerceau, and already revived at the Arsenal, was a favorite in Le Brun's arabesques. What is specially characteristic and essentially novel in painted arabesques is Le Brun's occasional use of moulded straight bars, or scrolls of flat bandwork connected by short horizontal or vertical bars—contrasting with the smooth flow of the acanthus leafage in the same panels (Figure 1). From the junctions of opposite band scrolls, as traditionally from the junction of acanthus scrolls, spring radiating leaf-motives, variations of the palmette. This is best illustrated at Vaux in certain painted friezes, where the intertwining of bands, from the scrolls of which diverge certain leaves of acanthus, foreshadows the treatment which was ultimately to be characteristic of plaster cove-cornices under Louis XV.

It was from such arabesques of Le Brun, obviously, that were derived the forms of many engraved models by such artists as Georges Charmeton (1619-1674), Nicolas Loir (1623/24-1679) and his brother Alexis (ca. 1630-1713).[73] Indeed those of the two latter correspond almost exactly with the character of Le Brun's composition at Vaux.

Similar forms appear in Le Brun's Gallerie d'Apollon of the Louvre, where the wainscot which covered the walls was richly ornamented with painted arabesques, while arabesques in stucco figure in the minor panels of the ceilings. The accounts are not specific as to the several parts of the decoration painted between 1666 and 1677—by La Baronnière, who had already worked at Vaux, by Gontier, Gervaise, and the Lemoines—or for the precise date at

[71] These and similar patterns were noted by Oppenord in his Roman sketchbook of 1692-1699, now in Berlin, p. 29 recto, 49 recto, etc.

[72] Nos. 5912, 5914, 8253, 8254, 8443 in J. Guiffrey and P. Marcel: *Inventaire général des dessins du Louvre* ... Paris, VII, 1912, VIII, 1913.

[72a] J. Cordey: Vaux-le-Vicomte, 1924.

[73] When in discussing the sources of Berain's arabesques, Berliner, *op. cit.*, 166, says that they cannot be derived from Berain's immediate predecessors such as Charmeton, he overlooks the basic common source in the painted arabesques of Le Brun.

which the arabesques of the walls were executed.[74] But the plates of ornaments of the gallery[75] engraved by Jean Berain (1640-1711) as his first work for the Crown, including six showing the piers (Figure 9), were paid for beginning in January, 1671, which gives a *terminus ante quem*. He was paid for nine plates by November, 1672.[76] Notable in them, as at Vaux, is again the presence of bandwork with scrolls from which diverge leaves of acanthus. While in the painted wall panels this bandwork is subordinate, in the ceiling panels in relief it is definitely characteristic. In one of these (Plate 7 of the engraved series, our Figure 10) it forms an inner border, turning into the pattern, uniting in opposite scrolls. The engravings also show the strips of ornament of the window jambs, still surviving, chiefly of interlacing bandwork, again with palmettes at the junctions of the scrolls, many of which are garnished with an acanthus leaf.

An equally advanced stage of decoration under Le Brun's direction is shown by the arabesques of the Grand Appartement at the Tuileries, as they appear in engravings by Lemoine in the same series.[77] He and his brother had worked at the Tuileries from 1669 (I, 334), and Germain Brice states that the Chambre du Roi had grotesque panels executed by them.[78] Here indeed, in certain panels, the bandwork even dominates over the acanthus. The essentials of the style which we call that of Berain are thus already present at a time before, or soon after, he first worked for the Crown.

If painted arabesques do not appear in the rooms of the Château Neuf at Versailles which survive from this period, we must remember that none of the private rooms of the time are preserved unchanged. Errard's arabesques of 1662-1665 were in the Petit Château, of which the rooms remained undisturbed only until 1678-1687. The apartment of Mme. de Montespan, where the decorations of 1671 by La Baronnière and the Lemoines (*Comptes* I, 509) may have been similar, was swept away in 1685. Of the nature of painted decorations of other private apartments we know nothing. In the Escalier du Roi the four simulated tapestries with arabesques, surrounding military scenes executed in 1677-1678,[79] have inner borders of bandwork analogous to others we have seen in the work of Le Brun.

Arabesques also figure in the designs for tapestry by Le Brun. This was the case notably in the suite of *Festons et rinceaux à fond de mosaïque*, "manière arabesque," woven at the Gobelins in 1668 and destroyed during the Revolution. As described in the *Inventaire du mobilier de la Couronne*[80] it had "rainseaux, oyseaux, et festons de fleurs, et dans le milieu de chaque pièce une

---

[74] Hautecoeur states, *op. cit.*, 117: "de 1670 à 1677 les Lemoine décorerent les trumeaux d'arabesques," but I do not find anything so definite in the accounts. Berain's engravings begin in the very year the Lemoines began to be employed at the Louvre, and would thus seem to be show work by the other men.

[75] Twelve plates engraved by him, of which the coppers are preserved by the Chalcographie du Louvre, were included with others in a series assembled in 1710 with the title: *Ornemens de peinture et de sculpture qui sont dans la Galerie d'Apollon au Château du Louvre et dans le grand Appartement du Roy au Palais des Tuileries. Dessinez et gravez par les Srs. Berain, Chauveau, et le Moine.*

[76] *Comptes*, I, 478, 544, 642. The payments for further plates, extending to 1677, as cited by R. A. Weigert: *Jean I Berain*, Paris, 1937, II, 40, are not specifically stated to be of ornaments of the gallery.

[77] Plates 26-29, *Lambris dans le grand Appartement des Tuileries*, of the collected series of 1710. The only plates for which he was paid were four in 1678 (I, 1089), which may thus well be these.

[78] *Description de Paris*, 1698 ed., I, 60.

[79] One of these, transferred to canvas is preserved at the Musée de Versailles, No. 155.

[80] Ed. by J.-J. Guiffrey, Paris, 1885, No. 71 of the tapestries, cited by M. Fenaille: *État général des Tapisseries des Gobelins*, II, 1903, 41.

médaille ovalle dans laquelle sont représentez les *Divertissements du Roy,* le tout sur un fond aurore de petits carrez d'or et de soye." It is our first mention of this characteristic background of *mosaïque,* which appears also in the overdoor panels of the Galerie d'Apollon, and later in many ceilings of the Château Neuf. In figural tapestries arabesques might appear, as initially in Raphael's tapestries, in the borders. Thus the borders of the suite of the *Histoire du Roi,* of which the first pieces were woven in 1668, have arabesques with rinceaux intertwined with horizontal bandwork, from the bars of which hang scalloped lambrequins, as in the friezes at Vaux.

Bandwork appeared likewise at Versailles in carved panel fillings, such as the surviving shutters of the Appartement des Bains, about 1672, and the doors executed for the Escalier des Ambassadeurs in 1678 by Philippe Caffieri, from Le Brun's designs of which we have spoken. In each of these the band is merely an inner border of the panel field, uniting at the axial points in opposite scrolls adorned with a leaf of acanthus. All such bandwork was still, and for a score of years to come, rigidly confined within the geometric outline of the moulded frame.

Our study of the remoter background has already, we hope, served to confute the old idea that the rococo issued directly from Italian baroque influence in France. We may emphasize several points particularly. Italian artists of advanced training worked in France during the high baroque without evoking the rococo; on the contrary, while employing many baroque forms, they reverted there to a more conservative spirit. French artists were in Rome at the height of the baroque, giving it particular and friendly attention. Baroque motifs were thus thoroughly domesticated in France long before the rococo, without generating it. The work of these artists in France, filled as it was with baroque forms, not only failed to create the rococo but assisted in evoking, by reaction, a pronounced classical academism. While the typically Italian baroque form of the cartouche was relatively neglected, and the trophy retained a conservative treatment, a new development, wholly French, was beginning to take place in arabesque surface ornament—a development independent of high-baroque forms. It was this French development, and not anything Italian, which, we shall find, ultimately led on to the rococo, the basic character of which, in spite of the continued survival of individual baroque elements, was essentially antithetical to the baroque.

Immediate Background:
The Central Period of Louis XIV, 1678-1699

A new outburst of activity corresponds with the central period of the reign, the last quarter of the seventeenth century, opening when the martial successes of France had brought Louis XIV to his apogee. The academic tendency which had emerged from 1666 onward, now became dominant. The advent of Mansart, as the ultimate agent of the King's artistic will, the decision to make Versailles the seat of the Court, coincided closely with the Treaty of Nimwegen, 1678, which opened a decade of peace with unexampled wealth.

More even than previously, it was the King who took the major initiatives. As between the Louvre and Versailles, who shall say that Colbert was right rather than the King, who insisted on creating at Versailles his unrivalled engine for the destruction of feudal independence in the nobility? We must emphasize, moreover, what tends to be forgotten: that the buildings of the Louvre and Tuileries—no matter how united and cleared of their ignoble encumbrances—were incapable, by their form and relations, of receiving a distribution at all in harmony with the functional requirements of royalty, Court and government, so admirably achieved at Versailles in spite of the early forebodings of Colbert. At Saint-Germain, which Saint-Simon thought should have been preferred, the remodellings and additions of 1680-1682 made only more obvious what the King already recognized: the total impossibility of creating from the irregularities and disparities of the buildings there a coherent practical and artistic whole, capable of receiving the entire Court.

As no programme for a building enterprise had ever been more wisely drawn, or more literally followed than the King's list of requirements of 1668[81] for the Château Neuf de Versailles, which Le Vau had so ably translated into plastic form, we can little doubt that the essential major demands for the transformation of 1678 were likewise ideas of the monarch, brilliantly embodied by Mansart. We know that it was the King's veto which ultimately saved the court of the château from the changes proposed by Claude Perrault, and we may thus suppose it to have been his decision also which now saved it from the elevation proposed by Mansart—thereby preserving the artistic dominance of the *étage du Roi* which Mansart's proposal threatened to extinguish. The basic artistic scheme of Marly, with its satellite pavillions, is implicit in the very conception of its practical requirements, and accordingly must also redound ultimately to the credit of the King, quite irrespective of the report to this effect mentioned by Charles Perrault. In the matter of taste—"le mauvais goût du roi en toutes choses" of the crabbed Saint-Simon—we have more than one example of the superiority of the King, as we shall see.

In the art of the central period, Colbert was no longer, as during the earliest years of his ministry and of his Surintendance des Bâtiments, the initiator and arbiter, but was now rather the energetic executant of the King's mature will. The system Colbert had created, a constellation of individuals in academies advising the minister, was subtly transformed, as we shall see, into a centralization of the Bâtiments under a single architect—responsible indeed to the Surintendant, but ultimately an instrument of the King. This new system, already existing since 1678, was recognized just before Colbert's death in 1683 by the revival for Mansart of the office of Premier Architecte. Multiplication of his subordinates followed under the Surintendence of Louvois. Except by the disfavour of Le Brun, the favour of Mignard, Louvois' action on the arts had little new personal direction, though his zeal and energy were equal to Colbert's. His own death in 1690 and the succession of the weak Villacerf increased the importance of the Premier Architecte, whose agency was the unifying factor in the architecture of this whole period.

In Jules-Hardouin Mansart, Louis indeed found and recognized the perfect executant of his artistic will. The purism of contemporaries and of later critics might indeed justly reproach him with a lack of that artistic conscience, of that correctness of motive, proportion, and detail so well exemplified by his uncle, François Mansart. All this was now beside the

---

[81] "Ce que le Roi désire dans son bâtiment de Versailles," *Lettres et instructions de Colbert*, ed. Clément, V, 1868, pp. 282-284. That the King and not the minister was responsible is shown by Colbert's demurrers on many points.

point. What was necessary was a breadth and readiness of conception, a rapidity of execution, only made possible by organization and by delegation of details to others. In stressing the large part of subordinates in the creation of artistic motive under Mansart's régime, we by no means deny him great and deserved credit for the plastic solution of the major architectural problems posed by the King. His was the responsibility, if not in all cases the initiative, for the masterly relationship to the château at Versailles of the great wings, of the Orangerie, of the Écuries, for the actual distribution at Marly and at the Trianon de Marbre. His was the responsibility for the choice of personnel, the recommendation of designs, as well as their realization with almost magical promptitude and efficiency, achieved by a body of subordinates with newly-specialized duties, of which, as we shall see, he himself dictated the organization.

We need scarcely detail the rise of Mansart except to assemble scattered evidence as to its early stages. Born April 16, 1646, he was scarcely twenty when we first hear of him as directing certain work for M. de Lesseville, mentioned in a subsequent deposition of December, 1673, in which, at twenty-seven, he is described as "architecte des bastimens du Roy,"[82] a term then still somewhat loosely used. By his marriage in 1667 to the daughter of a Trésorier de la prévoté de France he was definitely launched. The *Comptes des Bâtiments* do not mention him before 1676, when he was paid 500 livres as a member of the Academy of Architecture, following his appointment to it in 1675. The ground for his favour was his success at the Château de Clagny, begun in its first form for Madame de Montespan in the spring of 1674.[83] For the château as enlarged by the "nouveaux bastiment" begun in 1675, the specification for the joinery, in Mansart's hand, is dated June 14, 1676.[84] In March of 1677 he received the extraordinary sum of 6000 livres "pour les desseins et la conduite des bastimens de Clagny," beside other perquisites. From this year we have an ill-spelled letter of Mansart to Colbert from Clagny, September 10,[85] following an unannounced visit of the minister to the work in Mansart's absence, for which he pleads illness. He writes in great fear of Colbert's displeasure, especially as he had just had his first opportunity for employment at Versailles: "J'ai doné depuis peu le reste de touts les mesure pour les quabines de marbre que vous faite faire dans le parque de Versailles au cabinet de la Renommée."[86] From 1678 he was fully in charge of the immense new constructions at Versailles. In February, 1682, contrary to the statutes of the order requiring nobility, he was made a Chevalier de Saint-Lazare, being ennobled in September of the same year. Before Colbert's death, which took place on September 6, 1683, Mansart had been given the title of Premier Architecte.[87]

[82] J.-J. Guiffrey: "Jules et Michel Hardouin frères, architectes," in *Nouvelles archives de l'art français*, III, 1887, 289-294. In this deposition we find Mansart answering with a truculence already suggesting the self-confidence which was to carry him so far.

[83] C. Harlay: *Le Château de Clagny à Versailles, restitution-notices-iconographie*, n.d. (1912). Other documents in P. Bonnassieux: *Le Château de Clagny*, 1881, 50 ff. Cf. also Nolhac in *Revue de l'histoire de Versailles . . .* 1900, incorporated in *La Création de Versailles*, 1901 ed., which Harlay corrects in important regards.

[84] Cited by H. Jouin: *Nouvelles archives de l'art français*, 1885, 116-117.

[85] Quoted by Bonnassieux, 156-158, from G. Peignot: *Documents authentiques et détails curieux sur les dépenses de Louis XIV*, 1827.

[86] Payments for the model for a pavilion were made in April and May (*Comptes*, I, 959, 962).

[87] His nomination seems not to be preserved, but he was paid in this new capacity for the entire year, the first half-yearly payment being made July 25 (*Comptes*, II, 381).

As to how much or little Mansart himself could draw we have but scant authentic information. The younger Dargenville, to be sure, wrote, long afterwards, that Mansart "profiloit dans la dernière perfection et dessinoit grossièrement avec du charbon ou une grosse plume."[88] Dargenville was unborn at Mansart's death; even his father, with similar interests, could barely have known Mansart. Many of the younger Dargenville's notices were taken over entire from Mariette and other previous writers; others were merely journalistic compilations. In this instance his text seems to be based partly on scattered remarks of Jean-François Blondel's *Cours d'architecture*, 1771-1777, completed by Patte. One passage there (V, 41-42) speaks of certain mouldings at Clagny as "d'un excellent profil, partie dans laquelle Hardouin Mansart s'est toujours signalé avec le plus grand éclat." Blondel himself was not born until 1705, three years before the death of Mansart, and he speaks solely from knowledge of the finished buildings.

Actually we know of no single drawing which is surely from Mansart's own hand, at any period of his life. Many which have been called his and which have his signature have it merely affixed to an official approval "Bon à executer," itself written in another hand, not even that of the draughtsman. It is notable to what an extent Mansart adopted and adapted the existing designs of others. In the château of Versailles the system of the façades is merely that established by Le Vau—slightly modified and greatly extended. Hardouin Mansart's first designs for the chapel at Versailles, on a domed scheme, were adapted from sketches of his uncle for a funerary chapel at Saint-Denis, on which the scheme of the Chapelle Royale des Invalides was also based.[89] Nowhere do we find in the archives even any preliminary sketches which may be his. Nonetheless all public credit went to the Premier Architecte, who alone is always mentioned as having "donné les desseins."

It thus becomes vital to penetrate the official façade of the Bâtiments, which have masked in anonymity the personalities of all subordinates. Was it really to the great functionary, as Mansart soon became, or to other men, more modest in rank, that we should attribute the initiative in artistic creation?

Mansart's formal dominance in the Bâtiments dates from 1678. His title in that year was "Architecte," his basic salary 6000 livres. Aside from Blondel, "Professeur," each of the other academicians was now listed as "Autre Architecte" and, with a single exception, received merely the 500 livres paid for attendance at the conferences of the Academy.

The exception was François Dorbay, who had been in charge of the works at Versailles since the death of Le Vau and whose salary was 1000 livres. Dorbay also received in this year, as in the previous one, a gratification of 2000 livres "en consideration du soin qu'il prend des bastimens du Roy." Henceforth the functions of the academicians as such became nominal; the office of the Bâtiments was given an independent development. Dorbay continued to be second in command. When Mansart was named Premier Architecte Dorbay was named "Architecte" at 2000 livres, and he remained, until his death in 1697, second in pay—even after the appointment of De Cotte, Mansart's brother-in-law, to this rank in 1685. Mansart frequently looked to Dorbay for drawings, as we shall see.

[88] *Vies des fameux architectes*, 1787, 365.
[89] L. Hautecoeur: "L'origine du dôme des Invalides, "*L'architecture*, XXXVII, 1924, 353-360, and "Jules Hardouin and François Mansart," in *Bulletin de la Société de l'histoire de l'art français*, 1924, 120-121.

Background

Robert de Cotte (1656-1735), had begun his career as a contractor for masonry, with important royal work in 1682-1685. Marrying the sister-in-law of Mansart before 1683, he was made a member of the Academy in 1685, and in the same year was given a salary of 2400 livres as an architect in the Bâtiments, inferior only to Dorbay. He was to rise to fortune as Mansart's collaborator and successor. To remove the reproach of lack of academic training, he made in 1689-1690 a belated six-months trip to Italy, for which we have his journal, of the driest observations,[90] and a collection of drawings of churches, made with rule and square, in which several different hands may be recognized.[91] That De Cotte was not incapable of drawing we know from his slight and loose freehand sketches for his own hôtel of 1722, with their notes "ma chambre, mon cabinet,"[92] but we find no developed designs of interiors or ornament from his hand. His contribution will have been rather in larger matters of general conception, for which we have ample evidence of his great powers, both in his own correspondence,[93] and in the letters of Balthasar Neumann.[94] Indeed we must credit him, rather than Mansart, with some of the major conceptions of the period, for we find on the first study for the final scheme of the Place Vendôme,[95] 1699, a contemporary caption "Place Louis le Grand suivant l'idée de Mr. De Cotte."

Under Mansart, to a degree hitherto unknown, draughtsmen were regularly employed to assist the architect. True Le Vau had used Dorbay, Dorbay had used the young Desgodetz and sometimes Vigneux. But Mansart went further, even at Clagny, almost from the beginning. We find in the accounts there the following payments to Cauchy:[96] in 1675, "à compte de ses ouvrages, 300 livres,"—in 1676,"à compte des desseins qu'il fait, 600 livres;" in 1677, "à Cochery, designateur, pour plusieurs desseins du bastiment de Clagny, 500 livres." Cauchy, moreover, was not alone. There were payments at Clagny in 1675, 1676 and 1678 to De Langre, dessinateur, totalling 384 livres. Jomart was paid 300 in 1679 and 200 in 1680, "a compte des journées employées à copier les desseins du bastiment de Clagny." For the first time in France a considerable division of labor appears in the preparation of architectural drawings for a given project.[97]

At Versailles under Colbert, from 1678, during the years of greatest activity, Mansart had the help not only of Dorbay but of various draughtsmen for special tasks. The chief of these

[90] Bibliothèque Nationale, MS. fr. 14663-14664. Cf. Mlle. Jeanne Lejaux in *Bulletin de la Société de l'histoire de l'art français*, 1938, 31.

[91] *Ibid.*, Vf 7, with binders title *De Cotte-Églises d'Italie*.

[92] *Ibid.*, Va 270.

[93] *Ibid.*, Hd 135-135e, published in part by P. Marcel: *Inventaire des papiers . . . de Robert de Cotte*, 1906.

[94] K. Lohmeyer: *Die Briefe Balthasar Neumanns von seiner Pariser Studienreise, 1723, 1911*.

[95] Cabinet des Estampes, Va 441, No. 1808.

[96] So he signed his name to the minutes of the Academy of Architecture March 5, 1699, when Mansart came accompanied by "MM. les officiers des bastimens."

[97] None of the original drawings for the construction of Clagny survives at the Archives Nationales or at the Cabinet des Estampes, the earliest of many drawings (Cabinet des Estampes) being one from which Mariette's plate was engraved, drawn apparently by Lassurance, who did not enter the Bâtiments until 1684. None of the draughtsmen listed in the accounts for Clagny, to be sure, was capable of making the general design of Clagny, which is rightly called in a note in Blondel's *Cours d'architecture* (V, 192) "l'une des plus ingénieuses compositions d'architecture de ce genre." Is it possible that Mansart merely modified and executed a scheme of Antoine Lepautre, to whom Mariette attributed the first designs for Clagny? There are indeed generic similarities of design with Lepautre's work at Saint-Cloud.

was Desgodetz, who had earlier been employed under Dorbay. Now on his return from Rome, at twenty-five, he was paid in 1678 and in 1679 for "plusieurs plants des maisons royalles"; again in 1682 (after two years as clerk at Chambord) he received 1000 livres "sur les desseins qu'il a fait des bastimens de Versailles." On the Grande Écurie in 1679 Cauchy received 100 livres "à compte de ses desseins," Jomart, 200 "pour les journées employées à copier les plans, eslevations, et profils," and 120 more in 1681 "pour desseins des plants." On the Aile du Midi, he had 100 livres in 1680 "sur les journées qu'il a employées à dessigner les plants et eslevations."

It was, however, in 1684, after the advent of Louvois, that the supplementary staff was regularized and enlarged. In that year Cauchy and Chupin were regularly employed as draughtsmen. In 1685, beside De Cotte as architect, Daviler and Lassurance, then young men, were active as draughtsmen. Except for Lescuyer at Marly, and for the appearance of Boffrand from 1686 to 1691 and sporadically later, these continued to constitute the staff until near the end of the century. Cauchy was specifically qualified in 1685 as "dessinateur dudit Sr. Mansart," Daviler also in 1686 as "dessinateur sous le Sr. Mansart."

Simon Chupin had been at the Academy in Rome from 1672 to 1676,[98] where Errard had opined he would succeed better in military than in civil architecture, "n'avant pas de dessein." "Un garson soumis," he never rose, any more than did Cauchy, above the obscurity of an assistant.

Germain Boffrand (1667-1754), at the age of but nineteen, was employed on the drawings of the Place Vendôme in its first form, from its origins in 1686. April 13, 1687, he was paid 740 livres "pour ses gages de l'année 1686 sous le sr. Mansart à dessigner les plants et profils des bastimens de la place Vendosme et du Commun des Capucines (*Comptes* II, 1272). We find his handwriting on one of the earliest plans, to establish the levels.[99] In 1688 he was paid 600 livres, "pour avoir dessiné les plants et profils des bastimens de la place Royalle et du convent des Capucines de l'hostel de Vendome," in 1689, 600 livres for the same, "sous le Sr. Mansart en 1688;" in 1690, for the previous year, 300 livres; in 1691, 150 livres—all for drawings for this project. In 1693 he was paid only for taking plans of Fontainebleau and Choisy; and in 1694 for doing so at other places. We have not found any designs by Boffrand at this period for other new works than those of the Place Vendôme.

Charles-Augustin Daviler (1653-1700) was, along with Desgodetz and Chupin, exceptional among the staff of the Bâtiments for having studied in Italy, working at the Academy in Rome from 1676 to 1680. Soon after his arrival there, although he had previously worked at the school of the Academy of Architecture at the Palais-Royal, it was remarked by Errard that "Il manque du dessein,"[100] and this deficiency was considered to continue, for Colbert, on seeing his *envois*, wrote Errard in March 1679 "je n'ay pas trouvé, qu'il dessinait assez bien."[101] Mariette writes of him: "Lorsqu'il fut de retour de Paris, il continua encore pendant quelque temps ses études en son particulier; mais peu après M. Mansard, premier Architecte du Roi, qui connoissoit son mérite, le reçut au nombre de ceux qui travailloit sous

---

[98] *Correspondance des Directeurs*, I, 1887, 39, 64.

[99] Cabinet des Estampes, Va 441, not numbered. There are ample specimens for comparison in signed letters, e.g., Bibliothèque Nationale, Cabinet des Manuscrits, Nouv. acc. fr. 2768, fol. 27.

[100] *Correspondance des Directeurs*, I, 64-65.

[101] *Ibid.*

lui dans le Bureau d'Architecture. Il y occupa bientôt une des premieres places; & comme il ne se fasoit pour le Roi qui ne passât par ses mains, l'expérience augmenta considérablement ses connoissances."[102] During his activity in the Bâtiments, from the fall of 1684 to the spring of 1689, we do not find Daviler receiving any gratifications for special services, and, at least for interiors, the surviving drawings from the period of his employment are by other hands. Impatient for advancement, he left the Bâtiments in disgust at the beginning of 1690. After the publication of his *Cours d'architecture* in 1691, codifying the practice of Mansart's atelier at that time, he assumed the direction of the works of Dorbay at Montpelier, where he died in 1700.

It was Pierre Cailleteau, called Lassurance, who was the chief reliance of Mansart from the time of his appointment in 1684. He appears in the accounts from 1679 as *appareilleur* at Clagny, and thus learned building on the scaffold, like so many other French architects, without ever going to Italy. We know nothing of his birth, or of his life except in his profession; he died in 1724. Saint-Simon, indeed, after Mansart's death, twice made the exaggerated charge that Mansart's reliance of Lassurance was complete. In his additions to the journal of Dangeau, May 11, 1708, he wrote of Mansart:

> Il était ignorant dans son métier, et de Cotte, son beau-frère, l'étoit guère moins. Ils tiroient tout d'un dessinateur qu'ils tenoient clos et à l'écart chez eux, qui s'appeloit Lassurance, sans lequel Ils ne pouvoient rien.[103]

And, in his own memoirs for 1708:

> Ils tiroit leurs plans, leurs desseins, leurs lumières, d'un dessinateur des bâtiments nommé l'Assurance, qu'ils tenoient tant qu'ils pouvoient sous clef.[104]

We shall see that at least the drawings for interiors from 1684 to 1699 were from the hand of Lassurance.

Our survey of the Bâtiments at this period would not be complete without a renewed allusion to Le Brun, who in these years reached and passed the pinnacle of his career. As Premier Peintre in a period when there was no Premier Architecte he was indeed the leading officer of the Bâtiments down to 1683, the date of Mansart's elevation to the vacant post at the head of the architectural staff, which he had long headed in fact. Colbert's death soon afterwards exposed Le Brun, who may also have been regarded as representing a survival of baroque influences, to the force of Louvois' preference for Mignard; but he retained his favour with the King and his post as director of the Gobelins until his death on February 10, 1690. The immense body of his drawings preserved at the Louvre, includes many for works of the central period of the reign. The bulk of them are from his own hand; including at least the ornaments in certain designs for interior features other than paintings—where the mechanical outlines

---

[102] "Vie de . . . Daviler," in Mariette's edition of Daviler's *Cours d'architecture*, 1738, xxxix-xlii. Mariette was himself not born until 1694, and depended, as he says in the *Abecedario*, on memoirs and papers supplied him by the artist's brother.

[103] *Journal de Dangeau*, 1857 ed., XII, 134.

[104] *Mémoires de Saint-Simon*, ed. Boislisle, XVI, 1902, 39.

may have been drawn by assistants. We continue to find payments for such draughtsmen. The painter Claude Nivelon was paid 825 livres in 1680 as "dessignateur aux Gobelins pour ses appointements pendant les neuf derniers mois de l'année." There are small sporadic payments to others as draughtsmen at the Gobelins, as to Pattigny in 1681, Sebastien Le Clerc in 1681 and following years.

Not administratively subordinate to the Bâtiments was the office of Menus-Plaisirs, in which the artistic force was Jean Berain.[105] Born in 1640 in Saint-Mihiel, son of a mastergunsmith, he came in youth to Paris. After being occasionally employed by the Bâtiments, from 1670, as an engraver, he had been appointed, at thirty-four, by brevet of December 28, 1674, Dessinateur de la Chambre et du Cabinet du Roi. His predecessor, Henry de Gissey, whom a contemporary document calls the "maistre de M. Berain," may indeed have inducted him into pagaentry, but scarcely into the decorative arts, in which he was to unfold an extensive activity. Mariette wrote of him: "On ne faisait rein, en quelque genre que ce fût, sans que ce soit dans sa manière, où qu'il en eût donné les desseins." While the expenses of the Menus-Plaisirs by 1692, as described in the État de France, included among many other items those of "les Meubles et l'argenterie pour les appartements du Roi" their design is not mentioned in the charges of Berain's brevet of 1674, which were "pour toutes sortes de desseins, perspectives, Figures et habits qu'il conviendrait Faire pour les Comedies, Balets, Courses de bagues et Carousels . . ." Actually Berain's duties, in the early years at least, lay precisely in such fields, and we do not find specific references to designs for use in the royal interiors prior to those we shall mention in 1682-1684. Through these, and above all through decorative compositions diffused by engraving, he was to exercise an influence which was of very great importance.

In the central period of Louis XIV, even more than during his early personal rule, the creative works, decisive for artistic direction, were in the palaces of the Crown. Although these have been the subjects of so many monographs, it remains to place in a single chronological series the successive undertakings there which embody this creative line.

Of Clagny, substantially completed by 1680 and destroyed in 1769, we have only inadequate descriptions, drawings and engravings, many of them inconsistent and inaccurate.[106] The engraved suite by Mansart's brother, Michel Hardouin, 1678-1680,[107] gives us almost our only significant glimpse of intended forms in the interior—a transverse section of the central vestibule, a longitudinal section of the great gallery with its three salons, in the center and at each end (Figure 11). By contrast with the rooms of the Grand Appartements at Versailles as then existing, but following Le Brun's scheme in the Grand Escalier, they were distinguished by an order—which here was of Corinthian pilasters. As compared with the work of Le Vau and Dorbay, the growing academism was sharply accentuated by this use of

---

[105] Cf. Weigert: *Jean I Berain.*

[106] Assembled and reproduced by C. Harlay, *op. cit.*

[107] J.-F. Blondel: *Cours d'architecture*, Paris, 1774-1777 (completed by Patte), V, 41-42 alludes to this suite, often bound with Jean Mariette's series: "On peut compter pour rien, ou pour peu de chose, les plans qu'en trouve dans le receuil de *l'Architecture Françoise*, et qui ne sont que les premiers idées imparfaits que l'architecte," yet the plan is dated 1680, the other plates 1678. Blondel's work itself gives details of the niches of the salon (III, pl. XL) surmounted by a cartouche with flanking cherubs, and of two interior cornices (V, pl. VII), one with consoles—nothing fundamentally new.

Background

an order. In the two central salons an attic reigned above the cornice. Although Louis XIV had included a gallery, with a central salon if possible, in his program for Versailles in 1669,[108] the adopted plan for the main story did not provide these. Clagny thus anticipated the treatments soon to be adopted at Versailles, both in the gallery and the salons there. At Clagny, as at the Château Neuf de Versailles, the Chambre du Roi had neither panelling nor ordonnance. The chimney breast still projected; the chimney piece, with a relief on the tall attic, was crowned by receding mouldings.

At Versailles, Mansart's advent to power there in 1678 found work in the Château Neuf still continuing under Colbert, Dorbay and Le Brun. The last of the paintings in the Appartement du Roi were not placed until 1681; the Escalier du Roi was not completed until 1679; its adjuncts, the upper vestibule (Salle de Vénus) and the Salle de Diane, even without their future marble revetments, not until after 1680.

Mansart's first employment at the château of Versailles in 1678 was on new projects of greater importance than these completions and corollaries of old undertakings. They were, on the one hand, to extend the forecourt with new lodgings in its pavilions and wings; on the other, to provide a new monumental gallery with accompanying salons. These first enterprises themselves were but the prelude to the vast expansions projected in 1679 to provide accommodations for the entire Court: the wings along the gardens, beginning with the Aile du Midi; the two immense stables.

In the matter of a gallery, Louis XIV by 1678 found himself outshone both by his mistress at Clagny and by his brother at Saint-Cloud. At Versailles, there was still only the Galerie Basse. Its inadequacy had now become insupportable, especially since Mignard's dazzling decorations at Saint-Cloud had been revealed to the Court in October of 1677. The King's decision to house the Court at Versailles, to make it the true capital, rendered immaterial the existence of the Galerie des Ambassadeurs at the Tuileries, the completion of the unfinished Galerie d'Apollon at the Louvre. Versailles was no longer to be merely a country seat, however magnificent; it must have its gallery, the most splendid of all.

The decision to build the gallery must date from the spring of 1678, even before the peace of Nimwegen. The advance provisions for the year (I, 1013-1016) do not envisage the gallery, yet the terrace of Le Vau was dismantled for it by June 26 (1040), by which time the plan for remodelling the Château Neuf (Figure 12) must have been prepared.

The gallery was the product of intimate collaboration of Mansart and Le Brun, with their respective assistants.[109] Its calm pilastered ordonnance of marble represents the apogee, in the interiors of the time, of the academicism of the central phase of the architecture of the reign (Figures 13-14). The substitution of arches, in the gallery and its salons, for the square-headed windows previously in vogue,[110] gave an exaltation which prefigures the tendency of the coming years. In the vault, baroque motives, both in relief and in grisaille, still survived,

---

[108] Published in *Lettres . . . de Colbert*, V, 1868, 238. Cf. Kimball: "The Genesis of the Château Neuf de Versailles" (awaiting publication abroad).

[109] Kimball: "Mansart et Le Brun in the Genesis of the Grande Galerie de Versailles," *Art Bulletin*, XXII, 1940, 1-6, where their successive studies are illustrated, attributed and discussed.

[110] At Saint-Cloud, just before this, the pavilions by Antoine Lepautre, completed 1677, had arched windows, which appeared in the Salon de Diane, and at the end of the gallery, but the other windows of the gallery and of the Salon de Mars, while arched internally, were still square-headed on the exterior. Cf. Fleury, *op. cit.*

though the former are much diminished in plasticity. In the adornment of the walls there was not yet that freedom and delicacy brought only by the placing of their trophies after 1701. The mirrors which filled the openings in the inner walls of these rooms, reflecting the windows, made a monumental application of their use, hitherto mainly confined to small cabinets.[111]

The Salon du Roi (de la Guerre) at the north end of the gallery, was opened in 1682, though its completion, with that of the Salon de la Paix, required some years longer. As first described by the *Mercure*, its walls were of marble, with trophies in gilded relief. These trophies as originally proposed (Figure 15) had been dominantly symmetrical. We cannot be sure that the provisional ones first executed followed the first design, any more than that they prefigured those delivered in 1701, on which Ladoireau had worked since 1682. Over the fireplace was the immense equestrian relief of the King by Coysevox, in an oval frame suggested by many works of Bernini and of Borromini. A similar frame surrounded the panel in the corresponding salon, the Salon de la Paix, where the minor trophies were of attributes of peaceful occupations, executed with graceful naturalism.

For the central salon, adjoining the gallery on the east, the attic of the salons at Clagny was adopted—as indeed it was in the first studies for the end salons (which show also ceilings of a double cove as at Clagny). In this central salon, too, was a pilastered ordonnance, at first Ionic, to assume its Composite form in the changes of 1684 while awaiting the further modifications of 1701.

The building of the gallery and salons involved the destruction of the more private rooms of the Grand Appartement du Roi, the cabinets and garderobe, returning along the garden. It was impossible to undertake the gallery without replacing these facilities elsewhere. Mansart's project of 1678 (Figure 12) provided them with great ingenuity by taking as a Petit Appartement du Roi the five rooms of the Petit Château to the west of the Cour de Marbre. This new Petit Appartement du Roi, first executed in 1678-1682, was at first approached from the north, from the Grand Appartement which the King continued to occupy until 1682.[112] The rooms still were given, for the most part, wall coverings of tapestry and damask, as we see in the drawing of 1679, probably by Desgodetz,[113] for the Chambre du Roi and Petit Cabinet (Figure 16). In the former, only the side walls were panelled, with tall Composite pilasters flanking the chimney piece and opposite pier. These units projected, breaking the cornice, and each bore a large painting. The overdoors had paired sphinxes, a baroque motif derived from such Italian examples as Bernini's great doorway in the hall of the Palazzo Barberini. An attic, as in the central salon, was employed in the high rooms at each end of the suite—the Petit Cabinet and the Cabinet des Termes—the latter taking its name from its features in that zone. The chimney pieces remained in part, at least, undisturbed by this remodelling, or at

---

[111] In the gallery at Saint-Cloud, which had windows all along one side and part way along the other, the rest of this side had, as Tessin wrote, "autant feintes des glaces." "Relation de la visite de Nicodème Tessin à Marly, Versailles, Clagny, Reuil et Saint-Cloud en 1687" in *Revue de l'histoire de Versailles et de Seine-et-Oise*, 1926, 297.

[112] Cf. Kimball and A.-M.-E. Marie: "Versailles inédit: L'appartement du Roi, 1678-1701," awaiting publication. It is a source of great regret that I must anticipate here the results of this collaborative paper, while my co-author is inaccessible to communication in occupied France.

[113] For evidence of his technique we have the copy of his manuscript *Cours d'architecture*, with illustrations, made by Jean Pinard after 1742, Cabinet des Estampes Ha 23 and 23a. Cf. J. Duportal in *Revue de l'art ancien et moderne*, XXXVI, 1914, 153-157; also the relation of drawings to chronology developed by Kimball: "Mansart and Le Brun," cited above.

least continued to follow earlier types. That of the Chambre du Conseil, surviving until 1699 (Figure 22), still had the receding attic suggestive of a hood.

The filling in of the court on the north to provide for the Escalier du Roi and the Salle de Vénus had been followed by the filling of the corresponding court on the south, from 1676 onward,[114] to receive the chapel. This permitted the space previously occupied by the old chapel proper to be taken for a Salon de la Reine (equivalent to the Salle de Diane on the north side), and allowed the space occupied by the tribune to be added to the Escalier de la Reine, so that this might be rebuilt with greater magnificence. These last two units could not be remodelled until the old chapel was vacated in 1679,[115] and their internal designs are subsequent to those for the Grande Galerie.[116]

The Escalier de la Reine, envisaged, like the salon, for execution in 1679 (I, 1114), was built in the two following years from drawings probably by Dorbay, dated 1680, which survive (Figures 17-18). They offered little that was new after Le Brun's final designs for the Escalier du Roi, and follow them in using a marble revetment with the Ionic order.

After certain earlier payments for paintings for the room, we find by February, 1680, allusion specifically to the "salon de marbre . . . de l'appartement de la Reyne" (I, 1280)—later the Salle des Gardes de la Reine, as it survives intact (Figure 19). Scholars have not hitherto appreciated that this was the first of all rooms in the main story of the château, other than the staircases, to have a complete marble revetment, its execution preceding any of the revetments in the Appartement du Roi as well as those of the Grande Galerie with its salons. The scheme of the marble incrustation does not differ substantially from that of the Cabinet des Bains in its strictly geometrical panels, although greater unity is achieved both through subsumption within the tall architraves reaching to the cornice and through the rondels which unite, rather than divide, the panels of the piers.

In the ceiling, executed in 1679-1680, were used paintings first intended for the demolished Grand Cabinet du Roi. Between their frames, strictly rectangular, the angles had painted balustrades with figures looking down. It was the first example in the royal châteaux of this motif, familiarly employed by the Italian mannerists, as notably by the Alberti in the Sala Clementina of the Vatican, 1596-1598, and lately adopted by Le Brun in the chapel at Sceaux, 1674-1676.

The chimney piece of this room at Versailles may well be the oldest surviving example[117] of a new type, in which the moulded marble architrave is surmounted by a plain attic of marble, slightly set back, with a simple thin shelf of marble (not a cornice) at top of architrave and top of attic. It is not until 1682 that there were installed "les cheminées et les attiques du grand appartement."[118] It was doubtless to such works that François Blondel alluded at just this moment, when he wrote, in his *Cours d'architecture*, 1683: "L'on faisait cy-devant beaucoup de dépense pour la structure & les ornemens des Cheminées . . . que l'on

[114] *Comptes*, I, 881 ff.

[115] *Ibid.*, 1155, 1278.

[116] Kimball: "Mansart and Le Brun," *loc. cit.*

[117] At Clagny from February, 1679, the accounts mention "chambranles, *attiques* et foyers de marbre des principaux appartemens" (I, 1191), and at Versailles from April of the same year, "foyers, attiques et chambranles de marbre pour . . . les appartemens du Roy" (1164).

[118] Colbert to d'Ormoy, March 25, 1682. *Lettres . . . de Colbert*, ed. Clément, VII, clxi.

chargeoit excessivement: Mais presentement on les rend beaucoup plus legeres, & l'on les trouve plus belle dans leur simplicité."

The need of communication with the Grande Aile required a further displacement of the chapel, to a position, itself provisional, in a wing begun in May, 1681, to the north of the château, on the site of the future Salon d'Hercule. The unpublished designs of Dorbay, dated June 22, 1681, survive at the Archives Nationales (o¹ 1783). They show a continued use of herms in the principal story, here constituting the tribune, as had been first intended for the Escalier du Roi and its landing. Work was completed with the greatest rapidity, permitting dedication in May, 1682.

To reach the new chapel more handsomely, the old pavilion of the wing was remodelled, the northern portion becoming the Salle d'Abondance, which served as a vestibule from the Appartement du Roi not only to the chapel but to the Cabinet des Bijoux, des Curiosités, des Raretés, or des Médailles, which occupied the southern portion, raised by five steps. The raising of the roofs in this area in 1678-1679 permitted these new rooms also to have vaulted ceilings.

The Salle d'Abondance was executed in 1682, being described in the *Mercure* of that December, except for the ceiling, paid for in November, 1683. Its most striking feature was the marble doorway to the Cabinet, over which the cornice of the room was arched on consoles, framing a large medallion. This is a familiar Italian high-baroque motif used for instance in the drum of Pietro da Cortona's Santa Maria della Pace, adopted on a grand scale in the façade of the Hospice des Invalides, 1671, and partly anticipated in the overdoors of the design of the Grande Galerie approved by Colbert in September, 1678. The example in the Salle d'Abondance was the first to be executed in a French interior, henceforth there were many during the '80's and '90's. The design, in view of its date, will surely have been due to Dorbay. On the consoles of the cornice are cherubs' heads with butterfly wings.[119] The ceiling, unlike those of the older rooms of the Château Neuf, is not divided into compartments. Its celestial vault is bordered by a parapet with figures.

A series of rooms of a special character was opened by the Cabinet des Curiosités—or des Médailles, to use the name which ultimately carried the day—begun in 1682 and reaching substantial completion in 1684. Of its form, "ordonné" or "indiqué" by Berain,[120] we have had only very inadequate descriptions until the publication of that of Tessin from 1687,[121] now made intelligible by the discovery, by Alfred Marie, of a plan (o¹ 1768) and a section (o¹ 1775). This was the first of such cabinets in just this period, the forerunner of many others, as it was the successor of those of the earlier Versailles. Tessin wrote of the Cabinet des Médailles:

[119] Herms with butterfly wings, found in early Italian grotesques, are common in those of Berain, none of which, however, may be dated as early as this.

[120] According to the "Notes de Nicodème Tessin le jeune relatives à son sejour a Paris en 1687," in *Bulletin de la Société de l'histoire de l'art français*, 1932, 271. Tessin's special friendship for Berain, who supplied much of his information, occasionally led him, as we can judge in this case, to exaggerate the extent of Berain's responsibility.

[121] "Visite à Versailles," *loc. cit.*, 284-285.

Cette chambre est presque quarrée, mais, aux quattre coins il y a quatre niches ornées des glaces . . . et, dans la niche, on a faict comme les estages dorèes . . . avec leurs petits supports . . . en se diminuant . . . A costè de ces niches il y [a] un espece des petits pilastres estroits, representès des miroirs et bordès des orures [i.e. de dorures], devants lesquels on voit sur des petits soustiens posèes des petittes statües d'agathe; auprez de ces pilastres, de deux cotès de la niche, il y a des petits tableaux . . . rangès au nombre des trois l'un sur l'autre . . . à costè de ces trois tableaux nommès, il y a par tout des pillastres de rechef, ordonnès de mesme comme je viens de dire, entre les quells, du costè de l'entrèe, le chambranle de porte occupe l'espace; de même, vis-à-vis la fenestre, du costè gauche, la cheminée avec ses glaces en haut . . . â l'opposite de laquelle il est égualement ornè des glaces.

Above the cornice—in the frieze of which, as Félibien reports, were fifty recesses, lined with mirrors, for precious vases—was an oval dome on pendentives, its lunettes and drum pierced by dormers, all richly ornamented with gilded figures and festoons.

The chimney piece, as it appears in the section, is a new type with a frieze or attic and then a tall panel, successively narrowed, above the architrave.[122] Already in 1684 Le Nègre (or Le Nècre) was paid "pour avoir relevé les ornemens de cuivre doré de la cheminée . . . les avoir redoré où il était nécessaire, mis en couleur et reposez" (II, 459). Whatever was the case in 1682, by 1687, at least, the whole panel of the chimney breast was faced with mirrors, as we shall find them in the Chambre du Roi by 1684.

It was for the Cabinet des Médailles that Berain designed in 1684 (II, 497, 541) the famous Bureau du Roi executed in marquetry by Jean Oppenord (458) as were the twelve marquetry cabinets for the medals.

A related room—the Dauphin's Cabinet de Boulle—"son cabinet de marquetrie et de glaces"[123]—was begun in its first form in 1682-1683 (slightly later than the Cabinet de Curiosités of the King) for his apartment in the Aile du Midi. Much additional work was done by Boulle on its removal to the ground floor of the château in 1684, but we cannot doubt that it was from the very beginning, as Tessin says in 1687, "en compartemens octogons et quarrées, remplies de glaces all' imitation des incavatures antiques; les quatres murailles . . . fort jolÿment inventés et revesties des lambris, guarnies de touttes sortes des oeuvres de rapport d'otton, estain, etc.; le pavé . . . d'une marquetterie très fine," that it had, indeed, as Félibien later states,[124] "de tous côtez et dans le plafond des glaces de miroirs avec des compartemens de bordures dorées sur un fond de marqueterie d'ebène."[125] The floor of mar-

---

[122] Chimney pieces of not dissimilar type, but without mirrors, appear in Girard's suite of *Cheminées nouvellement faites*, 1686, in the *Receuil des oeuvres du Sieur Cottart*, 1686, and in Laurent Francart's *Nouvelles Cheminées*, n.d. One of this last suite is illustrated in Kimball: "The Development of the 'Cheminée à la royale,'" *loc. cit.*, on p. 266, and, as later revised to include a mirror in the attic, on p. 267. Pierre Lepautre, as we shall see, engraved some of the type with attic mirrors, and others appear in Daviler's *Cours d'architecture*, 1691.

[123] So Dangeau calls it, June 14, 1684, in speaking of the orders for its transfer to its new location (salle 50).

[124] J. F. Félibien: *Description sommaire de Versailles . . .* 1703. Other descriptions by Monicart, 1713, and La Martinière, 1729. As we have demonstrated, the familiar painting *Le Grand Dauphin dans son Cabinet* shows not this cabinet but that at Meudon, executed from designs by Berain in 1699. Cf. "The Development of the 'Cheminée à la royale,'" 268, 271 and *Burlington Magazine*, LXVIII, 1936, 185.

[125] La Martinière mentions consoles to receive bronzes and porcelains. Although Tessin does not mention them in 1687, they had apparently been installed in 1685 (*Comptes*, II, 618).

quetry had the arms of the Dauphin and Dauphine. Although no document connects the design of this cabinet with Berain, it is not improbable that he had such a connection in the case of this work for the Dauphin, as we know he had with the Dauphin's cabinet at Meudon seventeen years later, Berain being long the favorite artist of the heir to the throne.[126]

A new campaign in the interiors began after 1683 with the death of Colbert, the advent of Louvois to the Surintendance, the eclipse of Le Brun by Mignard. The man now primarily concerned with architectural design of interiors, as we have said, was Lassurance, appointed *dessinateur* in the Bâtiments in the fall of 1684.

The great enterprise of this year was the transformation of the rooms around the Cour de Marbre into a veritable Appartement du Roi. Since the return of the Court in May, 1682, when the eight northern bays of the gallery were opened, the Grand Appartement du Roi had become uninhabitable by the monarch. Although a state bed remained there for many years, the rooms began to be called Salles or Salons and the suite became known as the Grand Appartement rather than as the Appartement du Roi. The death of the Queen, July 30, 1683, rendered unnecessary the privacy of relationship between her apartment, henceforth assigned to the Dauphine, and the more intimate rooms of the King. The decision was made to take for the Appartement du Roi the whole circuit of the Cour de Marbre, to reverse the approach, utilizing the Escalier de la Reine, to provide a Salle des Gardes and Premier Antichambre by widening the Aile Gauche, and to turn the old Petit Cabinet into a Seconde Antichambre, giving public access to the gallery. This great change involved giving all the new outer rooms of the suite, which acquired the functions of the corresponding ones of the old Grand Appartement du Roi, a more monumental character, to adapt them, in their new uses, to the splendour of the monarch.

The new Salle des Gardes and the Premier Antichambre received a revetment of marble. The succeeding rooms of the Appartement du Roi were remodelled for increased magnificence. They were now characteristically panelled throughout in wood, richly carved and gilt: Antichambre des Bassans,[127] Chambre du Roi (Figure 20), Salon, Cabinet du Billard (Figure 21)[128]—"tous boisés" as Félibien describes them and as they appear in surviving designs revealing the style of Lassurance. Spatial unity and simplicity were heightened by elimination of the projection of the chimney breast, accomplished in the Chambre du Roi by carrying the cornice, unbroken, across the existing recesses at either side. The cornices themselves received a lighter treatment, as here. The new chimney pieces remained high, although in the Chambre du Roi a high frieze replaced the attic. In the panelling of the rooms, mirrors were now introduced over the chimney pieces, both of the Cabinet du Billard and of the Chambre du Roi, the

[126] As early as 1681 he had designed the costumes for the mascarade *Le Triomphe de l'Amour* given by the Dauphin, and in 1783 those of *La Noce du village* in which the Dauphin's disguises were particularly numerous and ingenious. Cf. Weigert, *op. cit.*, I, 77-81.

[127] This was actually panelled by mistake, as is clear from Mansart's letter to Louvois May 27, 1684 (o¹ 1762A), on which the Minister noted: "Le Roy n'avoit ordonnée que l'on boisast l'antichambre la plus proche de sa chambre, mais puisque cela est fait, Sa Majesté n'est pas fachée qu'elle soit boisé aussy bien que l'autre."

[128] From an engraved suite by Pierre Lepautre *Portes à placard et lambris dessinez par le Sr. Mansard et nouvellement executez dans quelques Maisons Royales*. It includes also the Cabinet de Monseigneur at Versailles, *ca.* 1684-1685, and several rooms at Trianon of 1686-1687. Possibly the panelling of the Cabinet du Billard was only on the chimney wall, as the number and size of the paintings which hung here seems to preclude panelling on the other walls.

latter rising to the main entablature. Thus appeared a feature, the tall pier-glass, which was to be of much significance in the subsequent development.

To a degree not generally realized, the Grand Appartement du Roi was also enriched at this time. The inner wall of the Salle de Vénus received its marble columns and revetment in the autumn of 1684.[129] The Salle de Diane, in November, 1684, acquired its supreme ornament, Bernini's bust of the King, in a new setting, designed apparently by Lassurance, again making use of the motif of an arched cornice resting on consoles.[130] Marble columns and recesses on the inner wall of the Salle de Mars, which have since disappeared, were added in 1687 (II, 1173). Here in that year Tessin states that "devant les deux piliers entre les croisées, il y a de grands miroirs." By their columnar ordonnance, these rooms of the Grand Appartement were made at once more monumental and more academic.

In 1684 a change was also made here in the floors. The need of washing the marble, which had tended to rot the joists below, led to the substitution of "parquet de menuiserie."[131] In general this was in the large diagonal squares still commonly known today as "parquet de Versailles." Such parquets "en lozange" were remarked by Cronström in 1693 both at Versailles and at Trianon.[132]

In the cornices of this time the scheme with consoles and sculptured metopes now became universal. Employed at Clagny and in the gallery at Saint-Cloud, it was adopted in the gallery at Versailles, and in such magnificent examples as those of the Salle d'Abondance, the Salle des Gardes and Premier Antichambre du Roi, from 1683 and 1684.

The ceilings of the two salons at the end of the gallery were attacked by Le Brun in 1685 and completed in 1686. Their frames were simplified, as compared with those of the old rooms of the Appartement du Roi, having, like the Salle de Diane, four lunettes under elliptical arches, with a central circular panel above. On the arches of the Salon de la Guerre there was a rich band of fronds of palm, recalling those of Borromini at the entrance of Saint John Lateran.

To Mignard the favour of Louvois assigned the flat ceiling of the Grand Cabinet de Monseigneur,[133] immediately after his completion of the vault of the Petite Galerie, and thus of nearly the same moment as that of the Salon de la Paix just above.

The work of Louvois' campaigns at Versailles included also development of the initiative taken in the Cabinets des Médailles and de Monseigneur. In 1684 the Cabinet du Conseil and the Cabinet des Perruques were revetted throughout with mirrors (Figure 22). A similar revetment was proposed in 1684 for the Petite Galerie, with its salons, as shown in the original design by Lassurance (Figure 23). Consoles for precious vases were to be placed against the glass, as we may see today in the Green Vault at Dresden (1721-1724), an imitation which has survived its French exemplars. A detail drawing (o¹ 1768, no. 50) shows that the frames were to be marquetry of lapis and tortoise shell. Tessin saw the whole work set up at the

---

[129] Reports of Louvois, November 10, cited by Nolhac: *Versailles résidence de Louis XIV*, 1925 ed., 103.

[130] Archives Nationales, o¹ 1768. Lassurance, previously employed as an "appareilleur," was paid on January 28, 1685, for his first quarter's work as a draughtsman, which could thus well include this drawing. The indication of the cherubs is closely similar to that of the same motif in a later drawing by him for the Ménagerie.

[131] *Comptes*, II, 610, and documents cited by Nolhac: *Création de Versailles*, 1925 ed., 175.

[132] R. Josephson: "Le Grand Trianon sous Louis XIV," in *Revue de l'histoire de Versailles...*, 1927, 24.

[133] Engraved by Gérard Audran.

Gobelins in 1687. He states that it had been "indiqué" by Berain; in view of Lassurance's general design this can only apply to the details. Apparently it was never installed at Versailles. By the inventories of 1695 as well as those of 1709-1710 we know that the walls of the Petite Galerie were hung with precious easel paintings.[134] Brice wrote in 1706 (I, 85) of the Galerie des Ambassadeurs at the Tuileries, "on distinguera encore dans même lieu les morceaux d'un tres riche lambris, que l'on avoit destiné pour la petite galerie de Versailles, orné de glaces et de moulures de bronze doré, sur des fonds d'écaille de Tortue et d'un lapis assez bien contrefait." The decision to devote the Petite Galerie to paintings led in 1690 to the installation of consoles for vases against the mirrors of the Cabinet de Conseil (II, 394-399).

The floor of the Petite Galerie and its salons, of which a drawing survives (Figure 24), was executed in marquetry by Jean Oppenord. It is possible that this was from a design by Berain,[135] whom we have seen providing designs for this ébéniste. The pattern is in compartments, with broken arcs not irrelated to those of the great series of Savonnerie carpets so lately completed for the Louvre. There is much interlacing bandwork, but without any mixture of acanthus or scrolls. The ceiling by Mignard, engraved by Gérard Audran, was in painted compartments against a background of delicate gilt mosaïque.

At Marly, first projected in 1679, the Pavillon Royal was begun in 1680, its joinery executed in 1680-1681, its carving 1682-1683. Of the initial form of its interiors we know very little. There is a manuscript section before the remodelling of 1699,[136] another after this remodelling (Figure 47).[137] The great octagonal central salon à l'italienne, suggested by the central circular hall of Palladio's Villa Rotonda, is adorned in the main story—here, as at Clagny, the ground story—by Corinthian pilasters, in the upper story by herms continuing the traditions of Le Brun and Dorbay. Prior to 1699 there were no fireplaces in the salon; "a chaque angle," wrote Tessin in 1687, "il y a, sur des piédestaux, des statues de marbre."[138] Here, as we shall see, the chimney pieces with mirrors were to be substituted in 1699.[139] The balconies of the room, introduced for music in 1686 (Comptes II, 922, 1045), were above the main cornice. The four vestibules with coved ceilings and heavy pedimented doors were adorned, below the imposts, with large paintings by Van der Meulen, and other paintings by him were placed in 1688 on the chimney pieces of the major apartments (Comptes III, 90). One of the rooms of the upper story—appearing, little modified from its initial treatment, in

---

[134] F. Engerand: Inventaire des tableaux du Roy, 1899.

[135] He was paid 1000 livres, August 19, 1685 "en considération de plusieurs desseins qu'il a faits pour le service de S. M." (II, 737), and again May 9, 1688, 1500 livres (III, 67).

[136] Archives des Bâtiments Civils, reproduced by Jean Verrier in L'architecture, XXXVII, 1923, 1.

[137] Archives Nationales, o¹ 1472, with title "Marly . . . 1714," pl. 5; an engraving of it for Mariette in Cabinet des Estampes, Va 351, re-engraved in A.-A. Guillamot: Le Château de Marly-le-Roi, 1865, pl. 3. I have not seen the drawings for Marly which Nolhac mentioned in 1901 as in the collection of Victorien Sardou. No interior designs are reproduced in C. Piton: Marly-le-Roi, 1904, which made use of the collection of Sardou. The diary of the German architect Pitzler contains sketches and descriptions of Marly in 1685, kindly called to my attention by Dr. Hans Huth, but they do not add to our information on Marly from other sources.

[138] "Visite à Versailles," loc. cit., 293.

[139] The trophies reproduced by J.-J. Guiffrey: Inventaire du mobilier de la Couronne sous Louis XIV, 314-315, with the caption "Trophées d'emblèmes sculptés et dorés du Grand Salon de Marly" are actually from a later room, now in the Hoentschel-Morgan collection at the Metropolitan Museum of Art, and have nothing to do with Marly.

the section of 1714—shows that here the inner walls had tapestries of the Maisons Royals series, above high two-tiered dados, and had narrow projecting chimney breasts with heavily moulded tabernacles later filled with mirrors.

The transformation of the Trianon de Porcelaine into the Trianon de Marbre took place in 1686-1688, two of the old pavilions being incorporated in the new building.[140] Here again, as at Versailles in 1679, windows arched externally were substituted for the old square-headed ones, although high vaults above heavy entablatures still held the internal opening of the windows, in their first treatment, down to the impost, with an elliptical *arrière-voussure*.[141] Of the early interiors here, from 1687, we have a drawing of the Salon des Jardins, and engravings of features in a number of other rooms (Figures 25-27)—all these rooms being designed by Lassurance. The Grand Cabinet is described by André Le Nôtre in 1694[142] as "remply de grande glasse depuis le bas jusque au haut"—doubtless then covering the entire walls as in the Cabinet de Conseil of 1684 at Versailles. In 1691-1692 was executed the Appartement du Roi of the Aile Gauche, likewise from designs by Lassurance (Figures 28-31). Its rooms were panelled throughout in wood, with marble chimney pieces having a high attic.[143] In two rooms the windows were pierced to the full height of the exterior arches; the effect must have been admired, for many others were pierced in 1694.

In the early panelled rooms of Lassurance, whether at Versailles or at Trianon, we find a variety of schemes, from survival of the old type of *lambris à l'hauteur d'un bras levé* with paintings above (Salon des Jardins) to ordonnance by columns or pilasters (Salon Rond, Salon "pour serrer le fruit," Salon de la Chapelle). In all, however, there was a multiplied articulation and superposition, involving universally some division of the wall by an impost. The rectangular panels, relieved only by a few oval or circular ones above the doors and chimney pieces, were of geometrical monotony. Carving was confined strictly to the friezes and to the principal frames, scarcely invading the panels themselves. Some of the cornices had consoles; more had continuous friezes with repetitions of balanced scrolls—sometimes of foliage, sometimes of broken bandwork—from between the scrolls of which spread radiating lines of shell or fleuron. At Trianon, mirrors were introduced in several rooms in 1691, being confined to the piers between the windows and to the attics of the chimney pieces, except in the Salon de la Chapelle, where after several studies, the pier opposite the chimney piece received a tall arched mirror with a cornice on consoles, the Italian motif employed just previously at Versailles in the Salon d'Abondance and in the Salon de Diane. The windows at Trianon had continuous archivolts without imposts, as in many Italian examples.

By 1692 Lassurance made the designs for the new Salon Ovale at Versailles (Figure 32) of elongated form with semi-circular ends. In alternating rhythm, between Corinthian pilas-

[140] Cf. on this point, R. Danis: *La première maison royale de Trianon*, Paris, 1927, which in some other regards is very untrustworthy.

[141] Kimball: "La transformation des appartements de Trianon sous Louis XIV," in *Gazette des beaux-arts*, VIe pér. XIX, 1938, 87-110.

[142] Letter quoted by R. Josephson: "Le Grand Trianon sous Louis XIV," in *Revue de l'histoire de Versailles . . .*, 1927, 20.

[143] We may remark that in the *Cours d'architecture*, 1691, of Daviler, who left the Bâtiments at the end of 1689, the chimney pieces are of types prior to those at Trianon; the complete interiors are not more advanced than the early style of Lassurance. Like most manuals, it codified the style of a moment before, rather than led the way.

ters, were four openings on the major axes for the doors and the window, four niches in narrower intervals between. Doorways and window were treated alike with carved architraves rising to the entablature; the niches rose freely into the upper zone between the pilasters. No impost divided the height; no chimney piece interrupted the lines—the effect was of a unity hitherto unexampled.

Later in the decade, in 1698, Lassurance was called on to design apartments for the little Duchesse de Bourgogne, at Trianon, and, a few months later, at the remodelled Château de la Ménagerie.[144] In the Chambre de la Duchesse at Trianon (Figure 33), the impost still survived, the multiplication of panels in the height still persisted, but certain arches, including two for mirrors above the chimney piece and on the opposite pier, broke into the upper zone, and sculpture invaded certain of the panels, above the arches and below the impost. These were the first of the new type of arched mirrors in the royal residences.[145] At the Ménagerie, in the Appartement d'Hiver, along with cabinets of varied spatial forms lined with mirrors and consoles—the last, by the way, of such cabinets in the French palaces—was panelling of almost stereotyped rectangular monotony (Figure 34). In the Appartement d'Été, however, while the impost was retained, with numerous tiers of panels, we find more varied schemes which embody fresh creative ideas. In the Antichambre the upper panels are rounded at top and bottom. In some of the rooms, the dado was eliminated, the piers up to the impost were punctuated only by a circular panel or rosette at half the height; in others narrow piers were unbroken by any impost. The marble chimney pieces here had broader shelves or tablettes without any attic,[146] their heads being arched or supported by herms. In the Antichambre (Figure 37), the mirror of the chimney piece was arched above the line of the impost, which itself was arched above this, almost to the cornice, with which it was united by a crowning motif of shell and cornucopia. In the Chambre (Figure 38), the semi-circular head of the tall mirror rose even higher, supporting a vase and cherubs which reached the cornice. These principal apartments being on the ground floor, with existing windows very close to the ceilings, which were flat or with the smallest of coves, the cornices were reduced to a thinness very exceptional at this period (Figures 35, 36). Most of them lacked any architrave. Their friezes and mouldings were richly ornamented, as were the frames marking the upper limit of the coves of the cabinets, these latter bordered with fringes of scrolls and palmettes.

The forms of work for the Dauphin at this time we know only through the accounts. His apartment at Versailles was enlarged and renovated in 1693-1695.[147] We note of the new chimney piece in the Grand Cabinet, February, 1694 (*Comptes* III, 991, 955), that there is no specific mention of an attic. Meudon, acquired in June, 1695, and included in the Maisons Royales, saw at once a few first remodellings. The Cabinet à la Capucine of the entresol took its name from the brown of its "boiserie de chêne naturel vernisée,"[148] a novelty and exception among interiors usually painted and gilt.

[144] Kimball: "Trianon," *loc. cit.*, and "Le décor du château de la Ménagerie," *Gazette des beaux-arts*, VIe pér., XVI, 1936, 245-256.

[145] Mansart had adopted it in 1695 at the Hôtel de Lorges, as we shall see.

[146] In 1699 it was proposed to substitute such low ones at Versailles, in the Chambre du Roi and the Cabinet du Conseil. Cf. "Versailles inédit: l'Appartement du Roi," previously cited.

[147] The beginning of the work is marked by Dangeau October 3, 1693, IV, 385.

[148] P. Biver: *Histoire du château de Meudon*, Paris, 1923, 134 ff.

Background

These works close the cycle of royal interiors executed under Mansart's direction before his succession to the Surintendance, when with a new designer, there was to open a new phase of artistic creation.

There were, to be sure, works of some importance executed at this period for the Dauphin at Choisy;[149] for Monsieur, a gallery was added by Mansart in 1692 at the Palais-Royal.[150] Both these works, however, like Meudon and Saint-Cloud, have suffered total destruction, as has Issy.[151] Here a pilastered salon recalled some motifs of the Grande Galerie de Versailles; one room at least had a square mirror above the fireplace. The little we know from drawings and documents does not indicate that these works embodied much in the way of artistic initiative.

In Paris relatively few private houses of importance were erected at this time when, of all other periods, Versailles was most completely dominant. In certain remodellings, however, we find some work of creative importance. Thus at the Hôtel de Mailly in 1687-1688 there were ceilings designed by Berain which we shall consider at length in our discussion of arabesques. At the Hôtel de Lorges,[152] though other parts of the house were still filled with workmen in 1698, the remodelling of the apartment of the Marshal was completed under the direction of Mansart by 1695. The *Mercure* of that year speaks especially of the views from the Grand Cabinet and their reflection, along with that of the central lustre chandelier, in tall arched mirrors over the chimney piece and on the piers of the other three sides—obviously a novelty.[153]

We are now in a position to sum up, more accurately than has been possible heretofore, the architectural character of interiors in the central period of the reign.

For wall treatment, in the state apartments at Versailles, complete revetments of marble added both monumentality and splendour. Elsewhere a unified panelling in wood, now embracing all the walls, became characteristic. In the cabinets equal unity was achieved by a facing of mirrors throughout.

Le Brun's adoption of an order in the Escalier du Roi at Versailles, followed by Mansart at Clagny and in the Escalier de la Reine, now led to more extensive employment of monumental forms. Unlike the galleries at the Louvre, the Tuileries and Saint-Cloud, the new gallery at Versailles had an ordonnance throughout, with full columns at the ends. Such columns were also introduced in the remodellings of the Salles de Vénus and de Mars. In

---

[149] B. Chamchine: *Le château de Choisy*, Paris, 1910, esp. pp. 29 ff.

[150] Champier and Sandoz: *Le Palais-Royal*, Paris, 1900.

[151] Designed by Bullet, it was spoken of by Tessin in 1687 as "new." "Séjour à Paris," 230. Certain motifs are engraved in Mariette's *Architecture françoise*, pls. 309-310 of the Hautecoeur edition.

[152] A. de Boislisle in *Bulletin de la Société de l'histoire de Paris*, XXXVIII, 1911, 199-208, where, as in notes to the *Journal of Dangeau*, V, 1855, 180, the documents regarding the house are assembled and quoted. Many drawings are preserved at the Cabinet des Estampes, Va 236 f, but no interiors before the period of occupancy by the Princesse de Conti, from 1713.

[153] Photographs of the Chambre du Lit at the Hôtel de Mailly, in its condition a generation ago (*Les Vieux hôtels de Paris*, IV, 1911, pls. 7-12) show such an arched mirror over the fireplace in connection with Berain's painted panelling of 1687. Tessin's description of the hôtel in that year, already cited, speaks of this panelling as being then in the "alcove," as being "ornes de glaces," but says nothing of the mirrors there being arched. The arched mirror may thus possibly date from the period of remodelling. If not, it would be the earliest of all the arched mirrors, preceding even those of the Hôtel de Lorges by eight years. It is almost impossible to believe that so long a time elapsed before adoption of the motif on a chimney piece anywhere else.

the new Appartement du Roi, as well as at Marly and Trianon, the more formal or more important panelled rooms had likewise an order.

When, toward the end of the period, interest came to centre mainly on more private accommodations, the use of pilasters diminished and the treatment of panelled rooms was one almost purely tectonic, stressing the doorways and chimney piece, with a multiplied superposition of rectangular panels, and carving confined chiefly to the major frames, without any pronounced baroque ornaments.

The use of mirror-glass reached an apogee at this period, overflowing from the cabinets into other rooms, even in the Grands Appartements, where hanging mirrors began to be replaced by glasses let into the walls. The inclusion of mirrors in the monumental treatment of the Grande Galerie—the Galerie des Glaces—made their vogue universal. In the Chambre de la Reine, in 1687, Tessin mentions, "au lieu de miroir, trois grandissimes glaces jointes ensemble." In the Salle de Mars and at Saint-Cloud, he noted their presence on the piers between the windows.

Important for the future was the placing of mirrors, instead of paintings, on the chimney breasts in rooms other than the glazed cabinets—*cheminées à la Mansarde* or *à la royale*[154] as they were later called. The first, as we have seen, were the large square-headed ones in the Chambre du Roi and the Salle du Billard at Versailles, both from 1684. This was prior to any architectural activity of Robert de Cotte, to whom the innovation was subsequently attributed.[155] At Trianon, where there were no such mirrors at first, small ones were introduced in the attics of the mantels in 1692, with others on the piers opposite.[156] Certainly at the Hôtel de Lorges in 1695, at Trianon and the Ménagerie in 1698, there were arched mirrors in this position, rising to the cornice.

Whereas the windows in the Galerie d'Apollon at the Louvre, in the first designs for the Château Neuf at Versailles and also in the gallery at Clagny (Figure 11), had stopped at a sill lining with the dado, those in the gallery at Saint-Cloud were spoken of by Tessin as descending "presque jusque à terre," and the very first designs for the gallery and salons at Versailles show casement sash extending quite to the floor. This scheme was quickly adopted elsewhere at Versailles. Tessin remarks particularly, in the Appartement du Roi in 1687: "Les fenestres montent depuis les pavées jusques sous les corniches par tout." Such a treat-

[154] Cf. "The Development of the 'Cheminée à la Royale,' " already cited, for these usages.

[155] J. F. Blondel, born in 1705, too late to have personal knowledge, mentions having heard this attribution, in his *De la distribution des maisons de plaisance*, Paris, 1737-1738, from which it was repeated without qualification by Pierre Patte in *Monuments érigés en France à la gloire de Louis XV*, 1765, and in his continuation of Blondel's *Cours d'architecture*, 1771-1776, V, 66, as well as by Dezallier d'Argenville, *Vies des fameux architectes*, Paris, 1787, 418, and universally by modern writers.

[156] Such mirrors appear throughout in Pierre Lepautre's suite *Cheminées et lambris à la mode executez dans les nouveaux bâtimens de Paris*. (An early impression issued by N. Langlois, belonging to the Metropolitan Museum of Art, shows that this included the following plates of the Jombert edition; suite 54, pls. 1-2; suite 55, pls. 3-6). The marble mantels, while simple in detail, show varied forms which anticipate later types: with a segmental opening, with baluster-like supports, and the concave *crossettes* at the upper corners. Similar attics with mirrors appear in three plates—which though unsigned, appear to be by Pierre Lepautre—of a suite incorporated in Jean Mariette's later collection *Architecture a la Mode* with the title *Cheminées nouvelles à la Mansarde*. The other three are from Laurent Francart's suite *Nouvelles cheminées gravé sur des dessein de Mr. Francard*, but have mirrors substituted for the bas reliefs originally shown in the attics and are otherwise modified in the direction of later taste.

ment—the "French window," used also at Marly, Trianon, and the Ménagerie—now became universally characteristic.

Thus was established the basic scheme which the French interior was to retain henceforth: a square room with symmetrical wall membering, double doors *en enfilade* balanced by false doors, windows rising from floor to cornice, doorways extended by overdoors to the same height, a relatively low marble frame for the fireplace, a chimney breast flush and treated as part of the panelling, already, like the pier opposite, with a mirror which might extend to the cornice. This abiding basic scheme attained its full embodiment during the last fifteen years of the seventeenth century.

The ceilings of the principal rooms, while still usually vaulted or with a high cove, tended to lose their traditional Italian character and thus also to approach the scheme which was to prevail in future. The frames of compartments in stucco were diminished in relief (Grande Galerie) and in complexity of outline (Salle de Diane, etc.), replaced by painted compartments (Petite Galerie), or eliminated entirely (Trianon). Where there was a story above, the ceilings of the ground story were usually flat, for instance at Versailles and in most of the rooms at the Ménagerie. This did not preclude their being painted, like Mignard's figural ceiling of the Grand Cabinet du Dauphin at Versailles; the ceilings of the Hôtel de Mailly "avec des voûtes tout à fait plates," as Tessin described them, gave occasion for a decoration of painted arabesques.

Except for a few rare instances of varnished woodwork *à la capucine*, the French panelled interior was painted and gilt. Tessin speaks repeatedly of white and gold: at Versailles, in the doors of the Escalier du Roi, in those of the Grand Appartement, and in the cornices there, as well as in the panelling of the central salon; at Saint-Cloud in the cornice of the gallery. The Grand Cabinet de Monseigneur at Versailles he describes as "tout garny d'or blanc et un peu d'azur." The arabesques of the ceilings of the Hôtel de Mailly were also in yellow, brown and gold, originally on a white ground. At Trianon alone there was at first no gilding: "le tout peint en blanc en detrempe," as Cronström wrote Tessin in 1693,[157] "et cela pour plusieurs raisons, premièrement pour eviter la dépense . . . à cause de celles de la guerre . . . et outre cela, pour gagner du temps, car les dedans de Trianon ont esté achevés avec beaucoup de précipitation."

It remains for us to speak of employment at this time of various motifs of ornament. The cartouche—sign manual of the baroque—sometimes with wings, sometimes with figural supporters, was now employed but rarely, almost solely to display an armorial bearing or a cypher. The trophy was employed as the principal ornament of the Salon de la Guerre. Le Brun's drawings for it (Figure 15), as we have seen, show trophies still mainly symmetrical, without the variety of movement of the trophies in bronze ultimately placed there, which, though begun in 1682, were not completed and installed until after 1701. The trophies at Issy, doubtless inspired by those in the Salon de la Guerre, are also of conservative form.

It was in the arabesque that a fruitful evolution continued. In the Maisons Royales of the central period of the reign, to be sure, we know no example of painted arabesques, which

[157] R. Josephson: "Le Grand Trianon sous Louis XIV," *loc. cit.* Later, J.-F. Blondel characteristically rationalized the absence of painted ceilings and of gilding, on the ground that the palace was to be occupied only in the pleasant season. *Architecture françoise,* I, 1752, 124.

there gave place to the monumentality of marble or the luxury of collected masterpieces of easel painting. Arabesques, however, continued to be used, increasingly in tapestries, and, by private clients, in painted decorations, where for the first time, they invaded a new field, the ceiling.

Although Le Brun continued to hold the direction of the Gobelins until his death in 1690, he was not called on under Louvois for designs of any new tapestry suites. His preoccupation until October, 1686, with the immense task of the ceilings of the Grande Galerie and its salons at Versailles might be regarded as a sufficient explanation but on its completion he was no longer employed in the palaces, and his disfavour with the Surintendant was a further reason why the Gobelins turned at just this time to other sources of design. It was equally significant that these sources were within the admired academic canon; the compositions of Raphael's *Stanze* of the Vatican, as copied by the pensioners of the Academy at Rome, the *Sujets de la Fable*, of Giulio Romano and Raphael, the *Scipio* and the *Fructus Belli* of Giulio Romano, and two suites of arabesques from models supposedly Raphaelesque.

Noël Coypel (1628-1707), pupil of Vouet, assistant of Errard, and himself from 1672 to 1674 Director of the Academy at Rome, was commissioned in 1684 to paint for the Gobelins "les desseins de Rabesques d'après Raphael," which became known as the Triomphes des Dieux, adapted from a sixteenth-century Brussels set.[158] Coypel's cartoons follow this older set very closely in composition, proportion and motif, but transform the figures and details into academic elegance. The background in both is of light columnar structures much in the style of Roman wall-painting. They nowhere contain any bandwork, even in the borders.[159] This revival of arabesque tapestries may well have given Berain a stimulus to design his own arabesque patterns, which began to appear soon after this time. By contrast with the prevailing trend to academism, stemming in French decoration from Errard and represented by Noël Coypel, Berain took up the creative line of the arabesque of Le Brun, in which he now further developed also the element of bandwork, in the form given it by French tradition. It is significant that this work was not in commissions for the royal palaces or for the Gobelins, but in decorations for private buildings and in models followed in tapestry at Beauvais.[160]

[158] Three of this set, woven by Franz Geubel apparently from designs by a follower of Van Orley, are preserved in French national possession. Two of them are reproduced by E. Guichard: *Les tapisseries décoratives du Garde-Meuble*, Paris, n.d.

[159] In 1687-1688 another Flemish grotesque set "dessein de Julles Romain, représentant les Douze Mois de l'année avec crotesques et paysages," was literally copied at the Gobelins, this time without new painted cartoons, except for two additional subjects by Coypel. The models then in French royal possession have been lost, but a set from the same designs, delivered in 1574-1575 by Jost van Herselle, "tapissier de Bruxelles," to the Duke of Lorraine, is preserved in the Viennese imperial collection, one being reproduced by H. Göbel: *Wandteppiche*, Erster Teil, Bd. I, 1923, frontispiece, with text on page 668. Thus was produced what has become known as the *Mois Arabesque*, of which the first set was hung at Trianon, just built. The central motifs, again of classic mythological figures, are framed in light structures of columns or lattice. In the fields of some of the set (August, or December) the lateral motifs are mannerist cartouche-medallions. Along with herms and other related elements, we find not only motifs of rollwork and pierced strapwork, but a number of flat bands of the step-like Roman type. In the French adaptations these bands become bars moulded as in Le Brun's arabesques.

[160] Doubtless by Berain's designs, engraved or manuscript, were inspired "les Grotesques à petits personnages" executed in tapestry at Beauvais from 1689 onwards, from cartoons painted by Jean-Baptiste Monnoyer and others. Weigert: "Les grotesques de Beauvais...," in *Bulletin de la Société de l'histoire de l'art français*, 1933, 7-21. We cannot be certain, however, that any of the surviving examples of these tapestries were of the earliest date, so that we do not take them into account in the chronological evolution of Berain's style.

Background

In 1687-1688, Berain gave the designs for arabesque decorations painted by André Camot at the Hôtel de Mailly in Paris. These decorations are described by Tessin at the time of his visit to Paris in 1687, naming the designer and the executant.[161] One of the ceilings of the hôtel is preserved, along with certain panelling; in addition we have several manuscript drawings of the ceilings.

The arabesques of the panelling[162] are closely similar to those of Le Brun (Figure 40). Again we find the broken opposite scrolls, with shells or palmettes radiating from their junctions, swirls of acanthus diverging from their volutes, with finials of interlacing bandwork. In many instances a figure occupies the incorporeal central tabernacle of bands and scrolls, a figure standing perhaps on a scrolled pedestal garnished with a lambrequin, and sheltered by a suspended valanced baldaquin. Such was the character and vocabulary of Berain's ornament in its beginnings, almost indistinguishable from what had gone immediately before.

It is in the ceilings, with their new problems, that we find Berain giving new developments to the established system. The different designs as shown in the drawings—alike in being composed symmetrically on the cardinal and diagonal axes—are not yet wholly homogeneous in style, although all of them display essential elements of Berain's patterns. The one for the "Salle ou Premier Antichambre" (Figure 39) is mainly vegetal, especially in a surrounding broad border—uniform in effect except for slight accents at the middle of the sides, and for others, made more emphatic by small wreaths, at the corners. Even in this border, however, there are traces of flat bandwork, formed of C-scrolls projecting at the corners in hawk's-bill form. Such bandwork is more conspicuous in the large central rosette, with radiating panels, not unlike Le Brun's rosettes of bat's-wing in the Galerie d'Apollon, but bounded outwardly by C-scrolls and bordered by lighter scrolls and tendrils. From their opposite pairs, here and throughout the series of designs, radiate palmettes of varying detail.

In the ceilings of other rooms (Figure 41) the bandwork dominates the vegetal elements; pairs of parallel bands united by contrasts of color give a firmer basis to the major pattern. The scrolls are characteristically joined by short straight bars, and the terminal volutes are reenforced by a divergent swirl of acanthus, henceforth typical of all Berain's touches. It is these elements, of which we have traced the rise in France—not the herms, masks, and candelabra-like forms common to Italian and Flemish arabesques—which now became the essential and characteristic ones in Berain's surface ornament.

The ceiling of the Chambre du Lit, the only one still preserved (Figure 13), is the most interesting of the four for its broad, embracing double band, so characteristically curved and broken, its elaborate diagonal standards of medallions (distantly derived from Pietro da Cortona and Le Brun) flanked by scrolls with profile masks having feathered headdresses, its

[161] His travel diary was first published by Oswald Sirén: *Nicodemus Tessin d. y. studieresor y Danmark, Tyskland, Holland, Frankrike och. Italien.* 1914; the Parisian portion, in translation, by Weigert: "Notes de Nicodème Tessin le jeune relatives à son séjour à Paris en 1687," in *Bulletin de la Société de l'histoire de l'art français*, 1932, 220-279, the passage on the Hôtel de Mailly occurring in pages 238-239. Weigert also discussed these decorations in the same *Bulletin*, 1931, 167-174, and in *L'architecture*, January 15, 1932, 31-36 where he published drawings of the ceilings secured for Tessin in 1696-1699 by Cronström, the Swedish minister, and preserved in the National Museum at Stockholm.

[162] Tessin describes it in place. It is now installed in the château of Vernou-en-Sologne. It is clear that the arabesques were not modified in the eighteenth century when important decorative works at the Hôtel de Mailly were executed by Cauvet, whose style is of quite another character.

interlaces of single bands, now substantially equivalent in importance with the acanthus. We note the employment, both in the broader bands and in the fields of the medallions, of *quadrillage* or *mosaïque* derived from the examples of Le Brun and henceforth commonly employed by Berain and others.

It is the engraved arabesque designs of Berain which have had the greatest attention, and which were doubtless most influential in diffusing his style. They come to us as collected by his son-in-law Thuret in 1711, the year of Berain's death. Their chronological evolution, important to establish, has not hitherto been emphasized.[163]

Fortunately we derive some fixed points from the lives of the engravers employed. The young Daniel Marot left France some time after the Edict of Nantes (October 23, 1685), and was in Holland certainly by the beginning of 1686.[164] It is perhaps significant that, while he engraved for Berain a frontispiece (1681) and three plates of court ceremonies which occurred in August, 1682, and September, 1683, he did none of Berain's arabesques, all of which we believe to be of later date.

We are able to date a number of them, engraved by Dolivar, as before 1693, through the fact that Dolivar's death occurred in that year. Several of these (e. g. Figure 42) show Berain's characteristic style well developed in the framing of the traditional central figure and baldaquin. Bandwork was now predominant, foliage subordinate. In the example illustrated, as in the ceiling of the Chambre du Lit of the Hôtel de Mailly, we find broad double bands of contrasting tone, themselves composed of interlacing fillets, their scrolls and bill-hooks garnished with acanthus.

It has not hitherto been remarked that none of the arabesques engraved by Dolivar, any more than those at the Hôtel de Mailly, are of the more attenuated type we are accustomed to associate with Berain.

We are fortunate in having certain designs by Berain, toward the end of the century, which show his use of major architectural forms. One is for the great organ at Saint-Quentin, from 1697; a whole series is for chimney pieces, from 1699. Both of these will be discussed in their relation to works of such types in the following period, to which they offer instructive contrasts. Of the same character with these works of Berain are the backgrounds of a series of tapestries in course of execution in 1698 for the Comte de Toulouse, woven from cartoons by Vernansal from lost designs which are justly attributed to Berain (Figure 43).[165] The foreground groups of marine deities, which recur in engraved arabesques of Berain, are framed in rustic columnar, arcaded loggias with a wealth of mannerist elements. The essential point to observe is that all this work is of massive architectonic character, by no means dissolved into the airy irreality of arabesque forms. While its frames are broken and overlaid by quoins, consoles, and figural elements, there is no suggestion of replacing these frames themselves by elements borrowed from surface arabesques.

---

[163] The plates reproduced by Berliner, however, are very correctly dated and placed in order.

[164] M. D. Ozinga: Daniel Marot, 1938, 17.

[165] Weigert: "La tenture des 'Triomphes marins' d'après Jean I Berain," in *Bulletin de la Société de l'histoire de l'art français*, 1937, 17-18. The attribution goes back to the early eighteenth century, for clearly these are the tapestries then at the Hôtel de Toulouse mentioned by Brice, 1719 ed., I, 161, as "sur les desseins inventez par le fameux Bérin, dont chacun sait le goût et la manière, et peint en grand par vernansal"—although Brice was mistaken in thinking they were made at the Gobelins for Madame de Montespan.

Background

Gifted artist as was Daniel Marot, whose career unfolded mainly after he left France, and admirable as are his engraved designs, we cannot allow him any share in the genesis of the movement we are discussing. In 1685 Berain's work was only in its beginnings. Marot thus knew it primarily through its subsequent diffusion by engravings. Some of these supplied direct prototypes for plates of Marot, modified only in minor regards. Daniel Marot's relationship to Pierre Lepautre is particularly instructive for us. Marot's suite *Nouvelle cheminees a panneaux de la glace de la maniere de France* obviously derives its title from Lepautre's *Nouvelles cheminées à panneaux de glace executées dans quelques hôtels de Paris*. It includes various belated types as well as one with a tall arched mirror, itself based on a plate of Berain of 1699. Other plates of Marot show derivatives from various engraved designs of Pierre Lepautre. The excellent biographer of Marot,[166] while mentioning such relationships, is at pains to stress the differences, in such plates, between his work and that of the French. He was indeed the creator of a national, provincial variant of the Louis XIV style, but he did not contribute, even by his engravings, to the formation of style in France itself.

In the central period of the reign Italian influence and baroque character were on the wane. So far from an intensified baroque, we have found a strengthening of academic reaction. So far from a progressive transformation of Italian forms in the direction taken by the future, we have found in French architecture a return to formulae essentially of the past, to which the eyes of the pensioners at Rome, like those of the Academicians, were now turned. Prior to 1678 the classical impulse of Colbert and Perrault had been felt mainly on the exterior of buildings; at Versailles, indeed, Le Vau had succeeded, to a degree, in escaping its sway. In the interior, at the time, the Raphaelesque academism of Errard had even given way before the tempered baroque of Le Brun. After 1678 academic tendencies gained the upper hand, inside as well as out; in the cabinets alone was a more playful treatment still permitted.

Le Brun himself, in conjunction with Mansart, became fully architectonic, monumental, and academic in the membering of the walls of the gallery at Versailles; his ceiling there, by contrast with his own earlier work, shows a diminution of baroque character, a diminution more appreciable still in the ceiling of the Salons and of the other rooms after 1680. For walls, whether panelled in marble or in wood, where there was no columnar "order," the treatment, as developed by Lassurance, was almost exclusively tectonic, not plastic; static, not dynamic. The panelled *assemblage* was of the most rigid geometry, in which the multiplied superposition of rectangular elements was relieved only occasionally by circular or oval frames, with carving confined almost entirely to an enrichment of these frames. Framework and painted surface ornament were kept sharply distinct.

Individual baroque members, already long domesticated, did indeed persist in certain instances. Their use, however, was entirely subordinate to the general tectonic character of the framework. Sculptured ornaments of baroque types were employed but rarely.

Only in the ornament of Berain, who had never been in Italy, do we find an original, creative impulse, derived primarily from French sources, and giving genial development to the fruitful initiative of Le Brun in this field. Only here do we encounter, prophetically, forms which were subsequently to become essential elements of the rococo.

His arabesque was still exclusively a surface pattern. It was through a transformation of

---

[166] Ozinga, *op. cit.*, especially pp. 11-14.

the scheme of panelling interiors, fusing frame and surface pattern, that, in the following period, the basic scheme of the rococo was to be created. Down to 1699, however, there was as yet scarcely a trace of this transformation.

In the spirit, as well as in the forms, it is only at the very end of the period that we find a prophecy of what was to come. It is significant that the words of this prophecy were words of the aging King himself, in reprobating Mansart's proposals of 1698 for the decoration of the Ménagerie. "Il faut qu'il y ait de la jeunesse mêlée dans ce que l'on fera."

Genesis

End of the Reign of Louis XIV, 1699-1715

WE should seek in vain in political, social and economic developments for any adequate explanations of the pregnant artistic innovations on the eve of the new century. The Treaty of Ryswick in 1697, to be sure, gave opportunity for return to the arts of peace, which continued even though the peace was of short duration. It was a favourable moment for great undertakings: the completion of the Invalides, the building of the Chapel at Versailles, the fulfilment of the vow of Louis XIII for a new altar at Notre-Dame de Paris, all authorized in the closing days of 1698,[1] and begun in 1699. Emulation of the splendours of Saint Paul's, which Louis XIV's antagonist, William III, opened to divine service on December 2, 1697, with a thanksgiving for the peace, may have moved the French king, a year later, to resume his great enterprises in religious building, improperly attributed to the devotion of Madame de Maintenon.[2]

At Court her influence was far from producing at this time any such restraint as has been imputed to it; on the contrary the advent of the young Duchesse de Bourgogne in 1697 led to a gaiety which even the disasters of subsequent campaigns could not quench. We have seen the small but significant remodellings which her advent occasioned at Trianon and at the Ménagerie. Now in 1699, new activity began at Meudon, Marly, Versailles, and Trianon on a scale truly regal, fully continuing the leadership of the Crown.

No broader social change, such as later coincided with the Regency, had yet been felt, and while the seeds of economic ruin were being sown, the harvest was still in the future. Paris still remained in the shadow of Versailles, though the Place Vendôme, transferred to the charge of the City, was begun anew. Its first hôtels were taken by the financiers, for whom others sprang up from the profits of the late war, soon renewed.

In the intellectual and cultural sphere we can indeed point to certain significant developments at the turn of the century. The literary quarrel of the ancients and moderns, unrolling from 1687 to 1701, in which Charles Perrault had championed the moderns on the basis of technical progress and of the advance of reason, had done much to destroy superstitious reverence for the authority of the ancients, and issued in agreement on esteem for the moderns. There was thus a self-confidence which might allow certain liberties, beyond those of Claude Perrault a generation before, with the rules of academic grammar and proportion.

The related quarrel of design and colour renewed from time to time since 1672 by the amateur Roger de Piles, resulted now in victory for the colourists, that is for the moderns. De Piles' *Abridgement of the Lives of the Painters*, appearing in 1699, while preserving much which was conventional, spoke for the artistic licenses of genius, which become new laws. He praised the Venetians, and, above all, Rubens. Thus he prepared the way for the contemporary colourism of Charles de la Fosse and of Antoine Coypel, both men long employed by the Crown, now on the eve of their great commissions at the Invalides and the Chapelle de

---

[1] As reported by Dangeau, December 20 and 21, *Journal*, VI, 1856, 477-478.

[2] Cf. the documents showing her opposition to these expenses, cited by Nolhac: *Versailles résidence de Louis XIV*, 1925, 355 and note.

The Creation of the Rococo

Versailles, both men not without influence on the future development of Watteau.[3]

It is difficult, nevertheless, to bring the innovations which were about to take place in architecture and decoration into any sequential relationship with developments of theory, or of practice in the other arts. These architectural innovations, indeed, while admired and adopted as a new and brilliant vogue, were not regarded as involving any breach with established theories, and thus evoked neither academic hostility nor a new theoretic justification. In these regards the situation was very different from the one which was to prevail about 1730, when the later, more pronounced phase of the new style called forth both attack and defense. The artistic revolution, which was ultimately to be recognized and opposed as such, was in its beginnings most gently insinuated and warmly welcomed.

The movement we are to trace, we observe, was, in its genesis, essentially an immanent, artistic one. Both its exact nature and its real protagonist are still to be ascertained. "Cherchez l'homme," as Lionello Venturi has said, "should be the motto of art historians." This search, superficially conducted in the past, we now undertake.

The Royal Works

Mansart's career was crowned, January 7, 1699, by his elevation to the high post of Surintendant des Bâtiments. Both before and after him this responsible position in the King's councils was held by a layman: a minister of state like Colbert or Louvois, a nobleman of rank like the Marquis de Villacerf or the Duc d'Antin. Advancement to it of a man of professional experience in the person of Mansart, already Premier Architecte, was a unique exception. Not only did this, in itself, imply that he had displayed high talents for administration, but it tended to plunge him still further into varied activities of an administrative nature.

Mansart's administrative talents were at once employed in a reorganization of the Bâtiments to handle efficiently the great increase in its tasks. In a series of long instructions[4] he established and defined in detail the duties of his principal subordinates, incidentally making plain what tasks he reserved for himself. Authority was closely centralized, the higher posts being in the hands of men bound to Mansart by ties of blood or marriage and wholly dependent on him for their rise to fortune. These instructions throw a clear light on the matter of personal creative responsibility within the Bâtiments.

De Cotte, Mansart's brother-in-law, with the rank of Architecte in the Bâtiments since 1685, was now formally established as second in command, by a brevet as Architecte Ordinaire and Director of the Academy of Architecture.[5] He kept the *bureau des plans* "où se seront tous les desseigns pour le service du Roi, qu'il fera faire sur ceux que nous aurons reglé." Beside this supervision of their preparation, he was charged with maintenance of orderly files of the drawings, with care of the copper plates, engraved and unengraved, and direction of the work of engravers, with records of the marbles in the various magazines, their employment and sale, as of the stocks of lead, copper, iron and other materials, with

---

[3] Cf. L. Venturi: *History of Art Criticism*, 1936, 134. Venturi, to be sure, overlooks the artistic forerunners of Watteau, and speaks as if, in this instance, criticism had outrun the evolution of art itself.

[4] Archives Nationales, o¹ 1246.

[5] Published by Mlle. J. Lejeaux in *Bulletin de la Société de l'histoire de l'art français*, 1938, 22-32.

the requisitioning of glass, with the papers of all the royal manufactures including the Gobelins and Savonnerie, their supplies and products, with all matters regarding the academies of architecture, painting and sculpture, and, not least onerous, with putting in final form all the specifications "que nous aurons dicté et reglé," distributing them to bidders and taking the bids. It is obvious from the enumeration of his duties that he did not have the time personally to make finished drawings, and indeed we find no developed designs of interiors and ornament from his hand.

The other principal official was Jacques Gabriel (1667-1742) whose mother was Mansart's cousin, his father a large contractor for masonry on the royal works. He had been appointed in 1688, at twenty-one, as one of the Contrôleurs Généraux, had accompanied De Cotte on his hasty trip to Italy in 1689-1690, and was now given the rank of Autre Architecte. He was the type of the efficient executive, and had developed marked practical and administrative ability. Mariette, who knew him well, states that he "étoit expert dans la conduite du bâtiment, mais il n'auroit pas pu dessiner le moindre bout d'ornement."[6] He asks "Est-ce là être architecte?" and continues, referring to his later succession to the leading place: "Et comment un premier architecte peut-il hazarder de juger sur les ouvrages des artistes qui lui sont soumis, quand il est lui-même dépourvu des connoissances qui sont si nécessaires pour diriger ses décisions?" For the moment his duties were all purely executive: keeping the files of *placets*, *mémoires*, and reports, the registers of orders and decisions, transmitting them to the proper persons, and so on.

Mansart himself, in spite of delegating so much, remained very fully occupied. His time was primarily employed in attendance on the King, whose orders, along with his own, he dictated to his secretary Marchand "sur des feuilles de papier volante," which were sent at once to Gabriel to be registered and communicated to those concerned. Marchand, or the under-secretary Beaulieu, were instructed to follow Mansart constantly about, paper in hand, "pour écrire tout ce que je dirai, soit pour les choses que je trouverai a faire dans les visites que je ferai, ou pour les ordres que je donnerai aux controlleurs ou entrepreneurs." Mansart held audiences and adjudications, dictated and signed letters, specifications, and contracts, and approved and signed the designs adopted. He was even farther than before from having the time, if he had the gifts, to prepare the preliminary designs for his buildings. We have no knowledge, either, that he had clarified any underlying aesthetic notions which may instinctively have governed him. It is, indeed, difficult to see how this driving opportunist could really have been the moving force in evolutions in the realms of thought and form. He continues to appear, as in the past, as a master of organization and efficiency rather than as an artistic creative genius.

We know that, in such ramified architectural organizations as Mansart was the first to organize, the chief sometimes still retains a true artistic initiative. To judge of this we need to know whether or not the character remains the same in the work of different designers in the organization at the same period, whether it evolves continuously in spite of change of

---

[6] *Abecedario*, II, 276. The comte de Fels, in *Anges-Jacques Gabriel*, 1912, cites no drawings by the elder Gabriel, whose later works he considers to have been designed by the son. Lemaistre (apparently Jean Pierre), who was also now appointed "autre architecte," though without equal responsibility, was paid in 1700 as "architecte et expert, pour le toisé et verification des bâtiments" (*Comptes*, IV, 684), and thus will likewise have been a practical man rather than a designer.

designers or changes sharply with change in the personnel—questions we shall devote ourselves to answering.

In the Menus Plaisirs, Jean Berain remained Dessinateur de la Chambre et du Cabinet du
Roi until his death in 1711, but Mansart was not the man to suffer encroachments on his department. Though Berain courted him at the beginning of his administration by dedicating
to him the suite of *Desseins de Cheminées,* he viewed Berain with no favour. Not once during
Mansart's Surintendance did Berain do any work for the Bâtiments reflected in the smallest
payment, and he continues to figure in our discussion only through the patronage of the
Dauphin. Even at Meudon, as elsewhere, his rôle as designer of arabesques was soon taken
over by the painter Claude III Audran, to whom we shall recur.

We have seen[7] that the chief designer of the Bâtiments, actually holding the pencil in the
period 1685-1699, was Lassurance, the accomplished "dessinateur sous clef" of Saint-
Simon's strictures. In interiors, which constituted the principal royal works of that time, a
sharp change in style had occurred on his first appointment as dessinateur by January, 1685;
the evolution during his tenure was relatively minor. On Mansart's appointment to the Surintendance, Lassurance's pay was doubled, and in 1700 he was advanced to the rank of
Architecte et Dessinateur at 5000 livres. From 1702 he was in charge of the Invalides and
had his office in Paris (*Comptes* IV, 912, 974), so that he will scarcely have been concerned
with the works which will occupy us here. From 1699 the design of interiors and of decorative features was left to other hands.

As other Dessinateurs in the Bâtiments there remained the veteran Cauchy, henceforth
carried as Ancien Dessinateur with the least pay,[8] and René Carlier the elder, employed occasionally since 1695, regularly since 1698.[9] These were now joined by Pierre Lepautre and
Rivet le fils.

We shall find that it was Pierre Lepautre who played the essential creative rôle in the
years from his appointment until his death,[10] and that a decisive turn in the work of the Bâtiments occurred, immediately on his appointment, in designs entrusted to him. They comprised precisely such interior features, domestic and religious, as first manifested the new
spirit, and continued to offer its most characteristic expressions.

Eldest of the children of Jean Lepautre (1618-1682), Pierre Lepautre was married at
Saint-Christophe in 1678.[11] We may thus place his birth in the neighborhood of 1648, perhaps a little later. Pierre-Jean Mariette, whose father published many of Pierre Lepautre's
engravings, and who must have known him well, recounts his varied training under Jean
Lepautre, his marvellous facility in etching, and his success as an engraver "dans le temps
qu'il en faisoit son unique profession." In this time, from his first dated plates of 1679, we
find him engraving illustrations for numerous volumes on architecture and related topics by

[7] Cf. the writer's papers on the Ménagerie and Trianon, already cited.

[8] He was made inspector at Meudon in 1700, and thereafter will scarcely have been concerned with the preparation of designs.

[9] We belive that to Carlier may be attributed the designs for remodelling the Cabinet de Madame de Maintenon
at Trianon, 1698 and the Appartement du Roi in the Aile Gauche, 1700, both of conventional and backward character. Cf. the paper on Trianon, cited above.

[10] Kimball: "The Creation of the *style Louis XV,*" *Art Bulletin,* XXIII, 1941, 1-15.

[11] H. Herluison: *Actes d'état-civil des artistes français,* 1873, 245. He is still frequently confused with his cousin
the sculptor Pierre Lepautre (1660-1744).

Desgodetz, Perrault, Daviler and others, with dates extending to 1698.[12] It is worth noting that, following his father and his brother Jacques (d. 1684), he engraved a number of designs by Jean Berain, those datable being of 1687, 1690 and 1693.[13] He received isolated payments in 1685, 1687 and 1689 for "planches et plans qu'il a gravez pour le service de S. M."[14] This was the justification for describing him as "graveur du Roy" in an accord of August 14, 1692, signed by him and by the engraver, Jean Liebaux.[15] He had also engraved privately in the 'eighties and 'nineties, as we have seen, several suites representing details and interiors from buildings by Mansart, among others, all very much in the style of Lassurance. Beside those already mentioned they include notably one "Fait par P. Le Pautre," the *Cheminées à la royalle à grand miroir et tablette avec lambris de menuiserie* (Figures 44-45).[16] It shows tall mirrors with heads both square and semicircular, crowned by acanthus scrolls, mostly rather heavy, invading the panels above. The closest analogy with any executed works is with the interiors of the Ménagerie, but Lepautre's designs are in some ways more advanced; he is groping toward the scheme which he will soon employ in designs of his own for the royal works.

For his later career the basic text is the following passage from Mariette's notice:[17]

> Comme il se trouva avoir assez de génie pour l'architecture, et qu'il possedoit toutes les parties pour la bien dessiner, Jules-Hardouin Mansart, surintendant des bastimens, jeta les yeux sur luy, fit créer en sa faveur une place de dessinateur et graveur des bastimens du roy, et, en cette qualité, se l'étant entièrement attaché, il se servit souvent de sa main pour rédiger et mettre au net ses pensées. Ainsy, Pierre le Pautre eut beaucoup de part à tous les ouvrages qui se firent dans la suite à Versailles, à Marly, et dans les autres maisons royales, tant pour ce qui regarde l'architecture que le jardinage. Il en fit presque tous les dessins; il en grava mesme plusieurs.

It was indeed precisely on Mansart's elevation to the Surintendance in January, 1699, that Pierre Lepautre first entered the regular employ of the Bâtiments, as "dessinateur et graveur" at a salary of 2000 livres (*Comptes* IV, 554), continuing until his death in 1716.[18] That Mariette was not in error in suggesting Mansart's dependence on Lepautre is shown by another significant document in the register of extracts and decisions for 1701:[19]

> Paultre represente qu'il a travaillé longtemps sous les ordres de M. Mansart du temps de Msrs. Colbert et Louvois sans estre payé de son travail.
>
> Que M. Mansart luy a promis de luy faire du bien en cette consideration. Il demande quelque gratification pour ce travail.

To which Gabriel noted:

> M. Mansart lui fera plaisir dans l'occasion.

[12] Listed by Destailleur, *op. cit.*, 124-127.   [13] Weigert: *Jean I Berain*, Nos. 234-241, 178 ff.

[14] *Comptes*, II, 785. The earliest of these may well have been the large perspective of the Hôtel des Invalides, signed and dated 1683.

[15] Archives notariales, minutier central, XLIX, 399, document communicated by the gracious authorization of Me. Faroux. This is the only signature of Pierre Lepautre known to me.

[16] Early impressions "Chez Langlois." Later incorporated in the Jombert edition as suite 54, pls. 3-6; suite 54, pls. 1-2.

[17] *Abecedario*, III, p. 188.

[18] This is the year given by Mariette. It is confirmed by the manuscript accounts, o¹ 2216 and 2217, which record payments to him for 1716, but not for 1717.

[19] o¹ 1081.

It was a promise never kept.[20]

As compared with Lassurance, his predecessor as Dessinateur, whose training was purely architectural, Pierre Lepautre was much more versatile, having learned from his father, as Mariette says, "l'architecture, l'ornement, la perspective et généralement toutes les différentes parties du dessin." In an engraved address he informs the public that "Pierre Lepautre . . . montre a dessiner l'Architecture, la Figure, l'Ornement, le Paysage, etc." Notably in his mastery of the figure he surpasses Lassurance, who rarely introduced any figural motives in his drawings, and then with but rudimentary indications.[21] We shall observe the greater freedom of line which appeared in the work of the Bâtiments with his advent.

Among surviving drawings for the royal works between 1699 and 1716 we find a considerable number made by a single hand, a hand not appearing before or after these dates, which are those of Lepautre's employment. Comparison of their technique with that of his engraved designs reveals that these drawings are indeed from the hand of Pierre Lepautre. In spite of varying media, and of varying degrees of care and of speed in preparation, they show a unity of technique as impressive as is their difference in technique from other drawings of the same milieu, even those of imitators and followers. They permit us, as we shall see, to identify as from Lepautre's designs a body of executed work which includes also certain works for which the original drawings are not preserved.

The works of various designers in the great year of 1699 require our individual scrutiny in their chronological order, as it was precisely in one of them—but not the first—that we shall find the decisive creative act of the period, becoming, as its significance was recognized, influential on other works in progress.

The earliest of the interiors of 1699 is a work of Berain for the Dauphin at Meudon—long destroyed, but known by documents—a work important not only for its own interest and novelty in some regards, but for its failure to show that decided initiative which Lepautre, taking his departure from Berain, was now to assume.

January 17, Dangeau notes (VII, 10), "Monseigneur . . . fait changer tout l'appartement où il couche." The changes, which began, as we shall see, with ceilings by Audran in the Chambre and Garderobe, were to involve the creation of the Cabinet de Monseigneur, represented, fortunately for us, in the well-known portrait of the Musée de Versailles, *Le Grand Dauphin dans son cabinet* (Figure 46). Its background has ordinarily been supposed to be one of the suite of Cabinets de Monseigneur at Versailles.[22] Actually it represents the Grand Cabinet de Monseigneur at the Château of Meudon, of which the chimney piece was exe-

---

[20] Lepautre did receive gratifications of 300 livres each in the years 1702 to 1705, but that was no more than was granted also to Rivet, Carlier and others. In 1706 he and Rivet were alike given 500 livres "en consideration des peines extraordinaires, veilles et voyages en 1705," after which the distress of war put an end to all supplementarly emoluments.

[21] E.g. the two cherubs in a drawing for the Ménagerie, reproduced above.

[22] Often erroneously assumed to have been the Cabinet de Boulle (Salle 50), executed in 1682-1683 for the Aile du Midi and transported to the ground floor in 1684. That room, however, as we have seen, was lined with mirrors and had an elaborate marquetry floor with the arms of the Dauphin and Dauphine. Nolhac presumed the picture to represent the second Cabinet (Salle 49), which the contemporary descriptions pass over in silence. Nolhac supposed the boy to be the Dauphin's eldest son, the duc de Bourgogne (born 1682); Pichon thought him to be the duc d'Anjou (born 1683); actually he can only have been the third son, the duc de Berry (born 1686).

cuted in the months from March to July, 1699,[23] the finished work being inspected by the King August 18.[24] The entries of the *Comptes* (IV, 479 ff., 546) correspond in all details with the chimney piece shown, which at that moment was absolutely unique:[25]

1er mars: à Hardy, sculpteur, à compte des modèles qu'il fait pour la cheminée du cabinet de Monseigneur, à Meudon	100 [livres]
15 mars — 21 juin: au nommé Boule, ébéniste et fondeur, pour les bronzes qu'il a fait pour la cheminée de Monseigneur, à Meudon, quatre bases, deux chapiteaux, deux pilastres et quatre bras (6 p.)	2492 [livres]
15 mars — 7 juin: . . . Au sr Desjardins, fondeur, pour les ouvrages de bronze qu'il a fait pour la cheminée de Monseigneur, à Meudon, deux enfants, mosaïques et trophées (5 p.)	1123 [livres]
15 mars: au sr Le Pileur, fondeur, pour les ouvrages de bronze qu'il a fait au dessus du ceintre de la cheminée de Monseigneur, à Meudon	481 [livres]
15 mars — 7 juin: a Soyer, fondeur, pour les ornemens de bronze du chambranle et consoles de ladite cheminée (3 p.)	340 [livres]
29 mars — 7 juin: au sr Sautray [fondeur], pour les consolles, testes et tailloirs et les deux bordures de table qu'il a fait pour la cheminée du cabinet de Monseigneur, à Meudon (5 p.)	1420 [livres]
29 mars — 5 juillet: a Dezaigres, marbrier, à compte de la cheminée du cabinet de Monseigneur, à Meudon (2 p.)	700 [livres]
5 juillet: à luy [Despardins, fondeur], sur les bronzes et dorures de la cheminée du cabinet de Monseigneur, à Meudon	400 [livres]
19 juillet: au sr Spingola [Lespingola], sculpteur, pour un modèle de cheminée pour le cabinet de Monseigneur, à Meudon	200 [livres]

But the conclusive identification of the room is by the inventories of paintings at Meudon:[26]

CABINET DE MONSEIGNEUR

Un tableau de Lanfrance representant Mars et Venus, figures de vingt a vingt deux pouces ayant de hauteur trois pieds sur trois pieds neuf de Large

This painting appears, in the correct dimensions, at the left of the rear wall over the bookcase.

Both the chimney piece and the bureau have been recognized in Berain's published engravings; we may add that the tall arabesque panel is also figured there on one of the plates of the series *Desseins de Cheminées* (Figure 115). We can thus attribute the design of the room to this favorite artist of Monseigneur.

[23] Cf. the writer's letter in *The Burlington Magazine*, à propos of Huth's erroneous identification as "A French Regency Interior by Boulle" (Vol. 68, No. 397, 1936, 185). Huth supposed the portraits to be of the Regent and the young Louis XV, which would place the work as late as 1722! It is inconceivable that the Regent would have been painted in such a setting at a time when Oppenord's new decorations and Cressent's furnishings of the Palais-Royal were complete. Edward Warwick, the distinguished authority on costume, also informs me that 1722 is much too late for the details of costume in the painting, which he places about 1700.

[24] Dangeau, VII, 132.

[25] Biver: *Meudon*, 154, recognized the similarity between this chimney piece, as detailed in the accounts, and the one in the painting (which he supposed to represent the Cabinet de Boulle at Versailles), but did not realize that they are one and the same.

[26] The inventory "B," after December, 1702, and before 1706. Biver, *op. cit.*, p. 457; cf. F. Engerand, *Inventaire*, 176-177, where the composition is described in detail.

The mirror over the chimney piece (as we see it here or in Berain's engraving) is richly framed with an arched cornice of triglyph voussoirs resting on panels crowned by consoles and ornamented by terminal figures of Victory. The mantel itself, as at the Ménagerie, rises but little above the dado, the architrave, as in one of the chimney pieces there, being abandoned for a low moulded band, here resting on panelled supports and for the first time bowed forward in an arc. At left and right are consoles on which are seated figures, their heads surmounted by branching candelabra.

Berain's plate of this chimney piece forms part of his suite with the title *Desseins de Cheminées dediez à Monsieur Jules Hardouin Mansard . . . surintendant . . . des bâtimens . . .*, a dedication which must fall after January, 1699. The great majority show tall mirrors with their heads arched or of broken curved outline. We cannot tell whether any others were executed, although very possibly they include other chimney pieces at Meudon listed in the *Comptes* as made in 1699.

The style of most of these designs is fantastic to a degree very unusual in the *grand siècle* in France, with architectural members broken in mannerist fashion, an extravagant use of curvature, and much interpenetration of elements. Some of the forms of Lepautre's *Cheminées à la mode* recur, endlessly varied and elaborated. Lateral consoles of balancing profile are common. The fireplace opening is given the most diverse forms, with its upper corners concave or convex, its intrados arched, scrolled or broken—even in a depressed arc. An architrave is rarely retained. The supports take the form of panels, herms, or consoles, with masks, shells, or palmettes. Although the turn which design took under Mansart's Surintendance was sharply away from the mannerist trend of Berain, some of his less extravagant forms entered into the general vocabulary of the period, and two decades later, under the Régence, as we shall see, many architectural details in the work of Vassé and Oppenord trace their suggestion to Berain.

How sharply such freedom contrasted with the conservative nay-saying of the Academy of Architecture, even a decade later, is illustrated by a report of one of its séances then, when the less extravagant of these forms had long been adopted by other designers.

LUNDI, 21 JUILLET 1710

> L'on s'est entretenu au sujet des ouvertures des portes et fenestres et des cheminées et l'on a examiné diverses manières qui s'introduisent, particulièrement à l'égard des cheminées, pour terminer le haut de leurs ouvertures. La Compagnie à désapprouvé plusieurs de ces nouvelles manières, qui sont défectueses et qui tiennent la plupart du gothique.[27]

It should be noted that, although the wall panels, both on the piers and above the mirror, are richly painted with arabesques of Berain's characteristic bandwork, this is confined within the recessed mouldings of the panels, which themselves retain a strictly geometrical outline. We shall see how fundamentally the work of Pierre Lepautre was to differ in this regard.

[27] *Procès-verbaux*, III, 344. Cited by B. Lossky: *I.-B. A. Le Blond . . . son oeuvre en France*, 1936, 210, in connection with Le Blond's edition of Daviler's *Cours d'architecture*, appearing in that year. The plates of this work, themselves engraved by Pierre Lepautre, are scarcely more than personal variants of his characteristic forms, with certain borrowings from Berain, notably in the form of the marble chimney pieces.

Genesis

The earliest of Lepautre's works in the palaces of the Crown,[28] the first to be executed and admired, the first to be influential, were his designs for changes at Marly. In them appear for the first time the characteristic forms of the last fifteen years of Louis XIV, already foreshadowing those of the following reign.

Beginning in April, Mansart's register records a series of orders for new chimney pieces:[29]

> Du 25 avril (1699). Le roy a ordonné de faire un dessus de cheminée au Cabinet de son appartement à Marly avec des glaces enfermées dans une bordure de bois sculptée et dorée depuis le dessus de la Tablette jusques sous la grande corniche . . .
>
> Du 26 avril. Le Roy a ordonné d'aller demain à Marly faire un dessin de cheminée de sa chambre . . .
>
> Du 27 avril. Le Roy a ordonné de faire des cheminées de marbre neuves dans sa chambre, son cabinet et sa garderobbe à Marly avec des dessus de Menuiserie ornées de cadres qui renferment des glaces depuis le dessus des tablettes jusques sous les corniches . . .
>
> Du 10 juin. Faire une cheminée de marbre avec des glaces jusqu'en haut dans l'anti-Chambre où le Roy mange[30] et dans le grand Cabinet de Madame de Maintenon . . .

There followed similar orders for the apartments in the attics of the Château (in part later countermanded) and also for those of Monsieur and Madame, and for the Appartement de Jeu. In one item there is specific mention of "cadres ceintrées par le haut renfermant des glaces."

The beauty of these new designs must have been instantly appreciated, for ones of similar type, with mirrors "en toute la hauteur,"[31] were ordered by August 20 for the diagonal faces of the Salon (cf. Figure 47).[32] In the autumn also was executed a redecoration of the Chambre du Roi,[33] shown in several drawings in the technique of Pierre Lepautre (Figures 48, 49),[34] eliminating the cove to raise the cornice much higher, and placing in the center of the ceiling an elaborate rosette in relief (Figure 49)—the first example of such a feature, which was to become characteristic in the following reign.

[28] As we shall see, the earliest of all his designs for the Bâtiments, preceding the domestic examples by a few weeks, was a religious work, but this was not executed until later and in a modified form.

[29] Archives Nationales, o¹ 1809.

[30] The disposition here was modified by order of May 3, 1702.

[31] The orders are in Mânsart's "Memoire des ouvrages . . . à faire au château de Marly . . . pendant le voyage de Fontainebleau et le restant de la présente année 1699." o¹ 1473, p. 56. The work is mentioned by Dangeau August 20 and September 1 (VII, 134, 140), and its executed form, with arched mirrors, can be seen in the section of the château previously cited.

[32] The flues of these new chimney pieces required the closing of the attic windows on these faces and the substitution of paintings. On a memoir for the salon, the King wrote, September 14, "Je suis de votre avis, il faut travailler à 4 tableaux comme vous le proposés, il faut bien choisir les paintres, et ne les pas presser pour qu'ils soient beaux." Lucas Montigny catalogue, cited by C. Piton: *Marly-le-Roi*, 1904, 117. Paintings of the Seasons are shown in these positions in the section of 1714. To introduce fireplaces at all in the Salon, without disturbing the central balance of its octagonal form, there had to be four, on the diagonal faces. Thus devotion to unity of form led from cold into the opposite extremity. Years later Madame de Pompadour was to write, one May, to her brother, from Marly: "J'ai un rhume assez fort . . . Je descends au salon ce soir, qui par parenthèse est diabolique pour les rhumes; il y fait un chaud enorme, et froid en sortant, aussi entend-on plus tousser qu'a Noël." *Correspondance de Mme. de Pompadour*, ed. by A.-P.-Malassis.

[33] Discussed in a paper presented by A.-M.-E. Marie December 2, 1938, at a séance of the Société de l'histoire de l'art français, and published in its *Bulletin*, Année 1938, 190-196.

[34] Cabinet des Estampes, Va 361 VI; an outline study for the rear wall, misclassified as for Trianon, is at the Archives Nationales, o¹ 1884.

The Creation of the Rococo

We find in the *Comptes* for 1699[35] payments to Antoine Rivet of 19,100 livres "sur la menuiserie qu'il fait aux cheminées de l'appartement du Roy et autres endroits du château de Marly"; to Pierre Taupin and André Goupy, 12,300 livres "sur les ouvrages de sculpture en bois qu'ils font dans l'appartement du Roy a Marly"; to various marble workers, large sums for marble chimney pieces, including those of the Chambre du Roi, the Apartment of Mme. la Duchesse, and the appartements du haut; to Lochon, fondeur, 2750 livres "à compte des moulures de bronze qu'il a doré d'or moulu pour la bordure des glaces des apartemens du château." These payments were completed by December, 1699, when the gilding of the Salon was executed. Already on October 23 the King had inspected the completed work, on the 29th it was shown to others, and the Salon was the object of admiration during the *voyage de Marly* of November 2.[36]

Designs of some of the chimney pieces of the apartments were published in the *Livre de cheminées executées à Marly sur les desseins de Monsr. Mansart Surintendant . . . dessinées et gravées par P. Le Pautre Graveur du Roi* (Figures 50-52).[37] These Marly designs, limited though they are to a refacing of the existing narrow chimney breasts, already embody the essential character of the new phase of style, soon to be employed in the remodellings of the royal apartments at Versailles in 1701 and at Trianon in 1702-1703. By contrast with Lassurance's work of 1685-1698, with its rigidly geometric, tectonic framework, its limitation of carved ornament to the decoration of mouldings and friezes, we now find a modification of the outlines of the framework and a free invasion of the panels by elements in relief.

The forms, though differently employed, were suggested by certain features of the painted arabesques of Berain. At Marly the scheme of flat bandwork in Berain's panel-fillings was taken over by Lepautre into the framework itself. Lepautre applied Berain's forms to the moulded outlines of the panels: he truncated their angles by C-scrolls ending in the hawk's-bill, each with a swirl of acanthus,[38] he flanked the palmettes of mask and headdress by opposite scrolls, interrupting or overlapping the mouldings. Some of these scrolls are of bandwork, others are realized as cornucopias, still others are of palm or of acanthus, occasionally terminated by sprays of naturalistic flowers, or joined by naturalistic garlands. In these it is not the motifs or the naturalism which is new—all this may be found under Le Brun, for instance in the ornaments of the Salon de la Paix—but the incorporation of such arabesque elements as features of the frame. So, too, where a mask is surrounded by scrolls, this is a derivative not of the baroque cartouche, with its corporeal plasticity, but of arabesque motifs, linear and ethereal.

Only where there are coats-of-arms or cyphers, as over the mirror head of the Chambre du Roi and in the firebacks, do we still find cartouches of plastic baroque character, with borders of rollwork—a survival of the types of Le Brun, as the circular or oval medallions, the wings in certain instances, make clear.

[35] IV, 513-518, 650.
[36] Dangeau, VII, 174, 178, 180.
[37] A precious example, unique so far as we know, is in the Print Department of the Metropolitan Museum of Art.
[38] Geymüller: *Baukunst der Renaissance in Frankreich*, 1901, 347, sees the "bec-de-corbin" motif in the scrolled ears of architraves by Borromini (e.g. at the Sapienza). These motifs, however, lack the acanthus leaf which clearly indicates Lepautre's dependence on Berain.

Genesis

We may compare Lepautre's treatment here with Berain's in his chimney piece at Meudon, in course of execution at the same moment, and in his engraved suite *Desseins de cheminées* (including that one) of which we have spoken, issued in 1699 or later. Berain's arabesque is a panel-filling. He may inscribe lines of bandwork with his typical motives, but he confines them within the mouldings, which themselves remain strictly geometrical—he does not transfer these motives to the frame. Lepautre, on the other hand, while modifying the moulded outline with such motives, abandons the painted arabesque filling. The only real filling in his panels is a uniform carved diagonal "mosaic" of neutral effect (itself common since the time of Le Brun) occasionally used as a foil to the airy whiteness of the background elsewhere. This transformation of the arabesque from a flat filling to a carved frame was a significant contribution of Lepautre, destined to have far-reaching influence.

There is an equal contrast between their major architectural forms: Berain's are of mannerist character, complex and broken, with academic proportions and bold projections: Lepautre's are relatively very simple, with slender proportions and slight relief. The lightness of Berain's surface arabesques was in sharp contrast to his own treatment of masses. Lepautre, having created a frame of plastic arabesque elements, now abandoned any massive architectural forms. Among the few survivals of architectonic elements are the pilaster strips which occasionally support the arches. They are themselves reduced to extreme slenderness, delicately panelled, with an invasion of relief ornaments at top, bottom, and centre. While in the design that serves as the title-page of Lepautre's suite the pilaster preserves a small capital and base, and the panel is geometrically outlined, in another design, where the strips support consoles, the geometrical outline is abandoned at the base, where the profile is given by a shell with pairs of opposite scrolls. The motifs are derived from Berain's painted bandwork in his pilaster-panels—the scrolls and palmettes being followed by an interlace and finial—but transposed from the flat to relief and already modifying the moulded outline on the panel, as Berain's never did. Thus Lepautre struck out the way which was henceforth to be followed.

Though, except in the Chambre du Roi, the new works at Marly were limited to isolated chimney pieces, and though we know them only from engravings, we can still feel their high artistic quality. From the marriage of frame and filling, of moulding and surface, of structure and ornament, of geometry and fantasy, had sprung a living entity, not only deeply new, but vitally perfect. It is a tribute to the perception of contemporaries that the quality of this creation was recognized almost instantly, that they could no longer accept anything which did not share it, or, in the end, possess it fully.

In the late spring of 1699 there had been proposals for certain changes in the Appartement du Roi at Versailles: eliminating the attics of the chimney pieces in the Chambre du Roi and the Cabinet du Conseil, and enlarging the latter room, without changing its treatment.[39] These proposals, drawn up by other designers with traditional forms, were regis-

[39] There were even suggestions for much more ambitious changes in the Chambre du Roi, one including the use of free-standing Ionic columns to frame the alcove—a scheme first adopted in the Chambre du Roi at Trianon in 1700. The design (o¹ 1773) has two old endorsements "Pour la Reyne" and "Encien dessein de la Chambre de la Reyne," but these are surely in error—error committed in filing after memory of this fugitive proposal had vanished. There was no queen from 1684 to 1725; none thus during the period to which the technique of this drawing surely belongs. The Chambre de la Reine was but 23 feet high and was 30 feet wide, whereas this drawing shows a

tered June 26, before the first of the new chimney pieces at Marly could have its effect. It was doubtless the dazzling novelty of their new ornaments, already realized, which led on August 21 to the abandonment of any minor undertakings in the Appartement du Roi, in favor of more sweeping changes to be made at a later day.

One enterprise at Versailles, which could not be postponed, was indeed carried through in 1699: the Appartement du Nuit of the Duc de Bourgogne, who was to be united with his young bride in the autumn. We know how skilfully this was provided, by a small block dividing the southern interior court and connecting the Antichambre du Roi with the Appartement de la Reine, which had been assigned to the child princess in 1697. The order for this construction was given July 28. The drawings for the interiors (Figures 53, 54), by an unidentified draughtsman,[40] are already under the influence of the new work at Marly, adopting some of the innovations of Lepautre, still but half understood.

That it was not Mansart or De Cotte who was responsible for originating the new treatment is shown by their failure to impose it not only on the designers of changes in the Appartement du Roi at Versailles but also on Carlier in his designs of February, 1700, for remodelling the Chambre du Roi at Trianon (Figures 55, 56). In these the coves are reduced, the cornices raised, but with a still further multiplication of the tiers of rectangular panels. The artistic failure of this work, in contrast to the brilliant success of Lepautre at Marly, was such that the triumph of the new style soon became universal. Mansart and De Cotte henceforth adopted the style of Lepautre for all interior works, and, as we shall see, called on him personally to make the drawings for the most important ones.

One of the orders for Marly indicated another treatment, a "transitional" one—really a compromise after the fact, like all "transitions." The entry reads:

> 10 juin . . . Faire quatre cheminées de marbre . . . dans . . . l'appartement de Madame
> la Duchesse de Bourgogne dans l'atique du Château de Marly avec des dessus de me-
> nuiserie, depuis le dessus de la tablette jusques sous les corniches ornez de glaces et *de cadres*
> *pour les tableaux.*[41]

Such chimney pieces, doubtless from the year 1699, are included in another rare suite of plates of Lepautre, the *Livre de cheminées executées dans les apartemens de Versailles sur les desseins de Monsieur Mansart Surintendant* . . . [43] The mirrors themselves are square or slightly oblong, rising half the height above the mantels. Their heads are sometimes straight, sometimes of varied forms, with corners eased by C- or S-scrolls and with a central mask, shell, or

room 27 feet high and 25 feet wide. Now the existing Chambre du Roi was 27 feet high, and was 25 feet wide in the clear between the chimney breast and the opposite pier. Doubtless the design forms part of the series of proposals of early 1699.

[40] Both the handwriting and the technique are very close to those of Carlier, but it is almost unthinkable that the author of these drawings, showing some receptiveness to innovation, should be the same man who, next year, was still immovably conservative.

[41] This order was cancelled in August when the princess was assigned the Appartement Bas, but the type was employed elsewhere, as we shall see.

[43] It has escaped the cataloguers of his work, but exists in the fine early collection of Lepautre engravings at the Metropolitan Museum. The heights of the cornices would indicate that the rooms were in the premier étage of the wings of the château. One might hope that the rooms concerned might be identified by the paintings, with the aid of the inventories published by Engerand, *op. cit.*, but this hope has proved vain, as Lepautre seems merely to have shown any painting of the right proportions, ignoring true sizes, as in the case of Raphael's St. Michael.

palmette. The characteristic tendency is to include the upper motive of the chimney breast within a single tall frame which embraces both the mirror and the painting or relief above it (Figure 57). In the marble mantels there is considerable variety, with several elliptical and segmental arches, with consoles and panels tending to replace the old plain architraves.

Great ladies of the Court must at once have chimney pieces in the fashion. There exist several manuscript drawings for ones on the order of those at Marly, the touch of which, identical with that of the Marly engravings, clearly established that they are by Pierre Lepautre (Figures 58, 59).[44] The fine pen-stroke does not differ essentially from the stroke of Lepautre's free outline with needle or burin, alike facile and flowing, with slight shading. The heads above the arches are expressively indicated with a few touches, a dot under the line of the mouth being particularly characteristic. Lepautre's handling of the brush, and of colour, is here revealed to us. Narrow shadows are drawn in boldly with a very sure line of the brush. While the tints chosen, for woodwork, for glass, for marbles, are those which had become traditional in the Bâtiments, the tonality is paler and more neutral than with Lassurance or Carlier. One of these drawings (Figure 5) is inscribed, "Cheminée de Mad^e La princesse de Conty à Versailles. Bon à Rivet menuisie et Tarlet marbrier. Le tout reglé le 15e Juin 1700. Mansart."[45] Another (Figure 6) seems to be for the chambre de Mme. la Duchesse de Chartres, ordered September 12, 1700.

By 1701 a remodelling of the Appartement du Roi at Versailles could no longer be postponed. It was executed, as we know, on a radical plan, taking for the Chambre du Roi the old central salon, with its greater size and height, extending the Antichambre to include the space vacated by the Chambre, and enlarging the Cabinet du Roi at the expense of the Cabinet des Perruques. The first two of these rooms remain substantially intact, among the chief monuments from the last period of the reign.

For the Chambre du Roi, designs survive at the Archives Nationales (o¹ 1768, No. 66) which seem to have escaped the earlier students of Versailles (Figures 60, 61). They show successive studies for the rear wall. Although the drawing under the wash is here in pencil instead of pen, there is no difficulty in recognizing the same hand as in the drawings by Lepautre which we have presented. There is the same free and sure drawing in of shadows with the brush, the same abbreviations for the scrollwork and *mosaïque*, the same notably for pilaster capitals. On the later alternates, more summarily sketched, the touch becomes progressively bolder, the figures showing the greatest mastery and economy of line, with Lepautre's characteristic shorthand for the faces.

While in this room the pilasters and doorcasings are survivals from the treatment of 1684, all else was, by successive orders, made new, and all was fused in the new spirit (Figure 62). The effect of height was increased by the genial invention of the great arch, and by the new arches of chimney piece and opposite pier "renfermant des glaces jusqu'en haut," with details clearly designed by the same hand as those at Marly. Reclining cherubs over the mirror have the butterfly wings we have seen a generation before in the cornice of the Salle d'Abondance, and meanwhile in Berain's arabesques. The old overdoors "trop

---

[44] Cabinet des Estampes, De Cotte collection, Ha 18, fols. 25 and 26.

[45] Only the signature is Mansart's, not the other writing. Nolhac was in error when, in the *Gazette des beaux-arts*, IIIe pér., XXVIII, 1902, 41, he captioned this drawing "Croquis de Mansart." The order for the work, 15 juin 1700, is included in Mansart's register.

pesants," were replaced; the heavy panels of the old doors were carved as best they could be with bandwork ornaments "riches et légers," the window heads and shutters were likewise carved in Lepautre's new vocabulary of forms.

The Chambre du Louis XIV has been universally recognized as an artistic masterpiece of the first order, both representative and absolute. There is a union of qualities rarely found together: nobility and grace, splendour and moderation, richness and refinement, monumentality and delicacy, strength and lightness, in the vital synthesis of the perfect work of art.

Of the designs for the Antichambre (the Oeil-de-Boeuf) and the Cabinet de Conseil, only rough office copies survive,[46] but many features reveal unmistakably the paternity of Pierre Lepautre. In the chimney piece of the Oeil-de-Boeuf (Figure 63), this is evident both for the mantel, with its oval arch, and for the great mirror with its concave upper corners—features both first found in the examples at Marly. The tympanums of the windows are merely so many Marly mirror heads; the concave window heads are rich adaptations of the same novel motives. Beneath the large paintings and mirrors of those rooms the panelling offered for the first time[47] large panels carved in the new manner, with a border of bandwork with scrolled bill-hook corners. By contrast with the doors of Le Brun and Caffieri in 1679-1681, where even the bandwork itself, united by gilding with major ornaments, constituted with them a panel filling, the treatment here may be thought[48] to represent a drawing together of the ornament into accented areas, contrasting with a nude background. It is truer genetically, however, to consider the scrollwork as an adjunct of the frame, invading the bare field at the ends and about a large central rosette. The motifs of this carved invasion of the broad panels are fundamentally the same as those of the narrow pilaster strips at Marly, although opposite scrolls of the interlace now enclose minor fields of appreciable area, filled with palmettes or fleurs-de-lys.

Many elements of the Oeil-de-Boeuf are actual remains of the old woodwork of the Chambre du Roi. The old pilasters were reused, merely elevated on dies to reach the raised position of the cornice, which itself was merely that of the Chambre du Roi extended around the enlarged room. The old overdoors remained, with a new frieze below of delicate scrollwork. After one has knowledge of the disparity of the elements of the wall one may find this somewhat disturbing, but as it has passed unnoticed by observers, one must concede that old and new are combined with remarkable skill and success.

The glory of the Oeil-de-Boeuf is its ceiling, which so genially takes advantage of every inch of height permitted by the roof construction and which masks the unusual resulting form by the superb inclined band above the cornice, incorporating the *oeils-de-boeuf*. The joyous, animated figures of playing infants by Van Clève and his fellow sculptors are relieved against a continuous background of gilded *mosaïque*, while branches of palm frame the openings. Here all was new, living, and beautiful.

[46] O[1] 1770, liasse 1, nos. 15 and 15 bis; and O[1] 1772, liasse 11, nos. 4 and 5. Cf. Kimball and A.-M.-E. Marie: "L'appartement du Roi," cited above.

[47] The great horizontal panel on the east wall is evidently later in date than the others there; it is closely related to panels of the Salon des Sources at Trianon, 1713, and to the doors of the chapel of Versailles at that time, having like some of those doors, a second, inner gilded band from which the interlaces of scrollwork take their rise.

[48] As by R. Sedlmaier, *Die Grundlagen der fransozischen Rokoko-Ornamentik in Frankreich*, 1917, 48 ff.

Genesis

In the Cabinet du Conseil (Figure 64) whereas proposals of the spring of 1699 had retained the full revetment of mirrors beginning at the floor with a division of the height at the top of the doors, the mirrors were now embraced in a more extensive framework of wood, rising unbroken from a dado to the main cornice. Arched heads with carved spandrels were placed over the mirrors at the cardinal points, as well as over the windows. It has not been appreciated that in the Cabinet de Conseil, again remodelled in 1755, much work of this period survives beside the window embrasures: the dado on the end walls, the friezes of the doors, and indeed the arched mirror frames themselves, with their spandrel ornaments, although the mirrors themselves may have been enlarged in an intermediate remodelling.[49]

Unlike the other rooms of the suite, this one was cast in a single jet; it was wholly an embodiment of the new spirit. To reconstitute it in imagination we may turn to the Cabinet des Glaces at Trianon (Figure 74), in which, a few years later, its scheme was again incorporated. There we may grasp and feel the artistic qualities of this first room which was wholly a work of Pierre Lepautre—instinct with smiling grace, with delicacy, with lightness.

It is small wonder, in view of the richness and novelty of all this treatment, that Dangeau should have written, on the return from Fontainebleau to Versailles, November 16, 1701 (VIII, 239): "Le roi trouva ici son appartement d'une magnificence, d'un agrément et d'une commodité non pareils."

Even in the Grande Galerie Lepautre was called on to make certain designs for modifications at this time. It is well known that the first set of bronze *chutes d'armes* were not delivered until 1701, when the King ordered them placed in the Salon de la Guerre,[50] and that it is not until this period that an order was given for additional examples for the gallery. It was to show their effect there, in place of the initial busts on consoles, that Lepautre made a long drawing of the gallery (o^1 1768), rendered in his characteristic manner.[51]

At Trianon, too, the King had to have an apartment in the new style, created in 1702 in the space hitherto occupied by the Salle de Comédie. From their character we cannot doubt that the details at least were drawn by Lepautre. These rooms, wholly new, exemplify the style more fully than could the remodellings at Marly and Versailles. The height of the walls was increased at the expense of the vaults, leaving the ceiling essentially flat, with a very small cove above the cornice. The panelling is of extreme importance, being the first in whole rooms of normal type treated in the new manner. We shall see that it embodies many innovations which have ordinarily been thought characteristic of a much later day.

The apartment consisted of Antichambre, Chambre, Cabinet, Grand Cabinet. The Grand Cabinet has long been swept away, the Cabinet absorbed in the enlarged Chambre, and the woodwork has been retouched in many places. Fortunately we have drawings (e.g. Figures 65-69)[52]—though small and summary ones—of the last three rooms of the suite, which enable us to verify what parts of the finish survive from 1703 and to describe it as it then was.

---

[49] Cf. "L'appartement du Roi," already cited, also A.-M.-E. Marie: "Le cabinet du conseil," a communication to the Société de l'histoire de l'art français, 1940, unpublished.

[50] Mansart's register, October 1701.

[51] o^1 1768, reproduced in "Mansart and Le Brun," *loc. cit.*

[52] o^1 1884. In our paper on Trianon, of which the proof corrections were not received in Paris in time to be incorporated, these are captioned as being drawn by Robert de Cotte; we consider them today to be office copies, some of the captions of which were indeed written by him.

The Creation of the Rococo

No longer are there any moulded imposts. Although the narrow piers on many walls are punctuated at half their height by rosettes or small ornamented traverses, the effect is now of a singe flight from dado to cornice.[53] On the broader surfaces, though there are again several tiers of shallow panels, they are differentiated, and subordinated to the general effect of height. Some of these panels surviving in the Antichambre have, within the rectangular outer moulding, an inner bead with scrolled crossettes—a multiplication of bands, as in the Cabinet du Conseil, which was to increase, in the most elaborate work, from double to triple. Already at Trianon, inside this inner ornamented bead, there is occasionally a further, third line, made by the moulded edge of a raised field, wholly nude, inscribed within the scrollwork of the crossettes—the forerunner of the fielded panels characteristic of the time of Louis XV. The bead itself is spirally wreathed with a delicate spray of flowers—the initial example of one of the favorite motifs of the coming reign. The modifications of the geometrical assemblage by carved scrollwork is carried into the pier glasses and into the overdoors, where in the Chambre du Roi the arched cornice on consoles, crowning the oval frame, is almost the only feature which preserves any academic or corporeal character. In the Grand Cabinet the overmantel mirror, square in a first study, is arched to the cornice. The weight and relief of all the mouldings is greatly reduced, and the whole panelling takes on an ethereal lightness and delicacy.

The marble chimney pieces shown need not detain us, as they are of types identical with those by Lepautre we have already seen.

In spite of the many losses and later retouches, we can, by an effort of mental reconstruction, recover something of the artistic effect of this suite, where, as in the Cabinet du Conseil at Versailles, all was new and coherent. No longer was there any substantial admixture of plastic survivals. Everywhere the linear, surface quality predominated, in a fine-spun net of delicate mouldings and carved scrolls—the mouldings themselves being now incorporated with the carving by spiral sprays. The framework was now fully autonomous and self-sufficient, an end in itself, delighting the beholder by its free play.

Lepautre's hand may be recognized beyond doubt in the subsequent work at Trianon. In 1705 there were new chimney pieces at Trianon-sous-Bois of which the mirror frames ring the changes on the Marly types. In 1706 there were new and more delicate cornices, placed higher, in many of the rooms of the Château. Several of these (Figures 70-72) are included, with others, in the engraved suite *Livre de différentes corniches executées dans le château de Versailles sur les desseins de Monsieur Mansart Surintendant . . . dessiné et gravé par P. Le Pautre*.[54] The great majority are still full entablatures; but there are some with merely an astragal in place of the architrave, as in that of the Salon de Musique. The frieze is now sometimes given a concave or reverse curvature as in the Salon Frais, where the concave frieze, divided by shallow consoles, and with playful figural ornaments, is already prophetic of future developments. Four feet was added to the wall in certain rooms, notably the Salon de Musique, where the overdoors are of this period. At this time also the Salon de la Chapelle received its present treatment with taller composite pilasters (Figure 73), and the Cabinet

[53] These piers, as we see them today, were later modified by the substitution of single tall panels: those of the Antichambre perhaps about 1712, those of the Chambre apparently after 1730.

[54] A rare copy, perhaps unique, is in the Print Department of the Metropolitan Museum of Art. It is datable from the Trianon cornices as after 1706.

des Glaces its graceful smiling decoration (Figure 74), confining the mirrors within arched frames as had been done in the Cabinet de Conseil at Versailles in 1701. Both are shown in other engravings by Pierre Lepautre.

Latest of the works at Trianon was that in the Salon des Sources, remodelled in 1713, where the carving of this time includes the large horizontal panels, the tall uninterrupted pilaster-like strips and the ovals of the piers, with their characteristic scrollwork.

In these and other works of Lepautre the profiles of the mouldings are not of new types, the basic form continuing to be the baroque ovolo or bolection. What is new in these profiles is their scale, reduced to a linear slenderness and lightness in complete contrast to the plastic massiveness of the baroque.

Even before Lepautre's first decorations were being executed in the royal châteaux, he had made for the Bâtiments the first design for a major religious work, the altar of Notre Dame de Paris. We are forced to discuss this project in some detail, for Lepautre's connection with it has not been appreciated and the evolution of the design itself has not hitherto been adequately established.[55]

December 19, 1698, Dangeau had noted in his journal[56] the King's gift of a large sum for this purpose, in fulfilment of the old vow of Louis XIII. Of the character of the first design, our chief idea hitherto has been derived from descriptions of the medal by Roussel and De Launay[57] placed in the cornerstone December 7, 1699, of which an example is now reproduced here (Figure 76). As Germain Brice wrote in 1713 (III, 264), it shows the altar "de quatre colonnes torses, d'ordre composé, posées en demy cercle, qui portoient un demy baldaquin."

The original design for the altar in this form has lain, apparently unobserved, at the Archives Nationales (o^1 1690, No. 52). It bears on the back the endorsement, entirely in Mansart's bold hand: "Arete par le Roy ce 19 mars 1699, Mansart."[58] The same date appears in his endorsement of a memorandum (No. 36), "Depense a faire pour l'Autel de Notre Dame," totalling 287,000 livres: "regle ce Jour duy—a Marly par le Roy pour estre executé—et depancer 40,000 par année a commancer de cel de 1699 19 mars."

This drawing, which we reproduced for the first time (Figure 75),[59] is from the hand of Pierre Lepautre. Drawn on a large fair sheet, it is inked with easy mastery and finely rendered in colour. The identity of technique with Lepautre's drawings and engravings extends to the indication of every individual motif of ornament—palms, bell-flower, acanthus, fleur-de-lys, shell, guilloche. The suggestion of the faces, the drawing of the figure, nervous and muscular, and of the wings all conform with the technique of Pierre Lepautre, indeed the crowning group is almost identical with one in the designs for the Chambre du Roi.

[55] M. Vloberg: *Notre-Dame de Paris et le voeu de Louis XIII*, 1926, reproduced some of the designs for the altar, but he apparently did not know those illustrated here, and thus failed to disentangle the evolution.

[56] VI, 477. December 21 he reports the amount as 500,000 livres.

[57] Their authorship of the medal is indicated by the *Comptes*, IV, 485, 488. In Mansart's register, o^1 1809, we find the authorization for it under date of 12 juin, 1699.

[58] *Ibid.*, 4 mars, 1699: "M. Mansart a fait voir au Roi le dessein en forme circulaire de l'autel de Notre-Dame, que sa Majesté a approuvé." Following preparation of the estimate, royal authority to proceed is also recorded here, 19 mars.

[59] "The Creation of the *style Louis XV*," *loc. cit.*

Lepautre's design of 1699 for Notre Dame, with its twisted columns, did not represent an isolated and radical adoption of a baroque type; Mansart had apparently adopted the scheme, the year before, for the high altar of the Invalides.[60] Lepautre's design is in many regards a conservative version of the baroque type, reverting to more geometrical lines. The plan is a semicircle; the canopy has a semi-circular arch, disguised but slightly by the fronds of palm—very different from the consoles at Saint-Peter's, the Val-de-Grace, or the Invalides. The spacing of the columns is uniform, instead of being unequal in balanced groups. Still architectonic and plastic, the altar and its canopy tend from energy toward equilibrium.

The treatment of the arcades of the choir and apse around the baldaquin deserves some attention, especially as, in the end, this treatment was to become dominant in the design. The Gothic piers were to be given a revetment of marble with round arches, above which were pairs of seated female figures supporting shields. The piers, with panels in slight relief, were to be adorned with trophies of arms.

The *Comptes* regarding Notre Dame reveal numerous payments in 1699 for the execution of a model of the altar in wood. The first stone of the foundations was laid December 7, 1699, and the model at full size was exhibited June 19, 1700,[61] but met with much criticism. The King inspected the model on his visit to Paris May 20, 1701, "le trouva mal placé," as Dangeau reports (VIII, 105), and called for a vote of the canons as to its location.[62] In September, 1703, the model was demolished.[63] In an unpublished contemporary resumé of the history of the project (o¹ 1690, No. 44) we read: "En 1703 M. De Cotte ecrivit au Chapitre en ces termes: 'Le Roy a vu le nouveau dessein de l'Autel de Notre-Dame; il ma paru content. Nous allons travailler en conformité tant à l'autel qu'au dessus de chaises et jubé.' Le dessein a été executé."

What appear to be the first tentative versions of the new design, thus datable probably from 1703, exist in three variants preserved at the Cabinet des Estampes (Va 259b).[64] The drawings (Figures 77-79), which we lately published for the first time, are likewise from the hand of Pierre Lepautre. This is shown not only by absolute identity of the tricks of hand with corresponding features in the design of 1699 (e.g., the crucifix) but also by independent analogies of indication with other drawings and engravings of Lepautre. The me-

---

[60] Francart was paid in October, 1698, for a "tableau en grand" and, in November, for "desseins en grand." From October, 1700, to November, 1704, there are payments for a wooden model or models. As executed in 1705 the baldachino had six twisted columns jointed by straight entablatures. An engraving of the work, long destroyed, is given in Granet: *L'histoire de l'Hôtel des Invalides*, 1736.

[61] We learn the date from a memorandum of severe "Observations," o¹ 1690, No. 37.

[62] From this time will come the studies for placing a similar baldaquin in other positions in the cathedral, reproduced by Vloberg, *op. cit.* One (pl. XXXVII), apparently by Lepautre, is a perspective showing it placed under the crossing. The colonnes torses are abandoned in favor of fluted Corinthian columns. Another (Figure 104), described by Vloberg as "Dessin de Robert de Cotte," is inscribed "Idée d'un particulier" and would appear to be one of the suggestions volunteered at this period. It places the baldaquin at the entrance to the choir, flanked by remains of the old jubé of the early XVIIᵉ century (cf. Vloberg, pl. XVII). From the technique and details of this design the "particulier" might well seem to have been Oppenord, just back from seven years study of the baroque in Italy and eager for employment (cf. *Grand Oppenord*, pl. LXXXXVIII).

[63] *Comptes*, IV, 957. Some late payments for further demolition of the "ancien modèle" occur in 1709 (V, 342).

[64] Courajod, writing in the *Nouvelles archives de l'art français*, 1873, 356-358, erroneously supposed these drawings to be of the period of 1699.

Genesis

dium is again the same—pen and coloured wash, with similar tonality—although there is a somewhat freer and bolder shading with the brush.

It was now proposed to abandon any boldly plastic central feature, and to develop the surrounding walls of the apse. Near the back of the apse was to be a low altar table like a sarcophagus, with a relief of Louis XIII kneeling before the Virgin with the dead Christ. Around the sanctuary, on pedestals flanked by consoles, were to stand angels holding flambeaux. In the first version an angel also occupies a niche in the central arch. The second version shows under the arch, instead, an elaborate tabernacle corbelled on consoles adorned with winged cherub-heads. In the third variant, from which the executed designs were later developed, the relief of the Pietà, with the monarch in adoration, is enlarged and removed from the altar-front to fill the central arch or niche, above which a glory with adoring angels replaces the royal coat-of-arms with its supporters. It was in harmony with the spirit of the new style that the scheme adopted should have been not the architectonic nor the plastic one, but the one in low relief, in which the surface dominated. The trophies of the piers below the imposts are now *trophées d'église*. Above are panels of *mosaïque* with rondels at half their height. The motifs meanwhile developed in domestic interiors thus begin to make a modest appearance in monumental religious work.

The execution of the altar was deferred until after the death of Mansart, with further modifications which we shall discuss in their place.

Meanwhile a project of related character, for the choir of the Cathedral of Orléans, had received the attention of the Bâtiments. The approved design for the stalls (Figure 80) was one presented in 1702 by Jacques Gabriel, Contrôleur Général des Bâtiments du Roi.[65] Now Jacques Gabriel, while an efficient executive, was, according to the passage we have quoted from Mariette, incapable of drawing the least detail of ornament. When we examine the surviving woodwork of the stalls and of the episcopal throne (designed in 1705),[66] we realize at once that he had recourse to the gifted designer of the Bâtiments, who had just created these new forms.

We see that Lepautre embodies here in church woodwork the ideas he had developed in the panelling of the palaces. While most of the panels are geometrical, those above the arches, like those above chimney pieces elsewhere, are truncated with scrolled hawk's-bills. In the panels of the pedestal below the episcopal throne are the rosettes and interlaces of the dados at Versailles. The scheme of the ovals within an arch on consoles is like that of the overdoors in the new Appartement du Roi at Trianon, designed the same year, and corresponds even more closely to one of Lepautre's engraved designs for interiors at this period (Figure 81).

It should be noted that the *trophées d'église*, here employed as a major decorative feature,

[65] Adjudication de 30 juin, 1702, published with other documents by G. Vignat in *Reunion des sociétés des beaux-arts des départements*, XVII, 1893, 722-756, and by G. Chenesseau: *Sainte-Croix d'Orléans*, 1921, 199-213. The carving of the stalls and of the throne was executed by Dugoullons (so he *signed* his name in one of the documents), the medallions of the life of Christ being from drawings and models furnished by Robert Le Lorrain, as the younger Dargenville notes in his life of the sculptor.

[66] The throne has been twice restored on different schemes, to incorporate the columns, the balustrade and basement, and the coat of arms with its supporters, which are original. We may doubt whether a scroll pediment, which today supports the arms, would have been used by Pierre Lepautre.

were the first conspicuous executed examples of this motif, foreshadowed in baroque Italy and henceforth so widely adopted. Its use was in contravention of a recent dictum of the Academy of Architecture, in discussing Blondel's remarks on trophies at its séance of June 3, 1697 (present: De La Hire, Desgodetz, Dorbay, Félibien): "il serait mal à propos de representer en trophée, mesmes dans les eglises, des chandeliers, des calices, des burettes et autres choses semblables, qu'on n'a pas coûtume d'attacher et mettre en trophée."[67] Thus a new freedom transcended academic bounds and pointed toward the future.

The stalls, restored in 1937-1938 to their original site though not wholly to their original relationships, speak to us today with ringing brilliance. Less delicate in voice than the house-music of the domestic interiors, theirs has a sonority and volume which is not less moving.

The succession of the Marquis (later Duc) d'Antin as Directeur-général des Bâtiments du Roi[68] and of Robert de Cotte to the post of Premier Architecte on the death of Mansart, May 11, 1708, brought little change, at first, in the artistic responsibility for design. Where the memoirs previously said "sur les desseins du Sr. Mansart," they now read "sur les desseins du Sr. de Cotte." In one case as in the other this was merely a uniform official formula, which tells us nothing as to the real authorship. Afterwards, as before, we find in the bulging dossiers of the organization, and equally in the rich collection of drawings which passed to the descendants of the Premier Architecte, no preliminary sketches from his hand for any of the royal works.

There were few important additions to the staff. Jossenet, Carlier cadet, Aubert and Lambert (d. 1709) who came in as draughtsmen in 1708, scarcely represent significant accessions in design. More important may have been the return of Boffrand, who was paid as Architecte from March 21, 1709, at the low rate of 1000 livres yearly, although again we find no drawings from his hand for decorative commissions. These were still handled by Pierre Lepautre, who continued as Dessinateur at the salary of 2000 livres.

One new force in the Bâtiments, destined soon to gain great importance, was the sculptor François-Antoine Vassé (1681-1736). Like Berain and Lepautre he was never in Italy. He had worked first with his father Antoine in the Arsenal at Toulon, for which Berain had furnished ornamental designs since 1687,[69] so that he must have been familiar from childhood with the basic ornamental forms of this godfather of the rococo. He may have come to Paris in 1698, at the age of seventeen. We hear of him there in the distribution of prizes to the students of the Academy of Painting and Sculpture, as winner of the first prize for the spring quarter of 1707.[70] This was presented to him by the Duc d'Antin, opening the series of awards made, belatedly, at the session of December 1, 1708, the first attended by the new Protector.

By September of this year 1708, under the administration of D'Antin and De Cotte, Vassé was engaged as a decorative sculptor at Versailles. He became, as we shall see, the

[67] *Procès-verbaux*, III, 11.

[68] Regarding this appointment, which evoked the jealous comments of Saint-Simon, cf. "Mémoires du duc d'Antin" in *Mélanges publiés par la Société des bibliophiles français*, 1822. Of De Cotte he says (p. 70), "homme de probité et de mérite"; of Mansart (p. 74), "je dois lui rendre justice, il n'a ni friponné, ni volé."

[69] Weigert, *op. cit.*, 116 ff.

[70] *Procès-verbaux*, LV, 73.

favorite sculptor of De Cotte.[71] His abilities were not limited merely to execution; by 1711 we shall find him also making drawings, and thus fully responsible for the advanced character of certain crucial works. In 1715, indeed, he was to be made Dessinateur Général de la Marine, a post of which Berain had performed the functions, although he had been refused the title.

In the years still remaining to Louis XIV, De Cotte was to have few opportunities to decorate domestic interiors in the royal châteaux. There was indeed one important work under construction, the Château Neuf at Meudon. The woodwork and carving fall in the years 1708 and 1709. The rooms of the Dauphin's apartment had boiseries carved by Dugoullons and his atelier, some being decorated *au vernis* by Claude Audran; we cannot doubt that they were generally similar to Lepautre's designs of just this time at Trianon. The destruction of the Château in 1870 leaves us with little evidence as to the precise forms of this work.[72] At the very end of the reign, in 1714,[73] there were extensive remodellings in the Appartement du Roi at Fontainebleau, but subsequent changes in the most important rooms leave us uncertain as to the exact identity of the elements there from this time. In minor rooms at Fontainebleau from this campaign the detail is closely similar to what we shall find just then at Bercy, to be discussed later.

The great enterprise in progress at De Cotte's accession was the decoration of the Chapelle de Versailles, of which the major forms, as executed, go back to designs of 1699.[74] They were magnificently recorded in the folio *Les Plans, coupes, profils et élévations de la chapelle du château royal de Versailles, levés & gravés par Pierre Lepautre, architecte & graveur du Roy*. It is not, however, on this his record of the completed work that we base our suggestion that Lepautre had a large share in the decorative design, where it was obviously desired to exploit as much as possible the new style he had created. There survive numerous manuscript drawings from his hand for this adornment.

The most important of Lepautre's designs are for the apse of the chapel with the high altar. One large sheet (Figure 82)[75] shows the whole breadth of the nave. No less than eleven flaps, now mounted separately (Va 361, tome VII), give alternate designs for the altar with its flanking figures. All these are rendered in wash in Lepautre's characteristic blond tonality, identical in touch and degree of development with the drawings of 1703

[71] Vassé's early success evidently went somewhat to his head, for we find him in 1713 demanding to enter first at the École du Modèle, before all the students and with the professor who posed the model, "s'estant mesme expliqué qu'il seroit autorisé dans sa prétention par Monseigneur le Duc d'Antin," a pretention which was rejected by the Protector and the Academy.

[72] At the Archives Nationales the drawings of Meudon in the carton o¹ 1524 include no interiors of the Château Neuf. Mariette's engraved section, taken on the axis, gives us only one panelled room, of little elaboration. One would expect that photographs of the interiors might survive, but our search for them has not been successful.

[73] *Comptes*, V, 786, 821, 823. Cf. Dangeau, XV, 219-220, Saint-Simon, XXV, 98. For the Salle du Conseil, modified first in 1738 and again in 1752-1754, we have a drawing by Gabriel at the latter period (pl. XLIII in E. de Fels: *Ange-Jacques Gabriel*, 1912) which shows at the left the work before his changes, but we cannot be sure how much of this goes back to 1714.

[74] We hope in future to say more than has yet been said as to the evolution of the general design of the Chapel to the form adopted. Lassurance, as surviving drawings show, had certainly a large part in it. In the ordonnance much depended necessarily on the masonry surviving from earlier beginnings, which was skillfully modified to give the whole a new character.

[75] Cabinet des Estampes, Topographie, format 6.

for the apse and altar of Notre Dame, with which they are also closely related in style and motif.

The basic drawing, already indicating all the wealth of sculptured ornamentation the chapel was to receive, shows this in forms antedating the execution of any of it, and was thus made not later than the spring of 1708.[76] Lepautre here treats the altar-front with his characteristic panel-work; above it he places a retable composed with motifs from Berain. Later alternates offer a variety of tabernacles and baldachinos, as well as large reliefs filling the arch: a Nativity, a Resurrection, a Pietà, and angels flanking a glory—the scheme adopted in the relief executed by Van Clève, on which he received a first payment May 25, 1708. In the several studies, the flanking figures are sometimes saints, sometimes angels, standing or kneeling, the last foreshadowing those finally carried out.

For the spandrels of the choir, Lepautre proposed groups of three angel-musicians; we know that, after Coustou had experimented with models of two angels, the scheme of a single angel with a cherub was adopted in execution. For the piers Lepautre proposed *trophées d'église* as in the stalls at Orléans—"les ornaments sacrés des églises," as Félibien says, "avec les armes que les rois de France ont fait servir a la défense et à la propagation de la foi."[77] Already in the drawing before us he suggests some of the motifs employed in a hundred variations of those which are the chief magnificence of the decoration of the chapel. The bands of interlace on the soffits of the arches are also indicated here generically; we cannot doubt that the motifs of the pendentives and the rosettes of the aisle vaults (Figure 86) as well as the backgrounds of *mosaïque*—all so consonant with his earlier work—derive also from Lepautre. Indeed the only surviving drawing for such elements (o¹ 1782), a very large one for a tapering compartment of the apse vault seems to be by Lepautre.

At the Archives Nationales are studies for several other architectural features of the Chapel;[78] all those surviving from the time of its first building may be recognized as in the technique of Lepautre. They include early projects for the altar of the Virgin, the altar of the Holy Sacrament, and the altars of the aisles. These altars, first discussed in a preliminary memorandum of January, 1707, were executed on a somewhat modified scheme from 1708 to 1710, when the Chapel was consecrated on June 5. Our drawings will thus be from 1707 or early 1708.

We may take as a specimen the altar of the Virgin, occupying the central chapel on the north at the gallery level.[79] The upper portion remains unchanged and enables us to identify two pencil drawings, closely similar, as preliminary studies for this altar (Figure 83). The indication of every motif—the heads, the scrolls, the acanthus leafage, the carving of the mouldings, the *mosaïques*—is identical with what we have seen in Lepautre's line drawings and engravings.

[76] The dates and names of executants are covered by L. Deshairs: *Documents inédits sur la chapelle de Château de Versailles*, 1906, reprinted with fuller detail from his paper in the *Revue de l'histoire de Versailles*, VII, 1905, 241-262. Van Clève had 4000 livres on May 28, 1708, "sur les ouvrages de bronze qu'il a fait pour le grand autel." The first payments for any of the stone carving shown in this drawing are of September 3, 1708.

[77] MS. published by Nolhac: *La chapelle royale de Versailles*, n.d. [1912].

[78] o¹ 1782, 1783.

[79] Its original form as executed is established by the engravings of the chapel and by Félibien's description, both included by Nolhac in *La Chapelle royale de Versailles*.

Genesis

The project for the altar of the Virgin is not based on Italian altarpieces, but is a composition of original type, of elements already familiar to us in his secular work. In the great frame of the painting, the outline repeats that of mirror frames at Marly and in the Oeil-de-Boeuf, though winged cherub heads—a Renaissance motif revived by Borromini, used occasionally by Le Brun and Jean Lepautre and by Oppenord in designs of 1704 as we shall see—form the central motif and replace the leafage at the upper corners. In the position, they constitute, with others in the Chapelle de Versailles, the earliest examples I know in French architecture of *têtes en espagnolette*.

That the superb doors of the chapel and its vestibules, carved in 1710, with their great oval rosettes (Figure 85) were made from drawings by Lepautre is a conclusion which is inescapable. Perfectly coherent in style with the projects for altar-frontals, as with the panels of this time at Versailles and Trianon, they show a culmination of his personal development, beginning with the chimney pieces at Marly, and have indeed served as classical paradigms of this phase of style.[80] The change from the work of 1699 and 1702 is most obvious in the liaison of the divisions by interpenetrating scrolls, and in the more impassioned curvature. In several instances an inner band reinforces the scrolled outline and defines the bare inner field.

More than a quarter century after completion of the chapel the obituary of François-Antoine Vassé said of him: "Il a fait tous les Desseins et Modèles des Archivoltes et Trophées des Piliers de la Chapelle du Château de Versailles, du grand Autel, Chaire à prêcher et les Tribunes du Roy et de la Reine, le Lutrin et plusieurs bas-reliefs."[81] This statement, which has escaped the writers of monographs of the chapel, obviously calls for careful verification.

We have seen that the first designs for the high altar were made by Pierre Lepautre, and that these show also the genesis of the reliefs of the spandrels, the archivolts and the pillars of choir and nave, with their trophies. Payments for the carving of these motifs of the ground story began September 3, 1708. As early as January 19, however, La Pierre was receiving a first payment on two of the reliefs of musical trophies in the tribune of the apse, reliefs which, with those of Le Lorrain at the same moment for the royal tribune, first set the style of execution for all the trophies of the chapel.

When we come to the pillars of the nave, we find that the first of all payments for them was to Vassé, September 3 (V, 216), this being also the first time that the artist, then twenty-seven, appears in the royal accounts. It was "sur quatre bas-reliefs de trophées d'église du pourtour d'un des piliers"—which we know from memoirs published by Deshairs was the fourth pillar on the right. This is also, as it happens, the only pillar where the trophy on the face was not carved by the same artist who executed the angel in the spandrel above—in this case Thierry, apparently later than the trophy. The other trophies of the face of the pillars, which we cannot exactly date, were carved each by a different artist, including men of such rank as Le Lorrain and Nicolas Coustou. April 20, 1709 (V, 214) Gaillard, Noël and Dugoullons were paid no less than 16,000 livres "sur les ornemens des trophees d'église des pilliers du rez de chausée"; these and many more by other sculptors were those of the aisles. From September, 1709, to January, 1710, Vassé again had 1050 livres on eight trophies for the pillars of the nave, some of these being on the sides and back of pillars of which the

[80] Sedlmaier, *op. cit.*, 52-53.   [81] *Mercure*, March, 1736, 531.

face was carved by others. His whole account, totalling 10,270 livres for such trophies and for carvings in wood for the pulpit was finally settled in October, 1710.

We see that Vassé was indeed largely concerned with the trophies of the pillars, that he may have carved the first of these to be executed and thus have established their depth of relief—less than that of the larger trophies above. Clearly, however, his work was subsequent to Lepautre's general design for the pillars, and follows the general suggestion and character of the earlier trophies by Le Lorrain and La Pierre above. That Vassé, the young newcomer, may have designed the trophies of the aisles executed by such men as Dugoullons and his associates is readily possible; that he gave designs for those by sculptors like Coustou and Le Lorrain is barely conceivable. More probably, after many years, the execution of eight out of over eighty trophies had become the designing and modelling of all.

In all these compositions, as in the military trophies of Ladoireau—so long ago begun, but so lately completed and placed in the Salon de la Guerre—any suggestion of symmetry is rare. There is a wealth of movement, not only in the placing of the major elements, but also in the lines of palm which so often add their reverse curvature. The endless variety and profusion, within the unity of scheme and treatment, make the adornment of the chapel incomparable in richness since the Middle Ages.

For the high altar, where the executed work differs in many ways from Lepautre's early designs, Van Clève's memoir of over 37,000 livres cover every phase of the work, including "60 journées a plusieurs petits modèles en terres et cires." The only payment to Vassé in connection with the high altar was a small one of 1711 (V, 533) "pour le modèle du nouveau projet du tabernacle"—the tabernacle which disappeared at the Revolution. On the other hand, Thierry, Vassé, Cayot and Desjardins were paid 7000 livres in 1710 "sur les ouvrages de bronze qu'ils font l'autel de la Vierge, et les cinq autels des bas-cotez" (V, 415)—altars of which the first designs, generally followed, had been drawn by Pierre Lepautre.

We turn now to the woodwork of the chapel, the ecclesiastical furniture, the oratories, the pulpit, the stalls and the organ—which include some of the freest and most advanced designs. Though so much of this is destroyed, we are not wholly without recourse as to its form. Some of it appears in Lepautre's engraved sections, and we have later drawings of certain elements.

The two oratories which stood at the western end of the aisles, later the Oratoires de Mesdames, had a crown of free profile—a concave pedestal with consoles at the corners, bearing a scrolled urn. Lepautre's section makes evident that the "changement" shown in a later drawing by Gabriel (Figure 84) was merely a rearrangement, on a new plan, of the existing elements which clearly reveal Lepautre's authorship of their original design.

The tourelles of the oratories of the royal tribune are shown in the engraved section. Oval in plan, they had, belatedly, the character of a baroque belfry, with crown of consoles. Vassé was the carver of these, the accounts (V, 493) confirming his obituary to that degree.

The form of the pulpit, which the obituary also attributes to Vassé, is preserved to us by certain graphic documents (Figure 88).[82] For perhaps the first time since the Renaissance,

---

[82] From an album of sketches, of which one is signed Tanche, 1770, in the Fromageot collection, it was first reproduced by Deshairs, *op. cit.* The pulpit also appears, more clearly, in the engraving of C.-N. Cochin the younger, *Cérémonie du mariage de Louis, Dauphin de France . . . dans la Chapelle . . . de Versailles le XXIII février MDCCXLV.*

it was a pulpit of circular plan; its profile was a reverse curve. The canopy, also circular, was of generally concave profile, buttressed at intervals by motifs of cartouche and scroll which clung very closely to the surface. The wax models were made by Bertrand, La Pierre and Vassé,[83] and Vassé, as his obituary stated, did indeed make the eagle of the lectern.[84] This was perhaps the extent of his carving on the pulpit, for which we have already seen he was paid in 1710.

It is the organ case, executed in 1709-1710 and still surviving (Figure 87), which most fully embodies the new spirit appearing in the decoration of the chapel. Here we are in an exceptionally favourable position for comparisons, with the organ of Saint-Quentin designed by Jean Berain in 1697,[85] just prior to Lepautre's first work from the Crown. That organ— itself representing great innovations in the traditional type—is extremely massive, in an effort to achieve academic proportions. Its broad base is panelled without other carving than garlands over certain rondels. We remark particularly that there is no smallest suggestion of a plastic modification of the geometrical outline of the panels, no trace of application to the framework of motives of Berain's painted arabesque—an application which we have signalized as Lepautre's decisive and fruitful contribution, transforming the evolution of style.

In the organ of Versailles we see, first, a reversion to the "Gothic" from which Berain expressly sought to escape.[86] The towers are accepted as the principal motifs; there is no effort to disguise the plate-faces by treatment à l'italienne. The pipes are supported by a spreading cove in a manner unused since the sixteenth century (Amiens, Rheims, Ecouen) but related to the cove of Lepautre's proposed tabernacle for Notre Dame de Paris in one of the projects of 1703. The case for the first time takes on a concave form, to remain characteristic throughout the following reign. The panel-frames of the substructure and of the cove have Lepautre's characteristic outline and ornaments, the frame of the fenêtre des claviers is richly scrolled with related motifs. The trophies of musical instruments, employed in pierced form by Berain, here continue the tradition of Lepautre from the stalls of Orléans; the royal arms with their supporting Victories have many analogies in his previous designs. The palm trunks rising at the angles were the first examples in interior decoration of the motif appearing in exterior designs for the Chapel at the extremity of the roof and executed in 1707 by the sculptors Guillaume Coustou and Lepautre. Naturally the gifted sculptors who executed the carvings had liberty to modify their details, but the instance of Saint-Quentin, where we can compare design and execution, shows that such modifications will have been minor and that the artistic credit rests primarily with the designer.

No mention of the organ is made in Vassé's obituary, and the accounts do not connect him with it in any way. The models for the Victories, the relief of King David, and the other figural motifs were made by Philippe Bertrand.[87] We cannot doubt, however, that in this

[83] Deshairs: *Chapelle . . . de Versailles*, 48, 49.

[84] His memoir of 4900 livres for it is noted, *ibid.*, 48.

[85] Cf. A. Sangel: *Les grandes orgues . . . de Saint-Quentin*, 1925, 18, which reproduces Berain's original design, and N. Dufourc: *L'Orgue en France*, 1935, 352-356 and pls. LX, LXI, which reproduce drawings of it by Berain *fils*, 1701, from the Tessin papers in the National Museum, Stockholm. Cf. Also Weigert, *op. cit.*, I, pl. XIV.

[86] Letter of Cronström to Tessin, October 16, 1700, quoted by Dufourc, *op. cit.*, p. 356.

[87] Deshair's *Chapelle . . . de Versailles*, 48, 49.

instance the essential responsibility for the design, as for so much of the decoration of the chapel, lay with Pierre Lepautre.

For the marble pavement of the chapel, there is a study (Figure 89)[88] which we cannot doubt was, like the engraved plan of the executed pavement, by Pierre Lepautre. The drawing of the royal arms in the centre is sufficient to identify his technique. The essential novelty in the design of the pavement was its use of marquetry of marble, the first suggestion for such a use of it in France. Within the main rectangles the outlines of the major panels, defined by bandwork, are of simple geometrical form—oval, octagonal, or lozenge—less complex in outline than Berain's in the wooden marquetry of the Petite Galerie. In the subordinate details, on the other hand, there is free use of Lepautre's characteristic motifs, C-scrolls with a suggestion of leafage, long panels with end interlaces and a central rosette, occasional backgrounds of diagonal mosaic. The proposed treatment proved, indeed, too elaborate for execution on such a scale in the unhappy years of war.[89] The wealth of novel ornament was transferred to the Savonnerie carpets from cartoons by Fontenay.[90] The one for the royal tribune from 1710 (or a duplicate supplied in 1734), preserved at Saint Eustache,[91] is quite in the new style created by Pierre Lepautre.

Work on the altar of Notre Dame was resumed November 3, 1708, with financial assistance assured in September by the canon Antoine de la Porte, who died December 24, 1710. The proposed treatment at about this period appears in the painting of Jouvenet, *La messe du chanoine de la Porte* at the Louvre, showing the monstrance he presented to the cathedral June 7, 1708. The background, reputedly painted by Feuillet (cf. *Biographie Universelle*, 1818, article Jouvenet), has an irreality which betrays that it was executed from drawings. The main group of the niche is now an Entombment, above which floats a group with God the Father upborne by angels. On the face of the altar is a relief of the Last Supper. More-advanced drawings for the work (Figures 90-91)—still made certainly prior to the end of 1711, as antedating the execution of features executed in 1712—we recognize as also from the hand of Lepautre.[92] They show a great elaboration of the ironwork, as carried out in 1713 (V, 692), in a development of Berain's style. The angels with their torches now stand on corbels or *culs-de-lampe* fronted by cartouches flanked with palms. At the entrance, on either side of the gates, appear marble altars in the form of a triptych, with the Madonna in a central niche flanked by saints.

For the altar table proper, Lepautre prepared certain early studies of moulded architectural profile,[93] but the final design (Figure 92) so richly sculptural, was made, as we shall

---

[88] O¹ 1783.

[89] The pavement laid in 1709-1712 from designs of Fontenay (*Comptes*, V, 315, 617) is purely geometrical, in a style almost indistinguishable from that of the Invalides, executed from designs of 1701-1705 by Lespingola and Fontenay (IV, 727, 846, 1175).

[90] V, 315, 340, 617.

[91] Cf. C. Jouhannaud in *Gazette des beaux-arts*, VIᵉ pér., VIII, 1932, 249 and P. Verlet, *ibid.*, XVII, 1937, 180-182. In the De Cotte albums at the Cabinet des Estampes, Ha 18, along with drawings by Lepautre, are certain designs for carpets, now inaccessible, which may have some bearing.

[92] Reproduced by Vloberg, *op. cit.*, XLI, and XLII, both attributed by Vlobert to De Cotte, among whose papers they are preserved at the Cabinet des Estampes. The latter drawing is also reproduced by M. Aubert: "Les trois jubés de Notre-Dame de Paris," in *Revue de l'art ancien et moderne*, XLIII, 1923, 112. Two additional minor drawings by Lepautre are included in the volume Va 254a, Nos. 2468, 2470.

[93] Va 254b, rendered in wash, all with the number 1862. Penciled details are preserved on the previous page of the same volume.

see, by François-Antoine Vassé,[94] who, with Cayot and Desjardins, executed in 1712-1715 the angels, bas-reliefs and other bronze ornaments (V, 609, 694, 787, 788, 875).

While we know of no signed drawings by Vassé,[95] we are not without resource to identify his draughtsmanship. There are a number of engravings after his designs. There are also several drawings for different works of De Cotte with which Vassé was concerned, both before and after the death of Lepautre—drawings which, by their own coherence of technique, totally different from that of De Cotte, we must conclude are by Vassé himself. Those which we consider to be by Vassé include the following:

1712	Altar, Notre Dame
1713-1715 ?	Chimney pieces for the palace at Madrid (Vb 147)[96]
1718	Study for the end of the gallery, Hôtel de Toulouse (Figure 125)
1718	Study for trophies of the gallery, Hôtel de Toulouse (Figure 124)
	Study for ceiling of the gallery, Hôtel de Toulouse (Va 232c)
1734	Design for a clock (Figure 177)

All these are drawn in ink with the greatest freedom, and rendered with india wash and colour, the gold being in a strong yellow.

As compared with most of Pierre Lepautre's work, Vassé's design for the altar (Figure 92) is much more freely plastic. The altar table proper is framed by diagonal pedestals, curved in profile and tapered downward, with consoles of a double reverse curve crowned by cherub heads. The bas-relief between, with concave upper corners, is flanked by floral pendants and, at the base, by pairs of cherub heads with bold scrollwork. The coffer behind spreads outward in reverse profile, buttressed by concave consoles. Its upper zone ends in bold volutes with fluted hollow, supporting a pair of kneeling angels—motifs influenced directly, as we shall see, by Oppenord's altar of Saint-Germain-des-Prés executed in 1704. In the center is a cartouche with a border of concave fluted scrolls and wing-like acanthus leafage. Only in the organ at Versailles and in the archiepiscopal thrones of Notre Dame do we find works of equally free character at this time.

Our attribution to Vassé, on internal evidence, of the design of the altar table gives support on this point to the statement regarding Notre Dame in his obituary of 1736, the other terms of which we must now scrutinize. After speaking of his work at the chapel of Versailles, extending as we have seen from 1708 to 1710 or 1711, it says: "Il fut chargé ensuite de faire les desseins et Modeles du grand Autel et du Choeur de l'Église de Notre Dame de Paris, et du Pourtour, avec la Chaire Archiepiscopale; les Modeles des Culs-de-Lampes qui portent les Anges, et il a executé une partie de ces Ouvrages." We shall consider these further assertions one by one in conjunction with the several elements of the work.

[94] *Ibid.*, reproduced as "dessin de Robert de Cotte" by P. Marcel in *L'architecte*, 1907, 32, and by Vloberg, *op. cit.*, pl. XL.

[95] None is catalogued as by him either at the Cabinet des Dessins du Louvre or at the Cabinet des Estampes, nor do I find mention of any in the published catalogues of the Musée de la Marine.

[96] Kindly called to my attention by M. A.-M.-E. Marie. The dates are those of the chimney pieces mentioned in the correspondence of Robert de Cotte. Marcel, *op. cit.*, 196-206, which mentions "sculptures en bronze doré de Vassé."

Obviously the statements cannot apply to the earlier designs down to 1711, which, as we have seen are by Pierre Lepautre. Vassé was first paid for work at Notre Dame in May and July, 1712, when he had a final payment of 2135 livres "a quoy montent les modelles et autres ouvrages qu'il a faits tant pour le maître-autel que pour l'autel des féries, pendant 1711 et 1712" (V, 609). His drawing for the altar was thus made some time in 1711. As it was precisely in this instance that he superseded Lepautre, we may presume this was the beginning of his activity at Notre Dame. The accounts themselves further show only that he executed, with Cayot and Desjardins, the sculptured ornaments of the altar proper, beginning June 8, 1713 (V, 694).

The form of the sanctuary as executed is shown in contemporary engraved plates.[97] Numerous changes of detail were made from Lepautre's latest design. On the surrounding piers, above the imposts, Lepautre had shown rondels and *mosaïque*. Brice complained in 1712 that the marble work was "d'une invention sèche et peu gracieuse"[98] and continued "Vassé travaille aux ornemens, & on espère beaucoup de son habilité." Thus while there are no payments to him for models of them, it is possible that he was responsible for the suggestion of substituting there, in execution, trophies of gilded metal, like those below the imposts. Only to this extent can he be credited with an influence on the "pourtour." The corbels or culs-de-lampe on which the angels stand follow closely the earlier design of Pierre Lepautre.

In the ultimate arrangement, the figure of Louis XIII was not included in the Pietà of the central niche, but placed on a separate pedestal in the flanking arch of the apse, balanced by a figure of Louis XIV—the sculpture being executed by Coustou and others beginning in 1712. The pedestals of the royal statues, buttressed by consoles, are fronted by winged cartouches, similar to many in the designs of Pierre Lepautre. The niche was surmounted by a glory with gilded rays, angels and cherubs. The pavement of the sanctuary, designed by Fontenay in 1712 (V, 615) is of marble marquetry in patterns suggestive of Lepautre's unexecuted design for that of the chapel at Versailles. The first of such works to be carried out in France, it was described by Piganiol de la Force as "surprenant."[99]

Payments to Jean de Nelle for the joinery of the stalls (Figure 95) had already begun by June 9, 1710, extending to January 2, 1711, on which date start payments to the carvers, Dugoullons, Taupin, Bellan, Legoupil and Lalande. Thus apparently Vassé was not concerned with their design, and indeed his obituary does not specifically name them.

The obituary, however, does name the archiepiscopal throne (Figure 93) as being of Vassé's design. The dates would not contravene such a possibility. Apparently it was begun in 1711, when a model in wax for the throne, paid for on November 11 (V, 510), was made by Bertrand, who, we remember, had collaborated with Vassé on the model of the pulpit at Versailles. May 12 of that year De Nelle and Louis Marteau received first payments on the joinery of the thrones, on the carving of which the sculptors had 11,000 livres on account in February, 1711.

[97] By C.-N. Cochin the elder. A memorandum of 1717 for them is noted by Marcel: *Inventaire*, 50. They are incorporated in Mariette's *Architecture françoise*, pls. 1-3 of the edition of Hautecoeur.
[98] 1713 edition, III, 266. The Approbation is dated June 1, 1712.
[99] 1742 edition, I, 392

Genesis

Brice does not state the authorship of the woodwork in any of the editions published in his lifetime (1713, 1717, 1725). The *Description* of Piganiol de la Force in 1742 (I, 392-397) correctly ascribes the execution of the ornaments of the altar to Cayot and Vassé, and the carving of the stalls to Dugoullons, but says nothing of their design. It was not before the mid-century that the guidebooks supplied attributions of the designs, and these do not carry any independent authority. Thus Dargenville's *Voyage pittoresque* of 1750 uses verbatim the passage from Vassé's obituary. When the 1752 edition of Brice[100] says "Les Stalles . . . sont du dessein de du Goulon . . . La Chaire Archiepiscopale [et] . . . une toute semblable . . . sont du dessein de Vassé," it is merely paraphrasing the earlier statements.

Let us examine the woodwork itself, so remarkably creative, to see both its own qualities and the internal evidence it may present as to the authorship of the designs. In such work the traits of the designer are to be sought in the general lines and major features, whereas the details of the carving derive from the executants.

In the panelling of the stalls we note particularly the crowns of the alternate panels, with curved corners flanked by twisted winged cherub heads—so closely similar to the crown of Lepautre's altarpiece of the Virgin in the chapel at Versailles. In the intermediate panels, above and below the oval medallions, the scrolls of the truncated corners—of the type originated by Lepautre at Marly—are almost identical with those which flank the circular medallion on the face of the altar in the same design of Lepautre. We cannot doubt that the basic design of the stalls was his.

In their aesthetic character, what is particularly to be observed is the relative lack of any bold plasticity. In total contrast with the baroque, where the forms spring forth from the mass, there is here a delicate play on the surface. The last remaining trace of academic memmering, still present at Orléans, has disappeared. So has any main division of the height. The tectonic feeling, still dominant at Orléans, is subordinated; the outer rectangular frames, slightly recessed, are dominated by the outlines of the major, inner panels, which are curved. In the fine-spun ornament—which here, instead of mere mosaic, fills the remainder of the field, above and below—the motifs are of small individual significance for us: branches of palm and of flowers, of much naturalism, garlands falling from acanthus scrolls. Cartouches, little projecting, bearing the royal cypher, and certain bas-reliefs, punctuating the narrow vertical strips, scarcely interrupt the flow of stems and leafage which constitutes a highly original form of arabesque, not yet fully digested. Most significant is the type of feature at top and bottom of these strips—developed from the terminal interlace of Lepautre's pilaster panels—now recurring also below the ovals in the wide panels: a flat field, in the plane of the background, surrounded by interlacing elements and itself usually enclosing some radiating palmette-like form. This feature, an equivalent of the cartouche without its plasticity, foreshadowed the characteristic cartouche of the rococo, in which the field—unlike the bulging field of the baroque cartouche—had the airy emptiness of the background of the arabesque.

The thrones also embody many features previously invented and used by Lepautre, but their general character, as in the case of the altar, suggests that their final design had another

<hr>

[100] IV, 201-202. The editor of this fourth volume, according to the *Bibliothèque historique* of Lelong, 1768 ed., was the Abbé Pérau, born in 1700, thus too late to have personal knowledge of the matter.

authorship. The line of development may be traced from the tabernacle shown in Lepautre's study for the altar of the Virgin at Versailles, in the profile of the crown and in the arch flanked by scrolled strips. The corbel below follows the corbels of the angels in the sanctuary. The departures from the scheme of the thrones at Orléans, however, are even more significant. Just as in Vassé's design of the altar, as compared with the design of Lepautre, there is an abandonment of academic, architectonic elements. No longer are there columns, entablatures, or balusters. The canopy, relieved of all massiveness by its suggestion of a valance, is supported by concave brackets. The rail, adopting Lepautre's scheme of panel design with rosettes against a background of diagonal *mosaïque*, is given a new lightness by piercing both. Its profile, a reverse curve, follows that of the pulpit at Versailles, carved by Vassé. Thus the character, as well as the date, of the thrones indicates that they may indeed well be of his design.

It is instructive to contrast the whole treatment with that of the woodwork of the choir of Saint-Paul's in London, which Grinling Gibbons had executed in 1695-1697, just before the beginning of work on the choir of Notre Dame. There all is heavily plastic, with high relief in the consoles, the garlanded friezes. The panelling of the stalls in London is boldly membered, with multiplied articulation, subdivision, and superposition of rectangular elements, and depth even through recesses, whereas in Paris it is smooth, unified in height, with suave curvature and liaison. In London, as upper termination of the stalls there is not merely an academic cornice but the additional firm horizontal of an attic; in Paris the thin canopy dissolves in a spray-like cresting. In London the thrones are flanked by three-quarter columns, with bold consoles, dominantly convex, and a massive, scrolled segmental pediment. Above rises an open crown in the form of a Borrominian belfry of consoles in two tiers, whereas in Paris all is flowing surface. In Paris, indeed, the work is not a derivative, but a negation of the baroque.

Beyond these relative values of priority and novelty in the choir of Notre Dame, are its absolute values of unending richness, inexhaustible fantasy, suavity, grace and ease.

The Salon d'Hercule at Versailles, occupying the position of the older chapel and leading to the vestibule of the new one, has passed usually as a work of the following reign, its decoration, with the brilliant sculpture of François-Antoine Vassé, having been completed in 1725-1736. Its masonry and joinery, however, were executed in 1712 (*Comptes* IV, 583, 585, 586). There is another significant item in the accounts (594):

> 8 janvier 1713: aux peintres, sculpteurs, maçons et autres ouvriers qui ont ésté employez au modelle des ouvrages du sallon neuf dud. château, pour leurs journées et autres menus dépenses faites à ce sujet. 3396 livres 17 s. 6 d.

Thus, and necessarily before the assembling of the marbles in 1713 and 1714, a design for the room existed. The north wall, indeed, appears in one of Lepautre's plates for the engraved folio of the Chapel published by Demortain in 1714. This shows the spacing of the pilasters, the arched doorways, the elliptical arch of the fireplace with a mask at the centre, the great frame above with its concave corners at the top, its consoles below—all that characterizes the general design of the room.

Genesis

Accordingly we are not surprised to discover a coloured section (Figure 94)[101] endorsed "Sallon de Versailles," showing the east wall as executed, in the technique of Pierre Lepautre, who was thus also the author of this supreme design. As envisaged at the end of the reign of Louis XIV, the room already incorporates so fully the style of the early years of the following reign that it has long been regarded as one of that period's most characteristic creations. Here were taken up again the marble revetment of the older state rooms which this room adjoined and continued, the ordonnance of pilasters of figured marble, but with a new graciousness and unity through the arching of doors as well as windows, through the advanced forms of chimney piece and pier.

When we reflect that the room formed the royal access to the tribune of the new chapel as well as the only communication, in the principal story, with the entire north wing, we realize that its forms, in an unfinished state, must have already become familiar during the last year of the life of Louis XIV.

We need scarcely discuss in detail other works for the Crown which are obviously from designs of Lepautre. Examples could readily be multiplied.[102]

We may however allude to the *Livre de tables qui sont dans les quelles son posés les bijoux du Cabinet des Medailles. Dessiné et gravé par P. Le Pautre, Graveur du Roi*, including at least one design of 1699,[103] as a work vastly influential in the design of furniture.

By the variety of work at the same moment under Mansart and De Cotte, by the changes in style when their designers changed, we know that the creative responsibility was not theirs. The true creative artist, as in other periods of fertile originality, was the designer who actually held the pencil.

We find that, as Mariette said with the utmost exactitude, "Pierre le Pautre eut beaucoup de part à tous les ouvrages qui se firent dans le suite à Versailles, à Marly, et dans les autres maisons royales"—that his part, down to 1712, was the decisive one. Marly, the Appartements du Roi at Versailles and Trianon, the stalls of Orléans, the altars and many other features of the Chapelle de Versailles, the choir of Notre Dame, the Salon d'Hercule—all the great royal decorative enterprises of the later years of Louis XIV—were all basically, when not completely, from designs of Pierre Lepautre. The authorship of these superb works of art establishes Lepautre, hitherto almost overlooked, as a great artist in his own right, the father of the rococo.

To a degree not hitherto appreciated, Vassé began, in the very last years of the reign, to assume a principal rôle. With his design of the thrones of Notre Dame and related works in 1712, he definitely took over the artistic leadership. In the second phase of the movement, thus inaugurated, characteristic of the Regency to follow, he was to continue in this

[101] o¹ 1768.

[102] Notably the work in the Appartement du Roi at Fontainebleau in 1714, *Comptes*, V, 820-823. While adding little to the idea of his work already gained, it is extremely difficult to disentangle, in some parts, from later additions. Thus in the Cabinet du Conseil, of which a drawing by Gabriel for changes in 1752 is preserved (o¹ 1424, reproduced by Fels, *op. cit.*, pl. XVIII) one cannot, in all regards, be sure what then survived from 1714 and what dated from changes of 1738.

[103] The "Buffet exécuté à Marly" shown on plate 6 is evidently one of the eight "tables angulaires" for the salon there executed in that year. *Comptes*, IV, 481, 583, 620. Doubtless some of the other tables are those still preserved, and lately adorning the Galerie d'Apollon. Coloured designs for the marble tops of certain of these survive in the De Cotte collection at the Cabinet des Estampes, Ha 18.

position of leadership, which he had then to share with the Regent's own designer, Oppenord.

The royal works at the time we have been discussing, so grievously fragmentary in preservation, known too often only through drawings or engravings, present unusual difficulties for us to see and feel them as artistic entities. When, however, we have successfully achieved their visual and emotional reconstruction, we appreciate that in these works were embodied not merely influential inventions but absolute artistic values of a new order. Baroque art, with its spatial and plastic energy, had been replaced by something wholly different, the rococo, a flowing organization of line and surface, rejecting the traditional forms of academic architecture, yet attaining a harmonious maturity in works deeply creative, of smiling ease and grace.

Private Buildings

The years from 1700 to 1715 were years of increasingly active private building in Paris, in which participated both the architects of the Bâtiments and those outside its favoured circle. Artistic initiative, to be sure, still remained wholly with the Crown: the new fashions of decoration were set, as we have seen, in the narrow royal circle of Marly, the Ménagerie, Meudon, Versailles, and Trianon. The centralizing power of Versailles had not been relaxed, nor was there, before the tragic deaths of 1711-1712, any lack of gaiety and life. Indeed the years prior to that, passed increasingly in the intimacy of Marly and dominated by the verve of the Duchesse de Bourgogne, had been of unsurpassed brilliance—even, for conscious effect, during the worst misfortunes of war.

Paris, though not the capital, remained the metropolis, and could attract the Dauphin and the Court itself by the unique entertainment of the opera at the Palais-Royal. Monsieur, until his death, and after him the Duc d'Orléans, there preserved a certain independence. Ministers like Pontchartrain and Desmarets had their hôtels in Paris, as did the financiers. Certain great noblemen like the Duc de Vendôme risked displeasure by setting up new establishments there although, as Saint-Simon makes clear, those closest to the King would not have dared this before the period of mourning for the Dauphin.

Among the men active in private building few new figures attained importance before the very end of the reign. Such practice was open to the officers of the Bâtiments, to the academicians, left in *otium cum dignitate* by Mansart's system, as well as to others.

The original academicians were now dead with the exception of Pierre Mignard, long retired to Avignon. There had been scarcely any appointments to replace them prior to Mansart's reorganization of the institution in 1699. The members as then named were:

First class: De Cotte, Bullet, de l'Isle, Gabriel, Gobert, Lambert, Le Maistre, de la Hire, Professor, and J.-F. Félibien, Secretary.

Second class: Lassurance, de l'Espine, Matthieu, Desgodetz, Le Maistre le jeune, Bullet le fils, Bruant le jeune, Cauchy, Gittard le fils.

Several of these were executives on the royal staff, controllers, inspectors or minor employees; others were interested chiefly in theoretical questions; the younger generation was not yet independently established. The only ones of these men having substantial private practice were Bullet, eldest of all, De Cotte, and Lassurance. After his attainment of the rank of Architecte in the Bâtiments in 1700, Lassurance was stationed in Paris from 1702, in charge of work at the Invalides (*Comptes* IV, 912), and seems to have had greater public reputation and opportunity to work also for individuals. De Cotte, with ever widening responsibilities, met them, as we shall see, by increasing the number of his draughtsmen and collaborators.

Outside the Academy were left, among men previously active, only Boffrand—still but thirty-two in 1699. He was occupied chiefly in Lorraine and in the Netherlands until 1709 when, under De Cotte's administration, he was taken into both Academy and Bâtiments, and began to be considerably employed in private building in Paris.

The men born after 1670 were also to have their importance mainly in the following period. We need mention here only four whose work began before that time: Oppenord, Delamair, Le Blond and Cartaud. Of these the first, both by his native gifts and by his prolonged study in Italy, was ultimately to be by far the most important.

Gilles-Marie Oppenord (1672-1742) was born in Paris as the son of the Ebéniste du Roy Jean Oppenord (1639-1715). Jean Oppenord was Dutch by birth, "natif de la ville de Gueldres," but naturalized in 1679 when "depuis plusieurs années il s'est habitué en nostre royaume."[104] We have seen him as the collaborator of Berain in 1685. Brought up in the ateliers of the Louvre, where his father was lodged since 1684,[105] the young Oppenord can scarcely be regarded as other than a French artist—although as with Watteau, another artistic innovator of the Regency—the blood of the Low Countries has been thought to tinge his reaction against the classic and academic.

Sent to Rome at twenty, in 1692, as a protegé of Villacerf, then Surintendant, he gave his prolonged studies there a different turn from that of most pensioners of the Academy. It was perhaps his facility and application which chiefly won him the constant praise of La Teulière, the director, although his taste was equally commended:[106] "Il escremera, pour ainsi dire, tout ce qu'il y a de bon en Italie." It was the ornaments and plastic forms which chiefly occupied him in his sketches: "un grand amas de tout ce qui peut estre propre à orner les ouvrages d'architecture de tous les accompagnens qui peuvent les rendre solides et agréables . . ." and, elsewhere: "non seulement pour les proportions, mais sur la forme des parties."

Three of Oppenord's sketch books survive, including many drawings made in Italy.[107] Particularly the one in Berlin overflows with hundreds of graphic notes dashed on the paper from Italian examples. Both from these and from La Teulière's letters we learn that Oppenord's observation was devoted less than usual to ancient Rome, far more to baroque Italy. From the Renaissance we find little; the arabesques of the school of Raphael, however, form

---

[104] J.-J. Guiffrey: "Lettres de naturalization accordées à des artistes étrangers," *Nouvelles archives de l'art français*, 1873, 258. Jean Oppenord, then "marchand ébeniste, demeurant dans l'enclos du Temple" is first listed as a witness in the parish register of Saint-Germain l'Auxerrois for 1675 (166), according to the Fichier Laborde of the Cabinet des Manuscrits of the Bibliothèque Nationale. In the same parish registers (63) a listing of Gilles-Marie Oppenord, as a godfather in 1690, when he was eighteen, gives his occupation loosely as "ébeniste du roy."

[105] Guiffrey: "Logements d'artistes au Louvre," *ibid.*, 371.

[106] *Correspondance des directeurs*, e.g., I, 327, II, 66, 169, 240, 400.

[107] Berlin, Staatliche Kunstbibliothek, OS2712 gr; Stockholm, National Museum, 89: 4: A; Lyons, collection of M. l'abbé Chagny, all generously made available to me for photographing. In addition we have the suite of Italian motives engraved by Huquier, after 1748 under the title *Livre de fragemens d'architecture recueillis à Rome*, familiarly known as the Petit Oppenord.

a significant exception. Page after page records the minutest details of the works of Bernini, and, above all, of Borromini, then dead less than a generation. The identity of a vast number of these may be recognized: "Tombeaux, tabernacles, fontaines, ornemens, chapelles, frontispices," as La Teulière says, among which figure prominently the elements of San Filippo Neri, San Carlo alle Quattro Fontane, Sant' Ivo, Sant' Agnese, the Propaganda Fide, and the Lateran.[108] Notable is the relative rarity of plans as compared with the abundance of profiles; the stress is on the plastic rather than the spatial.

Beside works in Rome, Oppenord drew and studied—by exception, and against Villacerf's objections—those of North Italy. There too he did not confine himself to Palladio and to Bramante's school.[109] The mannerists Giulio Romano, Pirro Ligorio, also find mention in the correspondence. Before leaving Italy Oppenord made designs for certain works of his own.[110] Certain details of them reproduced in the *Grand Oppenord* are of typical baroque character.

The profound study of the work of modern Italy, on the part of a man so gifted as Oppenord, failed to be immediately influential in France on his return in the fall of 1699 because of his failure to secure any post in the royal works. His patron Villacerf had retired as Surintendant in January; Mansart showed Oppenord no favor. He had tarried too long: when he arrived the reorganization of the staff, the appointment of Pierre Lepautre and Rivet as Dessinateurs had already taken place. Lepautre's first genial works were already visible, and their dazzling novelty and success were already apparent. An exotic design of high-baroque character, which, as we shall see, Oppenord submitted for the altar of Notre Dame, did not meet with favour, and he remained an outsider, never being taken into the Academy. In private employment he was at first little more fortunate. It was but gradually that his draughtsmanship and fertility of imagination brought him occupation as an engraver and a designer of altar pieces, his great opportunity was to come only after the close of the reign.

We get few glimpses of him in the first years after his return. In 1701, on his marriage to Antoinette Berard, daughter of a prosperous Paris bourgeois, he described himself as "architecte du Roy,"[111] a title only justified by his pension at Rome. We shall not find him receiving even private commissions for work in his profession before 1704. In the accounts for the engraving of the tomb of the Ducs de Bouillon at Cluny, for which he made the fair drawing for the engraver in 1708, he is called "Dessinateur du Roy,"[112] again loosely, for the Comptes des Bâtiments list no single royal payment to him under Louis XIV. A collection of engraved *Figures antiques*, after his drawings, was announced by the *Mercure* in 1709.[113] Brice states that the handsome catalogue of the works and collection of Girardon, issued in 1710, was "d'estampes dessinées et gravées correctement sous la conduite de Gilles-Marie Oppenordt."[114]

---

[108] It is worth observing that none shows the works of Sardi and others, beginning in 1691, cited by Marcel Reymond as inaugurating the rococo (as he uses the word for the late Italian baroque), although these were under way while Oppenord was in Rome.

[109] A large drawing of the altar of San Giorgio Maggiore is preserved at the Louvre, No. 31483.

[110] Brice, 1713 ed., II, 182-183 mentions those for a port for Innocent XII at Nettuno.

[111] Fichier Laborde, Saint-Germain l'Auxerrois, February 3, 1701 (177).

[112] *Nouvelles archives de l'art français*, 1872, 297.

[113] July, 203.

[114] 1713 ed., I, 121.

Genesis

During his long years of relative lack of employment there was ample time for the native tradition of French decoration to make itself felt on his own work. His hands were not idle; the new trends of French design gave occasion for further study, and he made full use of the opportunity to familiarize himself with them. While it is difficult to date the sketches he constantly added in his note-books, the subject matter of many of them indicates that they belong to this period, when he was absorbing the new motifs employed in executed works by Lepautre, Berain, Audran and other French designers. He sketched trophies in the Chapel at Versailles;[115] he designed, as we shall see, arabesques most nearly related to those of Gillot.[116] Such studies account for the profound difference of style between his Italian sketches and his own executed work in France,[117] a difference which begins to appear even in his earliest commissions.

By comparison with Oppenord, other new figures were, in the end, to play very secondary rôles. Pierre Alexis Delamair (1676-1745), had the precocious success of being entrusted, before the age of thirty, with the building of the Hôtels de Soubise and de Rohan. He was, however, almost immediately superseded at the Hôtel de Soubise by Boffrand, as regards the interiors, and, finding little other employment, devoted most of his later years to embittered writing of his humiliations.[118]

Jean-Baptiste Alexandre Le Blond (1679-1719),[119] gifted in drawing from earliest youth, and active in publication, was also employed in the construction of Paris houses, as we shall see, until his extravagance and quarrelsome humour led by him, in 1716, to accept an invitation to Russia, where he died in 1719.

Jean-Sylvian Cartaud, who had been with Oppenord at the Academy in Rome, though not as a pensioner, and who had been one of the witnesses at his marriage, built for Pierre Crozat in 1704 his house in Paris, and also built his château at Montmorency, at both of which Oppenord was later employed. Cartaud's oval salon in two stories at Montmorency, of which Mariette gives a section, closely follows that of Vaux, in spite of the two generations intervening—order below, herms above—with only slight nuances to suggest the later date. Clearly Cartaud, who in spite of his skill was not elected to the Academy until the age of sixty-seven, was not a force in decoration.

In the first decade or so of the century, Bullet was finishing for Antoine Crozat the earliest hôtels of the Place Vendôme. They were remodelled after 1750, and we have no evidence of the form of their first interior treatment. Bullet was an able planner and sound constructor, but we should scarcely expect decorative innovations in these houses, any more than in his Château d'Issy during the previous period.

[115] Those engraved by Huquier as Plate XII of the *Grand Oppenord* are in reverse, with trifling variations, from the pair carved by Robert Le Lorrain in the royal tribune. The left hand figure of Plate XIV is from the trophy of the second square pillar to the right on entering the Chapel.

[116] Cf. his manuscript arabesques preserved at the Staatliche Kunstbibliothek, Berlin (reproduced in part by C. Gurlitt: *Das Ornament des Rococo*, 1894, pls. 26, 27, 31, 35) with Gillot's engraved *Livre de Portières*.

[117] This difference is remarked by C. Linfert in *Kunstwissenschaftliche Forschungen*, I, 1931, especially 164-182, but we cannot concur in his attempted solution of the historical problems involved.

[118] Cf. Ch.-V. Langlois: *Les hôtels de Clisson, de Guise et de Rohan-Soubise*, 1922, *passim*.

[119] Boris Lossky: "I.-B. A. Le Blond, Architecte de Pierre le Grand, son oeuvre en France," in *Bulletin de l'association russe pour les recherches scientifiques à Prague*, III, 1936, 179-216.

The Creation of the Rococo

Lassurance built the Hôtels de Rothelin, toward 1700, Desmarets, 1704, d'Auvergne, finished 1708, de Bethune and de Maisons, 1708,[120] besides remodelling the old Hôtel de Pussort for the Duc de Noailles in 1715. Of these the Hôtels de Rothelin and de Maisons survive, much changed internally.[121] Of three of the houses, we are fortunate to have small engraved sections given by Mariette[122] and Blondel, themselves made later, after certain of the buildings had already been remodelled. These show that at the Hôtels de Rothelin and de Bethune Lassurance still used the geometrical panelling in many tiers characteristic of his early work. The Hôtel d'Auvergne was even plainer. At the Hôtel de Bethune we find, in the ground story, cornices with hollow friezes. Since, as in all ground-story rooms, even at Versailles, there was no cove above the cornice, one may say that these hollow friezes constitute cove cornices. Indeed it is in such instances, which we shall find as early as 1703, that the cornice first took on the form characteristic of the future.

Regarding the work of De Cotte, who built the Chancellerie, 1703, the Hôtel de Lude, 1710, and the Hôtel d'Estrées, 1713, we are better informed. True only one of these buildings still stands, and that one, the Hôtel d'Estrées, has been drastically remodelled.[123] But we have a small section of the Hôtel de Lude, and very full knowledge of the interiors of the Chancellerie.

The most important work of Robert de Cotte at this period not for the Crown, but having official aspects, was indeed the Chancellerie—remodelled from the old Hôtel de Lionne, Rue Neuve-des-Petits-Champs, for the Chancellor Pontchartrain. He had taken office in 1699. Although Dangeau reported the purchase as early as 1700,[124] it was not until March 27, 1703, that Pontchartrain completed its acquisition from the Duc d'Estrées, heir of M. de Lionne,[125] after which, as Germain Brice states "(il) y a fait faire des réparations et des embellisements considérables." A great mass of drawings for this remodelling survives in the De Cotte collection at the Cabinet des Estampes,[126] which gives us a unique opportunity to study the work of that moment.

The designs for interiors, to the number of thirty, are all in the technique of Pierre Lepautre. In one instance (No. 2146, Figure 96) we even have his own preliminary study, boldly shaded with a brush over pencil outlines. The schemes for the walls ring the changes on those of Marly and Trianon, showing mirror heads square with concave corners, or semi-circular, with or without breaks, and supported on pilasters or consoles. In one (Figure 97) a new form appears, a segment with concave corners, prefiguring still another scheme of the

---

[120] These dates, unless otherwise stated, rest on the statements of Germain Brice in the successive editions of his *Description de Paris*, of which those of 1707, 1713, and 1717 are contemporary with the period discussed.

[121] The present interiors of the Hôtel de Maisons come from a remodelling of about 1750 and will be discussed later.

[122] The drawings made for the engraver, chiefly by Chevotet, of which many are preserved in the Collection Lesoufaché at the École des Beaux-Arts in Paris, show some of these interiors more clearly, and were obviously meant to be highly faithful.

[123] This house, at 79, Rue de Grenelle, preserves certain interiors which have been thought to date from the time of its building. We would place them in the period around 1750. There are plans of the building at the Cabinet des Estampes which show it had already undergone certain modifications by 1727-1734.

[124] VII, 272. March 13, 1700.

[125] Note by A. de Boislisle in his edition of *Mémoires de Saint-Simon*, XV, 441.

[126] Large ground plans in Va 441, other drawings in Va 234 and Va 236e. There are many papers regarding the hôtel at the Archives Nationales, o¹ 1577.

Genesis

Regency. In general there are no imposts. For a few of the walls, where an impost with multiplied tiers of panels had been first proposed these are crossed off in favour of a single flight of panels above the dado, punctuated merely by an oval rosette, which still further emphasizes the vertical effect. The marble chimney pieces, in general, are of the types characteristic of Lepautre at this moment. The cornices are closely related in profile to those of Trianon at this period. Some with hollow friezes, and (unlike those at Trianon, where coves preexisted) with no cove above, constitute the very first examples of this treatment, which thus also was an innovation of Pierre Lepautre.

At the Hôtel de Lude, as shown in Mariette's section, there was a chimney piece of the type created at Marly. Here also the ground story has simple cove-cornices.

A later work, likewise destroyed, but likewise very fully known to us,[127] is the Château de Bercy, at the eastern gates of Paris, which, begun by François Le Vau in 1658, had stood for many years without internal finish. M. de Bercy, then Intendant des Finances, states very explicitly that he undertook the work of completion and decoration in 1712;[128] it must have been substantially completed before his disgrace in 1715. The caption of Jean Mariette's plot plan of Bercy gives the name De la Guêpière, doubtless Jacques who died in 1734, as architect of the distant stables of the château, still surviving, with bold naturalistic trophies of hunting dogs over the doorways. His name has been attached by modern writers to the decorations of the château itself—an assumption as easy as it is unwarranted.[129]

Many features of the decorations, such as the mirror heads (e.g. Figure 98) unmistakably betray, by their identity with those we have seen by Pierre Lepautre, his authorship of the designs of the interiors, which thus assume an immense importance as domestic works of his full maturity, unique in their integral character. The Grand Salon of the ground story, now installed at 2, Rue de l'Elysée, is of the greatest magnificence (Figure 98). Panelled Corinthian pilasters, with characteristic scrollwork, frame the bays, which contain, below oval frames with paintings, large panels closely similar to one type of those of the stalls of Notre Dame, completed in July of 1712. Their crowns, as in Notre Dame, have little cornices above concave crossettes; their bases, as at Notre Dame, are semicircular. The cherubheads of the religious work are replaced by scrolls, the bas-reliefs of sacred subjects by an inner bead with rich palmettes and scrollwork at top and bottom, by a light interlace in the center. Even within this inner ornamented bead, there is the third line of the moulded edge of a raised field which comprises the bare area of the panel, circumscribes the major outlines

[127] Beside the boiseries now installed elsewhere, we have the complete drawings of every room made in 1860 before its demolition, published by L. Deshairs, *Le château de Bercy*, n.d.

[128] Quoted by A. de Boislisle: "Topographie seigneuriale de Bercy," in *Mémoires de la Société de l'histoire de Paris*, VIII, 1881, 62. The date is further confirmed by the table prefixed to the 1713 edition of Germain Brice (the Approbation is dated June 1, 1712) which speaks of the château as "réparé et embelli en 1713."

[129] Of De la Guêpière we know very little, except that he was an academician of the second class from 1720. Mariette's caption for the plates of the Ménagerie at Sceaux, which Brice mentions in 1725 (IV, 396) as "bâti depuis peu," names "Mr. de la Guêpière" as the architect. In view of the dates we would presume this was also Jacques, rather than Philippe, who worked in Germany from 1752 to 1760 and died in 1773, if it were not that Dargenville says expressly in his *Voyage pittoresque des environs de Paris*, 1755, 195: "C'est la Guespiere, Directeur des Bâtiments du Duc de Wurtembourg, qui en a été l'Architecte." The interior of this pavilion, shown in Mariette's section, is of excellent conventional *régence* design, but nothing we know of De la Guêpière would indicate he was capable of such mastery of ornament as is displayed in the interior of Bercy, which we shall see was on the frontier of creative advance of its time.

of the upper and lower scrollwork, and itself bears the central interlace. It is a development of the initiative we have seen at Trianon in 1703, in a form frequently adopted henceforth. The panels of the doors, strictly rectangular, are given a similar treatment. The painted overdoors are framed with vertical consoles somewhat as in the Salon Frais at Trianon at just this time. As the cornice of this room, like those of all other rooms at Bercy, is a full entablature (although De Cotte's Chancellerie, Hôtel de Lude and several others already had simple cove cornices), we may assume that the proportions of those at Bercy were established by the pre-existing rough work. That of the Grand Salon has a concave frieze divided by consoles, the metopes being filled with light relief ornaments in which figures recline and slender grotesque sphinxes twine amid attenuated bands and scrolls. They trace their ancestry to Le Brun's tapestry borders, as developed in the arabesque of Berain and Audran. These cornices offer the earliest surviving example we have (unless in Boffrand's work at the Hôtel de Mayenne) of such a treatment, soon to become universal.

Other panelled rooms, often with very slender bandwork, ring the changes on familiar motifs, not without various innovations.[130] The library was greatly elaborated (Figure 99). Its doorway, like its mirror heads, was arched—a treatment just adopted by Lepautre for the Salon d'Hercule—their lunettes having pairs of sculptured figures not unlike those of the gallery at Trianon but with attributes of the arts and sciences. In the zone above the impost, between the doorways, were painted panels the frames of which have, for the first time, richly scrolled ends—pointing toward the scrolled overdoors of the future. The doors, as well as the walls beneath the imposts, have major panels with semicircular head and base, like those of the stalls of Orléans. As at Notre Dame, such panels at Bercy are inscribed in shallow outer rectangles filled with *mosaïque*, but the upper panels of the doors, with reverse curves at their ends, have no rectangular enclosure. Both here and in the rich boudoir there were certain panels which are treated much like those of the doors of the royal tribune of the chapel at Versailles, of about the same moment, with a central medallion, circular or oval, linked by the inner bead with the extravagantly scrolled borders of the ends.

The ceilings of rooms in the principal story still had low coves, lacking, as commonly, in the ground story. Everywhere the entablatures have hollow friezes, many undivided by consoles, with relief motifs of bandwork, scrollwork and figures, including some of playful monkeys, dogs, cats and birds. Such decorated cornices are the first examples of the sort we know anywhere, inaugurating a treatment characteristic of the reign of Louis XV. Indeed throughout the work at Bercy we find the most typical elements of Louis XV decoration, already fully established by Pierre Lepautre.

Of the marble chimney pieces of Bercy, all but that of the Grand Salon (the one preserved) were of the period of 1712. That of the library, with an elliptical arch on frontal consoles, was of the type originating about 1700. The others, however, were the first we know[131] of a new type destined henceforth to carry the day, their openings being flanked by consoles placed diagonally. Supports so placed (herms in that case) had appeared in one of

---

[130] Much material from them is recombined at the Hôtel de la Rochefoucauld-Doudeauville. The rooms there, though tastefully composed, contain a good deal that is modern and in many ways belie the character of Bercy. This is notably the case with the cornices, where in every case the coving of the ceiling above has been omitted and central and corner motifs have been added.

[131] Unless there be some in the Chancellerie drawings of 1703, now inaccesible.

the figures engraved by Lepautre for Le Blond's 1710 edition of the *Cours d'architecture*. What had there been but one of a variety of schemes, more or less bizarre, was now given the form which was to become most characteristic.

The stone vestibule at Bercy, enlarged in 1712, was adorned with an Ionic order framing wide and narrow bays, alike enriched with magnificent suspended trophies of arms, of arts and of the chase. We have come to the opinion that these, like the other decorations of the château, were from designs by Pierre Lepautre[132]—who had himself been so much concerned with trophies at Versailles and elsewhere. In these, his first secular examples, the artistic character is closely related to that of the religious trophies just executed in the Chapel at Versailles, with strongly asymmetric elements, and with a background of palm and other foliage. Conspicuously focussing the composition were stags' heads, one of them circled by a hunting horn—henceforth a favorite motif.

The adjoining room with a buffet offers us a unique glimpse, just before the Salon d'Hercule, of a marble revetment. It partakes of the change in design of wood wainscot, as it has but a single tier of tall panels above the dado, unlike the many-tiered marble wall engraved by Lepautre for Daviler's *Cours d'architecture* of 1691. A great oval frame over the buffet, reminiscent of Le Brun's in the Salons of Versailles, is flanked by narrow panels approximating pilasters, of which a mask with cartouche border replaces the capital. The heads of the frames of the diagonal niches recall those of Lepautre's mirror heads, with a great double shell surrounded by palm fronds. The fountains below, with basins of undulating shell, are the forerunners of many similar ones in the following period.

At Bercy, as earlier at the Chancellerie, was thus a house decorated throughout by Lepautre, of which the surviving fragments, welcome as they are, are a poor consolation for the loss of the consistent unity and wealth.

It has not been remarked that the modifications of the Hôtel Lauzun in the early eighteenth century may be recognized as from designs by Pierre Lepautre. This is obviously the case with the mirror frames of the chimney piece of the Grand Salon, with its arch and pilasters very close to those of 1705 at Trianon-sous-Bois. The other mirror frames are clearly from the same hand. The one opposite the chimney piece is our first example of a new form, its head a pair of S-scrolls of reverse curvature. Such curvature is thus transferred from the acanthus foliage to the mouldings of the frame itself. The *mosaïque* of the background also takes on curved lines for the first time. We may presume this work to have been done for the financier Ogier, who acquired the house in 1709.

Thus though Lepautre's main energies in these years were absorbed in his ecclesiastical work, he continued also in his domestic designs the freeing of the frame from the limitations of geometry, the progressive enfranchisement of the flowing line.

Among other artists at this time, we find ourselves in the case of Boffrand, one of the most gifted, lamentably ill-informed as to his work, whether in Lorraine or in Paris. We have available today no body of his drawings, since the disappearance from family hands, about 1918, of the *recueil Piroux* at Nancy, which had not been studied scientifically since

[132] In an early discussion of the work of Oppenord, published before we realized the extent of Lepautre's influence on him, we were led, on the basis of his trophies at the Hôtel de Pomponne and other designs, to attribute to him those of Bercy, as well as those of Rambouillet—an "expansionism" which we trust we have expiated in this book.

1864.[133] In Paris in 1704 he remodelled the Hôtel de Mesmes, demolished; by 1707, succeeded Delamair at the Hôtel de Soubise, where none of the earliest interiors survive; in 1709, remodelled the Hôtel de Livry, demolished, and the Hôtel de Mayenne, where little of the interior remains in place; in 1710, the Petit-Luxembourg (Présidence du Sénat) where much of the early decoration survives; in 1711-1714 the Hôtel du Premier Président,[134] demolished, and the Hôtel de Broglie in the Rue Saint-Dominique, gutted;[135] in 1713, a house for Melchoir de Blair, 18 Rue Vivienne, "décore très agréablement," of which the surviving stairway may well be Boffrand's.[136] Of none of these buildings do we have any engraved sections.

The best preserved of these buildings is the Petit-Luxembourg, as remodelled for the Princesse Palatine in 1710. Boffrand's staircase, now crowned by a modern ceiling, has monumental Composite pilasters framing arches with military trophies in the spandrels. The entablature, curved at the corners, has a broad concave frieze with scrolled bandwork and fronds of palm and laurel—one of the first of such treatments surviving. The overdoor which fills the arch on the landing has a circular medallion fringed with palm, flanked by a pair of griffins. Related winged animals frame supporting borders of palm for the semicircular overdoors of the Grand Salon (Figure 100). A uniform membering of arches—such as Blondel later notes[137] in the oval salons of the Hôtel de Moras—for the first time embraces the windows, the doors, the mirrors, again with corners and cornice slightly rounded. The spandrels, with gilded medallions surrounded by loose bandwork with playing cherubs, would seem to be surely original, as may be also the strange fringe of bandwork invading the high vaulted ceiling. The main wall panels however are obviously work of the period about 1730, as are some other interior features of the house. In the Chambre d'Apparat (Figure 101) is further work of 1710, of a general character not unlike that at Trianon at the same period. The mirror clearly shows its dependence on Lepautre's, though its consoles are turned sidewise, like earlier ones in Jean Marot's plates and in the Hôtel Lauzun. The *crossettes* of the panel above have a pronounced scroll, characteristic of Boffrand, and a central cartouche of residual plastic character. The overdoor, confined within a rectangle, is treated with arabesque in relief, derivative of Berain, quite unlike any other we know. To judge by the decorations here, which have not the perfect consistency and harmony of Lepautre's work, Boffrand was moving in the train of Pierre Lepautre, but with eagerness to retain his independence, and anticipating, in certain features, treatments of Oppenord under the Regency.

From the Hôtel de Mayenne, 1709, much of the woodwork was sold to M. le Comte

[133] P. Morey: "Notice sur la vie les oeuvres de Germain Boffrand," in *Mémoires de l'Académie Stanislas*, 1864, 203-282. A volume of tracings by Morey from the *recueil Piroux*, owned by the Musée Lorrain and kindly put at our disposition by M. Pierre Marot, naturally does not permit any certainty even of Boffrand's authorship of individual drawings, and those included do not surely belong to the early period, so as to establish any priority.

[134] For the documents regarding it see the *Bulletin de la Société de l'histoire de l'art français*, 1923, 338. Our date of 1709 is from the Comptes du prince de Vaudémont in the Archives de Meurthe-et-Moselle, cited by Langlois, *op. cit.*, 157n.

[135] The carved panelling from it preserved at the Musée Carnavalet (illustrated in *Les Vieux hôtels de Paris*, Quartier Saint-Antoine, pl. 13) seem surely to be of much later date, after 1730.

[136] Boffrand's interiors at the Hôtel de Villars, later than their generally reputed date, we shall discuss under the Regency.

[137] *Architecture françoise*, I, 118.

Cahen d'Anvers,[138] who installed it at the Château des Champs in the principal story, in the Chambre de Madame and the boudoir on the court of honour. Still in situ at the house are several rooms with various fragments of decoration of the period of Boffrand, mirrors, overdoors, and cornices, and cove-cornices with cherubs.

Boffrand, a master of disposition, did not fail also to build a number of new hôtels in Paris. The earliest of these, in 1700, was the house of Le Brun, nephew of the painter, which stands, dismantled. In 1704[139] he built one, in the name of the Abbé Dubois, for Madame d'Argenton, mistress of the future Regent, the ceiling of the salon being painted in 1708 by Antoine Coypel. It served from 1725 as the Chancellerie d'Orléans, and was repeatedly remodelled. We have numerous engravings after 1725 showing the salon, but its design as there seen cannot possibly be a work of the beginning of the century and thus will be discussed later.

With a business enterprise like that of Mansart and De Cotte, Boffrand erected a number of large hôtels at his own risk for sale. Thus in 1712 he built in the Rue Saint-Dominique a hôtel "dans laquelle on remarquera des dispositions extraordinaires & hasardées, lesquelles cependant paroissent fondées en raison pour plusieurs commoditez."[140] This, which promptly became the Hôtel Amelot de Gournay and later the Hôtel de Montmorency, had an oval court, a salon and a principal chamber flatly elliptical at the outer and inner ends, and a vestibule with rounded corners and two converging sides. Mariette's section shows the chamber panelled only at the chimney breast and at the doorways of the enfilade. The mirror head, with an arched cornice on consoles, is closely similar in type to examples by Pierre Lepautre, although the consoles here again are placed in profile. The overdoor, with a broken semicircular head of plain mouldings, is flanked by vertical strips such as we have seen in Lepautre's work at just this date. All the cornices throughout the house are indicated as having concave friezes with no architrave and no cove for the ceiling—in other words they are shown as simple cove-cornices. There is nothing in the details corresponding in novelty with the exceptional spatial inventions of the plan.

Also built by Boffrand as speculations were: his pavilion inaugurating the Faubourg Saint-Honoré (1712-1715), which became the Hôtel de Duras; a house in the Place Vendôme (1713), which was sold to Nicolas de Curzay (No. 24); as well as the Hôtels de Seignelay (1713 ff) and de Torcy (1714 ff). The interiors of the two latter have been wholly remodelled,[141] and Mariette's plates include no sections of them. We are no better informed as to the Hôtel de Curzay. Of the Hôtel de Duras, however, we have an excellent small section.[142] The mirrors are closely similar to those of Lepautre at the same period, with concave or reverse curves at the top, and sometimes with reverse curves at the bottom; some of them, as at the Hôtel Lauzun, have paintings above in frames composed essentially of a quatrefoil

[138] Cf. Champeaux, *op. cit.*, 148. The Comtesse d'Anvers has kindly verified for us their present location.

[139] Cf. J. Mayor: "L'Hôtel de la Chancellerie d'Orléans," *Gazette des beaux-arts*, IVᵉ pér., XII, 1916, pp. 333-359.

[140] Brice, 1713 ed., III, 153.

[141] The Hôtel de Torcy was completely redecorated under the Empire for Prince Eugène de Beauharnais. At the Hôtel de Seignelay, of which the present interiors have passed for work of the early period, they were actually, as we shall see, the result of a remodelling about 1750.

[142] Blondel: *Architecture françoise*, pl. 438 of the Guadet edition.

of four C-scrolls, henceforth the most common form also for overdoors. Here again all the rooms are shown as having simple cove-cornices.

Little of significance for us remains of Boffrand's work in Lorraine. In the Cathedral at Nancy, which Mansart had begun in 1703 and Boffrand continued after 1708, his high altar has a painted retable of which the semicircular head, lightly broken at the impost, follows the general type of Lepautre's side altars at the Chapel of Versailles. Not much which is his survives in the interiors of the châteaux of Leopold[143] or in the houses at Nancy, and such sections of these buildings as are given by Boffrand in his *Livre d'architecture*, 1745, give us small help in most cases. The exceptions are those of La Malgrange, begun in 1711. Work here was suspended in 1715, when the interiors were already well advanced, and the château was demolished by Stanislas. Boffrand gives sections of both his projects, of which the first was preferred to the second. In general there are few novelties worthy of remark, but one room deserves great attention: the salon of the first project (Figure 102).

This salon is oval, rising through two stories like Le Vau's salon of Vaux long ago, and like Cartaud's at Montmorency, built at much the same period as the Malgrange designs. Unlike these rooms, however, it has no order of pilasters or other boldly plastic architecture. The windows in both stories are arched, the heads of those in the upper story rising in penetrations of the cove, as later did those of the salons of the Hôtel de Soubise. The room, however, is far from anticipating these later salons fully, indeed many features point rather backwards than forwards. Thus a small academic cornice is arched over the heads of the upper windows, with breaks supported by tall herms in relief facing sideways, like the consoles we have previously noted in Boffrand's work. The cove is adorned with heavy garlands, from which depend large unsymmetrical trophies in the panels between the windows. In the lower story, below the impost, are square panels but slightly softened at the top by crossettes and a central shell. Above the impost pairs of figures seated on the arches support shallow iron balconies, while between them in the spandrels are large cartouches of little relief, with irregular fields and borders partly of shellwork. In spite of adherence to geometry, there is throughout a suggestion of graceful undulation which foreshadows that of Boffrand's future masterpiece.[144]

On the interiors of Le Blond we are better informed, thanks to the sections he himself published[145] of his Hôtel de Vendôme, built 1705-1706 and enlarged 1714-1716, which with the Hôtel de Clermont, 1708-1714, constituted his work in Paris.[146] Better still, we have the plates he added to his edition, 1710, of Daviler's *Cours*—plates, we may note, engraved by Pierre Lepautre (Figure 103). Mariette wrote of Le Blond: "Il touchait l'ornement avec une très-grande delicatesse."[147] There is, however, little that is new to us in motif;

[143] Cf. P. Boyé: *Les Châteaux du roi Stanislas en Lorraine*, 1910.

[144] The doors shown are remarkable for their free design, with curved rails, even one with a reverse curve. As such doors are quite unexampled elsewhere until after 1730, we may perhaps assume that they were indicated at the time the plates were engraved, in 1745.

[145] In his edition of Daviler's *Cours d'architecture*, 1710. Cf. B. Lossky in *Gazette des beaux-arts*, VIe pér., XII, 1934, 30-41. This paper, appearing before our discussions of Berain's and Lepautre's work, when Berain's chimney piece at Meudon was undated and wrongly identified, and when Lepautre's chimney pieces at Marly were still unknown, made claims of priority for Le Blond at the Hôtel de Vendôme which could not now be supported.

[146] A "Petite maison de campagne du dessein du Sr Le Blond," in Mariette's *Architecture françoise*, shows two rooms in section, which do not alter the idea we gain from the other works discussed.

[147] *Abecedario*, III, 89-92.

Genesis

the novelty, simplicity and variety which Le Blond remarks as now current, by contrast with earlier examples, are the qualities with which we have already become familiar in executed works. The designs of mirror frames represent personal variants of the schemes established a decade before by Berain and Pierre Lepautre. In some respects the forms are of belated types: many of the chimney breasts still project from the walls; some of the mirror heads, including one still square-headed, have unornamented, unbroken mouldings. There is much narrow bandwork of slight relief, suggestive rather of Berain's painted ornament than of Lepautre's transformation of it, and the bizarre forms of certain marble mantels—curved and broken both in plan and in elevation—recall Berain's designs of 1699. Two of these mantels have diagonal herms, never found in Berain's, hesitant forerunners of the diagonal consoles adopted by Lepautre by 1712 and henceforth typical. In the mosaic background we find in one instance the curved lines which Lepautre was then employing in the remodellings at the Hôtel Lauzun. The cornices, all full entablatures beneath a low cove, tend to have friezes also hollow, with figural ornaments—in form and decoration not unlike that of the Salon Frais at Trianon in 1706. Among the plates of "Nouveaux Lambris," "si differens de ceux qui étoient en usage il y a quelques années," we find again adaptation of Lepautre's motives, not well understood.

Delamair, so early superseded at the Hôtel de Soubise, retained his employment at the Hôtel de Rohan, subsequently much remodelled, abused, and "restored." The land was ceded July 22, 1705, the specifications and contracts for the construction range from 1705 to 1708, those for the carving and gilding, including that of the salons, being from 1706.[148] Of Delamair's original interiors there, certain early drawings survive,[149] which he included in a volume sent to the Elector of Bavaria in 1714. They show two sides of a room, one with a central arched doorway and very simple panelling. The mouldings of the lunette are strictly geometrical, there is no trace anywhere of the forms created by Pierre Lepautre. Busts are placed at the impost on consoles of free form; garlands follow the line of the arches, falling in one case from a simple cartouche. The cornice, with plain vertical frieze, is of academic form, though with only an astragal in place of the architrave, and is surmounted by a cove of substantial height. Clearly Delamair was not a pioneer in the decoration of interiors.

Delamair built also, before 1713,[150] for Chanac, abbé de Pompadour, a house which still stands in the Rue de Grenelle. The interior, however, was much remodelled under Louis XV and Louis XVI, and the plates of Mariette and Blondel include no section to confirm or modify our view of him.

Oppenord's earliest surviving works in France[151] are all ecclesiastical. One volunteered in 1699 for the altar of Notre Dame (Figure 104),[152] translates the baldaquin of Lepautre —the disapproval of which was itself doubtless partly due to its baroque aspects—into something still more baroque, and it also preserves the mannerist tabernacles of the old jubé.

[148] Langlois, *op. cit.*

[149] Royal Library, Munich, MS. fr. 540, reproduced by Langlois, *op. cit.*, pls. XLI and XLII.

[150] Brice, 1713 ed., III, 215.

[151] For the chronology of Oppenord's work see G. Huard's study in Dimier: *Les peintres français au XVIIIᵉ siècle*, I, 1928, 311-329.

[152] Cabinet des Estamples, Va 254c, No. 2220. It is marked merely "Dessein d'un particulier."

The altar of Saint-Germain-des-Prés was executed in 1704 from a design of Oppenord (Figure 105),[153] after he had made a multitude of studies on various schemes. Again it was a baldaquin, with scrolled baroque consoles above, their junction marked by winged cherubs' heads. The Gothic reliquary of the saint (for which Oppenord first proposed to substitute a baroque one) is held aloft by two angels who kneel on opposite volutes, as in Lorenzo Tedesco's ciborium at Santo Spirito in Sassia at Rome—such volutes, as we have seen, later taken up by Vassé, in 1712, for the altar of Notre Dame. One earlier study shows a revetment of the choir with *trophées d'église,* less like those which Oppenord had seen and sketched in Italy than like those of the new stalls of Orléans. The mouldings at the top of the panel take on something of the character of an early Lepautre mirror head, already with less geometrical character.

For the Abbey of Saint-Victor in 1706 Oppenord made designs of an altar, not executed, which were exhibited in the library of the establishment.[154] Our only trace is the study engraved in the *Grand Oppenord,*[155] which is of great scale and pronounced baroque composition, though by no means copied from any specific Italian model.

In the surviving altar of Saint John at the cathedral of Amiens, 1709 (Figure 106),[156] French traditions also begin to make themselves felt in the form of the great frame, which at first held a painting. It is cut at the upper corners by concave arcs as in overmantel mirrors by Pierre Lepautre at Marly and in the Oeil-de-Boeuf at Versailles, and as in the altar of the Virgin just executed from Lepautre's design at Versailles.

It was in 1712, according to the historian of the church,[157] that Oppenord presented a project for the altar of Saint-Jacques de la Boucherie. An engraving of this project is included in the *Grand Oppenord,* plate LXXXIII (Figure 107). The retable is framed between pilasters and beneath a cornice arched in the manner so often used in French decoration since 1685, and with a crowning ornament of a pair of cornucopias recalling many by Pierre Lepautre. A painted scene of martyrdom, with an unbroken rectangular frame, is crowned by a pair of floating angels supporting a cartouche of traditional plastic character. The altar table, of sarcophagus type, has a reversed curve profile and is flanked by consoles with cherubheads. On the face is an oval panel framed with palm. There is thus no such pregnant novelty of character as is so marked in Vassé's designs for the altar table of Notre Dame in the same year.

It was only in the period of mourning after the deaths of the two young heirs to the throne in 1712, following the death of the Dauphin in 1711, that princes and courtiers of the first rank, like the Comte de Toulouse, the Princesse de Conti, and the Duc d'Antin, "qui ne

[153] National Museum, Stockholm. The surviving preliminary MS. studies are there and in the Cabinet des Estampes (Va 269a)—one of the latter published by F. de Câtheu in *Bulletin de la Société de l'histoire de l'art français,* 1936, at p. 62. Other studies are engraved in the *Grand Oppenord,* pls. LXXVIII and LXXIX, and in the *Moyen Oppenord.* This altar was literally copied in 1710 at Sainte-Trinité in Caen, this replica now being at Notre Dame de la Gloriette there. Cf. Huard, *loc. cit.*

[154] Brice, 1713 ed., II, 182-183.

[155] Pl. CXVI.

[156] G. Durand: *Monographie de la cathédrale d'Amiens,* 1901-1903. A drawing for this altar is preserved at the Cabinet des Estampes. Va 401a.

[157] The Abbé Villain, cited by Huard, *op. cit.,* 316.

pouvoient decoucher de la cour," ventured to set up establishments in Paris.[158] It is particularly important to study the works of this last moment of the reign, in order to define exactly their character on the eve of the period of Louis XV. Bercy, from 1712, already discussed, sufficiently represents Pierre Lepautre at this time. Fortunately we have also reasonably adequate material on several works at the very end of the reign from the hands of other designers.

Oppenord's reputation had steadily grown since his return from Italy. In 1713 Brice spoke of him and of his house in the Rue Saint-Thomas-du-Louvre:

> remplie & decorée de quantité de bonnes choses, particulièrement des études qu'il a faites à Rome & dans tous les endroits d'Italie, sur ce que l'antique & les plus excellens modernes ont de precieux. Les beaux projets et desseins d'architecture qui sortent journellement de ses mains le font considerer comme un très habile architecte, ayant un connaissance parfait de tous les ouvrages de quelque genre qu'ils puissent être, et possedant le dessein à une haut degré de perfection.[159]

The first interior we know for which Oppenord was responsible was at the Hôtel de Pomponne, Place des Victoires, executed for Michel Bonnier in 1714.[160] There survive portions of the panelling (Figures 108, 109), twice moved, and two of Oppenord's drawings.[161] We observe first the great wealth of carving, richly figural, the invention of a fertile plastic talent. The large standing trophies of the chase in the major panels, with live animals as well as dead game, were doubtless suggested by Audran's Portière of Diana of 1699 with its standing trophy with hounds. The free grouping about naturalistic trees, which is such a novel feature of Oppenord's treatment, recalls the compositions of contemporary still-life painters like Weenix or Desportes. The filling of the subordinate panels (whether on the flat, or in the curved corners), likewise, is not confined merely to conventional leaf and bandwork, but playfully adopts, for the first time in carving, further arabesque motives. There are figures of Fame under valanced baldaquins, and naturalistic foliage such as is found in the arabesque Portières of Audran, and still more in the arabesques of Gillot and Watteau. The mouldings of the panels themselves, both large and small, are subtly curved and modified without departing from basic rectangularity. At the top only C-scrolls are used, but at the bottom we find already mouldings of reverse curvature.

One of Oppenord's drawings (Figure 110) shows two chimney pieces of related character. The marble mantels develop and vary types suggested by Berain at the turn of the century, doubtless now coming into wider use, as Le Blond's plates suggest—the marble curved both in profile and in plan, with a wealth of consoles and scrolls. In the hands of Oppenord, endlessly facile, there was no hardening of such types into new formulae. The heads of the tall

---

[158] Saint-Simon, XXIII, 176-177, 380-381. D'Antin bought in 1712 the Hôtel de Travers, which had been built for Chamillart; the Princesse de Conti, in 1713, the Hôtel de Lorge, redecorated by Mansart 1695-1698.

[159] I, 150. The passage recurs in the edition of 1717, I, 156, but disappears in the next one of 1725.

[160] Cf. the writer's paper "Oppenord reconnu," in *Gazette des beaux-arts*, VIᵉ pér. XIII, 1935, 42-58, which assembles the evidence for chronology. Brice (1717, I, 349) mentions "de fort grans changemens, et plus de soixante mille écus de dépenses pour décorer les appartemens et pour leur donner les agrémens de la mode nouvelle . . . dorures magnifiques"—made in 1714. We shall see that certain changes, at least on the exterior, were made by Oppenord at the house after 1723, but the panelling is fully consonant with the date of 1714.

[161] De Cloux collection, Cooper Union, New York, Nos. 231, 232.

mirrors over the fireplaces are freshly and lavishly invented: one bowed in reverse curves richly crested with a fan-like border; the other basically semicircular, to be sure, but with its regularity veiled by a diverging rim of shell. This adaptation of the rim of shell, which we have seen long ago in the cartouches of Stephano della Bella, was now a great novelty, which we shall also find, a moment later, in those of Vassé—a novelty which was to become a sign-manual of style under Louis XV. Scrollwork is not confined to the heads; the frame of one mirror breaks at the sides (as sometimes with Berain) into console curves, that of the other (far more freely than ever with Berain) waves at its base along the mantel, as does the mirror of the pier opposite. Without departure from the established general scheme, or a change in the tendency to greater curvature, the tendency is vastly accelerated, the scheme is given dynamic vitality.

It is worth observing that, in this first domestic design of Oppenord, to whom so much initiative has been attributed, the basic scheme was purely French—the scheme which was crystallizing toward 1700, with a low marble chimney piece and with a tall arched mirror above that, the single flight of panels above the dado, the modification of the geometrical frame, the linear character, the slight relief. There is a fertile originality in detail, but no fundamental modification of the constructive or decorative elements, to say nothing of any radical change of materials, or of aesthetic character.

The Comte de Toulouse, a legitimated son of Louis XIV, who had purchased in 1712 François Mansart's Hôtel de la Vrillière, began in 1714-1715 to remodel it under the direction of Robert de Cotte. Aside from the gallery, not disturbed until some years later, the chief decorative works were in connection with the vestibule and staircase. "La nouvelle escalier," wrote Germain Brice in 1717, "a de la grandeur, et le grand palier qui sert d'entrée aux appartements, est décoré de pilastres, qui soutiennent une cornice fort enrichie de sculptures d'un fini tout particulier, la plupart duquelles ont été executées par Du Mont,[162] sculpteur très habile, de l'académie . . ." It is only in later descriptions that we find the names of other sculptors. Thus in Piganiol de la Force's edition of 1742 (III, 83) he names Charpentier, Montean and Offhman as the sculptors of the staircase, while the 1752 edition of Brice, revised by Mariette,[163] mentions Vassé and Charpentier as sculptors specifically of the trophies. Vassé we know, was active elsewhere in the hôtel after 1715, but we cannot be sure he was concerned with the stairway.

For this stairway two architectural sections survive,[164] in the style of draughtsmanship established by Pierre Lepautre, not by his hand but inferior and labored.[165] Engravings of the work as executed were included in the *Architecture françoise* of Mariette (Figure 111).[166] In the principal story there were Ionic pilasters framing panels with large suspended *trophées de marine* and *trophées de chasse*. The general treatment is thus not unlike that of the vestibule at Bercy, with large panels bearing suspended trophies, here trophies of arms including

[162] Brice, 1717 ed., I, 332-338. The 1716 edition of *Les Curiositez de Paris* (I, 61), merely mentions work going on; the 1719 edition (I, 167) mentions no artists for the stairway, although it gives Vassé as the author of the sculpture in the Grand Cabinet.

[163] I (completed about 1740, see p. vii), 438-440.

[164] Cabinet des Estampes, Va 232e, Nos. 1585 and 1586.

[165] The author is not the same as that of the designs for the Château de Bonn, drawn by another imitator of Lepautre.

[166] Pls. 449-450 of the Hautecoeur edition.

shields sharply inclined. Two of the panels are not strictly rectangular, but have paired C-scrolls at the top. The newer motifs thus appear without pronounced modifications of general character.

De Cotte began at this time to be called in by foreign princes and their advisers. Thus from Spain, now a Bourbon kingdom, the Princesse des Ursins wrote in 1712 for his counsel on designs for the Cabinet des Furies (not preserved) and for chimney pieces in the Appartement de la Reine in the palace at Madrid.[167] In 1713 he was having executed in Paris the finish for "la pièce octagonale" at Madrid, including carvings by Dugoullons and associates, marble mantels, and bronzes by Vassé, billed in 1715. There survive at the Cabinet des Estampes (Vb 147)[168] a number of designs for chimney pieces at Madrid, some of them rendered in imitation of Lepautre's technique but not by him, four others, I believe, by Vassé. These last have flanking figures not unlike those we shall later see in the gallery of the Hôtel de Toulouse, where the arch of the fireplace rests on similar baluster-like piers, and there are similarities of detail also with the later ornaments of Vassé in the Salon d'Hercule.

The character of work of De Cotte's office at this moment for the provinces, without the participation of Lepautre or Vassé, is shown by drawings prepared in 1714 for rooms for the Marquis de Grammont at Besançon.[169] In their general ordonnance they follow the schemes of Lepautre about 1703, with square frames and medallions in the upper zones, and with the slightest modification of the geometrical assemblage. The Chambre (Figure 112) even retains an impost all about, and in all the rooms there are numerous superposed panels. The mirrors of the Salon and the Chambre still have semicircular heads; those of the Antichambre and the Cabinets have broken segmental heads like those of Lepautre at the Chancellerie. The marble chimney piece of the Chambre has the form now most characteristic, its inner moulding, of broken curves, flanked by diagonal consoles of slight projection and curvature.

It will be observed—contrary to the view of many writers—how completely private work at this time was under the influence of the initiative taken in the royal works. Versailles, so far from being conservative or backward, was in the forefront, by the remodelling of the Appartement du Roi in 1701, then by the decoration of the Chapel extending to 1710. Even between 1710 and 1715 the leadership remained with the artists of the Crown, at Notre Dame and elsewhere.

In the last years of the reign, as we have seen, younger men, while following and exploiting the tendencies established by Lepautre, began to show greater personal initiative. Thus Boffrand, always a finished master of spatial composition, showed, at least at La Malgrange, ability to devise new motifs for the treatment of surface. Oppenord brought a rich equipment which, especially in religious work, transcended adherence to formula and promised much for the future. At the end of the period, Vassé made himself felt as a vital creative force. The character of Oppenord's early work, to be sure, still tinged by baroque reminiscences, was not entirely in harmony with the essential spirit of the new style. It represented

[167] Marcel, *Inventaire*, 195-207.

[168] Not available for reproduction since the outbreak of war.

[169] Va ter, Nos. 794-805. Requested in October, 1713, and sent after June, 1714, according to letters abstracted by Marcel, *op. cit.*, 121 ff.

that "transition"—really a compromise after the fact—which follows, in the work of other men, the initiative of every great individual artistic creator.

The Ornamentalists

While Lepautre and his followers were creating the masterpieces of the time in architectural form, new developments had been proceeding in the painted decoration of surface, from which again were to come important suggestions.

Here the leadership was now taken by Claude III Audran (1658-1734). At thirty-three, on January 1, 1692, he had been received "maistre peintre, sculpteur, graveur et enjoliveur à Paris."[170] The next year Cronström, the Swedish Minister, wrote home to Tessin: "Celluy qui après M. Berain a la plus grande réputation en ce genre [d'arabesques et de grotesques] est Audran, neuveu d'Audran le graveur. Je croyois qu'on le pourrait disposer autant plus facilement a un voyage en Suède qu'il se trouve fort contre-carré icy par M. Berain à qui il fait ombrage."[171] In 1698 Cronström got from the Duc de Vendôme drawings from the arabesques executed by Audran at Anet. The Salon, as Dargenville tell us,[172] had a ceiling "de petites figures d'animaux, d'oiseaux et d'Amours peintes par Audran." Other rooms may also include his work: the Grand Cabinet, a gilded ceiling "avec quatre petites chasses," the Cabinet des Muses, "peintes en or sur les lambris," and the Cabinet des Singes with Savonnerie tapestries of monkeys in the four seasons. Cronström writes: "Afin de ne pas chagriner M. Berain, M. de Vendosme ne dira pas pour qui c'est . . . Audran estant le seul qu'il craint." This fear was well founded, for after 1699 Audran was to take the lead, receiving in four years over 70,000 livres for his work for the Bâtiments.

The momentous year of 1699 saw both artists employed on decorations for the Appartement de Monseigneur at Meudon. Berain's designs for arabesques on the panelling of the Cabinet (Figure 115) and elsewhere in the Château were executed by Guillaume Desauziers, gilder, who was paid from April 12 (*Comptes* IV, 544). The forms here and in other arabesques of this time—included, like these, in Berain's engraved series of *Cheminées*—are much more elongated than in his designs engraved before 1693. The double band disappears, although there are still contrasting areas, executed in gold, partly with *mosaïque*. The panels of the Cabinet are devoid of figural and animal motives, but one other panel of the *Cheminées* suite shows a seated Chinese figure of the type then just coming into vogue,[173] together with a pair of monkeys—the earliest example of each of these motifs in his work which we can securely date.[174]

Even before Berain's assistants adorned the walls of the Cabinet at Meudon, Audran had

[170] Registre des jurandes, Archives Notariales, Y9322, cited by Dacier et Vuaflart: *Jean de Julienne et les graveurs de Watteau*, I, 1929, 19.

[171] This and the following quotation are given by Weigert: *Berain*, I, 222.

[172] *Voyage pittoresque des environs de Paris*, 1755, 179.

[173] Cf. the general discussion of Chinese influence below.

[174] Monkeys appear in one of Berain's arabesques (Weigert, No. 191) of which Weigert, relying on a manuscript note of Mariette, attributes the engraving to Jacques Lepautre, who died in 1684, but the plate is signed merely "Le Pautre," and from its style we would attribute it to a much later date and its engraving thus to Pierre Lepautre. Such monkeys merely replace the fauns, in similar playful activities, familiar in early arabesques like those of Ducerceau.

already attacked the ceilings in other rooms there, being paid 6900 livres, February 22 and March 14 "sur la peinture qu'il a fait au plafonds de la garde-robe et de la chambre de Monseigneur" (IV, 544).[175]

The King visited Meudon and approved the work in the Chambre April 22. On April 25 Mansart received the Dauphin's order to efface an old ceiling in the Cabinet d'Angle "et y peindre un plat-fond de Grotesques comme celui de la chambre."[176] This order marked a definite preferment of Audran to Berain, and the end of Berain's employment for arabesques in the Maisons Royales.

Two sketches, "plafons de Meudon" (Figures 113, 114)—scarcely from Audran's own hand, but sketched from the work—survive in the Cabinet des Estampes (Va 358). The scheme of composition is still that of Berain's Chambre du Lit at the Hôtel de Mailly, composed on the cardinal and diagonal axes. Again as there, the fields are bordered by a double band, here, in one case, much more extravagantly scrolled. The single fillets and scrolls, however, are more isolated and looser in organization, a baldaquin on leafy supports is of the airiest proportions. Birds and monkeys, as well as human figures, perch on the scrolls.

Other royal commissions to Audran quickly followed. Already in April of 1699 payments to him began on "ouvrages de peinture qu'il fait pour la petite chambre de Madame la princesse de Conti" at Versailles (2500 livres to November 15, IV, 447).

On the reopening of the Gobelins in 1699, Audran was entrusted with a commission of outstanding importance, the "Nouvelles portières des Rabesques des Dieux" (Figure 117).[177] As compared with the earlier Triomphes de Dieux and Mois Arabesques, copied or adapted from old models, these embodied, for the first time at the Gobelins, the new character which French arabesque had meanwhile assumed. The light pierced baldaquins on tapered leafy gaines were surrounded by sprays of naturalistic foliage, by airy scrollwork, chiefly of acanthus, and by garlands of flowers—all delicately shimmering in pale colors on a gold background. We gain an idea of the admiration this suite evoked from its having been executed seven to nine times between 1701 and 1703.

With the advent of 1700, Audran, assisted by Desportes, began the painting of such arabesques for the apartments of the Duchesse de Bourgogne at the Château de la Ménagerie. Mansart had sent to Fontainebleau, September 8, 1699, a memorandum[178] proposing figures of Diana, Pomona, Thetis, Flora, Palès, Ceres, Minerva, and Juno. It was on the margin of this proposal that the King wrote his famous note, in which more than in all others, he showed his superior judgment and taste:

> Il me paroit qu'il y a quelque chose a changer que les sujets sont trop sérieux et qu'il faut qu'il y ait de la jeunesse mêlée dans ce que l'on fera. Vous m'apporterez des dessins quand vous viendrez, ou du moins des pensées. Il faut de l'enfance répandue partout.
> Louis, Fontainebleau, 10 septembre 1699.

[175] Cf. Biver: *Meudon*, 154.

[176] *Ibid.*, 154, citing Archives Nationales 0¹ 1473. Payments for this ceiling followed on September 27 and October 24. October 23 the work was inspected by the King (Dangeau, VII, 174, 176).

[177] Mansart's register, 0¹ 1809, carried on June 12 the order for these "suivant les dessins de grotesques que M. le Surintendant a fait voir à sa Majesté."

[178] Exhibited at the Musée de Versailles.

Audran's designs (Figure 117),[179] so admirably suited to the age and taste of the princess, were the result.

In the accounts for 1700 we find him paid no less than 22,000 livres "à compte des ouvrages de peinture qu'il fait dans les appartements de la Ménagerie"; the payments continue until November, 1701. The surfaces ornamented included the panelling as well as the ceilings.[180] We learn of the royal satisfaction by two passages from Dangeau:

> Jeudi 22 avril 1700. Le roi alla se promener à la Ménagerie, où Mme la duchesse de Bourgogne étoit allée pour le recevoir; il fut très content de toutes les dépenses qu'on y a faites, qui sont grandes et d'un goût fort recherché pour les boisures, les peintures, et les serrures . . .
> Mardi, 21 décembre. — Le Roi . . . monta en carrosse avec Mme. la duchesse de Bourgogne. Ils allèrent à la Menagerie voir les appartements qu'on à achevé de peindre et dorer; le roi les trouva magnifiques et charmants . . .

These decorations enjoyed considerable celebrity. Caylus, in his severe *Vie . . . de Watteau* read before the Academy in 1748, mentions them, remarking "la légèreté qu'exigent les fonds blancs ou les fonds dorés sur lesquels Audran faisoit exécuter ses ouvrages."

Three studies for arabesque ceilings on a gold ground, attributed to Audran, are preserved in the Musée des Arts-Décoratifs (Figure 117). The presence of a unicorn in one of them suggests that they were destined for the château of the little princess who was not yet united with her husband when the designs were first proposed.[181] They are of the most delicate, attenuated proportions, with ethereal canopies floating without any support. The central fluted sunburst becomes a ring of bat's-wing, itself with lace-like openings; the few remaining double bands are pierced and disconnected; other touches of bandwork become curved and calligraphic; fillets are replaced by single lines; and foliate scrolls are reduced almost to tendrils.

By such designs, in comparison with Berain's work of 1699, we are led to the conclusion that the lightest of Berain's arabesques were influenced by the victory of Audran and were executed after 1700. As pronounced examples, we may instance Berain's surviving engraved designs for ceilings (e.g. Figure 116),[182] which were drawn with single fillets only, though still, unlike those of Audran, with a firm organization. Without any change of fundamental scheme since the first ceilings of the Hôtel de Mailly, the pattern is lightened to the airiest of interlaces.

[179] One of three preserved at the Musée des Arts-décoratifs.

[180] Cf. the passage in Blondel: *Architecture françoise*, I, 1752, 125.

[181] This identification, proposed in my paper on the Ménagerie, is subject to correction by future study of the great body of Audran's drawings, about 1200 in number, from the Cronstedt-Fullerö collection, given to the National Museum in Stockholm in 1941.

[182] Weigert, No. 70b; also 70a and 69, of the same character. Weigert supposes these engravings to be among a dozen for ceilings mentioned by Cronström in a letter of 1693, in which however he says "il y a déjà quelque temps que cela est fait et le goût a un peu changé depuis." Now the style of a few years before, since changed, would have been the heavier style of the Hôtel de Mailly. There are none of the lighter patterns among the plates engraved by Dolivar before 1693. We must accordingly suppose that the dozen mentioned by Cronström are now lost.

Genesis

At this period, by 1703,[183] Audran also painted arabesques in the gallery of the Duchesse du Maine at Sceaux, which she had just acquired, works destroyed after 1775 by the Duc de Penthièvre.

In 1708-1709 Audran was paid the substantial sum of 7,471 livres for "verni" and "verni et dorure" in the Château Neuf at Meudon,[184] doubtless in arabesque patterns. In the same years the Gobelins executed from his designs, for the apartment of the Dauphin there, the series of narrow panels known as the "Mois Grotesques," with classical figures under light fanciful baldaquins. They do not differ substantially in style from his earlier work. Bandwork is subordinate but still present, sometimes with diagonal interlaces and almost a calligraphic character. In 1707-1708 and into 1709, Watteau, in his twenty-third and twenty-fourth years, was assisting Audran, so that it has been surmised that he may have collaborated on the designs. If so, his part was still receptive and secondary.[185]

In 1709 Audran painted for Marly his famous "tableau représantant un berceau où les singes sont à table,"[186] an exemplar of the surviving *singeries* of the next generation.

Germain Brice but expressed the general admiration of his contemporaries when, in his edition of 1713 (III, 71-72), he celebrated Audran as "consideré comme un des premiers dessinateurs du temps, sur tout pour les Arabesques & pour les ornemens de grotesques, dans le goût du fameux Raphael," and added "On voit de ses ouvrages en plusieurs endroits, particulierement au château de Meudon, & à la Ménagerie, où il a fait des choses dignes d'admiration, plus belles & plus ingénieuses, en ce genre singulier, que tout ce qui s'est encore vû en France jusques icy."

With forms suggested by the surface arabesque of Berain, Pierre Lepautre, transposing them, and transforming, in their spirit, the architectural framework itself, had created something new under the sun—the essential scheme which was to prevail in France under Louis XV and throughout Europe in all the development of the rococo. This creation, as we have observed, took place in fullness from around 1700, still under Louis XIV, at a period long before scholars have generally realized.

Contrary to received opinion, spatial impulses were not determining factors in this genesis, which took place chiefly within the pre-existing walls of rooms of simple cubical form. The relative absence of spatial variety in French work of the time has been thought due to lack of comprehension of this resource of the Italian baroque. Le Vau, however, had early been a master of this resource, of which he was expressly deprived in his later work by the rigor of French academism. Boffrand braved this rigor soon after the great creative moment, but Boffrand was exceptional in France for his interest in spatial variety, and it was Lepautre, not Boffrand, whose innovations were the crucial and prophetic ones. The spatial effects char-

---

[183] Madame wrote October 26, 1704: "I think I told you last year about the charming gallery and closet Madame du Maine has made for herself there." *Letters*, tr. by G. S. Stevenson, 1924.

[184] Biver: *Meudon*, 192, citing Archives Nationales, 0^1 2207.

[185] For the engraving of the series by Jean Audran, announced in the *Mercure* for 1726, three drawings in red chalk, in reverse from the tapestries and the engravings, are preserved at the Cooper Union, New York (Figure 118).

[186] *Comptes*, V, 340. Already in the Saturn of the Portières des Dieux, 1699, we find a monkey playing with the cherubs—the first instance, to my knowledge, which can be definitely dated.

acteristic of the reign of Louis XV, in the relation of interiors to one another and to the external landscape [187] were achieved with little variety in the forms of the units, and were themselves not the chief differentia of the new style.

It has been commonly believed also that in the genesis of the plastic forms of this style, Italian influences were predominant. Obviously many elements and motifs used by Lepautre, as by his predecessors, were of Italian high-baroque origin. The arched cornices on consoles, the occasional armorial cartouches, sometimes winged, with figural supporters, the valanced baldaquins, the winged cherub-heads were all features long domesticated in France. The outlines of his mirror frames and altarpieces, for which parallels may be found in Italy, were merely logical developments of the outlines of frames in Le Brun's painted ceilings, themselves based, long ago, on Italian baroque examples. The impact of the Italian high-baroque, as we have seen, had been felt in France well before the fundamental change of style we have described, and its influence had long been on the wane.

Quite otherwise significant was Lepautre's transformation of this traditional baroque material. In all his work one of the most striking qualities was the abandonment of plasticity: in architectural members and decorative motifs alike. The column soon completely vanished from his work, the pilaster, greatly attenuated and reduced in relief, survived only as a strip, its cap and base dissolving. The wall panels, increased in height, had their mouldings likewise diminished in projection. At focal points their outline was further etherealized by taking on the swing of arabesque bandwork with its adjuncts of acanthus. Interlaces and scrolls of these elements invaded the panels themselves at top and bottom and around the central rosette. Not the plastic baroque cartouche, which survived only as a shield of arms, but a smooth surface with surrounding bands and scrolls became the typical field for decorative enrichment. In the hands of Vassé the exuberance of line was heightened, the surface became curved without losing its smoothness.

For this genial transformation, Lepautre, who had never been in Italy, derived his first suggestion, as we have seen, from a French source, the painted arabesque of Berain. The derivative elements, Italian and French alike, he fused in a new creation, essentially distinct from either.

How completely distinct it had become from the art of Italy may be appreciated by a comparison of domestic interiors in their ensemble. The Italian rooms retained a high vaulted ceiling, with rich plastic ornament, in bold relief, often painted in full color with figural subjects; their walls were unarticulated, of plaster painted or covered with stuffs, in which the doors and windows, heavily framed, were pierced with little mutual relation. The French rooms, on the other hand, had an increase in the height of wall, a reduction in the depth of cove to a mere feature of the cornice, ceilings thus essentially flat, white or with ethereal arabesques; walls articulated in wood. Highly unified membering, delicate and of slight relief, brought out merely by gilding, embraced doors, windows, and chimney piece in a single organic whole, fusing functional elements with ornament.

This new French scheme was indeed almost equally far removed from the academic system hitherto prevailing in France itself, with its rigid distinction between the bold architectonic membering and flat surface decoration.

[187] Well analyzed by A. Schmarzow, *Barock und Rokoko*, 332-340.

Genesis

That it was appreciated by contemporaries as a new creation, in relation to what had gone before both in Italy and in France, is well evidenced by a remark of Germain Brice in 1713 (II, 31) regarding the Hôtel de Beauvais, which had been built by Antoine Lepautre in 1656:

> Dans le mois de Juillet de l'année 1704, les dedans de cette maison ont été entiere-ment détruits pour les mettre à la mode & dans le gôut moderne, qui est incomparable-ment plus commode & plus agreable, que celuy que l'on suivoit autrefois: & il est bon d'ajoûter à cet égard seulement, que les architectes François surpassent de bien loin en cet article, ceux qui les ont precedé, et les Italiens même; ce qui est d'une consequence infinie pour l'utilité & pour l'agrément que l'on en reçoit.

The pioneers in the new creation—Berain, Lepautre, Vassé, Audran—were purely French in blood, in training, and in tendency. Not one of them had studied in Italy. Italian elements, still surviving from earlier years, were secondary in their work; Italian influence was no vital factor in the new art they created. It is an art essentially French also in its grace, its gaiety and its gentleness, one of the most delightful flowerings of artistic creative genius.

Evolution

The Reign of Louis XV

ARTISTIC evolution in France during the reign of Louis XV falls into three main periods. The early years, in their very beginning under the Regency, saw a great outburst of creative energy from artists whose activity extended, without much inner evolution, to about 1730. The middle years began then with a fresh impulse under new leadership, to which ran counter a conservative tendency, issuing after 1750 in a trend to reaction. In the last years after 1760 this reaction, sharply intensified, gained entire mastery.

This whole evolution of art, down to the reaction, was a development of that initiative the genesis of which we have already discussed — an initiative which, as we have seen, was taken in the last years of Louis XIV. The opening of the new reign brought no fundamental change of direction, but only an exploitation of the paths in the new direction so lately taken. These varied paths were struck out by men of the artistic generation of the Regency. By 1730 a fresh artistic generation with fresh leadership was going beyond them in accelerated, heightened movement, always with the same general aim. It was only after the middle of the century that art began to turn in a new direction, toward new ideals.

The rise and fall of the rococo would once have been thought to offer a classic paradigm of analogy with the growth and decay of organic life. We know now the fallaciousness of such analogies imported into history from science. We shall see that in the rococo, as in the Gothic, there was no internal "decline," no diminution of quality or power. In the moment of its highest ultimate brilliance, still capable of new differentiations, a new force, originating elsewhere, was to sweep all before it.

Early Years of the Reign

The phase of style ordinarily called the *style régence*, marking the early years of the reign, extended beyond the years of the Regency proper (1715 to 1723), which saw its formation, roughly to 1730. In 1735 came the death of Robert de Cotte closely followed by that of Vassé and accompanied by the eclipse of Oppenord. Though new forces, inaugurating a new chapter, were felt by 1730, the men of the generation of the Regency thus continued their own work for a dozen years beyond its term. Official tasks and official dominance changed with the change of regime, so that the Regency and its aftermath call for separate treatment.

The Regency, 1715-1723

Louis XV, on his accession, was a child of five. The first eight years of his reign, till his majority was declared in 1723, were under the regency of the Duc d'Orléans, who died at the end of that year.

The seat of the Regency was not Versailles, but Paris — whither the boy-king was brought at once, and where he remained, at Vincennes and at the Tuileries, until 1722. Here was the Regent's own palace, the Palais-Royal; here now congregated the courtiers from an abandoned Versailles. Here too were the financiers and speculators of the post-war inflation of Law and the Mississippi Bubble—culminating in 1720—in which great noblemen were not above participating, along with lackeys. Courtiers, favorites, and financiers rivalled one another in housing themselves at the capital in the latest fashion.

Familiar generalizations, much too facile, have been made as to a rebound to frivolity from barren splendour and oppressive piety in Louis XIV's last years at Versailles with Madame de Maintenon. The artistic antithesis has been heightened by constrasting the Grands Appartements of Versailles with the Petits Cabinets of Louis XV, as if the Versailles of Louis XIV had not also had its own Petits Cabinets, swept away in the remodellings of the next reign. Actually the art of the last period of Louis XIV, retreating to the intimacy of Marly and Trianon, and renewed on the motive of youth at the behest of the aging monarch, already foreshadowed, in scale and motive, what was to come.

Philippe d'Orléans, licentious as he was, was no mere worthless debauchee, as he has too often been pictured, but an enlightened connoisseur with personal understanding of art. A passionate collector, he assembled in a few brief years paintings rivalling even those of the Crown. Works by French masters were few among them, but it is significant that among these was one by Watteau and that this was indubitably a commission.[1] The Regent himself drew and painted with a skill well beyond that of most amateurs. He exemplified the characteristic advantages of aristocracy at its best, for the patronage of art: eagerness to accept the latest in creative innovation, superiority to philistine and bourgeois timidity and reaction.

There is, to be sure, a certain measure of truth in the hackneyed formulation of social influences of the time. The personality of the Regent, informal and accessible, did tend to throw the centre of gravity further from the splendour of the Grands Appartements—which in his palace, too, had new forms of magnificence—to the luxuriance of the Petits Cabinets. The end and aftermath of war, with its characteristic sequels, gave the means for a burst of activity in private building and decoration, gave the mood of easy abandon.

A perfect artistic embodiment of this mood came in painting with Watteau, born in 1684, cut off by death in 1721, whose brief but immense productiveness coincides almost exactly with the Regency. Those who once applied the words frivolity or license to the shimmering gossamer of Watteau little thought of the incessant labour, the intense observation of nature, the endless wealth of preparatory studies, the artistic integrity, the personal asceticism of the frail genius of the *Fêtes galantes*. There is little need for us to analyse here the general character of his work, with its profound originality of subject and treatment. The specific character of his arabesque ornament, developed from that of Audran and Gillot, we shall discuss in its place.

It was doubtless more than a coincidence that, just on the eve of the period then opening, Shaftesbury had said with a new emphasis that art is not imitation but creation:[2] "To copy

[1] The minute *Les singes peintres* on copper, painted as a pendant to the Breughel *Musique des chats*. Listed by L. F. du Bois de Saint-Gelais: *Description des tableaux du Palais-Royal*, 1727 ff. Dacier and Vuaflart, *op. cit.*, I, 135.

[2] Cf. L. Venturi: *Histoire de la critique d'art*, 1938, in additions there made to the English edition of 1936. For the earlier realizations of this truth in Neo-Platonic thinking from Plotinus onward, cf. E. Panofsky: *Idea*, 1924, *passim*, especially 69-71 (Dürer), 121 (Leonardo, etc.).

what has gone before can be of no use ... To work originally, and in a manner create each time anew, must be a matter of pressing weight, and fitted to the strength and capacity of none but the choicest workmen." Like the true poet, the artist "is indeed a second maker; a just Prometheus, under Jove."[3] The very word creation, as applied to man's invention and imagination, was relatively new,[4] and its appearance marks a fuller recognition of artistic powers. Shaftesbury, indeed, had no sympathy with the art of his own time—still then baroque in England—which he spoke of as "a kind of debauch ... in gaudy colors and disfigured shapes of things ... the wild and whimsical, under the name of the odd and pretty," and held up the example of a Greece that he knew not, where "everything muse-like, graceful and exquisite, was rewarded with the highest honours." But art was not, in his view, to be subjected to any formula, even any formula of the ancients.

The French artistic pioneers of the Regency and of the 'thirties had certainly never heard of Shaftesbury, but artistic freedom, like English philosophic ideas, was in the air. Dubos in his *Réflexions critique sur la poésie et la peinture* (1719)—himself, like Shaftesbury, in the current stemming from Locke, opposed to *a priori* principles, restoring sensations to honour—made the application that art was not subject to intellectual laws but to sensibility: "Un ouvrage peut être mauvais sans qu'il y ait des fautes contre les règles, comme un ouvrage plein de fautes contre les régles, peut être un ouvrage excellent."

Critical reprobation for infraction of rules was not to fall for some time on the innovations of Oppenord and his fellows, any more than they were to receive, as yet, a formal defense on the new principles. The public of amateurs and patrons, eager to tell or hear some new thing, instinctively took them to their hearts.

The phase of interior style created by Pierre Lepautre, characteristic of the last years of the old reign, had received its harmonious and perfect embodiment at his hands in works from Marly to the Chapel at Versailles and the choir of Notre Dame; its protagonist was on the eve of his death. Already, since 1710, there had been stirrings and fresh impulses among other architects, sculptors, and ornamentalists. The moment was ripe for the men of creative talent among them to impress a new character on the work of the new reign.

In our study of men and works under the Regency we shall consider first the two leading creative designers, Vassé and Oppenord, and a basic work of each having major importance and influence: one for the Regent himself and by his personal designer; the other for a prince of the blood and by artists of the Crown, then without official commissions.

The advent of the Duc d'Orléans to regency gave Oppenord, then forty-three years of age, his supreme opportunity. Already at the death of his father Jean Oppenord, April 16, 1715—some months before the death of Louis XIV—we find Gilles-Marie Oppenord mentioned as "premier architecte du duc d'Orléans."[5] How long he had previously held this post we do not know, although Brice would presumably have mentioned it had Oppenord received the appointment by the time of his edition of 1713, as he does in those of 1717

---

[3] *Characteristics of Men, Manners, Opinions, Times,* 1711, cited from the 1790 edition, III, 5; I, 179.

[4] La Bruyère had used *créer* in this sense, though far less deeply than Shaftesbury, in his discourse on Boileau at the Academy in 1693. Leonardo, Lomazzo and Dürer, among others, had anticipated the conception of man as a second maker, God-like. Cf. Panofsky, *op. cit.*

[5] Burial certificate cited by G. Huard in L. Dimier: *Les Peintres français du XVIIIᵉ siècle,* I, 1928, 316. *Les Curiositez de Paris,* 1719 ed., I, 146, also speak of him as "premier Architecte de S. A. R."

Evolution

(Table of volume I), and of 1725 (I, 240). The surviving lists of household officers of the Ducs d'Orléans[6] include none between 1709, when he does not appear, and 1724, after the death of the Regent, when among the officers of his son, Oppenord is carried as "Surintendant et contrôleur des bâtiments et jardins," with a salary of 3000 livres. Among his younger contemporaries, Jacques-François Blondel called him "Premier Architecte de S. A. R. Monseigneur le Duc d'Orléans;[7] Huquier, in engraving his portrait and the title-page of his works called him "Directeur des Bâtiments et Jardins de son Altesse Royale."[8]

The other vital creative force in design under the Regency was Vassé, whom we have seen emerging toward independence in the last days of Louis XIV. He now, with the death of Pierre Lepautre in 1716, became the chief reliance of Robert de Cotte in decorative design, responsible for all that is of creative significance in De Cotte's later works, as Lepautre had been in the previous period.

The chief scene of the artistic activity of Oppenord under the Regency was the seat of the Regency itself, the Palais-Royal. Unchanged externally, it was transformed internally by the Regent, who employed Oppenord for a series of remodellings beginning shortly after his advent to power. Every vestige of Oppenord's work there has long been swept away, most of it even before the Revolution, but documents and descriptions enable us, in part, to reconstruct it.[9]

Among the first decorations, executed May to November, 1716, were those in the apartment of the Duchesse d'Orléans on the ground floor along the Jardin des Princes, ending with "une petite galerie du dessin & direction du sieur Oppenord."[10] For the treatment of this, alas, no evidence survives.

By the end of November, 1716, the Regent was occupying his new apartment in the Aile Gauche. The Cabinet des Poussins, with its rounded corners, we know only from plans of the palace. For the Chambre à Coucher we have a manuscript design by Oppenord (Figure 119), doubtless from this year, since it shows the room before an enlargement which was itself made by 1719. In this early form of the room there was little to mark any artistic change; the doors and the panels over them are rectangular and wholly unornamented, the walls being hung with crimson damask as a background for easel paintings from the superb collection of the prince. It is only in the treatment of the cornice that we note any innovation. Although the windows allow ample height for a full entablature, and although the presence of columns would hitherto have been thought to require it, there is now only an extremely low hollow, serving alike for architrave, frieze, cornice, and cove. The effort, from 1700 onwards, to secure maximum height of the wall proper, the abandonment of a full entabla-

[6] J.-J. Guiffrey: "Liste des peintres, sculpteurs, architectes, graveurs et autres artistes de la maison du Roi, de la Reine, ou des princes du sang . . . ," in *Nouvelles archives de l'art français*, 1872, 96.

[7] *Architecture françoise*, II, 1752 (plan of Saint Sulpice as reproduced by Blomfield II, pl. CXLVII).

[8] *Oeuvres de Gilles Marie Oppenord* . . . known as the *Grand Oppenord*. Though itself undated, it is datable by its dedication to Le Normant de Tournehem as Directeur général des Bâtiments (1745-1751) and by its quotation of Saint-Yves' *Observations sur les arts*, 1748, as between 1748 and 1751. The *Moyen Oppenord*, in which Huquier engraved other motifs of detail, followed, and the *Petit Oppenord*, with Italian sketches, preceded the *Grand Oppenord*, as its *Avis* states.

[9] Kimball: "Oppenord au Palais-Royal," in *Gazette des beaux-arts*, VIe pér., XV, 1936, 113-117, where the documents for the chronology are cited at length.

[10] *Curiositez de Paris*, 1719, I, 150-151.

ture, the fusing of cornice and cove, were here adopted even though this cornice must span the void between columns—a license which Oppenord was apparently the first to permit himself.

On quite another plane of magnificence was Oppenord's new termination of Mansart's gallery of 1692. This had meanwhile been decorated by Antoine Coypel in 1694-1705 with paintings of the story of Aeneas.[11] The ceiling was in compartments on a scheme not essentially different from schemes of Le Brun, united by cartouche borders of rollwork. The wall panels, with semicircular heads had spandrels haltingly derivative of the style of Lepautre. They were divided by pilasters, the entrance door was flanked by columns, all with rich gilding. Oppenord now designed an oval hemicycle at the end, completed by 1717. Its motif of a great central chimney piece and side bays framed by Corinthian pilasters (Figure 120)[12] may well have been inspired by Lepautre's treatment of the end of the Salon d'Hercule, the latest novelty of the end of the last reign, still unfinished. The use of pilasters, there resumed on account of the monumental character of the work, is in harmony with the bolder plasticity of Oppenord's tendencies. The mantel proper, with an oval arch like that of the Salon d'Hercule, is buttressed by great consoles. At each end groups of cherubs hold fronds of palm with a multitude of candelabra which, unlike those of Berain, branch irregularly though balancing each other. Above the immense mirror, filling the whole space between the pilasters, and breaking into the zone of the entablature, Victories flanking a great baroque cartouche with crown of shell draw aside a curtain with heavy baroque folds, as first by Borromini in 1660 in the Capella Spada at San Girolamo della Carità, and again in 1665 in the Sala Ducale of the Vatican. In the side bays, instead of the arched doors of the Salon d'Hercule, are pyramids in relief with rich military trophies and flying cherubs—"ornemens ... entièrement dorez, qui sont d'un grand effet." "Toutes les parties," Brice adds in describing the work with great admiration, "sont d'un profil nouveau et fort ingenieusement inventé."[13]

Parallel to the Grand Appartement of Mansart, Oppenord constructed for the Regent in 1717[14] two cabinets of novel form to receive some of the paintings of his collection. Both derived their light from elevated sources. For one, the plans[15] show shallow curved recesses in the longer walls, the shape of the room approaching a cross. The other, the Cabinet en Lanterne or Salon à l'Italienne, was elongated with an overhanging clerestory or monitor. Several of Oppenord's studies for this room, which presented new problems, were engraved by Huquier and included in his volume the *Grand Oppenord* (Plates CIX-XCI, Figures 121-123). In one of these studies (Plate CIX, at left) the motives are closely related to those of the hemicycle of the gallery—pyramids and trophies at the sides; cherubs, palms, and branching candelabra on the buttressed mantel—though of smaller scale. Over the segmental mirror head here is a heaped-up trophy of arms reminiscent of that of a pedimented

[11] Engraved by Duchange, 1719.

[12] J.-F. Blondel: *Cours d'architécture*, V, 1777, ed. by P. Patte, pl. LV.

[13] 1717 ed., I, 204. The word profiles here does not apply to the sections of the mouldings, as we shall see, but to the general outlines.

[14] Poërson in a letter of March 16, 1777 (*Correspondance des directeurs*, V, 66) speaks of "un cabinet que Monsieur Hoppenor fait orner." The Petits Cabinets are described in the *Curiositez de Paris*, 1719 ed., I, 148-150.

[15] Cabinet des Estampes, Ve 86.

doorway in G. A. de Rossi's Palazzo Altieri, which Oppenord had noted in Rome,[16] though it is also not unlike many French examples. Other studies (CIX, at right; CXI, at left) make use of elliptical arches circumscribing mirror head and door head—the first appearance of a treatment often adopted henceforth.

In this series, the large wall panels have rectangular tops with suspended oval frames, their mouldings still of academic weight and profile, interrupted only by radial crowning motifs of leaf and shell. At the bottom of the large panels on Plate CIX, however, we find a treatment of the carved terminal interlace analogous to that of Lepautre in the panels of the stalls of Notre Dame. The base of the panel is formed by two opposite acanthus scrolls, itself a novelty. At their junction, on the flat field, the usual central palmette is surrounded by a large rim, here of divergent width, scalloped internally and bordered externally with conventional flower-buds. As contrasted with the baroque cartouches, this frame—to become typical of the rococo—was not a plastic entity, which might be lifted entire from the wall, but has the irreality characteristic of arabesque. From the simple and delicate interlace at the top rises a tall light floral finial of acanthus leafage, with some more-naturalistic sprays. In basic motif, developed from that of the narrow panels of Notre Dame, the scheme anticipates the treatment of such panels not merely down to 1730 but even after that date. The historical filiation is unmistakable; the essential nature of the elements, here somewhat crudely juxtaposed, is far more obvious than in later, better assimilated ones.

There are also, to be sure, in these designs, several baroque cartouches of undigested forms still almost purely Italian and Borrominesque, by contrast with those of Lepautre. Thus in the clerestory (Plate XC) we find not merely an oval medallion having a slight cartouche border with wings, like those of some of Lepautre's fire-backs, but massive cartouches of broken outline with rolled leathery borders, some again with wings, almost undistinguishable from examples by Borromini at Saint John Lateran, where Oppenord had sketched.

Neither in these early designs nor in later works of Oppenord are the profiles of the mouldings of novel form. Like Lepautre's, they continue baroque types, but they follow Lepautre's use of these types in being greatly reduced in scale and thus denuded of plastic effect.

Such was Oppenord's work in the early years of the Regency.

Meanwhile Vassé was creating a work of equal programmatic importance, the gallery of the Hôtel de Toulouse. Its design and execution are subsequent to those of the Petits Cabinets and the hemicycle of the Palais-Royal, but prior to those of the Grands Appartements there.

The gallery of the Hôtel de Toulouse is the work among all others during the Regency on which De Cotte's reputation has rested. Here was no provincial or foreign task, to be dispatched according to routine formulae, but one in Paris for a son of Louis XIV. It has had the good fortune to survive when so many other works of the time, particularly those of Oppenord, have disappeared. Brice, describing the changes at the house in his edition of 1717, makes no mention of the gallery. In his edition of 1725 (I, 407) he adds: "En l'année

[16] Berlin sketch book, folio 12 verso, cf. D. de Rossi: *Studio d'archittura civile*, 1702-1711, I, 45.

1718, la gallerie . . . a été magnifiquement décorée, d'un lambris d'un nouveau dessein . . ."[17] Blondel in his *Architecture françoise* (III, 1754, p. 26), speaks of these augmentations, "qui ne furent achevées qu'en 1719." Indeed the *Curiositez de Paris* for that year (I, 168) says that work was then going on. All descriptions agree that, in the words of the caption of Mariette's plate:[18] "Toutes les figures et ornemens de sculpture qui enrichissent les lambris de cette Galerie ont été executés par le Sr. Antoine Fr. Vassé."

The remodelling of the gallery consisted of skillful modification of the existing painted ceiling by new frames of varied outilne, and a complete transformation of the walls, which previously had tall panels of trophies, without any pilasters.[19] The inner end, formerly square, was now rounded like the outer end.

For this remodelling a number of manuscript studies and drawings survive. None of them is by De Cotte, as both technique and handwriting show. We believe them, as we have said, to be from the hand of Vassé, to whom the design as well as the execution is thus due. Two are early studies for the outer end of the gallery with its fireplace and adjoining curved panels, for which not niches but trophies were then intended. Earliest of all, probably, since it shows Ionic pilasters instead of Corinthian, is a detailed study for these trophies (Figure 124).[20] One of the trophies is then sketched more hastily, but unmistakably, in a general design (Figure 125),[21] for which Corinthian pilasters are adopted.

The fundamental scheme of the study for the end of the gallery is the same as that of Oppenord in the gallery of the Palais-Royal, but it is clear that Vassé sought to give it a fresh treatment by different elements and a new character of detail. Again there was a hemicycle of three bays, again there were Corinthian pilasters and an attic, again the entablature was interrupted, again by a coat of arms with winged supporters and a background of drapery (here of flags) about the mirror. Again figures held aloft branching candelabra at the ends of the mantel. The differences, however, are substantial. In the curved panels, instead of Oppenord's massive obelisks, Vassé substituted trophies following the surface. The fireplace shows the most striking transformation. Geometry has wholly vanished. Instead of an ellipse, the arch of the opening has the line of a bow, with a pair of reverse-curved scrolls and a great central mask. The form of the supports with double consoles, frontal and diagonal, is obviously a development of those in Vassé's altar of Notre Dame, which is recalled also by the retreating attic buttressed by opposite scrolls.

The trophies, of the chase and of the sea, are of particular importance through their central cartouches, which are placed vertically but show a novel treatment. In the former the upper border is a pair of volutes with hollows fluted as we have seen in the volutes of Vassé's

[17] The *Curiositez de Paris*, 1719 ed. (the Approbation is dated February 27, 1718), I, 168, speaks of the gallery "dans laquelle . . . on travaille actuellement."

[18] *Architecture françoise*, 448 of the Hautecoeur edition, where pls. 446 and 447 are also devoted to the gallery.

[19] Cf. the section before the changes, in Blondel, *Architecture françoise*, III, 1754, pl. 328 of the Guadet edition.

[20] Drawing formerly in the Hoentschel collection, reproduced by R. Destailleur: *Documents de décoration au XVIIIe siecle*, n.d., pl. 12.

[21] M. Hans Haug, director of the museum at Strasbourg, who kindly communicated a photograph of this drawing to me in 1937, expected to publish it meanwhile with related material, including a larger version from the Sigwalt collection which passed by sale in 1937. In correspondence he seemed disposed to accept my suggestion of Vassé's authorship.

altar of Notre Dame. In the marine trophies the entire border is a mere rim of fluted shell — the first use we know at this period of the motif, which was to become the most characteristic detail of the work of the new reign. While we have noted anticipations of this shell border, long before, in the cartouches of Stefano della Bella, its use here seems to have been independent, suggested by the character of the subject.

In execution (Figures 126-127) the trophies of the curved end walls were abandoned in favour of niches with figures of Diana and Amphitrite, symbolizing land and sea. There are figures similarly placed in one of Oppenord's studies for the Palais-Royal. They here stand on corbels suggestive of Lepautre's for the angels of the choir of Notre Dame. In the chimney piece the reverse curve of the opening was abandoned for an ellipse, broken by a great rugged shell in the center. At either end of the mantel the opposite volutes, reversing those of Vassé's altar of Notre Dame, are now realized not as fluted hollows but as rims of shell. The great mirror, with a segmental head and concave corners, is crowned by an immense scroll, supporting a ship's prow with figures.

The arched doorway (Figure 128), which is equivalent to the chimney piece at the other end, is given a similar crown; its tympanum receives an elaborate development of radiating motifs between opposite scrolls; the main panels of the doors are carved with superb suspended trophies of the chase. The pilasters are continued along the side walls. Whereas in the gallery of the Palais-Royal the geometrical frames of Coypel's mural compositions were left unchanged, those of the Hôtel de Toulouse are given a treatment in harmony with the rest. The frames are richly curved at top and bottom, above a bold cartouche. The *bras de lumière* here, as on the chimney pieces, are unsymmetrical, pairing with their pendants on the other side of the bays.

In the wealth of carved detail Vassé deployed all his virtuosity, with many novel touches. "Tout," says Brice, "que la sculpture et la dorure ont pu imaginer de plus excellent, a été employé." The keystone of the doorway has a border half-shell, half bat's-wing. The bases of the pedestals are scrolled, on the suggestion of those in baroque vaulting. The central rosettes and the finials of the panelled pilasters are elaborated far beyond those of Lepautre's pilasters or any of intervening years, even exceeding those of the panels of Notre Dame. The *mosaïque* above the doorway and in the lower panels of the doors is given radiating lines as by Pierre Lepautre at the Hôtel de Lauzun. Numerous cartouches—below the wall panels and niches, over the door, and above the cornice—are given a large importance and development.

Of the ceiling two drawings are preserved at the Cabinet des Estampes:[22] one, in pencil outline only, shows its state before the remodelling; the other, in coloured wash, is for a skillful modification of the old rectangular outlines of the pre-existing paintings.

As compared with Lepautre's work, Vassé's gives a very substantial weight to the major frames, as well as to the cartouches, the fields of which are not flat but modelled. We appreciate that the designer was a sculptor, who thus—for a different reason than Oppenord, but with a similar result—reintroduced a more plastic character, and so participated in the transition after the fact.

---

[22] Va 232ᵉ, one with the number 1584. I cannot be certain of the authorship of these drawings, which are now inaccessible for reproduction.

The Creation of the Rococo

It is doubtless in 1719 that we should date certain engraved projects of Oppenord, unexecuted, for stables for the Palais-Royal.[23] The façade (Plate LXXXXVI) does not depart fundamentally from the familiar academic scheme of a two-story order over a high basement, any innovations being merely ones of detail. The section (Plate LXXXXVII, Figure 129), shows a Salon à l'Italienne, of which the attic appears in the following plate (Figure 130). In all these plates we find employment of the motif of a rim of shell: lobes of irregular outline in the border of the shield of arms of the façade; a continuous edge in the upper picture frame of the salon; fragments behind the eagle which crowns the same feature in the attic.

At the Palais-Royal itself Oppenord undertook in April, 1720, a redecoration of the Grand Appartement.[24] It was characteristic that marble was not employed, as it had been at Versailles even in the Salon d'Hercule; wood panelling was adopted throughout these large rooms, even in the Salle des Gardes and the Antichambre. In the *Grand Oppenord*, the designs of Plate CXIII are specifically titled as for this apartment and from their great height those of Plate CXII, also titled as for the Palais-Royal, are doubtless also for this suite. These designs are not only among the latest, but among the most advanced of the works at the Palais-Royal. Indeed it is only here and in the Hôtel d'Assy that Oppenord's forms are first fully integrated.

This advance is particularly notable in the large wall panels. In Plate CXII (Figure 131) to be sure, the panels above the dado are divided into three tiers by round or square panels at half the height, and their outer mouldings are all merely geometrical. But at the top as well as at the bottom these panels have a large development of carved ornaments, of the type we have previously noted at the bottom of panels in the Salon à l'Italienne. In most of them, on the flat surface, there is some linear equivalent of the cartouche, whether composed of scrolls or of floral sprays, with survivals of the palmette and interlace, and some spreading finial or pendant. The palmette is variously realized, with fleur-de-lis, with a mask and shell, or, in one case, with bat's-wing. In the narrow strips at either side of the mirror there are unsymmetrical motifs of leaf and spray, perhaps suggested by irregular *bras de lumière*, but here carved on the woodwork.

The wall panels of Plate CXIII (Figure 132) extend undivided for the full height. The panel outlines themselves, barely circumscribed by any rectangle, are given a curvature at the top as well as at the bottom; the hesitant lack of coordination of the Salon à l'Italienne in this respect is overcome. The profile at these points is formed by leafy scrollwork, in which the reverse curve now dominates over the C-scroll. A shell appears only once as the palmette, but here, characteristically, it tends to lose the former integrity of the basic scallop-shell, is indeed not even the outer, visible rim of one, but merely a radiating rugous mass, without a

---

[23] It was in that year that the Regent abandoned his former stables at the Hôtel de la Roche-Guyon, and purchased, to install new ones, the Hôtel Colbert at the corner of the Rue Neuve-des-Petits-Champs and the Rue Vivienne, where they remained at his death. The buildings were in such bad condition that they required repairs to the extent of 250,000 livres, carried out by the architect Ju. Champier and Sandoz, *op. cit.*, 323-324. Plans of this establishment are preserved at the Archives Nationales, N[III] 501.

[24] Dangeau, on April 8, April 19, and May 3 refers to this work, XVIII, 265, 276, 295. The apartment is described in the *Curiositez de Paris*, 1723 ed., I., 148-150, and in Brice, 1725 ed., I, 240-241.

centre. There is but one cartouche with a plastic, modelled field; elsewhere the linear frame on a flat surface is now constantly employed.

The mirror heads shown as variants on this plate, with their wealth of flowing or intersecting curvature, defy all geometrical definition. The motif of the *tête en espagnolette*, used by Lepautre in his altar pieces, and already adopted by De Cotte in the mirror frames at Bonn, as we shall see, is here given a lighter, more playful, less architectonic form, closer to its use in Berain's arabesque, as a fanciful derivation of the herm. We shall see it likewise at Oppenord's Hôtel d'Assy at the same moment.

The marble chimney pieces of the apartment are full of variety, by no means limited to the scheme with diagonal consoles, already hardening into formula in the hands of minor men. In the one case where there are such consoles they are no longer articulated geometrically, but their sides are united with the face of the mantel in a single curved surface, prophetic of the usual treatment of the future.

At least one of the cornices shown on Plate CXIII is a concave one, surmounted by a coved ceiling. In the concave frieze, which, like some of those at Bercy, is undivided by consoles, is bandwork with certain grotesque figural elements, now becoming characteristic.

The famous Salon d'Angle or Salon d'Oppenord, 1719-1720, was devised to give an axial approach from the Grand Appartment to the Gallery, and involved construction of extreme boldness, overhanging the Rue de Richelieu. This room, the "Lanternon" of contemporary versifiers, had also high side lighting. In a preliminary study which survives (Figure 133), the ends are elliptical, the upper zone is set back as a monitor. Reasons of prudence led in execution to flattening and thinning the ends, eliminating pilasters there, and to carrying the walls up vertically, interrupted only by a projecting balcony (Figures 134-135). Limited as it was by structural considerations, the form of the salon as executed nevertheless embodies a new and exceptional treatment of spatial form, more fluid than anything attempted in France either before or after, escaping from the geometrical lines which governed even the first design.

In the early study the doors are arched as in the Salon d'Hercule and the gallery of the Hôtel de Toulouse. The cornices of both wall and lantern are interrupted by segmental and elliptical arches. Into one of the former rises the great mirror of the chimney piece, no longer confined even to the full height of the order, with its head of broken curvature flanked by plumed *têtes en espagnolette*.

A "Projet de Plafond pour le grand salon du Palais Royal," doubtless an unexecuted one, is given in the *Grand Oppenord*, Plate CXXXIX. Its oval medallion is filled with a great rosette of bat's-wing, like a gored tent canopy, its sectors filled alternately with mosaic and with significant emblems.

Of the decorative treatment of the room as finally executed we have unfortunately no record.

Within the Regency, but without a specific date, may be placed Oppenord's "projet pour la reconstruction du Palais-Royal." Plate CII of the *Grand Oppenord* shows merely a garden pavilion of a single story, with related features. The section of a room in it is nevertheless useful as giving us another interior of the designer at this period. The chimney piece is merely another variant of his types already known to us. More significant is the placing of the arched window in a recess hollowed at the jambs as well as at the head, our earliest example of this treatment which was to become characteristic of the greatest works after 1730. The sash bars of the transom are given, for the first time, a curved outline. On Plate LXXXXIX the same window and the same chimney piece recur at larger scale. In the spandrels here Oppenord adopts the radial *mosaïque* first used at the Hôtel Lauzun about 1710, and uses for the mirror frame the wreathed moulding of Lepautre's panelling. The ceiling, in this room, which has no superstructure, rises with a shallow cove into the roof, the cornice being of conventional, earlier form with a vertical frieze and consoles.

It is hard to say whether Oppenord or Vassé in these decisive works of the Regency is more original or more influential. Certainly Oppenord, with the greater and more varied opportunity, is more fertile in invention, whereas Vassé, more limited by his commissions, is closer to what was to become the accepted canon of French decoration in the future. Both adhere to the established scheme of the French interior as opposed to anything Italian, both adopt essentially the scheme of Lepautre, with a linear surface treatment emphasizing height, and modifying the geometric, tectonic frame by arabesque elements of progressively freer curvature. Both adopt minor asymmetry in balancing opposite units, though only Oppenord admits this into the carving of the woodwork itself.

Meanwhile both artists were responsible for the designs of others decorative works.

While De Cotte, as we shall see, was extensively employed at Bonn by the Elector of Cologne, we read in a letter of December, 1716,[25] that the chimney piece of the Cabinet des Glaces there was from a design by Oppenord. It may well have been at this period that Oppenord made two projects for the Elector of Cologne, of which engravings appear in the *Grand Oppenord*, Plates LXXXXII-LXXXXIV. One is for a grotto or pavilion with a small attached room of geometric, architectonic treatment, the other for a circular salon with a gallery adjoining. They offer few points of interest to us, the only unit lying in the line of current development being the gallery, with arched windows and a spandrel treatment somewhat related to the one we shall see at the Hôtel d'Assy. If it was actually of 1716 it was the first of its type.

The vogue given to Oppenord's creative fancies by the patronage of the Regent, at once august and fashionable, had brought the artist active employment in Paris.

Jean-Pierre Chaillou, Secrétaire du Roi, added to the Hôtel d'Assy, on land purchased from the Prince de Soubise May 18, 1719,[26] the salon which now serves the Directeur des Archives Nationales (Figure 136). An engraved study by Oppenord (Figure 137)[27] identifies its author and permits us to follow its artistic gestation. Here, as first in Boffrand's salon of the Petit Luxembourg, complete unity is achieved between the four walls, by adopting for all a treatment with arches, all of which, conforming to the window heads, here became alike elliptical in execution. Doorway and overdoor, chimney piece and mirror, are uniformly subsumed beneath these arches. Between them, over the piers, are spreading spandrel panels convex at the base and curved also at the top, where in execution gentle reverse curves

---

[25] Marcel, *Inventaire*, p. 183.

[26] Langlois, *op. cit.*, 270-273, and Kimball: "Oppenord reconnu," in *Gazette des beaux-arts*, VIᵉ pér., XIII, 1935, 43-44.

[27] *Grand Oppenord*, pl. LXIV.

replace the broken convexity first suggested. The door heads, made segmental in execution, support overdoors with scalloped frames of palm, flanked at the base by plumed heads in profile like many of Berain. The mirror head, scrolled and crested, is supported by busts *en espagnolette,* and the relief ornament elsewhere is richly figural. In the engraved design the spandrel figures are enclosed in inner cartouche-like motifs with swelling field,[28] significantly omitted from the executed work where the surface behind the figures is plane and uninterrupted. The large wall panels assume convex lines, reversed and broken, at the base, still circumscribed by subordinate rectangular mouldings. The marble chimney piece, with the diagonal consoles now usual, was first designed with reverse curves in the soffit, but executed merely with a segment. Significantly, the corner panels of the room are rounded; the cove cornice of the ceiling no longed ends in a firm moulding but in a loose border of scrollwork, bent outward around major motifs which occupy the cardinal and diagonal points.

The fine preservation of this delightful room, lacking only its colour and gilding and suitable furnishings, a room which throughout is the creation of Oppenord, enables us here, as nowhere else today, to enjoy the fertile yet disciplined inventiveness of this gifted master.

Of the form of the interiors carried out by Oppenord in 1720-1721 for the Chevalier d'Orléans at the Hôtel du Grand Prieur in the Temple,[29] our only record is of several of the simpler rooms shown in the genre paintings by Ollivier executed during their later occupation by the Prince de Conti. One of these, *Le Thé à l'anglaise,* at the Louvre, shows the Salon des Quatre Glaces at the time of a performance by the child Mozart in 1763. The panelling is of extreme simplicity: the mirror heads form a semicircle with but the slightest interruption by scrolls beneath the masks at the top. The only important carved motif is a trophy of musical instruments, in which the circle of a hunting horn, as earlier at Bercy, centralizes the composition. *La Toilette de la Princesse de Conti* gives us a glimpse of an alcove with profile in reverse curves, perhaps the earliest of this sort. *Le souper chez le prince de Conti,* the famous *Souper aux chandelles* of the Musée de Versailles, shows a room of simple panelling painted with arabesques, doubtless the ones by Audran mentioned in his obituary in the *Mercure* for 1735. Above a light full entablature the ceiling has a low cove, itself with a fringe of painted ornament recalled in the central rosette.

To entertain the young King on the way to the Sacre in November, 1722, the Regent made some renovations in his château at Villers-Cotterets, which we may presume were executed by Oppenord, but of these no substantial trace now remains in the building, now degraded to use as an asylum.

No doubt for the Regent was the "Projet d'une Fontaine pour adosser sur le mur de Terrasse de montreton à S. Cloud," Plate LXXXXV of the *Grand Oppenord,* which we need only remark for the marine trophies in the flanking panels.

To the period of the Regency seems also to belong a set of drawings by Oppenord, pre-

[28] Sedlmaier, who knew only the engraving, cites this, *op. cit.,* 77, to stress the relation of the work to baroque Italy, and speaks of the overdoors "deren ganz ungewohnte Freiheit ohne die Errungenen aus dem römischen Barock schlechterdings ganz undenkbar wäre." They are indeed unthinkable without the baroque, just as baroque architecture is unthinkable without the classic, but to stress this is to miss the entire novelty and character of the French work, which — as the evolution of Oppenord's own design from project to execution shows — was essentially anti-baroque, linear and not plastic.

[29] Brice, 1725 ed., II, 74; Dangeau, XVIII, 265, 276, 295; and Buvat, *Journal de la Régence,* II, 256.

served at the National Museum in Stockholm,[30] for the "Salon du Château de La Grange" (Figures 138-140). Its identification is difficult, as there are more than twenty-five châteaux of some importance bearing this name in different parts of France, in none of which, so far as I am able to learn, does any room of this treatment exist today.[31] I offer the surmise that the design may have been intended for the royal palace of La Granja, where an old monastery was acquired by the Spanish Crown in March, 1720, and where the cornerstone of new buildings by the architect Teodoro Ardemans was laid April 1, 1721. Here also all efforts have failed to verify the existence of such a room, the palace having been much injured internally by fire some years ago. We know that René Carlier, an assistant of De Cotte, was active in the design of the park, and that it was to De Cotte, in general, that Philip V and his court turned for advice in France, but the possibility remains that, as at Bonn, Oppenord was also consulted.

To judge the date of Oppenord's drawings we have only the character of the design itself. We would indeed attribute it to a time about 1720. The large oval medallions of the broad panels are derivative from those of the stalls of Notre Dame. The small strips flanking the overdoors, though here given a herm-like form, are related to those of Bercy. The pilasters with their scrolled bases recall the treatment of the pedestals of the gallery at the Hôtel de Toulouse; the light frames in the narrow panels, those of the spandrels in Oppenord's own engraved design for the salon of the Hôtel d'Assy—both from 1719. The curved corners are found also in the Hôtel d'Assy. Nothing in the mantel or the overmantel would conflict with such a date.

Vassé, under De Cotte, was responsible for the sculpture and decoration of the chapel or rather altar of the Virgin in the south transept of Notre Dame, erected at the expense of the Cardinal de Noailles in 1718-1719. Only the figure of the Virgin survives. Certain crude drawings,[32] surely not by Vassé, and the enumeration of features in the old Paris guidebooks give us but an inadequate idea of the artistic form of this composition.

As another work of Vassé[33] at this period[34] we know only the salon of the château of Petitbourg,[35] which had been reconstructed by Lassurance for the Duc d'Antin, and was demol-

---

[30] Nos. 5108-5112. Two other Oppenord drawings for interiors, Nos. 5940, a ceiling ("Chambre de Parade"), and 5184, seem to be of similar date.

[31] In the effort to determine this, I had the advantage of the remarkable and richly illustrated manuscript dockets on the châteaux of France assembled by my friend Ogden Codman of the Château de Grégy (Seine-et-Marne).

[32] Va 254c. Cf. Marcel: *Inventaire*, 46.

[33] Named in his obituary in the *Mercure*, March, 1736, 532.

[34] We are unable to date the work with certainty; the style suggests a date around 1720. Louis XIV's first visit to the reconstructed château, September 12, 1707, is described by D'Antin, 62-63, by Saint-Simon, XV, 258-262, by Dangeau, XI, 461, and by Sourches, X, 397, but Vassé's work in the Salon must surely have been subsequent to this. Dangeau on August 30, 1714 (XV, 219-220), describes the King's last visit there "où il à été bien content de tous les changements qu'il y a trouvés. Son appartement est bien commode, bien plus beau, et il est meublé magnifiquement . . . Généralement tout ce qu'on a fait est du meilleur goût du monde." If the salon was among these works, it was the first major domestic interior by Vassé. But although the Court ceased to come to Petitbourg during the minority of Louis XV, we cannot assume that D'Antin ceased to redecorate. We have been unable to examine the album of MS. drawings of 1715, presumably prepared to show the changes of 1714, and sold with the Destailleur library in 1894. The album prepared in 1730, perhaps made to show further changes, and preserved at Vaux-le-Vicomte, gives the room in its final form, substantially as shown in the section of Mariette's *Architecture françoise*, pl. 325 of the Hautecoeur edition.

[35] Always written as one word by the owner, the Duc d'Antin. His memoirs, already cited, also give no clue to the date of the salon.

ished after D'Antin's death in 1736. As we see it in Mariette's section, the room, with Corinthian pilasters, had a chimney piece and mirror much like that of the Hôtel de Toulouse, but simpler, and overdoors of the form now become conventional.

In all his works of the period we see that Oppenord, far from following essentially Italian models, pursued the line established in France by Pierre Lepautre. A familiar process was repeated: a gifted artist, steeped in a foreign style, returned to be drawn into a vital current of events at home, to which, without changing its direction, he gave added force and sweep. In the work of Oppenord, it is the pre-existing French scheme which predominates over the added Italian elements: the French arabesque dissolves and absorbs the baroque features; the heritage of Berain and Lepautre triumphs over the intrusions of Borromini but is left enriched by them.

The character of Oppenord's interior designs under the Regency achieves a new ease, movement, and fluidity, not less consistent than the harmonious accord of Pierre Lepautre. Curvature becomes more pervasive, the arc tends everywhere to be replaced by the flowing line, intersecting and interlacing now with greater complexity. Though there are occasional variations of spatial effect, the typical form still remains cubic, the treatment linear and superficial—again, with one or two exceptions, the most striking innovations are made on the walls of pre-existing rooms, without spatial modification.

In the work of Vassé at this period, as in that of Oppenord, we find plastic, baroque elements such as the cartouche, intruding into the linear treatment of surface. Such greater survival in their work, as compared with that of Pierre Lepautre, of undigested baroque elements, disappearing in the sequel, is typical of a moment of transition after the fact, universal in a process of artistic creation and evolution.

Although other architects and designers had meanwhile not been idle, we shall see that their contributions in this period do not compare in importance with those of Oppenord and of Vassé.

In the Bâtiments du Roi under De Cotte, the existing staff continued to be carried during the Regency,[36] but without any additions. Pierre Lepautre disappeared after 1716; Cauchy no longer received his pension after April 1, 1717. That left, as salaried Architectes, Lassurance at 4000 livres and Boffrand at 1200 livres; as Dessinateurs, Jossenet and Carlier. Not faced, in the King's minority, with any important tasks in the Maisons Royales, De Cotte and the other architects were free to devote themselves elsewhere.

De Cotte, sixty years of age at the beginning of the Regency, was, as Premier Architecte des Bâtiments du Roi, the leading architect of Europe. With new royal undertakings in France suspended, he was overwhelmed with commissions from other quarters, requiring a large force of assistants.

In his later years De Cotte's trusted lieutenant, at least in general concerns, was his son, Jules-Robert de Cotte (1683-1767), who received in 1718 one of the three posts of intendant and ordonnateur in the Bâtiments.[37] The best idea of the activity and relationship of

[36] Manuscript accounts, o¹ 2216-2222.

[37] *Mémoires de Saint-Simon*, ed. Boislisle, XXXV, 166 note. One might hope to derive an idea of Jules-Robert de Cotte's draughtsmanship from the drawings of an independent commission of 1711-1712, the church at Domfront (Orne), preserved at the Cabinet des Estampes Va 146. Their technique, though competent, is a little

father and son, a few years afterwards, we derive from the letters of Balthazar Neumann, who came to Paris in 1723 to consult regarding the designs of Würzburg.[38] He speaks of Robert de Cotte's time as being very precious, "in deme er alzeit beym König ist." Nevertheless Neumann conferred repeatedly both with the father "vndt sein Herr sohn, der so guth als der vater darin ist." He says "dass . . . Mons. de Beaufrand nicht der beste seye sondern Monsieur de Coti vndt sein Herr sohn;" "ich finde Zwar ihne vndt seinen sohn von grosser vernunft;" and "ich habe mit seinen leithen (Leuten) gesprochen, die gar guthe architecti sein vndt die arbeit machen helfen."

Even before the death of Pierre Lepautre in 1716 Robert de Cotte, as we have seen, was employing other draughtsmen. In his account of expenses for the King of Spain we find an item: "Paiement de cinq dessinateurs en 1714: 1800 l."[39] Several different draughtsmen were used even for interiors: by 1714 we have found the drawings of more than one man who imitated both the style and the technique of Lepautre with superficial similarity but without the same freedom and verve.[40]

We shall observe that De Cotte himself and most of his later collaborators offered little in the way of artistic initiative, but mainly repeated as formulae the forms created by Pierre Lepautre and developed by Vassé.

An important early commission of De Cotte under the Regency was the Electoral Palace at Bonn, of which the interiors were undertaken in 1716-1717.[41] Although little remains of these, we have numerous drawings for the chimney pieces. The drawings for the chimney pieces of the "Plan noble," 1716 (Figure 141) show De Cotte's own handwriting and may be inked over his pencil indications. These chimney pieces, "Touttes . . . dans l'epaisseur des murs," are mostly of types already sufficiently conventional. Three of the mirrors shown have semicircular heads with a marked impost. Two of these are flanked by pilasters, either of academic form or panelled with carved rosettes and finials. Another mirror has an oval head supported on rather heavy consoled *têtes en espagnolette*, the earliest of the examples we have encountered. In the Cabinet des Glaces there is a more advanced treatment, with reverse curves, with a garland hanging before the mirror, a feature new to us. Concave C-scrolls softened by leafage cut off the corners of the panels. The indication of ornament is rudimentary: it says little more than the frames were to be carved, the backgrounds, in some cases, to be of *mosaïque*, the shield of arms in the Cabinet de Bavière to be flanked by fronds of palm. The marble mantels show little variety, being mostly flanked with diagonal consoles, as already commonly since 1712. It was perhaps this monotony of De Cotte's designs which led, as we have seen, to the execution of the chimney piece in the Cabinet des Glaces from a design of Oppenord.[42]

arid; the human figure is sufficiently well drawn and rendered, without real facility. But we may presume that these drawings also, for such a minor construction, were the work of assistants in the office.

[38] *Die Briefe Balthazar Neumanns von seiner Pariser Studienreise*, 1723, ed. by K. Lohmeyer, 1911, 15-23.

[39] Marcel: *Inventaire*, 206.

[40] The hands of at least two such imitators are recognizable: one in the designs for the Buen Retiro at Bonn, 1717, and for the Chambre du Régent at Versailles; another, even in Lepautre's lifetime, in the drawings for the vestibule and staircase of the Hôtel de Toulouse, 1714. These are in addition to hands of which the technique is less similar to Lepautre's.

[41] Marcel: *Inventaire*, 182-186.

[42] Letter of Hauberat to De Cotte, December 17, 1716. *Ibid.*, 183.

Evolution

The rooms of the wing at Bonn called the Buen Retiro, commissioned in the autumn of 1717,[43] are shown in a whole series of designs (Figures 142-147) by a draughtsman who imitates Lepautre's technique and also his style. The Antichambre, Chambre du Lit and Petit Cabinet might almost be copied from the old drawings of Lepautre for the Chancellerie of 1703, or, at latest, those for Bercy. The mirror heads include semicircular and segmental forms, as well as broken and reverse curves. The marble mantels show simple segments as well as some wavy scrolls, and plain architraves and pedestal supports as well as some diagonal consoles. There are cove cornices everywhere except in the gallery. The wall panels are of types current about 1712. Evidently the style of that moment was quite good enough, five years later, to offer foreign princes. Indeed a much earlier fashion is represented by De Cotte's suggestion, accepted by the Elector and adopted in the Grand Cabinet, for a "cabinet tout en glaces." Its design follows the scheme of French examples from the period of Lassurance, with consoles against the glass, but now embraced within arcades on pilasters, arches and pilasters being of the types of Lepautre's mirrors. Similar arcades, which we meet in these Bonn designs for the first time, appear in the Chambre du Lit pour les Bains, which was to have the more modern and fashionable treatment of lacquer panels with Chinese subjects. Motifs half-sphinx, half-dragon support the oval panels of the overdoors. In the gallery we meet for the first time, so far as there is surviving evidence, painted overdoors with the general outline of a cartouche, the winged frames being realized with segments concave, convex and reversed. With this exception—perhaps really dependent, like all the rest, on earlier examples elsewhere—the atelier of De Cotte appears in such secondary designs as an industrial manufactory, rather than a hearth of creative fire.

The gallery of the Hôtel de Toulouse was not entirely isolated in De Cotte's work at this time; there was a somewhat similar treatment at the Hôtel de Conti in the Rue de Bourbon, no longer standing. This was begun in 1716, was still under construction in 1717, and is mentioned as if completed in 1719,[44] when it was acquired by the Duc du Maine. It is thus substantially contemporary with the work at the Hôtel de Toulouse. Mariette gives a section[45] which shows a simple and somewhat backward treatment in most rooms. The salon of the principal story, however, is richly elaborated with pilasters flanking a very large central mirror. The doors at either side have overdoors framed with scrollwork which includes bold reverse curves. Whether Vassé was used here we are not in a position to say.[46]

Another building in Paris with which De Cotte was concerned is the Hôtel de Bourvallais in the Place Vendôme, now the Ministry of Justice. Bourvallais, "the first tax-gatherer of the kingdom," had bought the site in two parcels in 1706 and 1709, being installed by 1710. Brice said in 1713, "l'appartement de Marie-Suzanne Guithou, son épouse, mérite d'être

[43] *Ibid.*, 186-189. 186-189. The designs were requested October 30 and their receipt was acknowledged December 22.

[44] Brice, 1717 ed., III, 280: *Curiositez de Paris*, 1719 ed. (the Approbation is dated February 27, 1718), II, 490.

[45] Pl. 269 of the Hautecoeur edition. Blondel, in reproducing this, *Architecture françoise*, pl. 279 of the Guadet edition, wrote in 1752: "Le sallon . . . est décore avec quelque richesse, mais son ordonnance n'en mérite pas plus l'éloge, les portes êtant trop petites, la partie du milieu trop grande et les pilastres d'à côté, d'une proportion trop courte et revêtues d'ornemens peu convenables."

[46] The war has precluded a search for drawings at the Cabinet des Estampes which might determine this.

vu par les étrangers," and spoke in 1717 of "les riches meubles et les ajustemens magnifiques," especially in this apartment. Bourvallais was sent to the Bastille in 1716 and the house was acquired in 1717 for the Chancellerie de France. Dagusseau, the Chancellor, fitted up an apartment for himself in the rear,[47] using De Cotte for the remodelling.[48] The character of the surviving salon (Figure 148) points to this period. It is closely related to the work at Bercy, but clearly somewhat later. The overdoors, with unbroken oval frames, are flanked by pilaster strips. The mirror heads have reverse curves, as commonly since the remodelling of the Hôtel Lauzun, with ornaments still much in the style of Lepautre. The main wall panels, with oval central medallions, have large C-scrolls at top and bottom, indicating a date after 1715. The cove cornice, divided from the ceiling by a heavy moulding, curves out to frame corner motifs of winged cartouches, the first instance we know of such a ceiling treatment.

On the return of the Court to Versailles June 15, 1722, the Regent occupied the former apartment of the Dauphin in the ground story, which had been restored for him in that year. The design of a new chimney piece for the Chambre (Figure 149) is preserved in a volume of the De Cotte collection at the Cabinet des Estampes (Ha 18, no. 28). This drawing is identical in technique and indication with the drawings for the Buen Retiro at Bonn; the design is merely another conventional repetition of formulae now familiar, with panelled pilasters, a mirror head with *têtes en espagnolette*. To the Regent, accustomed to Oppenord's fertile invention of ornaments, the work of the Bâtiments must have appeared very banal. He had, however, but a brief time to inhabit the apartment, where he died suddenly on December 2, 1723.

Among private works of De Cotte we may cite one of exceptional importance, considering its location, the decoration of the Château de Saverne in Alsace for the Cardinal de Rohan. Rebuilt after a fire of 1709, it again fell prey to the flames in 1779, but numerous drawings for interiors survive.[49] The earlier of these, of the period soon after 1709, are of the most conventional and conservative character. Some twenty others relate to the Appartement de Parade, with documentary dates of 1721 and 1722. These include detailed designs for the carved panelling, which show how little discretion was left to the executants. Certain large wall panels have moulded crowns of reverse curves with a rich palmette; other panels frame elaborate trophies of arms recalling those of the doors of the Hôtel de Toulouse, but without equal fire and variety (Figure 150). We reproduce also a design for a ceiling rosette (Figure 151), representing approximately the same phase of design found at the Hôtel de Bourvallais and at Chantilly. I am unable to identify the technique and handwriting of these drawings; the technique, however, is a freer, more competent one than that of any minor hack.

The measure of De Cotte's own very moderate power of invention in ornament appears in his drawings for the house he built for himself on the Quai d'Orsay in the years 1721 and

[47] Dangeau, September 8, 1717, XVI, 159.

[48] Plans, marked "Chancellerie," and thus for 1717 or later, with designs including the new Chambre à Coucher, are preserved in the De Cotte papers, Va 422 and 234.

[49] Cabinet des Estampes, De Cotte collection, nos. 1224-1257; and Bibliothèque de l'Institut, both discussed by J. Duportal in *Bulletin de l'art ancien et moderne*, August 10, 1921, 126-128. Some correspondence of De Cotte regarding work of 1727-1730 is published by Marcel, *Inventaire*, 148 ff.

1722[50]—the latter date appearing on one of the interior details. Numerous hasty sketches for the chimney pieces (e.g. Figures 152-153) are preserved at the Cabinet des Estampes (Va 270a). That they are from De Cotte's own hand is evidenced by the scrawled notes "ma garderobe," "mon antichambre," etc. The marble mantels are of the variety of simple Régence types then long familiar. The mirror heads, sometimes semicircular or segmental, are mostly of paired reverse curves, with the mouldings little broken or elaborated. A few have oval frames above for pictures; one or two suggest conventional carved trophies in that position. There is nothing in the forms beyond what had long become common property.

Boffrand continued active in Paris and in Lorraine, where he had been named Premier Architecte of Duke Léopold in 1711, and his advice, like De Cotte's, continued to be sought abroad.[51] Many of his works in this period, as in the preceding one, are lost to us, but we are fortunate in having remains of the decorations of two of his Paris houses from this time.

Claims for Boffrand of priority in work of Régence character have rested on certain decorations at the Hôtel de Villars, in the belief that they were executed as early as 1713.[52] Following his purchase in 1710 of the old Hôtel de Navailles, the Duc de Villars, as Brice wrote in his edition of 1713,[53] "y a fait faire une nouvelle porte en 1712 sur les dessins de Bofrand." The plan of Paris by Jean de la Caille, 1714, however, still shows the building unchanged in extent, without the wing added on the west which survives at 118, Rue de Grenelle under the name of the Petit Hôtel de Villars, and which contains the decorations under discussion.[54] Brice in his edition of 1717 indicates that further work followed Villars' great victory of Denain, 1713, and the peace of 1714. He now mentions not only the gateway but "quelques adjustemens sur les desseins de Boffrand, qui l'ont considérablement embelli. Les dehors ont été réparez & les dedans accomodez à la mode."[55] We may infer that the wing now constituting the Petit Hôtel was part of the work described in 1717, and that the surviving decorations are the work of Boffrand at that period.

We see them today as restored in 1924 by the architect Perrin; it is by no means easy to be sure how much is old, how much new or newly embellished. Antique would seem to be at least the oval panels with their paintings, the arched doorways with their scrolled over-

---

[50] Brice, 1725 ed., IV, 146-147. Cf. C. Ponsonaille: "La maison de Robert de Cotte," in *Réunion des Sociétés des beaux-arts des Départements*, XXV, 1901, 508-516.

[51] Notably by the Prince-bishop of Würzburg, through Balthazar Neumann. Neumann's published letters of 1723 from Paris, already cited, show that he consulted not only De Cotte but Boffrand, "mit welchen ich pflege freyer umzugehen" (p. 44). Boffrand at this period had evidently several draughtsmen, as Neumann speaks of drawings, which "ich . . . von seinen leithen copiren lassen." Among them we may presume his two sons, whom Dargenville states applied themselves to architecture, dying young, in 1732 and 1745. Boffrand was to send his revisions to Würzburg, and in his published works he includes designs "sur lequel projet le Prince me proposa d'aller en 1724, sur les lieux," as he did. Cf. W. Boll: "Balthasar Neumann und die Vorgeschichte des Würzburger Residenzbanes," in *Frankenland*, VIII, 1921, 23 ff; R. Sedelmaier and R. Pfister: *Die Fürstbischöfliche Residenz zu Würzburg*, 1923, 33-35. The engraved section shows the monumental stairs and Salle des Gardes, with motifs not unlike those of the Petit Luxembourg. These are not greatly to our purpose.

[52] J. Vacquier: *Les vieux hôtels de Paris*, XVI, citing only the 1713 edition of Brice, gives the date of the surviving work merely as "après 1713." This year has since been taken by various writers, notably M.-J. Ballot in *Le décor interieur au XVIIIe siècle*, as the date of these decorations which have thus been cited as the earliest of all works in the Régence style.

[53] III, 123-124. The Approbation is dated June 1, 1712.

[54] This wing appears on the next important plan of Paris, that of De la Grive, in 1728.

[55] III, 156. The wording of the 1725 edition remains unchanged.

doors (Figure 154) and the magnificent wall panels with trophies of arms (Figures 155). As we shall see also at Boffrand's Hôtel de Parabère, an impost survives, though it is turned upward to form the crown of the large panels, giving, with the arches, such a pervasive undulation as at La Malgrange. There is a boldness of swing in the enlarged scrolls of the crossettes of the minor panels, a new freedom in the stems with twisted vines which, as first in Lepautre's work at Trianon, form the inner bands of the great panels.

Decorations of Boffrand, slightly later but closely related to those of the Hôtel de Villars, are some of 1718-1720 from the Hôtel de Parabère, 22, Place Vendôme, now installed in modified form in the apartment of M. le baron Fould-Springer (Figure 156).[56] Champeaux described the small salon before its removal;[57] it then was of very different form. He states that it had one window, two bays on each side (one with a door), curved panels with carved dragons and arabesques leading in to a chimney piece at the inner end, and a painted balustrade above the cornice. Although Champeaux speaks of the painted upper panels as "oblongs . . . entourés de bordures à coquilles," we do not doubt they are the same as the rounded ones surviving, beneath arches, which, as at the Hôtel de Villars, rise from an impost. Again we have the vertical mosaic strips, again the sphinxes. Again the scrolled crossettes are very bold; here indeed the upper lines of the spandrel panels are swung in reverse curves. Most notable and freshest is the elaboration of the large wall panels, the whole base of which is filled with carving: a small basket of fruit on a light fanciful stand, surrounded by scrollwork very loosely joined, and twined with the most delicate tendrils.

The dazzling virtuosity of execution in these works, which makes us so much regret we do not know the names of the carvers, and even the unquestionable power and beauty of the designs, which freely develop prevailing formulae without really basic innovation, do not suffice to establish for Boffrand a position in the first rank among the creators, coordinate with Oppenord or Vassé, to say nothing of Pierre Lepautre, the pioneer of the previous generation.

Lassurance continued to have much private employment; Blondel describes him as "celui qui a le plus bâti à Paris." The original interiors of his Hôtel de Monbason, built in 1719, we know only by the section of Mariette,[58] which shows nothing novel for its date. The three important works under construction at the time of his death in 1724 were still unfinished and of their interiors he was responsible only for the vestibule of the Palais Bourbon,[59] which shows nothing of any great novelty. We may remark only the small horizontal frieze above the door casing, serving as a base for the overdoor—a feature henceforth often adopted. The interiors of the Hôtel de Roquelaure (1722 ff.) were executed under Leroux; all others of the Palais Bourbon (1722 ff.) and of the Hôtel de Lassay, under Gabriel and Aubert. Only a

---

[56] In the earlier literature there has been much confusion regarding the hôtels of the Place Vendôme associated with Boffrand and with Madame de Parabère, mistress of the Regent, who had already been given a house there by 1717 (Dangeau, April 17, XVIII, 66). Boffrand built and sold No. 24 as we have seen. Madame de Parabère lived at No. 20 (from 1718, succeeded by her daughter 1735), and at No. 22 (1720-1732). For these two latter the old guides are silent on Boffrand. J. Vacquier in *Vieux hôtels*, IX, 26, which illustrated the decorations, states that the lot at No. 22 was sold May 10, 1718, for 28,500 livres to Boffrand, who built and sold for 153,000 livres in 1720 to Madame de Parabère.

[57] *L'art décoratif dans le vieux Paris*, 1898, 287.

[58] Pl. 68 in the Hautecoeur edition.

[59] *Ibid.*, pl. 475, "du dessin de M. Lassurance."

grotesque error has associated the name of Lassurance I with the Élysée.[60] There is nothing to suggest that he played any part in the evolution after his own important early contributions before 1699.

Jacques Gabriel, no longer able to lean on Lepautre and not yet able to lean on his son, Ange-Jacques, born in 1698, took, as we shall see, a new collaborator, Jean Aubert (d. 1741). In the service of the Bâtiments as a Dessinateur from 1703 to 1708, Aubert was admitted to the second class of the Academy in 1720. Already employed by the Duc de Bourbon at Saint-Maur in 1709-1710, he became in his own right the favorite architect of the house of Condé, responsible for many fine interiors but not a leader of the first rank.

Aubert's work during the Regency may be seen at Chantilly.[61] The rebuilding of the Grand Château was begun in December, 1718, and the apartments there were sufficiently advanced by November 4, 1722, to receive the King and Court on their return from the Sacre. The Regent was lodged in the Petit Château, in "l'appartement nouvellement restauré qui est un des plus beau à Chantilly."[62] The harmony and splendour of the familiar rooms there, which survive with little modification, have distracted attention from their conventionality as compared with prior works of others who had created the style.

The ceilings call for more remark. All the rooms have coves above full entablatures (even where there is no order), entablatures in which the frieze is also hollow: that is to say they are "transitional" in treatment. In addition to the light scrollwork in the frieze — now adopted universally, though handled here, especially in the gallery, with great freedom and beauty — gilded ornaments in relief rise into the upper cove. In the Chambre de M. le Prince and in the Salon de Musique (Figures 157-158), large motifs, developed from the scheme of the terminal interlaces of the panels, rise at the cardinal and diagonal points. In the gallery, beside such motifs at these points, there is a continuous fringe of delicate scrollwork, punctuated at each bay.

One might suppose that Armand-Claude Mollet (1660-1742), enobled in 1722, should be numbered among the important artists of the Regency, since he was architect of the Hôtel d'Évreux (Palais de l'Élysée). It was built for a favorite companion of the Regent, who graced its formal occupation on December 14, 1720. The interior of the house as Mollet left it, however, contained very little of the woodwork we see today. Three of the original rooms, "du dessin de M. Mollet," are engraved in Mariette's *Architecture françoise* (Figures 159-161).[63] Of these only the Chambre de Parade retains today any of the material shown,

[60] In speaking of the modifications under way there for Madame de Pompadour by Lassurance (II), d. 1755, Blondel in his *Architecture françoise*, III, 1754, says "Voir ce que nous avons dit de cet architecte dans le premier volume, p. 235a," but what we find there is a notice of Lassurance I, who died in 1724.

[61] Aubert's connection with the decorations there is not established by documents, but rests on his relation to the Duc de Bourbon, exemplified at just this moment (as in other instances) by his responsibility for the design of the stables at Chantilly. Cf. H. Lemonnier in *Bulletin de l'art ancient et moderne*, September 25, 1920, 165-168. Cf. also G. Macon: *Les arts dans la maison de Condé*, 1903.

[62] Relation de Faure, quoted with other documents by E. de Ganay: *Chantilly*, 1925, 22-26. He cites a memoir of 1725 in the accounts of Chantilly "pour la fourniture des plaques de cheminée 'posées partout,' " which seems to indicate the entire completion of the work in the château by that year.

[63] Pls. 488-491 of the Hautecoeur edition. In two of these the engraver has filled in paintings by Watteau, not owned by the Comte d'Évreux. Those of the Chambre de Parade, *La finette* and *Les charmes de la vie*, establish a *terminus post quem* for the plates, since engravings of these subjects were not available before July and

and this room has been much modified, with new overdoors, new mirror heads, and additional decoration in the cornice. Initially there were tapestries toward the alcove, oval paintings above the doors and mirrors, in outer borders of somewhat freer outline than commonly hitherto, in the reverse curves at top and bottom not circumscribed by any rectangular panel. The only surviving features of importance are the broad panels toward the windows, now duplicated on the other side of the mirrors. Even they have been modified by addition of large center ornaments, and by substitution, toward the base, of crossed cornucopias and birds for the original baskets there. The Seconde Antichambre shown by Mariette (apparently the future Salle des Aides de Camp) has been greatly modified and the Antichambre or Salle de Bal entirely destroyed. The former was of simple character, by then entirely conventional; the latter, with arched doorways was distinguished only by the double inner border of scrollwork in its large rectangular panels. Clearly Mollet, in spite of his inherited prominence as an official, was too old to participate deeply in a new decorative movement, and had nothing really personal to offer for the design of interiors.

The same was true of Jean Courtonne (1671-1739), who built the Hôtel de Noirmoutiers in 1722.[64] In a contract of just that time he is described as "maître maçon, entrepreneur des bâtiments,"[65] though in 1728 he was admitted to the second class of the Academy. Champeaux[66] and other writers, without citing documents, state that after the house was acquired by Mademoiselle de Sens (1735) it was decorated by Lassurance, but I have been unable to confirm this. The house, in recent years used by the État-Major Général, formerly contained some admirable panelling, in large part removed. One fine room survives, characteristic in style of about 1730, and remarkable only for having, somewhat exceptionally, reverse curves without circumscribing rectangles in the main door panels, as well as in the wall panels and overdoors. Courtonne also designed the Hôtel de Matignon, contracting with the Prince de Tingry in 1722 for its erection, but he was superseded there in 1724, as we shall see. Courtonne was very assiduous at the Academy, being elected Professor in 1730, but nothing in the proceedings suggests that he was a force in the field of decoration.

Among the artists who accompanied Le Blond to Russia in 1716 the most gifted was certainly the sculptor Nicolas Pineau (1684-1754), whose work there we shall now examine.[67]

He was the son of the carver Jean-Baptiste Pineau, who appears in the royal accounts from 1680 at Versailles and elsewhere, but who died in 1694 when his son was only ten years old. We have no documents on the son's work prior to 1716, when, at thirty-two, he went to Russia along with the architect Alexandre Le Blond and others. Emile Biais,[68] writ-

August, 1729, when they were announced in the *Mercure*. Dacier and Vuaflart, *op. cit.*, I, 134-135, are in error, as we shall show, in thinking the plates must be prior to 1727.

[64] Brice, III, 426. Both Courtonne's own *Traité de Perspective*, 1725, and the *Architecture moderne*, published by Jombert in 1728, give several plates of the house, *Courtonne, inv.*, but they include no sections.

[65] Documents on the Hôtel de Matignon published by L.-H. Labande in *Gazette des beaux-arts*, Vᵉ pér., XIII, 1935, 257 ff.

[66] *Op. cit.,* 119-121. Lassurance I died in 1724, so it could only have been Lassurance II. Blondel, *Architecture françoise*, I, 235, speaks only of "changemens dans les basse-cours . . . de peu d'importance," and does not mention Lassurance.

[67] The following account of Pineau's early work first appeared in *Art in America*, XXX, 1942, 233-237.

[68] *Les Pineau*, 1892. He published many of Pineau's drawings, then in his collection. Many others were reproduced and catalogued by Léon Deshairs: *Nicolas et Dominique Pineau*, n.d. [1911].

ing fifty years ago, supposed Nicolas Pineau to have worked on certain buildings prior to that time: the Hôtel de Villeroy (which he presumed to be the Hôtel de Lesdiguières, inherited by the Duc de Villeroy in 1716), and the Château de Petitbourg. Pineau's work for Villeroy, however, as the drawings show, was in the later remodelling of the Hôtel Desmares, which Villeroy acquired in 1746. I am not aware of any evidence connecting Pineau with Petitbourg, where the salon was carved by Vassé, as we have seen. That Pineau may have worked for Le Blond on the Hôtel Vendôme, as Biais also supposed, was merely an unverified assumption.[69] Clearly he was not yet a figure of importance in France during the last years of Louis XIV.

By Pineau's Russian contract he undertook to make "doors, chimney pieces, frames, table frames and other ornaments and designs"[70] and at first was concerned mainly with carving. The death of Le Blond in 1719, however, left Pineau the leading French decorative artist at the court of the Czar, called on even for certain architectural designs, as well as for a great variety of decorations, on which the documents have been assembled by Serge Roche. His contract expired in 1726, but, although he had already sought to be released, he was persuaded to remain a little longer. Our last specific mention of him in Russia was in March 27, 1727, though it would appear from certain designs that he was still there at the time of the death of Catherine I on May 16 of that year.[71]

Among Pineau's first works in Russia must have been the design for a surtout de table with the symbol of the Empress Catherine I. There is little here that might not have been inspired by the work of Berain, whose influence appears also in the designs of tombs for Romane Bruce (d. 1720) and for Peter himself (d. 1725).

His chief surviving work in Russia is the carving of the Cabinet of Peter the Great in the Grand Palais at Peterhof (Figures 162 and 164).[72] It was shown by the Czar on August 1, 1721, to Bergholz who speaks of it as "made by one of his French sculptors."[73]

The room, unlike many works executed by French artists abroad, is purely French in character, with the characteristic scheme of large central mirrors flanked by carved panels and double doors. That the general design of the panelling was due to Le Blond may be established by comparison with plates of his edition of Daviler's *Cours d'Architecture*, 1710. We reproduce one (Figure 163) of a pier glass, which embodies the same scheme of a segmental head with concave corners, a small cornice and carved crossettes. In certain features, like the reverse curve at the base of the mirror, the room is more advanced in style than the engraving, but there is nothing which was not already familiar in France by 1716.

The glory of the Cabinet is its carvings, of which we are happy to reproduce several unpublished details (Figures 166-169).[74] For these carvings there survive a number of manu-

---

[69] B. Lossky gives no support to such a view in his works on Le Blond, already cited.

[70] Imperial Archaeological Cabinet of Peter the Great, 89, 1.651, cited by Serge Roche: "Les dessins de Nicolas Pineau pour la Russie," *Staryé Gôdy*, May, 1913, 3-21, translated from the Russian for me by Arthur Berthold. The references to works in Russian have kindly been supplemented for me by Mrs. K. N. Rosen.

[71] *Staryé Gôdy*, 1907, 602, cited by Roche, *op. cit.*

[72] *Les Trésors d'art en Russie*, II, 1902, pls. 83, 84. The Cabinet de Travail at Marly in the Peterhof group is illustrated on pl. 92.

[73] *Diary*, I, 131-135. I. Grabar: *Histoire de l'art russe*, 1910-1915, III, 132-134, supposes that the carvings were executed about 1717-1719.

[74] Supplied by courtesy of I. Baltzutevitch of the Department of Parks and Palaces, U.S.S.R.

script drawings by Pineau (Figure 165),[75] which show that he was entirely responsible for their design.

Four of the major panels have superb military trophies. With dazzling brilliance of execution, and with the novelty of including Russian helmets and weapons, they do not differ in essence from French examples like those of the stalls of Orléans, 1703-1705, and of the Chapel of Versailles, 1708-1710, of which they continue the tradition. As in all these—and indeed in the bronze trophies of Ladoireau for the Salon de la Guerre at Versailles, begun in 1682 but not completed and placed until 1701—they include sharply inclined shields and other elements unsymmetrically grouped, with a freedom permitted in such representative sculpture long before it was adopted in purely ornamental elements.

Other wall panels have symmetrical central cartouches with medallions or cyphers and with attributes of the arts and sciences. The shutters and door panels are of arabesque elements, including herms, and show certain suggestions from the stalls of Notre Dame executed in 1710-1712. Extreme elaboration is everywhere given to the double bordering beads, which are foliated and enriched beyond any seen in France at this time.

It is the overdoors which offer the greatest interest. Here the dragons which flank the central tripods do not face and balance one another, but are turned in the same direction with a novel and decided asymmetry. It is, however, but a slight instance on which to base any general claims for priority of Pineau in this regard.

In none of his other works in Russia do we find any similar liberty. Roche, carried away by his subject, dates before 1727 the designs for chimney pieces for Levenvolde or Ouchacoff (Ushakov) in which the central ornaments are decidedly unbalanced. We must agree with his earlier view, cited by Deshairs in the description of his figures 105 and 106, that these designs were made later in Paris during the reign of the Empress Anne, 1730-1740. Roche also reproduces an unsymmetrical cartouche (no. 46 of Deshairs' list) as "avec le chiffre de Pierre le Grand." Deshairs himself saw in this "le chiffre L. P. (?)." The cypher is indeed not unlike that of Peter, but would pass equally well even for that of the Regent, or many others with a P. The extremely advanced character of the *rocailles* below is unlike anything in Pineau's Russian designs, and closely similar to those of his work in the 'forties.

It is not surprising, in view of his isolation, that Pineau—in spite of his brilliance as a designer and carver—scarcely participated during his absence from Paris in the general creative movement by which French style was meanwhile transformed at the hands of Vassé and Oppenord. It was on his return that, absorbing with genial rapidity the new spirit and the new vocabulary of forms, he was able to take, with Meissonnier, a leading position in the following phase.

Another ornamental sculptor, who has been credited with large initiative under the Regency, was Bernard Toro (1672-1731).[76] We are by no means to assume from this spelling, which he ultimately adopted, from among the numerous early spellings of his name, that he was of Italian origin; his father, Pierre, signed as Teurreau, and his grandparents were

---

[75] At the Musée des Arts-décoratifs in Paris. One is reproduced by Deshairs as his figure 58, two others (nos. 163 and 164 of his list of unpublished drawings) are reproduced by Roche. The one illustrated here is no. 164.

[76] The most recent studies to assemble the material on Toro are the article in *Les Artistes décorateurs de bois* by Vial, Marcel and Girodie, 1922, 166-167, and the chapter by Robert Brun in Dimier's *Les Peintres français du XVIIIe siècle*, I, 1928, 350-363. They repeat, however, many early attributions no longer tenable.

French also. Born in Toulon, he worked, like his father, as a carver at the Arsenal, where, after the time of Puget in his boyhood, the dominant influence, by 1687,[77] was from the designs supplied by Berain. In 1706 the archives place him at Avignon, carving in the chapel of the Pénitents Blancs; in 1710 at Aix in relation to a patron, Boyer de Bandol. A new sojourn at Aix extended from 1713 to 1716.

The attribution of executed carvings to Toro, and the building up for him of a legendary fame as one of the chief pioneers of the art of the Regency, was the work of a group of scholars in the 'sixties of the last century.[78] It is only fair to say that, in the absence of specific documents for the authorship of various carvings, and of developed notions of style, they were carried away by local patriotism and piety to their subject. Thus Toro's earliest surviving work has been supposed to be the doors of the Hôtel d'Artalan at Aix, adorning a building assigned the date of 1695-1700—an attribution resting only on the high quality of the carving. Leon Deshairs has rightly pointed out the lack of relation with the style of Toro's engraved plates and the much later character of the work, for which he even suggests a date around 1730. If these doors have anything to do with Toro at all, they are from his later years.[79] So far from showing any priority or initiative, they are late provincial derivatives of the work of Pierre Lepautre—compare the tympanum and its rosette with one at Trianon—into which have crept a few details of a generation later.

A goldsmith of Aix, Honoré Blanc, engraved, with collaborators, presumably before 1716, the first suites of Toro's of *Desseins à plusieurs usages*. It was at this juncture that Toro entered the consciousness of the capital through the issue of these and other plates in Paris, as announced in the *Journal des Savants*, August 10, 1716:

> Le Sr. Dubuisson, architecte du Roy, achève de faire graver et imprimer chez lui les oeuvres de M. Toro, designateur et sculpteur du Roy, pour les ouvrages du port de Toulon. — Ce sont des compositions des plus neuves, des plus variées et du meilleur goût qui aient encore paru: elles représentent des soleils, des ciboires, des calices, des lampes, des candélabres, et autres pièces à l'usage des églises; des trophées, des têtes, des cartouches, des pieds de table, des vases, des cuvettes, des surtouts et d'autres pièces d'orfévrerie et de sculpture; des arabesques et des grotesques de toute espèce . . . Cette grande suite est divisée par livres de six feuilles de chaque espèce . . .

All told, nearly a hundred and fifty plates are known.

Toro himself was in Paris at this period; we have later letters of his mentioning his presence there April 26, 1717, and asserting "j'etois beaucoup chargé d'ouvrages que j'avois enterpris à Paris pour des puissances." A copy of one of his engraved suites has a dedication to De Cotte, but it seems to have gained him little favour. Toro's stay in Paris was brief; he returned to Toulon in the course of 1717, and in 1719 succeeded to the post of master sculptor of the arsenal. His pretensions to work from his own designs were rejected, and the designs were supplied by Vassé as Dessinateur Général de la Marine. We know from documents of the same year that Toro gave the design for the marble high altar of the cathedral

---

[77] Weigert, *op. cit.*, I, 116.

[78] I. Pons: "J. Bernard Toro, sculpteur provençal," in *Archives de l'art français*, VI, 1860; L. Lagrange: "Toro," *Gazette des beaux-arts*, Ire pér., XXV, 1868, 345-352, 477-508, "Catalogue de l'oeuvre de Toro," *ibid.*, IIe pér., I, 1869, 289-296.

[79] *Aix-en-Provence*, n.d., xii-xiii and text to pl. 19.

of Saint-Saveur in Aix, but this was never carried out. From letters and contracts we know of several executed works, unfortunately not preserved. Collectors and biographers have been very free in attributing to Toro carvings at Aix of every quality. They have added, without the smallest justification, the doors at Nos. 118 and 120, Rue du Bac in Paris,[80] but these, from their style, are certainly of a date prior to his Paris sojourn.

Actually we know the art of Toro only through his drawings and engravings. One of the former preserved at the Cabinet des Estampes, a large cartouche with the arms of the Dauphin, bears this note: "Le cartouche cy a côte a esté commencé par le S. Toro . . . et n'a pus estre fini par luy, ayant été attaqué d'apoplexie le 28 janvier 1731 . . . Ce sculpteur travailloit le bois avec une si grande délicatesse que les ouvrages qu'il a faits, en pieds de tables, pendules, et consoles, n'étoient susceptibles a aucune dorure, et même que les vernis qu'on pouvoit y mettre dessus y faisoit tort; tous ces ouvrages étoient entièrement finis, et il leur donnoit toute la perfection qui pouvoit servir à son génie et à ses doigts."

Drawings and engravings alike show the same character, a verve, a life, a fantasy often touched with the grotesque. Sphinxes and dragons are tormented by birds and satyrs, cherubs play with helmets too big for them, frowning busts are flanked by delicate sprays. Their character derives from his free personality, which his employers found "capricieux et fantasque." For many elements, however, Toro was dependent on Berain and, more distantly, on Le Brun. This was particularly true of the non-figural elements: vases, consoles, pedestals with their fields of *mosaïque*. Most striking of innovations in French ornament were the cartouches unsymmetrically placed (Figure 170): inclined, or seen diagonally if not actually unsymmetrical in design like some by Mitelli in Italy more than two generations before. These remained for the moment without imitators.

The wealth of sculptured ornaments did not end that of painted ones, indeed these were never more in vogue than under the Regency.

Audran was still active, as indeed he remained almost until his death, at seventy-six, in 1735. Among the works mentioned in his obituary, those at the Temple, the Château de la Muette, the Hôtels de Toulouse, d'Antin and de Verrue, may well have been executed under the Regency, while those at the Hôtel Peyrenc de Moras must have been as late as 1730. None of these decorations survives, unless the cabinet with an arabesque ceiling at 8, Rue d'Assas, of a character related to Audran's known work, formed part of the adjoining Hôtel de Verrue, which disappeared in the piercing of the Boulevard Raspail.[81] They do not differ substantially in character from his earlier works, on which they show little development.

We have exceptionally few fixed points to assist us in dating the arabesques of Claude Gillot (1673-1722).[82] A great number of Gillot's drawings for arabesques are preserved,[83]

[80] Best illustrated in the *Vieux hôtels de Paris*, I, pls. 1-2.

[81] Reproduced by P. Gélis-Didot: *La peinture décorative en France*, n.d., pls. 131-135. Gélis-Didot doubts that the two buildings were originally united but considers it probable that they were erected by the same architect and decorated by the same artists.

[82] Cf. E. Dacier "Gillot" in Dimier: *Les Peintres français du XVIIIe siècle*, I, 1928, 157-215.

[83] Many at the Staatliche Kunstbibliothek, Berlin (two reproduced by R. Graul: *Decoration und Mobiliar*, 1905, figs. 7 and 8), a few at the Louvre (nos. 4226-4230 of the published *Inventaire*; four of them reproduced in *Dessins d'ornement du Musee du Louvre*, n.d.), and elsewhere.

derivative from the work of Audran, with which they are very closely related indeed in their spirit, composition, and details. In the great majority—as always in Audran—the figures are classical, Gillot's concern with the theatre being but rarely reflected by adoption of figures from the Italian comedy. Naturalistic sprays of foliage, as well as angular, inclined bands and fret-like interlaces, all found already in Audran, multiply in the arabesques of Gillot.

Of Gillot's arabesques he himself began the engraving of one suite, the *Portières des Dieux*, left unfinished at his death and completed by Cochin in 1737 (Figure 171). Doubt has been expressed whether their vapourous naturalism on which the impression of advanced character rests, was due to this later hand, but the surviving proofs of Gillot's first unfinished state establish that this was by no means the case.[84] The *Livre de principes d'ornemens*, posthumously engraved, is of earlier character, almost devoid of naturalistic features, and with its light, conventional elements very evenly distributed over the background.

Contemporaries thought very highly of the arabesques of Gillot. Huquier in his frontispiece to the *Principes d'Ornemens*, speaks of him as "l'un des plus grands artistes en ce genre et reconnu pour tel par ceux qui en font profession," and Mariette writes that the plates of the *Portières* were "commencés avec tout l'art et l'esprit possible." Nevertheless we cannot feel that, in relation to Audran's, they show any deep originality.

Apparently from Audran or Gillot, more than from Watteau, whom Oppenord knew and admired,[85] came the direct influence reflected in Oppenord's own arabesques of which a number of drawings are preserved in Berlin (Figure 172)[86] and of which several were engraved after his death. They are of quite a different character than those which he had sketched in Italy, and show how fully Oppenord had been caught up in the main current of French decorative art. They do not, however, bring anything vitally personal.

Pineau's arabesques likewise developed under the influence of Audran. Those designed surely during his stay in Russia[87] are reminiscent of the *Mois grotesques*. That he made greater use of the cartouche and other elements of substantial weight was due partly, at least, to their being intended for carving, rather than for painting or tapestry.

By contrast with those of Gillot and Oppenord and Pineau, the arabesques of Watteau (1684-1721) show a fresh personal impulse. He had worked with Gillot, probably from about 1706 to 1707, before going to Audran. Doubtless the questions are insoluble[88] whether Gillot had then already taken up the arabesque of Audran, and whether Watteau himself subsequently influenced the later designs of Gillot. Certain it is that Watteau

[84] Cf. Dacier, *loc. cit.*, 210, and B. Populus, *Gillot*, 1930, where the states are carefully distinguished.

[85] The Goncourts signalize (L'art du XVIIIe siècle, 3d ed. 1880, 41) a portrait with the inscription "Antoine Watteau . . . d'après nature par son ami Gilles-Marie Oppenord," drawn in wash on the back of the title-page of the *Figures de différents caractères*, which however, was not issued until 1726. Doubtless they met through Pierre Crozat, with whom Watteau lodged in 1712 and again after 1714 as Oppenord did after 1730 and for whom Rosalba made a portrait of Oppenord in 1721. Oppenord owned at least two paintings by Watteau. Dacier and Vuaflart: *Jean de Julienne et les graveurs de Watteau*, I, 1929, 45; II, 1922, Nos. 30 and 77. Oppenord himself also owned the engraved *Figures de différents caractères*. Among his sheets of sketches in Berlin are two drawn on plates of the series. One is a group of figures of the *Assemblée galant*, the other is the frontispiece, Boucher's engraved portrait of Watteau, about which Oppenord has drawn an elaborate tabernacle.

[86] Staatliche Kunstbibliothek. Several are reproduced by Jessen: *Das Ornament des Rococo*, 1894.

[87] Deshairs, *op. cit.*, figs. 133, 134 and no. 166, more fully discussed by Roche, *op. cit.*

[88] Thus conclude both Berliner, *op. cit.*, 167-168, and Dacier: "Gillot," *loc. cit.*, 162, 189-190.

The Creation of the Rococo

derived from Gillot his interest in the comedians as subject matter, appearing in the arabesques of both artists along with the classical deities which alone occur in those of Audran. Some of Watteau's arabesques, engraved posthumously from 1735 onward, follow Audran very closely, as in the Venus and Cupid engraved by Caylus (D. and V. no. 207). Others like *Les Singes de Mars* are closer still to Gillot. No doubt these are his earlier compositions, from the formulae of which Watteau must soon have enfranchised himself. This enfranchisement is well in progress in the suite painted for the Hôtel de Chauvelin, including the *Feste Bacchique*,[89] where the tabernacles, the bandwork are still recognizably derivative from Audran, the central scenes are already pure Watteau.

We know the arabesques of Watteau[90] today mainly through engravings made after his death. Some of them (*Watteau pinxit*) were made after arabesques painted by him. Among these were the panels painted for Chauvelin, and the screen of six leaves of the Groult collection. Others (*Watteau invenit*) were after drawings by the master. The question has been raised whether these latter were perhaps merely rapid indications, to which the engravers felt free to add features belonging to a later phase of the movement. Deshairs based his belief that this was the case on the sketches of the Groult collection, the only drawings for arabesques he felt confident were from the hand of the master himself. With these the engraver has indeed taken certain liberties. Thus Deshairs was led to suppose, very plausibly, that it was the engraver, Huquier, who added below *La Voltigeuse* or *La Danse bachique* opulent *rocailles* as yet unknown in the time of Watteau, more in the style of Meissonier and of Lajoue.

In the genial hands of Watteau the central feature of the arabesque became fully naturalistic. The conventional figures of the gods gave way to personages of the Italian comedy, and to groups which are wholly Watteau's own, the *Pastorales* and *Fêtes galantes,* bowered in foliage. Naturalism invaded also the surrounding elements in varying degree. Such plates as *Le Berceau* or *Le Duo champêtre* are merely scenes of figures in landscape within an outer frame of arabesque or cartouche elements, reduced to the greatest attenuation and wreathed or branching with leafy sprays (Figure 173). Usually, however, there are vestiges, at least, of an inner tabernacle or medallion for the figures, perhaps itself dissolved into feathery trees, and arabesque elements unite the real and the unreal of central field and outer border. Sedlmaier has rightly emphasized[91] the essential flatness of the whole surface, in spite of all "plastic" or "spatial" motives, of all perspective play. The last echoes of baroque massiveness disappear in evanescent incorporeality.

The part of China in the development of the rococo has often been considered a large one.[92] We are led to the opinion that genetically Chinese influence was a minor and secondary

[89] These compositions, says Mariette, *Abecedario* VI, 107, were painted on the panels of the cabinet of M. Chauvelin, Gardes des Sceaux. The house no. 43, Rue de Richelieu was occupied by Chauvelin from 1695 to 1719.

[90] E. Rahir: *Antoine Watteau peintre d'arabesques*, n.d. [1920]; Fourcaud: "Antoine Watteau peintre d'arabesques" in *Revue de l'art ancien et moderne*, 1908, II, 1909, I; Deshairs: "Les arabesques de Watteau," in *Mélanges offerts à M. Henri Lemonnier*, 1913, 287-300; Dacier and Vuaflart, *op. cit.*

[91] *Op. cit.*, 69.

[92] H. Havard: *Dictionnaire de l'ameublement*, n.d. [1887-1890] I, article "Chine," especially p. 842. E. Molinier: *Le mobilier au XVIIe et au XVIIIe siècle*, n.d. [1898] 90, 99; Geymüller, *op. cit.*, 268; R. Graul: *Ostasiatische Kunst und ihr Einfluss auf Europa*, 1905; H. Belevitch-Stankevitch: *Le goût Chinois en France au temps de Louix XIV*, 1910, v, 180; H. Cordier: *La Chine en France*, 1910.

factor. At most it may have encouraged the vogue of asymmetry, the impulse to which was already present in European ornament, in the treatment both of the cartouche and of the trophy.

The French were very late, as compared with the Portuguese, Spanish, English and Dutch, in entering the China trade and in taking up Chinese motives of decoration. Chinese porcelains and curios, brought by traders of other nationalities, were collected in France from the time of Mazarin. La Fontaine's description of Versailles in 1668 mentions Chinese stuffs in the Appartement du Roi.[93] The Trianon de Porcelaine of Louis XIV, 1670, first of the garden structures of oriental pretensions, was painted with figures in blue "à la manière des ouvrages qui viennent de la Chine,"[94] but the result was little nearer to China than Delft. The textiles brought by the Siamese ambassadors in 1686, "brodés . . . de fleurs, figures, animaux et autres de la Chine," were used at Trianon-sous-Bois,[95] and doubtless also in the Nouveaux Appartements of the Marquise de Seignelay at Sceaux in that year.[96] The voyage of the *Amphitrite*, begun in 1698, gave a new interest, and even before her return in August of 1700, Chinese motives were adopted in Berain's divertissements in January and February of that year. Some furniture of Meudon at this time was decorated with Chinese grotesques[97] and Martin Lister in 1698 saw lacquer panels in the Appartement de Monsieur at Saint-Cloud.[98]

We have seen Berain introducing certain Chinese figures in his arabesques of just this time. This, however, was merely a change of detail, without influence on the general nature of the pattern which remained symmetrical and otherwise unaffected. The dragon was a European as well as an Oriental monster; it was familiar in Italian ornament and in Ducerceau before it appeared in the engraved plates of Berain and of Toro, as well as in decorations of Boffrand and Oppenord. The asymmetry of Toro's cartouches derives not from anything Chinese, but from such Italian examples as those of Mitelli.

The most notable of the "Chinese" decorations were the painted panels of Watteau engraved as *Figures chinoise et Tartares, destinées au Cabinet du Roy au château de la Meute*, derived doubtless from some imported drawings.[99] The Château de la Muette, sold by Catelan to Fleuriau d'Armenonville in 1707, and by him to the Regent for the Duchesse de Berri in 1716, was acquired in 1719, after her death, for the boy king Louis XV. The descriptions of the château in the mid-eighteenth century fail to mention the panels, and we cannot be sure they were ever put in place. In addition Watteau made the designs for two engraved arabesques with the titles *Empereur Chinois* and *Divinité chinois*. Here the figures are very secondary, in settings which do not differ substantially from those of Watteau's other arabesques.

We have reproduced De Cotte's designs of 1717 for the Chambre du Lit pour les Bains at Bonn, with its lacquer panels. We may cite also a signed study of Oppenord for a Chinese panel of that general period, without any indicated destination.[100] Was it, perhaps, for the

[93] Cited by Nolhac: *Création de Versailles*, 1924, 122.
[94] A. Félibien: *Description sommaire . . . de Versailles*, 1674; cf. Danis, *op. cit.*
[95] H. Belevitch-Stankevitch, *op. cit.*, 113-115.
[96] F. de Câtheu in *Gazette des beaux-arts*, VIe pér., XXI, 1939, 98.
[97] Biver: *Meudon*, 137.
[98] *A journey to Paris in the year 1698*, 1899.
[99] Cf. Belevitch-Stankevitch, *op. cit.*, 248-250.   [100] Berlin. Staatliche Kunstbibliothek, D114, Hdz 2136.

"Cabinet de la Chine rouge" of the Duchesse d'Orléans, of which the porcelains are listed in the inventory[101] made in 1723 after the death of the Regent?

We have seen that, in spite of such examples of Chinese workmanship and of Chinese influence in the details of decoration, there was no instance of asymmetry in the outlines of panelling at this period—indeed there was none before 1730, when it appeared under quite different circumstances.

Aftermath of the Regency

The coronation and official majority of the young King found the new style fully formed and universally adopted. For nearly a decade there was within it no significant fresh movement, no vital new force in design. The Bâtiments du Roi recovered their official leadership, the artists of the Regent had to seek other commissions, but the same men, without significant additions, continued active inside and outside the royal buildings, their work retained the character already established. It is thus entirely valid to extend the term *style régence*, according to French practise, over all the work down to about 1730.

Versailles resumed its central position in the life of the monarchy without, however, effacing Paris to any such degree as during the glory of Louis XIV. No longer were there substantial additions to the palace; the tasks of the royal artists lay wholly in the interiors. As the apartments from time to time required adaptation to their new occupants,[102] with different requirements, different temperaments and habits, they were given an artistic treatment in line with the changes of style which had meanwhile taken place elsewhere.

The marriage of the young Louis XV to Marie Leczinska in 1725 occasioned redecorations in the Appartement de la Reine. By the standards of the new century work of the decade of 1670 must have seemed very forbidding for the bedroom of a young queen, even as a *chambre de parade*.

In the Chambre de la Reine De Cotte and Vassé undertook extensive changes, step by step. A new chimney piece with bronzes by Vassé was placed in 1725;[103] it disappeared under Marie Antoinette. The walls were not attacked until 1730, after the birth of the Dauphin in 1729. We have a long "Memoire des ouvrages de sculpture en bois ... suivant les desseins de Monsieur de Cotte ... par Du Goulons, Le Goupil et Verberckt dans les six premier mois de l'année 1730."[104] It is our first mention of work for the Crown by the young Jacques Verberckt, of whom we shall hear much more. This makes clear that the principal motifs of the room, the mirrors of the three great piers with their frames of palm (Figure 174)—of which only the one between the windows survives—were of this time. The doorways and overdoors (Figure 175), for which the paintings were ordered in 1734, also fall within the period of De Cotte's administration.

[101] Archives nationales, X¹ᵃ 9162.

[102] It was Pierre de Nolhac who disentangled the history of the château at this period: first, and in most detail, in *Le Château de Versailles sous Louis XV*, 1898, resumed and summarized in his *Versailles inconnu*, 1924, *Versailles au XVIIIᵉ siècle*, 1926, *Louis XV et Marie Leczinska*, 1928, and *Louis XV et Madame de Pompadour*, 1903, 1931, Their conclusions, with certain corrections based on independent study of the documents, are here embodied in a single chronological series, as contrasted with Nolhac's mainly topographic arrangement.

[103] O¹ 2225.

[104] Published by P. Francastel in *Revue de l'histoire de Versailles*, 1927.

Evolution

In 1730 De Cotte was seventy-four; we shall scarcely expect to find him personally taking new initiatives in design, any more than Dugoullons and the other executants, likewise mostly of great age. Vassé, admitted to the Academy in 1723 and lodged in the Louvre, would surely have been De Cotte's reliance for design of work of such importance, and in fact, as we shall see, it was wholly coherent with his work in the Salon d'Hercule at the same period.

Mirrors and overdoors alike were framed by palm stems, spreading freely at the top, of a weight in harmony with the large scale of the room. Those of the mirrors were spirally wreathed with sprays of olive. Garlands united the palms with the rich frames of the paintings above (now replaced), crowned by wings against a background of *mosaïque*. The ornaments of the frieze between doors and overdoors, are very similar to Vassé's trophies of the Salon d'Hercule.

The panels of the narrow piers, so different in style, were undertaken by Ange-Jacques Gabriel and Verberckt in 1735 and will be discussed later.

Another principal task in which Vassé was concerned was the completion of the Salon de Marbre, henceforth to acquire, from the motifs of its decoration, the name of Salon d'Hercule (Figure 176). Vassé was at work from 1729 to 1736 on the sculpture, including the superb bronzes of the chimney piece: the head of Hercules, the lion masks, and the rugous cornucopias. The consoles above the mantel merit particular attention. Like the motif at the key of the arch in the gallery of the Hôtel de Toulouse, they show rims of irregularly fluted shell, ending below in lobes wholly unsymmetrical, as are the spirally fluted shells in the corresponding consoles at the other end of the room. Vassé's also were doubtless the two great frames for the paintings, with bold crossettes of palm so closely related to his ornament of the Chambre de la Reine. Over the large Veronese opposite the chimney piece the winged cartouche with the royal arms had also the irregular border of shell, which, as we have seen at the Hôtel de Toulouse, had been adopted chiefly on Vassé's initiative.

The immense ceiling by François Lemoyne, as finally fixed in design in 1732 and unveiled in 1736, was the first of all those at Versailles to be undivided into compartments. It was also, in the French decoration of the time, to be the last of the painted vaults of figural subjects.

As late works of Vassé we may cite three designs—two for clocks, one for a lectern—engraved by Charles-Nicolas Cochin the younger (1715-1790), who was but twenty-one, and at the beginning of his independent activity, when Vassé died. For one of these the original drawing, in reverse, is preserved,[105] a precious basic evidence for Vassé's technique (Figure 177). In each of these pieces, the general design is symmetrical, with but minor departures except in the sculpture, where, in the clock not reproduced, the unbalance is violent. Vassé evidently participated to the end in the tendency toward increased movement, without violating the principles which had governed his earlier work.

Vassé, "après avoir été cinq ans malade," died in 1736. His ability and creative achievement were well recognized by contemporaries; the *Mercure*[106] speaks of his "talent heureux et très abondant pour les Ornemens."

[105] Musée des Arts-décoratifs, Salle 35, No. 110. Certain impressions of the engravings bear the inscription "Inventé par Vassé, 1734," others merely "A. Vassé invent deli."

[106] March, 1736.

The Creation of the Rococo

"Vassé étoit décorateur," wrote Mariette,[107] "et c'étoit principalement dans cette partie qu'il brillait." He remarks the "gentilesse" of his work as contrasted with the "goût solide et mäle" of the antique. Briseux, writing in 1743 of the decoration of apartments, speaks of "la manière dont quelques Génies distingués ont traité depuis peu ces ornemens," and adds this striking passage:

> Rien n'étant plus juste que d'inspirer à la posterité de la reconnaisance envers ceux qui ont perfectionné l'art sur lequel on écrit, ni plus utile que d'exciter dans les Eléves une louable émulation, on croit, par ces deux différens motifs, devoir dire ici, que le feu Sieur Vassé, Sculpteur du Roi, a été de nos jours le premier qui ait sçû tirer de l'obscurité la Sculpture propre à decorer les appartemens: Ses formes sont des plus nobles, & elles ont un accord merveilleux avec ses ornemens. C'est dommage qu'il ne nous ait laissé que peu de productions de cette espèce.[108]

In other designs of the Bâtiments at this period, where we have no reason to presume the intervention of Vassé, we find no trace of any new impulse. De Cotte is described in 1733 as "très vieux et aveugle,"[109] his other designers had not the force to rise about banal repetition of old formulae.

Among their first works at Versailles had been the Cabinet de la Reine. Following the death of Marie-Therèse in 1683 the queen's apartment had lost, beyond recall, its old more intimate quarters which had lain along the Cour de Marbre. For the new queen, doubtless in 1725, these were replaced by a remodelling of the former Appartement de Nuit of the Duc de Bourgogne, created in 1699, which now became the Petit Appartements des Bains de la Reine. It comprised a Pièce des Bains and a Cabinet en Niche. For the latter we reproduce a drawing (Figure 178),[110] which serves to show that the artistic effort here was of the very slightest.

From the first return to Versailles of Louis XV as a boy of twelve, had begun, already in 1722,[111] the installation of the Petits Cabinets du Roi. They lay about the interior court, thenceforth called the Cour des Cerfs, from the stags' heads then placed there as decoration. From 1727 they began to invade the level of the attics, where a small library was created; the next year a larger room was added at this level in the building between the courts, with baths below, a Cabinet des Fourneaux and a roof terrace above. In 1732 library, "laboratoire," and terrace were doubled in size, and kitchens were added at this roof level; later a story of offices was to be added even above that. In 1732, with substantial payments for carving in the library and cabinets, we again encounter, among the carvers, the name of Jacques Verberckt.

A room to receive the Cabinet des Médailles[112] at the Bibliothèque du Roi in Paris (Fig-

---

[107] *Abecedario*, VI, 40.

[108] *L'art de bastir des maisons de campagne*, 157-158.

[109] Document quoted by Lemonnier: *Procès-verbaux*, IV, xxxviii.

[110] O¹ 1773.

[111] O¹ 2222, fol. 299, cited by Nolhac: *Le Château sous Louis XV*, 1898, p. 174. The drawings showing all these transformations are in O¹ 1771. An important MS. description prepared for the King, preserved at the Cabinet des Estampes, Va 363, published *ibid.*, 180, and *Louis XV et Marie Leczinska*, 1928, 308-309, establishes the exact dates.

[112] J. Babelon, "Le salon Louis XV au Cabinet des Médailles," in *Revue de l'art ancien et moderne*, XXXVII, 1920, 37-47; and *Le cabinet du Roi*, 1927.

ure 179) may have been designed at the end of the administration of Robert de Cotte. It was above the Arcade Colbert, uniting the library with the Hôtel Lambert, which the Crown acquired in 1724, and took possession of in 1733. The medals, to be sure, remained at Versailles until 1741, and the paintings for the room, on a program outlined by Jules-Robert de Cotte, were not executed until 1741-1746. To the long walls, where the windows have elliptical embrasure heads, is applied the scheme of Oppenord's salon at the Hôtel d'Assy, meanwhile adopted elsewhere in the work of other men. Spreading spandrels, bowed downward at the base, make up, with the window heads, a continuous undulating line.

After the death of De Cotte in 1735, he was occasionally credited with a larger share than we have allotted him in artistic creation. Thus Jacques-François Blondel, born in 1705, wrote in 1738 of the employment of mirrors: "J'ai entendu dire à feu M. de Cotte . . . qu'il avoit été le premier à les introduire sur les Cheminèes."[113] We have seen that the first of such mirrors, from 1684, antedate even the beginning of his activity in architecture. The remark reported by Blondel was merely a compliment to the aged dean of the profession. In 1737 Delamair, as part of his systematic denigration of Boffrand, speaks of Boffrand's "gratieux badinage d'ornemens des dedans . . . dont il faut avouer que la veritable et plus vertueuse origine doit s'attribuer au célèbre decorateur feu M. de Cotte."[114] This was indeed true in a measure, but only in the measure that De Cotte had employed Lepautre and Vassé.

Oppenord, though still excluded from the circle of the Academy and of the Bâtiments du Roi, did not fail to find other clients, both ecclesiastical and secular.

Charles de Saint-Albin, a natural son of the Regent, created Archbishop of Cambrai in 1723, purchased by 1725[115] the Hôtel de Pomponne, in which Oppenord had already worked for Michel Bonnier in 1714. Oppenord now made external changes illustrated in the *Grand Oppenord*, Plates XVI-XVIII. While characteristically free, they do not show any significant innovations in detail.

At this period, to judge by their style, additional decorations were executed at the Hôtel d'Évreux (Élysée), in the Grand Salon, the Grand Cabinet (Salle du Conseil des Ministres) and Seconde Antichambre (Salon des Aides de Camp). We have ventured for these an attribution to Oppenord,[116] maintained on grounds of the Comte d'Évreux's close attachment to the Regent and of the character of certain details. Chief of these are the mirror heads of the Grand Cabinet (Figures 180-181) with their incomparable wealth of motif and delicacy of execution in the fluted crestings, eagle heads and trophies of arts, so closely comparable with pages of Oppenord's sketch books (Figure 182). The overdoors here (Figure

[113] *De la distribution de maisons de plaisance*, II, 1738, 68. The passage was later paraphrased by Patte in *Monuments érigés à la gloire de Louis XV*, 1765, p. 6; and by Dargenville, *Vies des fameux architectes*, 1787, 418.

[114] *La pure vérité*, MS., 198, cited by Ch.-V. Langlois, *op. cit.*, 160.

[115] He is mentioned as owner in the 1725 edition of Brice, I, 427, the Approbation of this edition being dated February 22 of that year. The house was put up for sale in February 1723, after its confiscation from Madame Chaumont, according to J. Buvat, *Journal de la régence*, 1865, I, 449.

[116] "Oppenord reconnu," *loc. cit.* Lady Dilke, in her *French Decoration and Furniture of the XVIIIth Century*, 1901, 29-30, attributed the carving of this period at the Élysée to Pineau, on the basis of resemblances with his manuscript drawings for other works. She cites "the same vigour of the scroll terminations . . . the same strident heads of beasts or birds," but these are scarcely more than generic characteristics of work at this moment, as is shown by her other loose attributions to Pineau.

184) with their unique arabesque panels of figural relief and rugous horns of plenty (a motif based on Borrominian examples sketched by Oppenord, and used also by Vassé in the Salon d'Hercule) may be compared with the figures under similar baldaquins in his work at the Hôtel de Pomponne. The superb military trophies of the Grand Salon (Figure 183), far surpassing those of the Hôtel de Villars a decade before, have a new fluidity of line and are paralleled only in Oppenord's numerous studies for plumed casques (Figures 185-186). The Salle des Aides de Camp, though much enriched from its original treatment shown by Mariette, is of more conventional character, but even here we find motifs analogous with Oppenord's drawings.

The date of these remodellings, which had already taken place before the making of Mariette's general section of the house,[117] would fall after 1729, in view of what we have said regarding Mariette's engravings of the earlier decorations.

A design of Oppenord's which may well come within this period is that for the Hôtel Gaudion, at the corner of the Rue des Veilles-Audriettes and the Rue du Grand-Chantier.[118] Pierre-Nicolas Gaudion was Garde du Trésor Royal from 1731-1749, so that the inscription "Trésor Royal" in a cartouche over the door doubtless places the project, which may never have been executed, as probably from 1731 or soon afterwards. This extremely competent and ingenious design is full of admirable but not unconventional spatial effects, achieved with units exclusively rectangular in plan. There is nothing in the details, however, which involves any innovation.

Oppenord was employed by Pierre Crozat in 1730 for additions to his house built by Cartaud in the Rue de Richelieu—where Oppenord himself, like Charles de la Fosse and Watteau before him, was lodged in 1740[119]—and for the orangery at Montmorency, but we know nothing of these which is significant for our purpose.

Oppenord was in charge also of the major religious work of the time, the continuation of Saint-Sulpice,[120] which had been taken up with great energy by the curé Languet de Gergy in 1715. In 1719 the Regent had made a substantial contribution to the cost, on the occasion of his laying the first stone of a tower.[121] Oppenord's work included completing the transept façades, building the nave, furnishing the choir, and making a design for the altar, of which he

---

[117] *Architecture françoise*, pl. 118 of the Hautecoeur edition. It is impracticable, unfortunately, to determine exactly the date of these plates and of most others of the interiors contained in that work. Although the title-pages used for the first three volumes are dated uniformly 1727, the first, as ordinarily found, contains a plate of Saint-Roch with the date of 1739; the second includes the Hôtel de Janvry, with the dates 1732 and 1733, and even the Hôtel Demares, "avec les nouveaux changemens . . . faites . . . depuis que cette maison est devenue l'Hôtel de Villeroy," i.e. surely after 1744. The interiors in volume III, sometimes found with a title-page of 1738, include one of the Hôtel de Rouillé, executed about 1732, according to Blondel, and the Salle à Manger added by Villeroy to his hôtel after 1744.

[118] Of the fifteen signed drawings belonging to the Musée des Arts-Décoratifs, two, including an important section, are reproduced by P. Alfassa in a well documented article in *Musées de France*, 1914, 56-60; and three by H. Mayeux in *L'architecture*, XXVII, 1914, 129-131.

[119] Will of Pierre Crozat cited by Huard "Oppenord," *loc. cit.*

[120] Contemporary allusions to his connection with it may be found in Brice, 1725 ed., III, 384 ff; *Mercure de France*, March, 1725, 473 ff, 548; Piganiol de la Force, 1742 ed., VI, 380-381. Many of Oppenord's manuscript drawings, preserved at the École des Beaux-Arts and elsewhere, are published by E. Malbois: "Oppenord et l'église Saint-Sulpice," in *Gazette des beaux-arts*, VIᵉ pér., IX, 1933, 34-46.

[121] J. Buvat: *Journal de la régence*, 1865, I, 465.

is named as the architect in 1725, but of which the first stone was laid under Servadoni's direction in 1732.[122] This, with the stalls, was destroyed at the Revolution. Unlike those at Notre Dame, the stalls had no high backs, but the two thrones at the entrance, while much heavier in treatment, took several suggestions of detail from the ones in the cathedral; so did the main altar and the *autel des féries*, though both had spatial relationships quite different from their exemplars.

In the sacristy at Saint-Sulpice there is a wainscot carved with magnificent ecclesiastical trophies. In these the scheme of the trophies at Versailles is given a fire and swing which makes us suspect—pending possible archival discoveries—that the designs were by Oppenord. As in one of his drawings in Berlin,[123] a scroll of leafage crosses the curved moulded frame in a way very characteristic of him, representing a heightened movement by contrast with anything found before 1715.

Several designs survive, though not a general elevation, for the façade and western tower as intended by Oppenord. His studies offer many alternatives, one of which anticipates Servadoni's use of the Doric order below, but both the grouping of the supports (in most studies) and the details, are markedly influenced by the Italian baroque. Notably a study for the window of the portal, "a laquelle je me fixe," notes Oppenord, "comme plus convenable," is of extreme baroque character. While in its crossettes there is an adaptation of Lepautre's hawk's-bill with acanthus, its cornice, waved and scrolled, and indeed its ensemble, is far closer to Italian examples, toward which Oppenord tended to revert throughout the design of the façade and its adjuncts. Such a revision, apparently inacceptable to the taste of Languet de Gergy, may have been quite as largely responsible as the impending failure of Oppenord's wooden central lantern,[124] taken down in 1731, for his being superseded as architect of the church. In 1732 Servadoni appeared in this capacity.[125]

Oppenord was likewise responsible for designs for the church of the Oratoire, of which some are preserved at the École des Beaux-arts. One is for a high altar. The table, with frontal and diagonal consoles, with kneeling figures flanking the retable, is not irrelated with Vassé's at Notre Dame. A detail for completion of the old façade, not yet undertaken when Brice wrote in 1725 (I, 215), is similar to Oppenord's baroque studies for details of the facade of Saint-Sulpice. The work did not proceed on this design; Brice's passage remained unchanged in the edition of 1752 (I, 227).

Designs for a jubé with its altars at the Cathedral of Meaux, commissioned in 1729, are

---

[122] E. Barbier: *Chronique de la régence*, 1857, II, 333.

[123] Published by Sedlmaier, *op. cit.*, pl. IX, and by Jessen, *Das Ornament des Rococo*, pl. 39.

[124] Oppenord's lantern itself had been adopted to replace a heavier dome projected by his predecessor, Gittard, but proved itself too much for the supports. Huard's "Oppenord," *loc. cit.*, and *Bulletin de la Société de l'histoire de l'art français*, 1925, 37-39, make Oppenord responsible not only for this misjudgment, but for the fall of a portion of the Hôtel Crozat in the Rue de Richelieu in September, 1721. Buvat's *Journal de la régence* for that date (II, 295), makes clear, however, that the failure there was due to an architect named Roquet, and the whole affair was prior to Oppenord's employment by Crozat. Oppenord was a bold, even rash, constructor, but we cannot assume that structural rather than aesthetic reasons were responsible for his later eclipse.

[125] Blondel's *Cours*, III, 1772, 345-349, speaks of a "competition" for the design of the façade of Saint-Sulpice, won by Servadoni, and thus supposedly held in 1732, in which Meissonier participated with others. We shall see that Meissonier's design was offered in 1726, while Oppenord was apparently still in full control. Dargenville, *Vies des fameux architectes*, 1787, 483, speaks of an invitation to Boffrand to take charge, which he declined.

shown by an engraving of the *Grand Oppenord*. One of the alternate proposals for the retables is derivate from Lepautre's in the jubé of Notre Dame, now given a concave plan. The other shows a baroque head of Italian profile and character, distantly recalling the main altar of Sant' Ignazio in Rome, though less strongly plastic in its forms. It has a terminal figure of pronounced movement backed by a great shell of which the unsymmetrical outline is rather exceptional even in the sculptural compositions of Oppenord.

In the transformations of the style of the Regency which was to establish the *genre pittoresque* Oppenord played no important rôle. At the time of Meissonnier's first use of "contraste" in silverwork, Oppenord was fifty-six; he was sixty at the date of Pineau's decisive interior designs of 1732. Oppenord's design for the Hôtel Gaudion, shortly after this date; his work begun in 1730 for Pierre Crozat (by whom he was lodged in 1740), may have continued for some years.[126] Neither shows any significant change of style. In his sketch book at Berlin are notes on the execution of a salon at Torcy in 1740, on which we have nothing further. Aside from these, we know of no designs for buildings or interiors in his later years, but only book illustrations and similar minor works.[127] We must imagine Oppenord then—like Meissonnier, as we shall see—to have passed much of his time in the spinning of facile, ideal designs, which French taste—now definitely hostile to their baroque Italianism—left unexecuted.

Among these, and very probably of this period, were certain decorative studies, engraved after his death by Huquier in the *Moyen Oppenord* (e.g. suite A, no. 2), which participate in the picturesque movement by their considerable assymmetry as well as by their fusion of cartouche motives with naturalistic elements,[128] while others depart little from old formulae derived from Bernini and of Borromini. Berliner speaks of the "victorious Italian tendency" of this plastic development under the leadership of Oppenord. We find him personally defeated, and Meissonnier victorious only in the crafts and in the taking up of his new type of composition in engraving and, to a minor degree, in painted panel-filling. As for Italianism, it was limited to the derivation of the cartouche, dissolved and absorbed in such compositions, where the principle of fusion of the decorative and naturalistic elements, however different individually, goes back to the French initiative of Watteau. In interior woodwork the plastic Italianism of Oppenord and still more of Meissonnier was wholly overcome by the French linear, surface tendency, triumphant with Pineau.

It was indeed always for his drawings, rather than for executed works, that Oppenord was particularly celebrated. We have seen what Brice wrote of them as early as 1713. After

---

[126] Huard, "Oppenord," *loc. cit.*, lists various designs, some engraved, some manuscript, which he cannot date: for work at the church of Saint-Marcel, at the Château de Bove near Lyons, at the Séminaire d'Orléans, etc. None of them shows a character more advanced than that with which we are familiar.

[127] E.g. his two vignettes for the Molière of Boucher, which appeared in 1734. Among his drawings at Berlin are a number for initials and frontispieces, some of which may be of this last period.

[128] Berliner, *op. cit.*, 169, citing a design of the *Moyen Oppenord*, says that Oppenord was the first to effect this broader treatment, which we have seen by 1734 in the engravings of Meissonnier, whom he does not mention. We are by no means justified, however, in assuming that Oppenord's designs of this type, few in any event, are of earlier date. Rather we are of the opinion that Oppenord, then over sixty years of age, in whose dated work there had never previously been anything of the sort, was trying his hand in the new genre inaugurated by the younger artist. A further instance is a coulisse-like sketch, very closely related to Meissonnier's composition but unique among Oppenord's, preserved in the National Museum, Stockholm, bearing the cryptic legend "Fait pour lx Vxrx."

Evolution

Oppenord's death in 1742, the engraver Huquier, bought over two thousand of them.[129] About 1748 he published the collections familiarly known as the *Petit, Moyen*, and *Grand Oppenord*. Saint-Yves in his *Observations sur les arts*, 1748[130]—where he calls Oppenord "le Le Brun de l'architecture" and speaks, strangely to our ears, of "les ornemens antiques . . . si simples, si élégans, si majestueux que le sçavant Oppenor dont le génie si vaste & si fécond a tout osé, craignoit de s'éloigner de leur goût—says "Les mêmes hommes qui de son vivant s'étoient déchainés contre lui, donnerent après sa mort l'or à pleines mains pour avoir de ses desseins." Cochin, hostile to Oppenord in tendency, conceded that "il s'étoit fait un grand réputation par ses desseins . . . (qui) ne faisaient pas le même effet, en exécution," and, long afterwards, Dargenville echoed both these passages.[131]

Our estimate of the position of Oppenord is borne out by literary testimony. In 1755 in the famous ironic defense of the extremes of the *genre pittoresque*,[132] Cochin wrote of their origin: "Le fameux Oppenor nous servit dans commencements avec beaucoup de zéle . . . Il se servit abondamment de nos ornamens favoris, & les mit en crédit. Il nous est même encore d'une grande utilité, & nous pouvons compter au nombre des notres ceux qui le prennent pour modele." But he makes his protagonist add, quite truly, "Cependant ce n'étoit pas encore l'homme qu'il nous falloit; il ne pouvoit s'empecher de retomber souvent dans l'architecture ancienne, qu'il avoit étudiée dans sa jeunesse." Oppenord had indeed been early a notable champion of the free tendency, but his reminiscences of Italian baroque plasticity, his surviving architectonics, had kept him from taking any prominent part in the ultimate phase of the French rococo.

Our idea of Aubert's position is not changed essentially by several works of this time in which he served as designer for Jacques Gabriel.

At the Palais Bourbon, although the land was acquired in 1720, Brice mentions only the foundations in 1725. Begun by Giardini, forwarded by Lassurance, who died in 1724, it was completed by Gabriel and Aubert, as was the neighboring Hôtel de Lassay, also begun by Lassurance. "Par malheur," wrote Piganiol de la Force of the designers of the Palais Bourbon, "le plus habile est venu le dernier." In spite of the sumptuousness of the decoration which, Pierre-Jean Mariette said in 1740, "surpasse en ornemens et en magnificence tout ce qui s'étoit fait jusqu'à présent dans ce genre,"[133] there is little fundamentally novel in either of these buildings.

Of the Palais Bourbon, Jean Mariette, in his *Architecture françoise*, gives six plates of interiors,[134] which are welcome because of the great transformations the building has under-

[129] He speaks of these in his introduction to the *Grand Oppenord*.

[130] 131-132. In a footnote he speaks of Oppenord's published designs as "dans un goût tenant de l'antique, mais plus riche."

[131] *Vies des fameux architectes*, 1787, 434-440.

[132] *Mercure de France, loc. cit.*

[133] Brice, 1752 ed., prepared by Mariette in 1740, IV, 142. Blondel, indeed, criticizes the too great profusion of ornaments and gilding here: "La dorure doit aussi être employée avec ménagement, & lorsque l'on veut dorer tous les ornemens, au-moins faut-il mettre ces derniers avec discretion . . . parce que cette sculpture que l'on affecte quelquefois dans le milieu des pilastres, des frises, ou des panneaux, cause une trop grand confusion, aussi qu'on peut le remarquer dans l'intérieur des appartements du Palais Bourbon." *Architecture françoise*, I, 1752, 121.

[134] Pls. 475-480 of the Hautecoeur edition. Neither the Archives Nationales (o¹ 1578) nor the Cabinet des Estampes offers anything of significance on the early period of the building.

gone both before the Revolution and subsequently. On the walls with the windows, arched or with elliptical *arrière-voussures*, the spandrels are treated very much like those of Oppenord at the Hôtel d'Assy, now so commonly followed. The Grand Cabinet shows in its treatment of the oval medallion above the mirror, of the heavy fluted reverse-scrolls and dragons of the overdoors, a character which had meanwhile become essentially conventional.

At the Hôtel de Lassay, of which Mariette gives merely one plate of the vestibule,[135] the interiors with their panellings "dues pour le plupart à du Goullon,"[136] are better preserved, in spite of some barbarous changes. In the Grand Salon (Figure 187) the main wall panels, with triple bands, have large central fields of free outline—no longer merely oval—with figural reliefs, which are repeated by smaller fields at top and bottom of the panels. The doors and indeed all surfaces are richly ornamented. The most personal touch is in the multitude of C-scrolls which make up the bands of *mosaïque* and reappear in the mirror heads and overdoors of other rooms. The chief glory is that of the cornices, heavy with medallions and other large gilded areas, ribbed and pierced, which evoked Blondel's criticism. In the Grand Salon and the Salon des Saisons (Figure 188) the upper moulding is interrupted by cardinal and diagonal features with which it is combined, not too organically, by subordinate scrolls. In the Salon de Musique and the Salon des Jeux (Figure 189) it is carried around the room in an oval, creating large pendentives at the corners, in which the motifs are but loosely combined. These were two different approaches to the ultimate solution of the problem, to be achieved by Pineau a few years later.

At the Hôtel Peyrenc de Moras (de Biron), erected in 1728-1731 by Gabriel and Aubert, little is left of the original woodwork to supplement the small sections given by Blondel, who also describes the changes, rather minor, made by the Duchesse du Maine, who took possession in January, 1737.[137] That little—mostly doors and dadoes—is closely coherent with the corresponding features at the Palais Bourbon and the Hôtel de Lassay. The two elliptical salons had the unified arched treatment initiated by Boffrand at the Petit-Luxembourg, which had meanwhile become common property. So far as our information goes, it confirms our impression of Aubert as a highly gifted representative of a school already established.

Boffrand is represented in Paris at this period by the remodelling of the Hôtel d'Argenton for Comte Marc Pierre d'Argenson, who occupied it from 1725 as the Chancellerie d'Orléans, and was given it in 1743.[138] The ceiling and doubtless the cornice of the salon remained unchanged. The new treatment of the walls is illustrated on Plate XXXIV of Boffrand's *Livre d'architecture*, 1745 (Figure 190), which shows the room in the same state as Mariette's small section.[139] A consistent range of semi-circular arches frames the windows, doors, and chimney piece. At the crowns of the arches are cartouches having bulging central fields; at the base of the spandrels are similar frames—likewise with narrow serrated rims

---

[135] Pl. 481 of the Hautecoeur edition.

[136] Dargenville: *Voyage pittoresque de Paris*, 1752 ed., 362.

[137] *Architecture françoise*, II, 1752, 205-207, Brice, 1752 ed., IV, 30. J. Vacquier: *Ancien hôtel du Maine et de Biron*, 1909, gives the documents and illustrates some remains of the decoration. The purchasers of others are indicated by A. de Champeaux: *L'Art décoratif dans le Vieux Paris*, 1898, 131-132.

[138] Cf. J. Major: "L'Hôtel de la chancellerie d'Orléans," *loc. cit.*, The house, including its salon, was much modified again by Charles de Wailly after 1783.

[139] *Architecture françoise*, pl. 63 of the Hautecoeur edition.

of shell—surrounding fields apparently flat, though ending below in a subordinate plastic cartouche. Not only in the spandrels but also on the piers is a uniform circular *mosaïque*, related to that of Aubert at the Hôtel de Lassay.

In the year 1724 Boffrand visited Würzburg and there established the interior designs for the first episcopal suite of the palace.[140] Certain surviving drawings made there by the stucco worker Johann Peter Castelli of Bonn under Boffrand's direction and bearing his handwriting are of purely French character (Figure 191). They show a very sober version of style for that time, equivalent to De Cotte's decorations for his own house, depending for enrichment almost wholly on the mirror frames, without carving in the panels. Certain mirrors are arched and slightly scalloped, others even remain square. This panelling was swept away in 1776, but the ceilings of 1725 by Castelli remain, with rosettes and cartouches closely related in design to French models, without innovations which we could suppose to be Boffrand's.

Jean-Baptiste Leroux (1676?-1746)—a pupil of Dorbay, admitted to the Academy in 1720, Professor in 1730—has passed as the author of many important interiors, but we shall find that these were actually by other hands. He is indeed specifically mentioned, with Le Grand and Tannevot, by one of Jean-François Blondel's interlocutors, as "ne sachant guère que faire des plans," and having recourse to other designers.[141] The engraved plates issued with his name are in part from the time of his young manhood after 1700, under the influence of Pierre Lepautre,[142] in part, as we shall see, from designs of Pineau after 1730.

As a work of Leroux at just this time there is only the Hôtel de Roquelaure (Ministère des Travaux Publiques) begun in 1722, which he continued after the death of Lassurance in 1724 and completed in 1726.[143] Mariette's *Architecture françoise* gives six plates of interiors,[144] all captioned as "du dessin de M. le Roux." Of these rooms, three survive as shown: the Vestibule, with arched doorways and Ionic pilasters, an Antichambre and the Petit Cabinet (Figures 192-195).

In the last of these, as we see it today (Figure 196), the only change is the substitution of panelling for the very large mirror opposite the windows. This is indeed a very lovely room, by its wealth of fine carving integrally preserved, still somewhat heavy in width and relief, by its fine ceiling and cornice with angle ornaments. Essentially it offers little new: its quatrefoil overdoors, its mirror head with reverse curves, surmounted by an oval panel—all these had become traditional since 1710. Characteristic for its time are the outlines of the cupboard door panels with reverse curves truncated by concave corners. A feature we have not hitherto encountered is the coiled dragon replacing the swirl of acanthus in certain crosettes here and elsewhere in the house.

The surviving Antichambre shown on Mariette's Plates 483 and 485 (Figure 193), has

---

[140] R. Sedlmaier und R. Pfister: *Die Fürstbischöfliche Residenz zu Würzburg*, 84-88 and figs. 81, 82.

[141] *Les amours rivaux, ou l'homme du monde eclairé par les arts, par un homme de lettres* (J. F. de Bastide) *et feu M. Blondel*, 1774, 102 ff.

[142] Six chimney pieces without title-page, and a suite of *Nouveaux lambris*, both included in the Mariette collection entitled *Architecture à la mode*.

[143] Brice, 1752 ed., IV, 47; not mentioned in the 1725 edition.

[144] Pls. 482-487 of the Hautecoeur edition. The small section of the house in Blondel's *Architecture françoise*, I, 1752, pl. 70 of the Guadet edition, shows another room of similar character, doubtless also from the time of first building.

large wall panels with reverse-curved crowns. Otherwise the room, with its low rectangular mirror on the chimney breast, its mantel with frontal consoles, is relatively backward in treatment.

Of the additional interiors shown by Mariette—the Antichambre où est la Chapelle (Figure 192) and the Chambre à Coucher—the former is of simple geometrical conventionality. The Chambre (Figures 194 and 195) has handsome large panels with central rosettes of rich interlace. With all their excellent disposition of ornaments, we find, in these first interiors at the Hôtel de Roquelaure, merely an accomplished version of the style already current.

Among the younger men, Claude-Guillot Aubry (1703-1791) built in 1724 for the dancer Madamoiselle Desmares a house which survives, much remodelled, as the Ministry of Agriculture. Blondel's section[145] is interesting to us, since it shows the salon as wholly identical in design with Oppenord's of 1719 at the Hôtel d'Assy. From this designer, who was to enter the Academy in 1739, we shall accordingly expect no great originality.

Aubry also built in 1730 the Hôtel de la Vrillière, sold in 1732 to the Princesse Douarière de Conti (Ministry of War).[146] Here one handsome room of the period survives. Its most notable feature is the ceiling, where a great circular medallion is inscribed on the flat surface within the cornice, the spandrels being filled in with a diagonal network. The overdoors, again resting on a narrow retreating frieze, have naturalistic reliefs, instead of paintings— doing away with the dark spot over the door which had been conventional, and thus increasing the unity of the room.[147]

The Hôtel de Matignon, while begun in July, 1722, from plans by Courtonne for the Prince de Tingry, was purchased when well advanced, July 25, 1723, by the Comte de Matignon, who dismissed Courtonne and entrusted the completion of the work to Mazin "ingenieur et directeur des plans du Roi."[148] Courtonne listed profiles of the internal cornices among the drawings he had furnished, and certain of them had then already been executed, by Louis Herpin and other sculptors. Some of these were modified by Mazin, who substantially completed the interior by 1726, although carving in wood was still being executed in 1731. As some remodellings were undertaken in 1751 and again in 1760, to say nothing of brutal redecorations a generation ago, it is not possible to identify any of the surviving work as belonging to the first decorations. We shall have occasion later to discuss the work of 1731.

We may mention also certain fine surviving rooms in other buildings of the period, for which we have not succeeded in establishing the authorship, or even the exact dates.

In the Hôtel de la Fare,[149] 14, Place Vendôme, Messrs. Morgan et Cie. preserve a most

[145] *Architecture françoise*, pl. 5 of the Guadet edition.

[146] Brice, 1752 ed., IV, 50. The Academy of Architecture was requested to adjudicate the accounts of workmen there in 1737, which may mark the end of further operations, perhaps including decorations. *Procès-verbaux*, V, 161-164.

[147] Blondel in 1752 recommended such use of reliefs: "ceux-la se lient d'avantage avec l'ordonnance de la pièce," and deplores the prejudice still existing in favour of paintings. *Architecture françoise*, I, 119.

[148] The documents, preserved in unusual fulness, are published by L.-H. Labande in *Gazette des beaux-arts*, VIe pér., XIII, 1935, 257-270, 347-363. The engraved designs of the house, *Courtonne inv.*, in the *Architecture moderne* published by Jombert in 1728, include no sections.

[149] The Marquise de la Fare, favored by the Regent, sold his house, acquired in 1704 by his father-in-law, Paparel, in 1716 to M. de Souvré; after the cancellation of this sale it was acquired in 1719 by Salomon Le Clerc, for whom this room would seem to have been executed some years later.

delightful little cabinet (Figure 197). Its inner end is curved, its cornice crowned with a balustrade with scrolled pedestals and with vases profiling against the unbroken painted vault. That the room, with such suggestions from Oppenord's hemicycle and from the gallery of the Hôtel de Toulouse, was executed a half dozen years after those works, we may judge by the contorted dragons which form the crosettes flanking oval paintings over the little doorways, recalling those of the first interiors of the Hôtel de Roquelaure.

Such dragons also occur in a similar position in a room from the house at 18, Place Vendôme,[150] the Hôtel Cressart, which, with another fine room of the house, shows further analogies with the first woodwork of the Hôtel de Roquelaure.

In works of this character, however handsomely embodying the taste of the time, we scarcely find fresh creative ideas, which were now to appear from other quarters.

In ornament, soon to undergo a great upheaval, artists were still mainly occupied in exploiting the initiatives of the Regency. So it was in the decorations of the wonderful room formerly in the house at 23, Place Vendôme,[151] acquired by Jean de Boullogne in 1728 and decorated by Lancret, obviously at just that time. The panelling itself is closely related to that of three works we have just discussed, the Hôtels de Roquelaure, de la Fare, and Cressart, with dragons on the crossettes and sphinxes flanking the overdoors. The arabesques of Lancret are derivative from those of Watteau's middle period.

The painter Christophe Huet (died 1759) belongs in the great line of decorative designers stemming from Berain and Audran. It was he, doubtless, who painted the Grande Singerie and the Petite Singerie at Chantilly, of which the latter bears the date 1735, the same date appearing with the signature of Huet on ten paintings of Chinese and other oriental subjects executed for the Duc de Bourbon and likewise preserved at Chantilly.[152] The Grande Singerie adorns a simple panelling of 1722 which has been adapted for the paintings by an inner frame of very richly curved but symmetrical profile, the intervening space being filled by a fine diagonal *mosaïque*. The arabesque itself outdoes even Watteau in its atmospheric dissolution of the tabernacles, to which, however, the naturalistic elements are kept subordinate. In the vault, as well as on the ceiling of the Petite Singerie, the schemes of Audran are realized even more airily, without any touch of the innovations of the rocaille which had been launched the year before in the engravings of Meissonnier, to which we shall turn.

It is as appearing at this time that we should speak of the early works of Jean-Jérôme Servadoni (1695-1766).[153] Born in Florence as son of a French father, Jean Servan of Lyons, and of an Italian mother, he became the pupil of Panini, from whom he derived the style of his compositions of Roman ruins such as his diploma picture for the Academy of Painting in Paris, 1731. Meanwhile he had had many wanderings, to Grenoble, to Portu-

---

[150] The treasurer, Herlaut, owned the land from 1710 to his death in 1716, but (according to documents kindly supplied me by my friend André Carlhian, who owned the rooms in 1939) it was still without buildings when acquired by Cressart, "syntic des rentes à l'Hôtel de Ville," March 18, 1723. It was he who built the house, which he sold in 1733 to the Sieur de Tournelles. Clearly the decorations, as their style shows, are from the period of Cressart's ownership, and the house should be called the Hôtel Cressart rather than the Hôtel Herlaut.

[151] Dispersed by sale in 1896. Cf. G. Wildenstein: *Lancret*, 1924, Nos. 729-737 of the catalogue, which cites the literature but does not attempt to date the work.

[152] Macon, *op. cit.*, 1903, 73-75, citing the earlier literature.

[153] M.-L. Bataille: "Servadoni," in Dimier: *Les peintres français du XVIIIe siècle*, II, 1930, where the documents and literature are assembled and the stage models illustrated.

gal, where he worked for the opera, to England, where he married. His first appearance in Paris was in 1728, where he made a great success with the settings for Orion at the Opéra. He continued there as Décorateur-en-Chef for eighteen years. Any idea that his early stage-settings were of classical severity is dispelled by the models belonging to the Marquise de Castelbajac, exhibited in 1929, a "Chinese" temple, purely French, of light baldaquins, a garden portico of contorted treillage. Extravagant as these are, their elements, by contrast with many baroque designs, are placed parallel with the stage, and they contain no trace of any asymmetry.

Thus the second impulse in the creation of the rococo, given by the artists of the Regency, began to lose momentum, on the verge of a third impulse at the hands of a new generation.

Middle Years of Louis XV

With the middle years of the reign, after 1730, we encounter a fresh creative movement, which was to carry the style in France to its culmination. Again, as in the last years of Louis XIV, it was no political, social or economic change, modifying those already visible under the Regency, which evoked this new artistic development. Again it depended on personal initiative of gifted individuals, and was essentially immanent to the field of art.

There are, naturally, obvious parallels in other artistic branches, but in painting the great creative achievement, the great personality—that of Watteau—had appeared and disappeared with the Regency. The death of Watteau, so prematurely, left no one of equal stature to carry on a vital development of painting into the middle years of Louis XV. In decoration, on the contrary, these saw an extension of the movements of the Regency, at the hands of men of powerful orginality.

Their initiative was taken entirely in private buildings. In those of the Crown, at the moment, the only tasks were the completion of the Chambre de la Reine, and of the Salon d'Hercule, both already well advanced. Nothing new was undertaken before 1738, when the King, at twenty-eight, avowing his course of infidelity, remodelled his private apartment and created the Petit Appartement above. Meanwhile men outside the circle of the Bâtiments, working for private clients, had renewed and vitalized the design of interiors. From their work came the fresh influences later to be felt even in the Maisons Royales. We shall speak first of the beginnings of the new phase in the hands of its protagonists, then of its acceptance by artists of the Crown and others, before reaction set in.

The Creators of the "genre pittoresque," 1730-1735

Through the hardening established lines of the French interior, about 1730, rustled a fresh breeze, bringing new life and movement. The novelty and import were recognized by contemporaries, who, within a generation were to call it the "goût nouveau" or the "genre pittoresque," and to remark on its most striking characteristic, asymmetry—"le contraste dans les ornemens."

It is doubtless worth while to glance briefly at the appearance and usage of the words by which the new phase of style was characterized. The Venetian Boschini, enamoured of colourism, in his *Carta del navegar pittoresco*, 1660, had used "picturesque" as applying to pictorial form generally: "The painter forms without form, or rather with form deforms the formality of appearance, seeking thus picturesque art." The word was already domesticated in France early in the eighteenth century, and had even passed to England, where Steele used it by 1703 and Pope spoke in 1712 of certain lines of poetry "as what the French call picturesque." Yet we do not find it defined in print in France prior to the *Discours sur la peinture* of Charles Coypel, read at the Academy in 1726 and published in 1732, as "Un choix piquant et singulier des effets de la nature . . ."[154] This has the overtone which the word has preserved, corresponding exactly to the effects in decorative art which were appearing just at this moment.

As for symmetry, which Pascal had still used as a synonym for proportion, by the time of Montesquieu's *Essai sur le goût* in the mid-eighteenth century, it was commonly applied to bilateral identity. The word and its opposite both appear in his dictum "L'âme aime la symétrie, mais elle aime aussi le contraste."

Asymmetry in itself, to be sure, was not wholly a novelty in French ornament. The trophy, such a favorite motif since the time of Lebrun, had long comported unsymmetrical arrangement, so notably exemplified in the famous examples of Ladoireau at Versailles. After these were put in place, from 1703, the uses of the trophy multiplied, as we have seen, in the Chapelle de Versailles and elsewhere, with corresponding increase in the familiarity of asymmetric motifs of decorative sculpture.

More significant was the unsymmetrical form which the cartouche had occasionally assumed. In Italy we find examples well within the seventeenth century; several were sketched by Oppenord in his sketch book now in Berlin, where we find also holy-water basins with cartels of related form. In the suites engraved by the Italian Mitelli (1609-1660) we find cartouches with frames and fields of violent asymmetry. Asymmetric cartouches, as we have seen, appear much closer at hand, in the work of Toro after 1716.

All this time, however, the panel outlines, the mirror heads, had remained rigidly symmetrical. In panel fillings of ornamental motifs other than representative sculpture, we have found only a single minor exception, even in the work of Oppenord, to the rule of self-contained axial balance.

Of the genesis of this new phase of style we have two familiar accounts by younger contemporaries, men of academic sympathies, both writing after 1750 when reaction was beginning.

One occurs in *Les amours rivaux, ou l'homme du monde éclairé par les arts, par un homme de lettres* [Bastide] *& par feu M. Blondel*, published in 1774. Jacques-François Blondel, who died in that year, was born in 1705; he had himself sponsored early engraved designs by Pineau.[155] He was thus in the best possible position to know who were the innovators in interior design after 1730. A propos of the Hôtel de Mazarin (1735), he makes one of his interlocutors say: "Ces dessins charmants ont été donnés par M. Leroux, architecte du Roi, et ont été exécutés par Pinault, artiste à qui nous devons toujours une reconnaissance et une admiration infinies pour toutes les jolies choses qui embellisaient nos demures . . ." The other replies: "Les Le Roux, les Le Grand, les Tannevot ne sachant guere qui faire des

[154] Quoted by Abbé J. Lacomb: *Dictionnaire portatif des beaux-arts*, 1750, 2d edition, 1759, 483.

[155] Dargenville, writing in 1787, states that Blondel was a pupil of Oppenord, but Blondel himself in his biographical note on Oppenord in his *Cours d'architecture*, III, 1772, 330n, says nothing of any such relationship.

plans, eurent recours au prestige des embellisemens et s'addressèrent aux Pineault, aux Meisonnier, aux Lajoux," whom he names as "les trois premiers inventeurs du genre pittoresque."

Cochin the younger (born ten years after Blondel) published in the *Mercure de France* in 1754 an attack on the style, and the next year a satirical defense.[156] After attributing to Oppenord the initiative in the previous phase, he says of Meissonnier:[157] "il inventa les contrastes, c'est à dire qu'il bannit la symmétrie," and adds: "L'on peut dire que nous n'avons rien produit depuis dont on ne trouve les semences dans ses ouvrages." Pineau, just dead, he does not name, but devotes a long passage to him, which terminates as follows: "On peut dire à sa gloire que tout ce qui s'éloigne du goût antique lui doit son invention, ou sa perfection."

Pineau and Meissonnier: for each of them primacy has been claimed by modern writers.[158] We shall attempt to define their several priorities and contributions more precisely.

Juste-Aurèle Meissonnier was born in 1695 in Turin. Much has been made of this Italian origin, as bearing on his later style. His father, however, was Provençal,[159] his uncle, Alexandre Meissonnier, was "officier du roi" in France. We first hear of Juste-Aurèle as a goldsmith or silversmith; his engraved works illustrate a piece of silver executed in 1723. At twenty-nine he was admitted to the *maîtrise*, on September 28, 1724, by a brevet as *orfèvre du roi*, working at the Gobelins.[160] We know, however, no single piece of silverwork surely executed by himself; the surviving examples after his designs bear the marks of various silversmiths, of whom Duvivier was the most important. Two years later, on December 6, 1726, he was appointed Dessinateur de la Chambre et du Cabinet du Roi,[161] the post held formerly by Jean Berain and meanwhile by his son. This charge Meissonnier held until his death in 1750. In 1742 we find him listed as in possession of a lodging in the Galeries du Louvre.[162]

His earliest known design, for the "Seau à rafraichir executé pour M. le Duc en 1723," engraved as Figure 58 of his collected works,[163] is still entirely symmetrical, with moulded profiles of Louis XIV character. Any new feeling appears only in the rugous forms of the triple borders of the armorial cartouche and of the marine figures and dolphins which form the handles.

[156] "Supplication aux orfèvres," December, 1774, 178-187 and "Lettre à M. l'Abbé R." February, 1775, 148-171.

[157] The full passage on Meissonnier is quoted, more accessibly, by Destailleur: *Notes sur quelques artistes français*, 1863, 224-226. He does not quote the passage on Pineau, which, although referred to by Deshairs, has thus escaped the many who have relied on Destailleur, at second hand, for the text of the *Mercure*.

[158] For Meissonnier, M. L. Bataille in L. Dimier: *Les peintres français du XVIIIᵉ siècle*, II, 1930, 365-378; for Pineau, E. Biais: "Nicolas Pineau, inventeur du contraste," in *Reunion des sociétés des beaux-arts des départements*, 1899, 384. The following account of the early work of Meissonnier appeared in the *Gazette des beaux-arts*, VIᵉ pér. XXII, 1942, 27-40.

[159] Obituary of Meissonnier in the *Mercure*, October, 1750, 138-141.

[160] The documents regarding him, including also the inventory after his death, are cited by R. Carsix in the *Revue de l'art ancien et moderne*, vol. 26, 1909, 393-401.

[161] O¹ˣ 68, fol. 257. The appointment was reported in the *Mercure*, January, 1727, 133-136, which describes the design for fireworks "sur lequel il a été agréé."

[162] Piganiol de la Force, 1742 ed., II, 162, a mention which seems to have escaped other students.

[163] *Oeuvre de Juste Aurelle Meissonnier, peintre, sculpteur, architecte, et dessinateur de la Chambre et Cabinet du Roy. Première partie executée sous la conduite de l'auteur. à Paris chez Huquier*, n.d.

Evolution

In the "Cadran à vent de Mr. le Duc de Mortemar en 1724" (Figure 198), engraved as Meissonnier's Figure 98, while the frame of the dial is itself symmetrical, the whole effect is made violently asymmetric by the diagonal pose of the unbalanced figures above and below. We cannot confidently assume that its architectural setting, in the engraved plate, was not supplied subsequently; certainly it cannot have been found acceptable for actual execution at so early a date. In the large wall panel, extending to the floor without any dado, there are not merely loosely straying stems; the central leaf below is twisted out of frontality. The shutter is even more advanced in character, with both the central, distorted cartouche-like motif and the terminal scrolls and sprays wholly unsymmetrical, in a way not found executed anywhere in interiors before 1730.

The "Garde d'Epées d'or pour les presens du Mariage du Roi en 1725," Figure 51 of Meissonnier's folio, were no doubt among his first works for the Crown, even prior to his appointment in the Menus-Plaisirs. It is hard to see anything particularly free or novel in them.

Another early dated work of Meissonnier, which received the praise of the *Mercure*, is the "Soleil Executé en argent pour les Religieuses Carmelites de Poitiers en 1727," Figure 78 of the engraved folio (Figure 199). An instructive comparison may be made with the related monstrance given to Notre Dame in 1708 by Antoine de la Porte (Figure 200).[164] As seen from the front this is entirely symmetrical except for the variety of the Apocalyptic figures, themselves disposed with general symmetry. The support of the glory is still articulated, with consoles and other architectonic elements. The monstrance of Poitiers has, to be sure, a base of sufficiently conventional form, derivative from Berain or Boulle. In the shaft, however, clouds wind spirally up from the base among symbolic ears of wheat and sprays of grape. The interpretation in the *Mercure*[165] concludes: "Ce morceau est tout-a-fait dans le goût des célèbres Pietro da Cortona & Puget, dont l'École a toujours fait l'objet des études de l'Auteur." A new development is in germ, but as yet in germ only.

By 1728, however, the germ had developed, in silverwork, into almost full flower, as we see by the "Chandeliers de sculpture en argent inventé by J. Meissonnier Architecte en 1728," which were engraved as Figures 10 to 12 of his works (Figure 201). These three are actually three views of the same candlestick from different sides—something which would never have been necessary with more uniform, earlier works, showing that Meissonnier clearly appreciated that this one was the manifesto of a new character. Even in the base, its three elements, equally spaced, are all varied in detail: the shells and scrolls which buttress it are unlike; the scrolls which rise to support the stem are both unlike one another and unsymmetrical in themselves. Above it is not merely the figures of cherubs which are unbalanced, it is the entire stem and socket, composed of a multitude of characteristic elements: distorted scrolls, a twisted cartouche, spiral fronds of palm, all differing in every aspect. Just this very work—of which the illustrations are missing in many copies of the engraved folio, and which has escaped the attention of scholars—is the crucial one in the origin of the *genre pittoresque*, which shows it fully formed at the hands of Meissonnier—so far as craft objects are concerned—in the year 1728.

[164] From a contemporary engraving of the design at the Cabinet des Estampes, Va 254b. The monstrance also appears on the altar in Jouvenet's painting *La messe du chainoine de la Porte* already cited.

[165] January, 1727, 135-136.

If the prevalent beliefs as to Italian influence on the formation of Meissonnier's style were justified, we should expect to find works of Italian silverwork which anticipate the character of this piece. Actually I have been unable to find there anything remotely related to such a design.

One might be tempted to suppose that Meissonnier had actually looked in quite another direction, to the north, and derived a hint from the designs of such artists as the Dutchman Adam van Vianen (d. 1627). There had indeed been considerable asymmetry in the designs of these northern artists before any in Italy, from the time of Christian Jamnitzer's *Grotteskenbuch* of 1610. The designs for silverwork issued as Adam van Vianen's by his son,[166] actually with some additions of his own, appeared about 1652-1654.[167] They have obviously some superficial resemblance to Meissonnier's much later work, and he may indeed have been familiar with them and have derived some stimulus from them.

When, however, we analyse the basic schemes of these late mannerist silverworks, we see they are far from anticipating fully the *genre pittoresque* of the rococo. Vianen's pitchers, ewers, and sauce-boats are uniformly shown in profile, and thus their representations are inevitably unsymmetrical. It is rare, though, for them to have any thoroughgoing organic asymmetry in all aspects, such as characterizes the work of Meissonnier. Their vocabulary of forms is also very different. Its basis is the baroque cartouche with bulging plastic field, here with an auricular border. In Meissonnier's work, on the other hand, the chief elements are those developed by the early rococo, the scroll and the palmette realized as a shell. In spite of some apparent similarities, Meissonnier's designs were essentially new.

"Pittoresque" also is one of the chief pieces of surviving silverwork after a design of Meissonnier which is datable by its marks. They are those of Claude Duvivier and of the period 1734-1735, on a candelabrum reproducing the model on Figure 73 of Meissonnier's engraved works.[168] Here base, stem, and socket, of cartilagenous scrollwork, are all spirally twisted, the basic baluster-like profile disguised by leaf, shell and flower, again fully unsymmetrical. So are also the terrines of the marvelous pair executed in 1735 for the Duke of Kingston,[169] illustrated in Figure 115 of Meissonnier's works (Figure 202).

The aesthetic value of such works is very high, from their inner fire, their molten unity of form, carrying into every part the unequalled verve and energy of the artist.

Interesting features may be observed in Meissonnier's designs for the frame of the "Carte Chronologique du Roy fait en 1735," of which several details were engraved. The cartouches which crown the several panels end in varied unbalanced shell motifs. The flanking pilasters are filled, in part, with distorted and fragmentary cartouche scrolls. Very probably of the same time, as we shall see, are the details of a "Bordure pour le portrait du Roi," likewise included in the sixth book of his engraved works. Here the mouldings at the sides of the frame are interrupted by disjointed scrolls, and unsymmetrical cartouches or trophies are

---

[166] *Constighe Modellen*, with title also in Latin and in French: *Modelles artificiels.*

[167] W. R. Zülch: *Entstehung des Ohrmuschelstiles,* 1932, 97 ff.

[168] Sold at the Hôtel Drouot March, 1911, passing to the collection of David Weill. Illustrated by M. Rosenberg: *Der Goldschmiede Merkzeichen,* 3d ed., IV, 1928, pl. 107; Nocq, Alfassa, and Guerin: *Orfevrerie civile française,* n.d., I, pl. 28.

[169] A pair of this design, from the Polovtsoff collection in St. Petersburg, sold in Paris in 1909 to Seligmann, is illustrated by Carsix, *op. cit.*

applied at this point. Thus, at an early date, though in a small way, the *genre pittoresque* penetrated the intimacy of the royal cabinets at Versailles, in a degree scarcely repeated.

Meissonnier was most ambitious, as his obituary recalls, for employment in architecture. As before in the case of Berain, a predecessor in the post of Dessinateur de la Chambre et du Cabinet, he was to find the royal architects too jealous of their own prerogatives to permit his occupations for the Crown to extend beyond the sphere of designing festal decorations and household objects, so that for the fulfilment of greater ambitions he could look only to private clients.

Even before his official appointment he had made a design for the façade of Saint-Sulpice, later engraved as Plate 105 of his works with the legend "Presenté à M. le Curé . . . en 1726." At this date and until 1731 Oppenord still had full charge of all work at Saint-Sulpice and Servadoni was not called in until after that. It is not impossible, nevertheless, that Languet de Gergy was already prepared to entertain proposals from others, though it would not have been out of character, either, for Meissonnier to have volunteered the design. It has often been considered a manifesto of the extreme phase of French rococo. Actually it is little more than an effective union of familiar Italian baroque motifs, without fundamental originality. In plan it may well have been suggested by a project of Pozzo for San Giovanni in Laterano, published in his works;[170] the convex portal there, with kneeling angels above, is taken directly from Bernini's Sant' Andrea del Quirinale. There are relationships also with Guarini's Palazzo Carignano in Turin, begun 1679 and completed after the death of the architect in 1683.[171] Only in the roof, which participates in the swing of the other lines, was there any real innovation. Neither by nature nor by influence—for there was substantially none on French executed works—did this design of Meissonnier have any vital relation with the evolution of architectural style in France.

There is also a "Projet de la chapelle de la Vierge de St. Sulpice . . . fait par ordre"—Meissonnier says this time, with subtle distinction—"de M. le Curé . . . en l'année 1727." If we may believe this statement, we see that Languet de Gergy, already knowing Meissonnier's proposal for the façade, was still prepared at least to receive a design of similar qualities for another part of the church. This too (Figure 203) is a purely baroque design, boldly plastic, of a character close to that of works of the same moment in Turin. Nothing of this kind, either like the altar itself or like the heavy stuccoes of the vault, was executed in France after the beginning of the eighteenth century.

In addition, there is a "Projet fait pour le Maitre Autel de l'Eglise de St. Sulpice," without date, but doubtless of the same moment. It unites motifs of Vassé's altar of Notre Dame and Oppenord's of Saint-Germain-des-Prés, with kneeling angels, no longer so closely equivalent, supporting a monstrance not unlike that of 1727 for the Carmelites. Below the pair of broken scrolls is an inscribed cartouche of violent asymmetry. The scrolled candle branches follow the suggestion of those of French chimney pieces dating back to 1717.

We need not analyse other projects, undated but early, for altars of Saint-Leu at Paris and of Saint-Aignan at Orléans, to which many of the same remarks would apply, nor the minor "Projet d'un Tombeau fait pour Mr. Le President de . . . à Dijon en 1733."

[170] *Perspectiva pictorum et architectorum*, 1693-1700.

[171] The publication of such works in Guarini's *Architettura Civile*, 1737, was posthumous and subsequent to Meissonnier's design.

The Creation of the Rococo

In all these there is heightened movement, energy and plasticity: in spite of the French elements the effect is baroque and Italian. In France such designs of Meissonnier were to remain unexecuted, isolated and uncharacteristic.

The sole design we have of Meissonnier for an entire house is that of the "Maison du Sieur Brethous," a tall "maison bourgeoise" on a block front with converging side-streets — the ancestor of innumerable apartment buildings in the nineteenth-century Paris of Haussmann. Meissonnier's engraved plan permits the site to be readily recognized, from the river Nive, on the quai of which it stands near the Pont Mayou — that is, in Bayonne.[172] The location, on the Spanish frontier, is doubtless characteristic for Meissonnier, who was employed for interiors also by Polish and by Portuguese clients but found little acceptance for such extreme designs in Paris.

The date of the design for this house can fortunately also be established, owing to its proposal to incorporate a public passage from the Place to the Quai. In the Archives de Bayonne are a number of documents of 1733[173] dealing with land conceded to Léon de Brethous for the enlargement of his house, and his request for permission to cover the corner there on condition of providing public access by a passage at the corner. This permission was granted, and the house was accordingly built. It still stands, the most conspicuous in the town, occupied by the Chambre de Commerce. Meissonnier's published design, which shows this passage, may thus be dated in 1733. It is the earliest of his known domestic works, subsequent, however, as we shall see, to a number of interiors in Paris designed and executed by Pineau.

The house is planned very ingeniously to give the rooms a regularity of form in spite of the irregularity of the site. The rounding of the corners of these rooms, while carried through in unusual degree, was not unexampled: there were rounded corners in several rooms of Oppenord at the Palais-Royal, and others we have seen.

The interior treatment follows the traditional basic scheme of French decoration: wainscoted walls, a coved cornice, a central chimney piece with mirror, and, beyond narrow panelled piers, flanking double doorways with painted overdoors (Figures 204-205). Nothing, however, could be more uncharacteristic of France, either before or after, than the turn which Meissonnier gave to this established scheme by the unwonted plasticity of the frames, particularly in the *bel étage*. The over-mantel mirror here has heavy consoles supporting the projecting ends of a massive undulating crown. The door casings, subsuming the overdoors, end in bold volutes. Curvature is made more pervasive by the abandonment of a level cornice, or its interruption by major curves. Quite secondary to the plastic boldness we have remarked was the asymmetry of mirror motifs of the carving of certain panels, both of the piers and of the doors.

All this evidences a strong influence from the late Italian baroque. To assume, however, as German scholars have constantly done, that this Italian influence, in such uncharacteristic works, was the fructifying force in the genesis of the Louis XV style — imagined to be a creation of the Italianate Oppenord and the "Italian" Meissonnier is to misconceive the whole course of chronological development and, particularly, Meissonnier's place in it.

[172] While Destailleur correctly identified the location, it has several times been misstated as in Paris.

[173] Cf. E. Ducéré: *Histoire topographique et anecdotique des rues de Bayonne*, II, 1889, 72-73; *Variétés d'histoire bayonnaise*, 1899, 61-69; *Dictionnaire historique de Bayonne*, 1911, 192. A fire of 1896 affected only the third story and the roof, subsequently restored.

Evolution

Another domestic interior by Meissonnier which is datable is the "Cabinet de Mr. Bielenski, Grand Maréchal de la Couronne de Pologne, executé en 1734," engraved as Plates 87-90 of his works (Figure 206), where a sofa dated 1735, appearing as Plate 94, is for the same client. This Bielenski would be Francois, whose father with the same title died in 1713. François cast in his lot with Stanislas in 1733 and joined him at Danzig, which was besieged from October, 1734. On its capitulation June 30, 1735, he was reconciled with Augustus, who named him grand marshal. The chronology, as we see, is closely related with the design and execution of the room, "d'une construction absolument nouvelle," which was set up by Meissonnier at the Tuileries and received a laudatory description in the *Mercure* of July, 1736.[174] It was a room in which architecture, sculpture and painting, all apparently by the same hand, were richly combined. Large painted wall panels of allegorical subjects filled the space between the central mirrors and the curved corners. The description, which certainly reflects the views of the artist, stresses especially, everywhere, the liason of the different elements. The crown of the window frames "porte immediatement sous la corniche, et paroît la soutenir et former l'architrave." The mirror frame has rich contours "qui ont leur liason avec le chambranle de marbre." Above the chimney piece the cornice "fait ressaut en suivant les mêmes formes qui entourent le haut de la glace." The crown of the contorted dado "s'éleve et vient se lier avec le montant des panneaux de chacun des coins." In describing the frames of the painted panels, the author stresses that "les orillons aux coins . . . sont variés avec goût." Though he speaks of the marble chimney piece as "de forme nouvelle," it was little different from many others of its date. Each half of the double doors has a single panel of the full height, with crosettes of slightly varied form, and with a large flat cartouche of extreme asymmetry in the center. Most exceptional, for a domestic interior of this time, is the ceiling, which returns to the traditions of monumental painting of Pietro da Cortona, with simulated balustrade and arches of heavy baroque form, and with floating figures in the center. Just in the degree, however, that the treatment differs from what was characteristic of the prevailing treatment of French interiors—above all in the breaking of the cornice, and other emphasis on plasticity—the innovations failed to find acceptance and imitation.

There is an interesting relation, not hitherto observed, between the commissions for this room and for the "Appartement fait pour Me. la Baronne de Bezenval," of which an engraved detail is included as Plate 91 of Meissonnier's works (Figure 207). The tablet to the baron Jean-Victor de Besenval—who had been envoy in Poland from 1719 to 1721—designed and executed by Meissonnier at Saint-Sulpice, states that he died at the age of sixty-four, March 11, 1736, and that it was erected by his wife "Catherine Comtesse Bielinska, fille du grand Maréchal de Pologne."[175] We thus learn that the apartment was decorated after 1736, and for a sister, doubtless, of François Bielenski. The one client, like the other, was thus a Pole, so that the Baronne de Besenval should not be cited[176] against the justified

[174] Pages 1691-1694.

[175] Piganiol de la Force, 1742 ed., VI, 405; cf. also the *Mercure* for March, 1736, 604-605. The design of the monument, given as pl. 100 of Meissonnier's engraved works, is conservative in character, without substantial asymmetry.

[176] As by E. Donnell: "Juste Aurèle Meissonnier and the Rococo Style" in *Bulletin of the Metropolitan Museum of Art*, XXXV, 1941, 254-260.

generalization that Meissonnier's interior designs found no acceptance by Parisians, but only by provincials and foreigners. One must avoid also confusing this work, which I cannot localize, with the house later occupied by the more famous Baron de Besenval, Pierre-Victor, son of Jean-Victor and Catherine. That was the old Hôtel Chanac de Pompadour,[177] bought by Besenval in 1767, where he assembled his famous collection and added baths from the designs of Brongniart in 1782.

The design is much less extreme in basic character, with the cornice unbrokenly horizontal, the doorway and overdoor merely rectangular. Even allowing for a certain subjection to French taste, we may surmise that it was for redecoration of wainscot already existing. The mirror frame is composed of a multitude of disjointed scrolls, the doors are handled like a single wall panel with central symmetrical cartouche, the carving of the shutters is freely asymmetric. In this single instance of an interior installed in Paris, Meissonnier restrained himself to a treatment little more extravagant—indeed more conservative in many ways—than the interiors of Pineau. We cannot feel, perhaps because of the restraint or limitations, that it was either the most consisent or the most successful of Meissonnier's designs.

Already by 1734, and thus earlier than any other engravings we know of such character, had begun the issuance of engraved suites after his designs, nearly fifty plates being then ready. The *Mercure* for March of that year carried a brief review of them—reserved, but without hostility—which is significant in wording:

> Il paroit une suite d'Estampes en large, dans le goût d'Etienne la Belle, qui doivent piquer la curiosité du Public et de Curieux du meilleur goût. Ce sont des Fontaines, des Cascades, des Ruines, des Rocailles, et Coquillages, des morceaux d'Architecture qui font des effets bizarres, singuliers et pittoresques, par leurs formes piquantes et extraordinaires, dont souvent aucune partie ne répond à l'autre, sans que le sujet en paroisse moins riche et moins agréable. Il y a aussi des especes de plafonds avec figures et animaux, groupez avec intelligence, dont les bordures sont extrément ingénieuses et variées. Le cartouche qui sert de Frontispice, porte ce Titre : Livre d'Ornemens, inventez et dessinez par J. O. Moissonier, Architecte, Dessinateur de la Chambre et Cabinet du Roy.
>
> Ces Estampes se vendent rue S. Jacques chez la veuve Chereau, aux deux Pilliers d'or. Il y en a près de cinquante gravées par Laureolli.

The *Mercure* in June, 1734, mentioned the appearance of an additional plate, but nothing further.

The cartouche with the title described (Figure 208), appears, with the number 20, among the figures included in the folio of collected works published by Huquier, of which the first part, at least, was issued within the artist's lifetime.[178] The plate with the early title is indeed "en large"—*en largeur*, horizontal—but of small size, about eight by four inches. From the dimensions and character, we may conclude that the series referred to in 1734 surely included the figures numbered 20 to 26, and 28 to 34 (this last group having the title *Cinquieme Livre d'Ornemens inventés par J. A. Meissonnier*). The small vertical plates of the *Livre de legumes inventées et dessinées par J. Me*, with the numbers 13 to 19, are doubtless also early, and may well have been included.

[177] Cf., *Vieux hôtels*, III, 1910, 4-5.

[178] Some time after 1742, the date appearing in the watermark, as in those of other papers subsequent to an edict of that year.

Evolution

The suite *Maison du Sieur Brethous*, of small plates, partly vertical, included in the folio with the numbers 1-9 (in addition to two marked A) could indeed have been engraved at the time the house was designed in 1733, but as nothing of such practical character is mentioned in the *Mercure* I incline to believe it was renumbered later to bring it at the beginning of the book. We must also assume that the large Plates 10-12 (showing the candlestick of 1728) and 35-41 (showing the Carte Chronologique of 1733) were later given these numbers and substituted for some plates of the original series.

The *Livre de Legumes*, presumably at least a year or two earlier than 1734,[179] has for its title an unsymmetrical cartouche, which, while lighter, is not basically different in character from many by Mitelli, so long before, and like Mitelli's is charged with flowers and fruit. Except for those of Toro, it was the first composition of this sort in France. The other plates of the suite show single motifs, four of them variants of the characteristic shell-palmette flanked by scrolls, where the fertile variety of the accessories need not obscure what is still an essential conventionality of scheme.

It is precisely in the plates of what we may baptize the fourth book, with the title-page of 1734, that the fullest originality of Meissonnier was embodied in forms henceforth so widely influential. These seem to be the earliest of what became known as "Morceaux de fantaisie" or "Morceaux de caprice," the most extreme, characteristic and novel expression of the rococo. Basically they are developed, as the *Mercure* recognized, from the cartouche, but its elements are realized in the most varied ways, half plastic, half visionary: broken scrolls, an airy edifice, a cascade in diagonal perspective (Figure 209). As in Watteau's arabesque, otherwise so different, frame, field, and filling became indeed inextricably interwoven. At last, above all in Meissonnier's Figure 34 (Figure 210), the cartouche-work itself becomes architecture. From it came later the architecture of the rococo outside France, never within France itself.

In the *Mercure's* review of these plates we note first the significant allusion to the manner of Stephano della Bella—a relationship by no means superficial, whether it concerns certain elements, like the rim of shell, or the general spirit. The *Mercure* recognized also what was not derivative, but was new, whether in element or in mode. In mode it was the *pittoresque*, "formes . . . dont souvent aucune partie ne répond à l'autre"—our first encounter with the word in this specific sense. In collocation, of which it would be easy to exaggerate the significance, occurs also the word *rocailles*. To exaggerate, because here it is part of the subject matter of cascades and fountains, where concretions, stalagmites, shells had been common since the sixteenth century. The word is still used in its original meaning, which it never wholly lost, but its appearance in this context is nevertheless significant: the *rocailles*, the *coquillages*, were now becoming characteristic elements of the rococo.

These are the works of Meissonnier which can be dated in the earlier years of the *genre pittoresque*. He had indeed vastly contributed to the establishment of its character, not so much by any architectural designs, as by his silverwork, and, ultimately, by his ideal compositions.

[179] One might suppose, from the lack of mention, in the title, of Meissonnier's official post, that it was engraved before 1725, but the title of the fifth book — presumably, like the fourth, as late as 1734 — also omits the author's title of honour.

The Creation of the Rococo

"Meissonier," wrote Jacques-François Blondel,[180] avoit pour principe, disoit-il, de créer de neuf." In these fields, at least, he was successful to a superlative degree in fulfilling the call for creation which, contrary to the doctrine of academism, had so lately been recognized by philosophy as the task and mission of art.

Though Meissonnier was thus chiefly responsible for the impulsion toward asymmetry in France, he was not the first to attempt its application to the design of interiors. Here we shall find him anticipated by Pineau, whose executed works in Paris precede any of the designs of Meissonnier in this field. Moreover, as we shall see, it was he, and not Meissonnier, who gave the French interior the character it was now to assume.

The life and work of Pineau have been very fully studied.[181] In age, a dozen years younger than Oppenord, he stood at the head of the coming generation. Lajoue was younger by two years; Meissonnier, by eleven years. Leaving Russia apparently in 1727, Pineau was doubtless soon back in Paris, although we have no definite record of his presence there until toward 1732.

We have already seen the character of his work in Russia. Symmetry is preserved in it throughout the frames of the panels; except for certain dragons, only the trophies have the freedom of asymmetric composition which had long been commonly allowed them as sculpture.

"De retour à Paris avec sa famille," writes Blondel, "Pineau crut pouvoir y exercer l'architecture comme il avait fait en Russie après le mort de Leblond; mais surpris de trouver tant d'architectes dans cette capitale, il reprit la sculpture; et comme il dessinait bien et composait facilement, il eut une vogue extraordinaire."

In many works he was associated with the architect Leroux. That Blondel has correctly defined their relationship, and that credit for the ornament in these works must be given to Pineau is established by many surviving drawings from his hand. The earliest of the executed examples which can be securely attributed and dated are as follows: decoration of the Hôtel de Rouillé, "vers 1732"; gallery of the Hôtel de Villars, 1732-1733; certain decorations of the Hôtel de Roquelaure, 1733; remodelling of the Hôtel de Mazarin, 1735. Except for the Hôtel de Roquelaure, these crucial works have long been destroyed. Their destruction is responsible for the slight attention paid them, and for the consequent failure to appreciate the full importance, in the history of art, of the rôle played by Pineau. Ample material survives, however, both in his original drawings and in engravings, to permit analysis of their forms and appreciation of their significance.

Even before these works, we venture to suggest, Pineau may well have given the designs for a room in the Hôtel de Matignon, where the sculptor Robillon, at work since 1724, was still active in 1731.[182] The Antichambre of the ground floor (Figure 211) is of a character and a merit quite superior to all others surviving there, with great delicacy and attenuation of carving. We are emboldened to propose its attribution to Pineau not only on internal

---

[180] *Cours d'architecture*, III, 1772, 350.

[181] Biais, *op. cit.*, L. Deshairs: *Nicolas et Dominique Pineau* (Dessins originaux des maîtres décorateurs), n.d., G. Huard in L. Dimier: *Les peintres français du XVIIIe siècle*, I, 1928. In addition to Pineau's manuscript drawings published by these authors there are several (Nos. 246-256) in the De Cloux collection at Cooper Union, New York.

[182] H. Labande, *op. cit.*

grounds, but because of a graphic evidence, hitherto unremarked, connecting Pineau with the house. The rosette of the ceiling in one of the rooms of the principal story (Figure 212) follows identically a plate of "Nouveaux desseins de plafonds inventés par Pineau" included in Mariette's *Architecture françoise*.[183] In the antichambre also the rosette, while not identical in detail, is very close to a design by Pineau.[184] In this room the most strikingly novel detail is the piercing of the mirror head in several oval apertures, letting the glass and the background penetrate the frame. Now we find this appearing at the same moment at the Hôtel de Rouillé, and, a moment later, in one of the new plates (ggR) added to Mariette's 1738 edition of Daviler's *Cours d'architecture*, plates for some of which manuscript drawings by Pineau survive.[185] With these hints we may recognize the room as the work of Pineau.

There is nothing at all revolutionary here—merely an extremely suave, light, gay version of established schemes. Main wall panels with a principal field, as here, falling short of their full height had appeared already at the Élysée, even in the earliest rooms there. It was, however, a favorite treatment with Pineau, which we shall encounter in his work at the Hôtel de Roquelaure and in the gallery of the Hôtel de Villars, not to speak of manuscript designs. Already in these works of Pineau at the Hôtel de Matignon we find a delicacy of relief, a freedom and fantasy in the play of interlace and tendril, which foreshadow the highest achievements of his art.

Of the decorations executed in the old Hôtel de Villequier, Rue des Poulies, on its occupancy by the minister Rouillé, illustrated by Jacques-François Blondel,[186] he writes "elle fut restaurée et augmentée considerablement, vers 1732, sur les dessins de M. Blondel"— that is, as notes make clear,[187] of Jean-François (1683-1756), uncle of the writer. At the Musée des Arts Décoratifs are many original drawings by Pineau inscribed "M. Rouiller, rue des Poulies,"[188] which leave no doubt that he designed the decorations. From these drawings and from the engraved plates included in the fourth volume of Mariette's *Architecture françoise*[189] we are well informed as to the interiors, although the buildings was destroyed soon after 1760.

In the details (Figures 213-216) we remark first, as Cochin observed of Pineau, the extreme attenuation of mouldings and ornaments. The doorways no longer have conventional architraves, but narrow mouldings recessed within a thin outer frame rising to the cornice. The emphasis on height thus secured is further accentuated by the treatment of the doors and the dados, which also offer new fields for the invasion of curvature. While the doors are square-headed (perhaps, in this remodelling, because of the existing form of the opening), the number of their panels is reduced to two by the elmination of any traverses, and in certain rooms their rails sweep in reverse curves, both at the top and at the lock.

[183] Pl. 538 of the Hautecoeur edition. The rosette of our Antichambre is very close to Pineau's drawing reproduced as fig. 117 in Deshairs' *Pineau*, though not identical.

[184] Fig. 117 in Deshairs' *Pineau*.

[185] Deshairs' fig. 104 is the original of pl. 59d; fig. 116, for pl. 101e. All the plates are entirely coherent in style and we cannot doubt that all were from designs of Pineau.

[186] *Architecture françoise*, III, 174, 58-60, and pls. 348-350 of the Guadet edition.

[187] *Ibid.*, III, 58, note *a*, and II, 114, note *a*.

[188] Deshairs, *Pineau*, figs. 83-86, 118, and nos. 145-146.

[189] III, pls. 469-474 of the Hautecoeur edition.

The Creation of the Rococo

In several rooms the familiar moulded dado-rail is abandoned for scrolls with carved motifs uniting the upper and lower panels of the pilaster strip. In some instances the artist employs decorative elements which are unbalanced, finding their reversed equivalent in a corresponding panel on the other side of the central feature. This is the case with the panels flanking the door of the Grand Cabinet de Monsieur Rouillé in Mariette's plate, where the inner mouldings themselves are oppositely scrolled with unbalanced shell-motives supporting sprays of naturalistic flowers.

Pierced rims of such shellwork crown the mirror of the Chambre à coucher de Madame Rouillé, which is bordered by ethereal tapered gaines, pierced and flower-twined—the first of such features used in this way. Elsewhere we find every variety of radiating motif: the scalloped cresting of the mirror in the Cabinet de M. Rouillé, the bat's-wing crowning the panels there, the baskets, fleurons, and sprays, at the central junctions, sometimes with discreet asymmetry.

Pineau's manuscript drawings show whole sides of several rooms. The "Cabinet de Monsieur Drouiller," like the Antichambre at the Hôtel de Matignon, has rounded inner corners, here with unsymmetrical panel mouldings and carving. The small central cartouche above the broad inner panel is set sharply at an angle. The most important feature, however, is the treatment of the pier opposite the chimney piece in this room. As first in the window recess of Oppenord's designs for reconstructing the Palais-Royal, there is a shallow recess with rounded corners, here framing the mirror. This feature was a favorite with Pineau; we find it in numbers of his manuscript designs,[190] one for the Hôtel de Mazarin being, like this one at the Hôtel de Rouillé and the windows of the gallery of the Hôtel de Villars, prior to any example we know in the work of other men. We shall see what importance it assumes in the later development of the style.

The drawing for a ceiling of the Hôtel de Rouillé, like another of substantially identical character,[191] is marked by a great development of the cartouches at the cardinal points, and by a curvature of the upper moulding of the cove, which no longer parallels the wall but sweeps boldly from one cartouche to the other. It is a treatment here found for the first time, which was to be widely adopted. One motif which is surprising, at this time and in this connection, but which was frequently employed by Pineau, is the classical bust in profile which occurs in medallions both in these ceilings and in a mirror head of the Hôtel de Rouillé as engraved.

In the Hôtel de Rouillé, as we can picture it in imagination, there was a freedom, a grace, beyond anything hitherto found in the French interior. Unlike Meissonnier's designs for rooms, with their strong baroque plasticity, Pineau's were all delicate line and surface. His effects of asymmetry, of contrast, were achieved within the characteristic scheme of the French rococo.

The gallery of the Hôtel de Villars, as we learn from the title of the suite of nine plates published by Jacques-François Blondel [192]—was "batie de 1732 à 1733 sur les plans et dessins de l'architecte Leroux." Two drawings for it by Pineau were in the Biais collection, a cartouche and an overdoor with the inscription "Hôtel de Vilars."[193] That Pineau was indeed

---

[190] Deshairs, figs. 1, 9 (1735), 31, 61-64 (1744), 73 (1736), 82, 113 (1750).   [191] Deshairs, figs. 118, 119.

[192] Publication of this suite was announced in the *Mercure*, December, 1746, p. 147. Certain of the plates were later incorporated in Blondel's *Nouveau livre des cinq ordres . . . de Vignole*, and in his *Cours d'architecture*.

[193] Bias, *op. cit.*, 167.

responsible for the ornaments is confirmed by the presence of his name, with that of Bernard, among the payments for sculpture in the accounts for the construction,[194] which was still incomplete at the death of the Maréchal de Villars in 1734.

The gallery (Figures 217-218) occupied the eastern wing of the building, balancing the wing now constituting the Petit Hôtel de Villars. The chimney piece, itself not merely crowned but also flanked by mirrors, was at the outer end; at the inner end there was not a single door—as in the galleries of the Palais-Royal and of the Hôtel de Toulouse, with their central doors—but two glazed doors flanking a central pier, its mirror reflecting that of the chimney piece. The profusion of mirror glass is carried to a point beyond that of any other example.

The tall windows are set in rounded recesses with elliptical *arrière voussures* rising to the cove cornice, of which the lower moulding is the only level, uninterrupted line above the dado, here itself broken at each pier. The upper moulding of the cornice, interrupted by large rocaille cartouches at the center and at the rounded corners, ends against them in large leafy scrolls. Above it the fringe of scrollwork takes on a movement and variety of outline hitherto unexampled, finally dissolving in sprays of delicate naturalistic flowers and tendrils.

On the walls, the repeating piers with mirrors terminate in cartouches with paintings, the corner piers in elaborate scrollwork without any enclosing rectangular moulding. The principal mirrors, like one at the Hôtel de Rouillé, are bordered with fronds of palm spirally wreathed with flowers, suggestive of those in the Chambre de la Reine. One is crowned, like those, by a winged cartouche, the other by wavy rims of shell, themselves ending in smaller wings. Asymmetry—except for the minor twisting of certain central ornaments—appears only in the two narrow panels flanking the chimney piece, where, as in an example at the Hôtel de Rouillé, there is a pronounced unbalance in the scroll motifs, reversed at the two sides to answer one another. Little is left of acanthus anywhere, but bandwork, rollwork, shellwork, palm, garland and spray are united with the plausible irreality and inexhaustible fantasy characteristic, in other periods, of the arabesque.

The marble chimney piece is of the well-established type with herms supporting branching candelabra, little different from the simpler examples by Vassé.

The gallery of the Hôtel de Villars was marked, among the works of the French rococo, by a masculine boldness, in character both with its more than ordinary size and with the personality of the old marshal, its owner. Completely unified, it was a masterpiece the loss of which we cannot fail deeply to regret.

Blondel speaks[195] of the Hôtel de Roquelaure, built by Lassurance, as "continué et decoré intérieurement en 1733 par M. le Roux pour Antoine-Gaston-Jean-Baptiste de Roquelaure" the marshal, who died in 1738. In view of the collaboration of Leroux and Pineau at the Hôtel de Villars just in 1733, we are not surprised that there exist several drawings by Pineau for the decoration of the Hôtel de Roquelaure.[196] The only one now accessible (Figure 219) "pour M le marechal de Roclaure," a mirror with wreathed mouldings and diagonal key, cannot be identified with any of the surviving motifs, but is most closely related to

---

[194] Cited by A. de Champeaux, *op. cit.*, 110.
[195] *Architecture françoise*, I, 1752, 246-249.
[196] Listed by Biais, *op. cit.*, 166; and Deshairs, no. 154.

those of the "Salon Rouge." We may scarcely doubt, from the multitude of features characteristic of Pineau, that both this room and the Grand Salon of the ground story were modified according to his designs. Neither of these rooms conforms to Mariette's plans of the house as first built,[197] which were evidently made before 1733.

In the Grand Salon (Figure 220), of which the shallow recesses in the center of the long walls existed in the original construction, the fireplace, initially at the back, was moved to the recess on the inner long side. An aesthetic motive for this change can be inferred: in its original position the mirror of the chimney piece came opposite a window; now it was placed opposite a wall, where it could be reflected in the mirror of the pier. The change involved a re-panelling of the inner wall, and of the recesses, but not of the projections. Once we appreciate this, we observe that the doorways (still square headed, with heavy, academic casings), and the doors themselves (still with traverses), survive unchanged from the period of 1726, their rigid lines betraying their earlier character. The new work is very suave and flowing, with a wealth of naturalistic detail. In the narrower panels hang delightful trophies of music and gardening, closely related to those of Watteau of which the suite engraved by Huquier was announced in the *Mercure* of March, 1734. The large panels have an inner border of stems wreathed with delicate sprays, in the large frame at the top the palmette is realized as a radiating network of the slenderest leafage. The floral scheme is carried throughout: the whole room is alive with flowers. The cornice appears to have been renewed on designs by Pineau, with scrolled curving upper moulding. Trophies of music again form its principal features among the band- and scrollwork. The corner cartouches have a border of curling feathers, which reappear in the crosettes of the great mirrors. There is endless fertility of gracious imaginings.

In the Salon Rouge (Figure 221), with its curved inner corners, the ceiling is treated much like the one at the Hôtel de Rouillé. The upper moulding of its cove, continuously curved, is here the true cornice of the room, given a suggestion of scrolled pediments over the central elements of wall below. The curvature is heightened beyond anything previous, with numerous double-reverse curves; in the crossettes, in the frames of the overdoors, with the fewest exceptions, there are no longer any smooth mouldings or bands. Everything is foliate, twined, spriggy. Above the mirror and in the equivalent field over the inner door the leafy sprays meander with little firm organization. Though the main lines remained traditional, and though asymmetry is confined to small details, Pineau himself must have felt he had gone too far; never again so far as we know, did he carry dissolution of the elements to such an extreme.

A superb carved panelling formerly ornamented a salon "terminé en hemicycle à deux fenêtres" of the Hôtel Gontaud Saint-Blancard, near the corner of the Rue Saint-Dominique and the Rue du Bac. This house, destroyed by the piercing of the Boulevard Saint-Germain, is one on which I have been unable to secure any helpful documentation. The salon itself has been installed for the past half-century in the Hôtel Pillet-Will, 31, Faubourg Saint-Honoré, where, in our opinion, the three arched doorways must come from another source.[198] The woodwork from the Hôtel Gontaud is apparently from the period around 1735 and

[197] Pls. 223-227 of the Hautecoeur edition.

[198] Their design is surely derivative from that of the doorways in the Chambre du Roi at Fontainebleau, 1753-1754.

from the cycle of Pineau, with a strong resemblance to his work at the Hôtel de Roquelaure.[199]

The Hôtel de Mazarin, for which numerous drawings by Pineau survive,[200] stood on the site of 59-61, Rue de Varenne, and was remodelled by the Duchesse de Mazarin (previously Marquise de la Vrillière) after she had sold her house in the Rue St. Dominique to the Princesse douarière de Conti. Blondel spoke of the new Hôtel de Mazarin as "une de nos maisons particulières à Paris décorée intérieurement avec le plus de magnificence, les ornemens et les meubles sont d'une grande beauté et travaillés dans le goût le plus moderne; les curieux sont intéressés à visiter cet hôtel dont la restauration et les embellissements, tels qu'on les voit aujourd'hui, sont de M. Le Roux . . . et furent faits en 1735."[201]

It is of the Hôtel de Mazarin that Blondel's interlocutors, two amateurs, partisans of the older and newer styles, speak in *Les amours rivaux*, published in 1774. Here Blondel himself obviously espouses the triumphant classical reaction, but not without permitting his antagonist to make an able presentation of the claims of the rococo. The latter says: "Les dedans . . . sont les plus agréables . . . les plus variés que j'aie jamais vus . . . Tout, dans les appartements, prêsente une contraste admirable. On ne remarque pas une ligne droite, ni dans les plans, ni dans les élévations. La symmetrie en est bannie. La composition et l'élégance des ornemens n'ont jamais rien offert de plus satisfaisant; idées riantes que la magie des glaces répète encore et semble multiplier à l'infini . . . Ces dessins charmants ont été donnés par M. Leroux . . . et ont été exécutés par Pinault, artiste à qui nous devrons toujours une reconnaissance et une admiration infinies pour toutes les jolies choses qui embellissaient nos demures . . ." To which Blondel's protagonist replies severely: "Les Le Roux, les Le Grand, les Tannevot, ne sachant guère que faire des plans, eurent recours au prestige des embellissements et s'addressèrent aux Pinault, aux Meisonnier, aux Lajoux, qui, dans la suite eurent des imitateurs dans les Mondon et les Cuvillier, et ceux-ci achevèrent d'introduire le mauvais goût dans les ornemens, consequemment dans l'architecture."

Inwards from the porte-cochère, with its curved recess and cartouche, its extravagantly carved doors,[202] we follow the fragmentary designs available to us, noting indeed the prevalence of variety and "contraste"—always some touch of asymmetry, with occult equivalence. But, alas, the building itself, so highly vaunted, is gone, and these designs, mostly of single details, by no means enable us to reconstruct it mentally. We learn just enough to guess the depth of our loss.

Of other executed work of Pineau in the 'thirties,[203] we know only his designs for the re-

---

[199] This resemblance was noted by Vacquier: *Vieux hôtels*, VI, 9, but he nevertheless repeats the attribution to Boffrand suggested by Champeaux, *op. cit.*, 113, who reports the original form of the room.

[200] Deshairs, figs. 8, 926, 109, and nos. 60, 82?, 150, 151, 187, 189, beside five others mentioned by Biais, *op. cit.*, 163.

[201] *Architecture françoise*, I, 215 note a. Piganiol de la Force, 1742 ed., VII, 104, says "vers l'an 1735."

[202] Engraved in Mariette, *Architecture françoise*, pl. 454.

[203] Two writers who were very loose in making attributions to Pineau were Champeaux and Lady Dilke, writing in 1898 and 1901 respectively. They assigned him the carvings of the Élysée and many other buildings merely on the ground of their high quality and his own celebrity. Even their casual allusions to his name have since led it to be applied without qualification, as for instance to the room from 43, Boulevard Beaumarchais acquired by the Kunstgewerbe-Museum in Berlin, remaining in the building now occupied by the Staatliche Kunstbibliothek. Cf. R. Graul: *Dekoration und Mobiliar*, 1905, 32-38. This good but not exceptional work, without the smallest trace of asymmetry, has obviously no connection with Pineau.

modelling for Boutin, in 1738, of the house which stood at 77-79, Rue de Richelieu,[204] which add little to the idea we have gained from the richer surviving interiors we have seen. We note, however, the door head of the Salle de Compagnie (Figure 222), where the opening itself is of wavy outline, the first of the sort we have encountered.

We make bold to attribute to Pineau a group of designs for interiors of the Hôtel de Soubise engraved on eleven plates of Mariette's *Architecture françoise*, captioned as "du dessein du Sieur Harpin," or, in many cases, "executés sur les desseins du sieur Harpin, sculpteur du Roi." These designs have always presented a puzzle, for no such works survive anywhere in the palace. It has been said[205] that there is no reason *a priori* to doubt the positive affirmation of the captions that these works were executed; we find, however, ample reason against this *a posteriori*. The dimensions of the rooms shown cannot be reconciled in most cases with any of those in the plans of the executed building.[206]

"Harpin," no doubt, was Louis-Jacques Herpin, who had executed carvings with Dugoullons, in 1709, at the Chapelle de Versailles (*Comptes* V, 320) and already had worked for Boffrand, from 1709 to 1714, in the transformation of the Hôtel de Mayenne.[207] We have seen him at work for Courtonne at the Hôtel de Matignon in 1723.

The best evidence for both the authorship and the date of these designs is their own character. We have only to compare one of them, for a Salle de Compagnie (Figure 224) with designs of Pineau we have already seen to appreciate that they were from his pencil, notwithstanding their being nominally credited to someone else, as was frequently the case with him in other instances. In other plates we note particularly the characteristic pilaster capital which Pineau had invented. We have seen Pineau designing for Leroux and Mouret, there is no reason he should not have done so for Herpin. The pronounced asymmetry of the crowns of the panels, the design of the doors—so close to that of doors at the Hôtel de Rouillé—would indicate a date around 1732. That was the year of the marriage of the Prince de Soubise, and was but three years before the great remodelling of the Hôtel de Soubise, which followed not these designs but designs furnished by Boffrand.

An initiative so novel and so brilliant as Pineau's was not long in gaining diffusion by engraving. In the fourth volume of *Architecture françoise* of Jean Mariette, of which the title-page is dated 1738,[208] and in the later collection given the title *Architecture à la mode*, are assembled no less than sixty plates engraved after Pineau's compositions, mostly of earlier style than those published elsewhere. Pierre-Jean Mariette's new edition of Daviler's *Cours d'architecture*, 1738, contains five designs for which his authorship is certain;[209] the coherence of the other newly-added plates of decoration enables us to conclude that all of them are from his drawings. Jacques-François Blondel's first book *De la distributions des maisons de*

---

[204] Deshairs, figs. 28, 71-75, and nos. 45, 139-142.

[205] Ch.-V. Langlois: *op. cit.*, 157-158.

[206] In the case of the "Grand Cabinet dans le Grand Appartement" (pl. 457 of the Hautecoeur edition), only, the width and the position of the chimney piece correspond with those of the Grand Cabinet adjoining the oval salon.

[207] Accounts of the Prince de Vaudémont, already cited.

[208] We have seen that the plates of this volume include some of buildings of a date as late as 1746.

[209] On pls. 59d, 59e "executez à Paris sur les dessins du Sieur Pineau, sculpteur" (for which the manuscript designs are reproduced by Deshairs, figs. 104 and 89) and 101e, without name of designer (for which Pineau's drawing is reproduced by Deshairs, fig. 116).

plaisance, 1737-1738, also includes two figures[210] which, though signed "Blondel inv. et f.," are, nevertheless, from surviving drawings by Pineau. We need scarcely raise the question, as did Deshairs, whether they are after sketches by Blondel; the case of the Hôtel de Rouillé, where Blondel also gives no credit to Pineau, yet all the sketches are from Pineau's hand, is a sufficient answer. Indeed we cannot doubt that here also further designs (e.g. Figure 223), irrespective of their legends, are from designs by Pineau.[211] The same is true of the suites of *Divers décorations de cheminées* issued without date in the name of Jean Mansart de Jouy, and later reengraved in part for Blondel's Vignola. Pineau, we shall see, worked for the brother of this grandson of the Premier Architecte; it is, however, not on such a relation, but on the character of the designs themselves, that we base our attribution.

Mariette, in the text of his edition of Daviler's *Cours*, stresses several times the need for new plates in a work where the edition of 1720 had been unchanged from that of Le Blond in 1710: "La décoration intérieure des appartemens à eprouvée de si grands changemens qu'elle a tout a fait changée de face," "les lambris qu'on fait présentement sont si différens de ceux qui était en usage il y a quelques années, qu'on a trouvé à propos d'en donner de nouveaux dessins."

The character of all these ideal designs does not differ substantially from that of Pineau's executed works already discussed, though they anticipate his later executed works in certain further freedoms. Thus we find doorways where the head of the door itself has a fluid curve,[212] as in the Hôtel Boutin of the same year; rooms where the dado is curved below the main panels;[213] others where, in the main panels, the mouldings themselves are curved unsymmetrically, finding their pendants in those on the other side of the chimney piece (Figure 225).[214] In these plates and in the manuscript designs we find the creations of an inexhaustible fantasy.

As a further analysis of Pineau's work we cannot do better than quote, hostile as it is, Cochin's ironic passage on Pineau, which has not, to my knowledge, been reprinted. His pretended champion says:

> Nous fîmes enfin la découverte du héros dont nous avions besoin. Ce fut un Sculpteur, qui n'avoit point pû se gâter à Rome, car il n'y avoit point été, bien qu'il eût vû beaucoup de pays. Il s'étoit formé avec nous, & avoit si bien goûté notre maniere, & si peu ces prétendues régles anciennes, que rien ne pouvoit restreindre l'abondance de son génie. Il sçavoit assez d'architecture ancienne pour ne pas contrecarrer directement ceux qui y tenoient avec trop d'obstination; mais il la déguisoit avec tant d'adresse qu'il avoit le mérite de l'invention, & qu'on ne la reconnoissoit qu'à peine. Il allégea toutes ces moulures[215] & tous ces profils où Oppenor & Meissonnier avoient voulu conserver un caractere qu'ils appelloient mâle; il les traita d'une délicatesse qui les fait presque échapper à la vûe; il trouva dans les mêmes espaces le moyen d'en mettre six fois davantage; il s'affranchit tout d'un coup de la loi qu'ils s'étoient follement imposée de lier toujours

---

[210] I, pl. 93 and II, pl. 53, from drawings reproduced by Deshairs, figs. 56 and 218.

[211] Many of the same plates, reengraved, are included also in Blondel's Vignola.

[212] Daviler-Mariette: *Cours d'architecture*, pl. 99H.

[213] *Ibid.*, 99D and Blondel: *Distribution des maisons de plaisance*, II, pl. 62 (fig. 223).

[214] Daviler-Mariette, pl. 57.

[215] The statement is exactly correct, the profiles of Pineau remain of the same types, but still further attenuated and lengthened.

leurs ornemens les uns aux autres; il les divisa, les coupa en mille pieces, toujours termi-
nées par ce rouleau qui est notre principale ressource; & afin que ceux qui aimoient la
liaison ne s'apperçussent pas trop de ces interruptions, il fit paroître des liaisons apparentes,
par le secours d'une fleur, qui elle-même ne tenoit à rien, ou par quelque légereté égale-
ment ingénieuse; il renonça pour jamais à la régle & au compas: on avoit déja banni la
symmetrie, il rencherit encore là-dessus. S'il lui échappa quelquefois de faire des panneaux
semblables l'un à l'autre, il mit ces objets symmétriques si loin l'un de l'autre, qu'il auroit
fallu une attention bien suivie pour s'appercevoir de leur ressemblance. Aux agrafes du
ceintre des croisées qui ci-devant ne représentoient que la clef de l'arc décorée, il substitua
de petits cartels enrichis de mille gentillesses & posés de travers, dont le pendant se trouvoit
à l'autre extrêmité du bâtiment. C'est à lui qu'on doit l'emploi abondant des palmiers, qui
à la verité avoient été trouvés avant lui, & que votre auteur blâme si ridiculement. Il
établit solidement l'usage de supprimer tous les plafonds, en faisant faire à des Sculpteurs,
à bon marché, de jolies petites dentelles en bas-relief, qui réussirent si bien, qu'on prit le
sage parti de supprimer les corniches des appartemens pour les enrichir de ces charmantes
dentelles. C'est notre triomphe que cette proscription des corniches; rien ne nous donnoit
plus de sujétion que ces miseres antiques dont on les ornoit, & ausquelles votre écrivain
paroît si attaché. Il y falloit une exactitude & une justesse, qui pour peu qu'on y manquât,
se déceloit d'abord à des yeux un peu severes. Nous regrettons encore ce grand homme,
quoique ses merveilleux talens ayent été remplacés sur le champ par quantité de Sculpteurs,
non moins abondans que lui dans cette sorte de génie. C'est à lui que nous avons l'obligation de cette supériorité que nous avons acquise, & que nous sçaurons conserver; & on peut
dire à sa gloire que tout ce qui s'éloigne du goût antique lui doit son invention, ou sa
perfection.

After all we have seen, we can no longer doubt that it was Pineau who was primarily responsible for the creation and the adoption of the *genre pittoresque* in French interiors. Earlier
than Meissonnier, he designed and executed rooms fully incorporating the crucial innovations. Far more than Meissonnier or any other, he fixed the character and type of detail destined to prevail in France. Among all the works, his own were to remain unsurpassed.

Blondel named the painter Jacques de Lajoue (1686-1761),[216] with Pineau and Meissonnier, as one of the "trois premiers inventeurs du genre pittoresque." Some of his works of
this character are indeed early in date. Son of an "architecte et maître maçon," he first appears in 1721, when he was *agréé* at the Academy of Painting, with an architectural view
and two landscapes. In such paintings he was deeply indebted to Watteau, with whom he
worked as he worked also with Lancret, and in 1729 with Boucher. In 1731, beside certain
canvases for the Crown, he painted an illusionistic perspective in the library of Sainte-
Geneviève.

Two painted architectural compositions of Lajoue, dated 1734, constituted overdoors of
a cabinet of the collector Bonnier de la Mosson, presumably at the Hôtel de Lude as remodelled by Leroux.[217] One of these (Figure 227)[218] shows a cabinet of physical apparatus, of

[216] Cf. Huard: "Lajoue," in Dimier: *Les peintres français du XVIIIᵉ siècle*, II, 1930, 347-361, where the material regarding him is best assembled.

[217] Brice, 1752 ed., IV, 45. While we might presume that Pineau would have been active here, as in other
works for Leroux at this period, we cannot establish this: Bonnier's name does not occur on any of the manuscript
drawings we have by Pineau, where there appear those of so many other clients.

[218] The property of M. Georges Wildenstein, who kindly signalized to me the presence of the other, never
photographed, in a private collection in Paris. Presumably they are the same ones which passed by sale in 1774.

which Bonnier was a devotee. Although it has been supposed to show a room of the house, we cannot doubt that it is purely fanciful in design, not representative of any actual construction.[219] It embodies spatial forms of a richness and variety much beyond anything executed in France.[220] A domed room, its arches borne by Ionic columns, and, on one side, by an intermediate pier formed by a tall clockcase, opens into neighboring alcoves, with hollowed niches and bulging counters for the instruments. The forms of mass and detail offer us nothing new; it is a fantasia in which the elements are familiar.

Another ensemble of decorative paintings, less significant for our purpose, was executed in 1737 for the cabinet of the Duc de Pecquigny.

Lajoue designed also a great number of suites of engraved ornament. They bear no dates, but some of them can be identified with suites mentioned in the *Mercure* from 1734 to 1736.[221] Another is dedicated to the Duc d'Antin, who died in 1736. Once more, as in 1699, it is essential to pay close attention to the dating, to determine priorities in these very crucial years.

The earliest seems to be the *Premier Livre de divers morceaux d'architecture, paysages et perspectives*, these plates apparently being the "Cartouches gravés" noticed in the *Mercure* for September, 1734. The frames are circular, with light cartouche borders of scroll- and shell-work, with floral adjuncts, all perfectly symmetrical. Within these are views of architectural compositions, chiefly fountains in which shells are conspicuous — fountains themselves symmetrical, seen sometimes frontally, more often diagonally — with adjuncts of curving stairways flanked by consoles and with backgrounds of foliage recalling Watteau. As compared with Meissonnier's plates described in March of the same year, the architecture of Lajoue's is more practicable, less fantastic by far, the frames are more conventional, and there is no such fusion of filling and frame. There can be no doubt that it was Meissonnier who was in advance.

It did not take Lajoue long, however, after the issuance to Meissonnier's early suites, to come abreast of the younger leader. The *Troisième livre de cartouches* (which must follow the *Second livre de cartouches*),[222] is dedicated to the Duc d'Antin, and was thus surely engraved before his death on December 2, 1736 — perhaps appreciably before that. In these ingenious examples, with trophy-like attributes of the arts, of the sea, and others, the cartouche proper is realized in various corresponding forms, as a painter's canvas, as a great shell, and so on. This time all is *contraste*, notably in a cartouche of striking dissymmetry with attributes of gardening, not irrelated to Meissonnier's *Livre de légumes*.

The *Livre nouveau de divers morceaux de fantaisie* is noticed in the *Mercure* for May, 1736, as "12 feuilles . . . gravées par les meilleurs Maîtres et qui mérite bien de l'être . . . des sujets

[219] A drawing "Coin du cabinet de physique et mécanique de Bonnier de la Mosson," signed "Courtonne, 1740" (i.e. not Jean Courtonne, who died in 1739), shows the actual forms of the room, shelves framed by palm stems with extravagant unsymmetrical branchings. Reproduced in *Revue de l'art ancienne et moderne*, LXIX, 1936, 70.

[220] The only approach to it in an executed work is in the library, itself very much simpler, at the Hôtel Lambert, executed doubtless in the tenure of Marin de la Haye, after 1746.

[221] September, 1734, 2027.

[222] The *Livres de buffets*, dedicated to Bonnier de la Mosson, is noticed in the *Mercure* for July, 1735, 1611, which also mentions a plate "*la Fontaine*, d'aprés M. de la Joüe, en large . . . un Morceau fort agréable," engraved by Aveline.

de fantaisies singulières et très élégantes, de la Composition de M. de la Joüe." They are indeed well named: the flights of fancy outdo even the wildest of Meissonnier's, whose scheme of union of cartouche, frame and filling they adopt for their violently asymmetric motifs of fountains, treillages, canopies, and grottoes, employed with variations appropriate to the titles in such plates as the *Fontaine glacée* (Figure 226) the *Naufrage*, and the Turcquerie *Trône du Grand Seigneur*. Other plates of Lajoue exploit Chinese motifs.

While the suite *Nouveaux tableaux d'ornements et rocailles* (like its sequel the *Second livre de tableaux et rocailles*) is not among those which can be specifically dated, the symmetrical, relatively backward character of its plates places it as early as any of Lajoue's, and thus as early as 1734. In this instance, though there are fountains with incrustations, it would appear that the word *rocaille* was indeed beginning to take on a wider meaning than its traditional one.

Lajoue, we see, designed nothing to be actually built. His influence toward freedom, like his whole work, is in the realm of fantasy. In this general movement of the arts he can scarcely rank in importance with Pineau and Meissonnier.

As immediate "imitators" of the "three first inventors" Blondel, as we have seen, named Mondon and Cuvilliès, both active within the 'thirties.

Jean Mondon le fils, whom the *Mercure* in its first notice of April, 1736, calls a "jeune homme," "sculpteur en bijoux, ciseleur," dated in that year his third, fourth, fifth and sixth suites continuing the series begun by his undated *Premier livre de forme rocquaille et cartel* — a title in which the word rocaille first appears, to my knowledge, as an adjective characterizing the genre we are discussing. Cartel was a common equivalent of cartouche. The forms were thus described as rocaille-like or cartouche-like. They are most extravagant in composition as well as in their motifs, which include Chinese figures, dragons, phoenixes (Figure 228). There is little here of incrustation in the older sense of rocaille. A few plates, to be sure, show fountains, but even these have little or no stalagmite work; in the majority there are no fountains or grottoes at all. It is easy to see how the word came, especially in modern works, to apply to all pronounced examples of the *genre pittoresque*.

François de Cuvilliès (1695-1768), born in Hainaut but with French training, worked entirely abroad. He became before 1711 one of the pages of the Elector Max-Emmanuel of Bavaria, then in exile in France, whom he accompanied on his return to Munich in 1715. After preparation for military engineering, he was sent to Paris, where he appears to have studied from 1720 to 1724 under Jean-François Blondel. From 1725 he had the title of architect to the Court of Bavaria and held posts of increasing dignity under successive electors until his death in 1768. We need concern ourselves here only with his first engraved suites of ornament.[223] They were themselves published in Munich, though no doubt, as later suites expressly state, also offered for sale in Paris.

The earliest of all is the *Livre de Cartouches* of 1738 (Figure 229), followed at intervals, down to 1745, by suites of other subjects in the same general series. As no other work of such advanced character had been executed in Paris at the time of Cuvilliès' earlier studies there, he must have acquired his own familiarity with the intervening developments through engravings. The very first cartouches are unsymmetrical, derivative doubtless from those of men we have discussed, although never slavishly imitated. Cuvilliès distinguishes designs as

[223] Catalogued by J. Laran: *François de Cuvilliès*, Paris, n.d. (*Les grands ornemenistes*).

"irreguliers" or "reguliers" on the criterion of symmetry, and includes suites of both kinds. The prime source for the interior designs, like the *Livre de Lambris* (Figure 230), was the engravings of Pineau. While I have found no single motif copied literally, the family resemblance is extremely close. On Pineau's schemes and motifs, Cuvilliès, in such earlier suites, rang the changes with inexhaustible facility. Lajoue was also a source of inspiration: his title *Morceaux de fantaisie* was taken over by Cuvilliès for a suite which reflects the Parisian artist's rocaille fountains and trellises. Clearly, however, in spite of this facility, he was not a pioneer creator of the first order.

Boucher is not mentioned by Blondel in company with the men so far discussed, yet this artist, so much more highly gifted than some of them, would well have deserved it. François Boucher (1703-1770) developed precociously, winning the grand prize in painting at twenty, going to Italy at twenty-four and returning to be made a member of the Academy in 1731. Beside his tireless activity in painting and tapestry design, he was busily occupied both as an engraver, for instance of some of Watteau's arabesques, and as an independent designer. He contributed illustrations, as did Oppenord, to the famous Molière edition of 1734. Few of his suites of ornament are dated, but certain of them fall in the second half of the 'thirties. Some follow the scheme of the arabesques of Watteau, but with greater use of the cartouche as an adjunct; others develop the initiative of Meissonnier.

Among the latter the fountains of a suite engraved by Huquier, datable by the *Mercure* of April, 1736, are richly sculptural, with shelly basins irregularly composed, as are the frames of certain more purely ornamental compositions committed to copper by the same engraver. Others, symmetrical, are closer to Lajoue's early work. A suite of arabesques engraved by Cochin and Duflos includes compositions related to Lajoue's *Morceaux de Fantaisie* of 1736, but may probably be later than that, as neither of these engravers is known to have worked for Boucher until after 1740. One of these plates bears as a title merely the word *Rocaille*, although including, beside shellwork, the most diverse motifs of the period.

Of critical opinion of the first reception of the *genre pittoresque* we have few testimonies.

The *Temple du goût* published in 1733 by Voltaire, fresh from Palladian England, brushes it lightly in its social satire of the palace of the parvenu:

> Le tout brisé, verni, sculpté, doré,
> Et des badauds à coup sur admiré

and, by contrast, in the account of the Temple du Goût itself, prophecy of a reaction still far in the future:

> Il n'a point les défauts pompeux
> De la chapelle de Versailles,
> Ce colifichet fastueux
> Que du peuple éblouit les yeux
> Et dont le connaisseur se raille.
> Simple en était la noble architecture
> Chaque ornement, à sa place arrêté
> Y semblait mis par la nécessité,
> L'art s'y cachait sous l'air de la nature
> L'oeil satisfait embrassait sa structure
> Jamais surpris et toujours enchanté.

The Creation of the Rococo

The Academy of Architecture, in its deliberations, gave no utterance. It continued to discuss, with the utmost pedantry, the minutiae of the orders, while passing over in silence the freedom which, in practice, some of its members admitted in interiors. Its dictum of December 17, 1736: "La Compagnie . . . verra . . . avec plaisir l'émulation s'appliquer à de nouvelles études et . . . elle croit devoir son sufrage aux découvertes dont il résulte plus d'élégance et de noblesse dans la composition, plus d'ordre et d'arrangement dans les parties" was given not on such designs as Pineau was executing for Leroux, but merely on a proposal of Tannevot for handling the minor details of the Doric entablature."[224]

The *Mercure*, as we have seen, reviewed Meissonnier's plates of 1734, of the fullest extravagance, as designs "qui font des effets bizarres, singuliers, et pittoresque, par leurs formes piquantes et extraordinaire . . . sans que le sujet paroisse moins riche et moins agréable." Its notice of Meissonnier's Cabinet for Bielenski, which, it said, would give in Poland "une idée très-avantageuse du progrès des Beaux-Arts en France,"[225] was more in the nature of a puff. Lajoue's plates, as we have seen, were also favourably noticed.

As regards interiors of the new character, the first published comments are those of 1737 and 1738 in the *Maisons de Plaisance* of Jacques-François Blondel—always an advocate of the golden mean between pro and con. Regarding unsymmetrical ornaments "dans le goût du temps," which he illustrates, he speaks more than once of "la prudence dont il faut user à l'égard de ce derniers," and of "ces contrastes qui appartiennent si peu à la bonne architecture," and adds "c'est dans la décoration des petits appartemens destinés au délassement que l'on peut seulement s'abandonner à la vivacité de son génie à l'égard des ornemens." He is more severe in the matter of confusion of attributes: "les plus respectables paraissent confondus avec des ornemens qui ne doivent leur naissance qu'à une imagination bisarre . . . l'on trouve partout un amas ridicule de coquilles, de dragons, de roseaux, de palmiers et de plantes, qui font à present tout le prix de la décoration intérieur." In making acknowledgments for certain plates, he speaks of Pineau "que la fecondité de son génie a rendu si célèbre"; and elsewhere says of such plates "on pourra s'apperçevoir que les examples [sont] variés, sans avoir trop donné dans le goût de ce siècle." Fortunate it was that the timidity of academicians and critics could not stifle this taste.

Thus came to fulfillment, in an advanced phase, one of the most fanciful, gayest, most delightful of all artistic creations, now fully worthy of a name of its own, the rococo. For the moment public admiration was almost universal. The fire of the rococo was now to sweep all Paris, all Europe, and, what was more difficult, to penerate even the massive walls of the royal palace of Versailles itself.

Other Designers, 1735-1745

The Bâtiments du Roi

The long régime which had governed the Bâtiments since 1708 was now drawing to a close. The Duc d'Antin, dying at the end of 1736, was succeeded as Director-general by the

---

[224] *Procès-verbaux*, V, 201. Cf. Lemonnier's introduction to vol. VI, xxix-xxx. He speaks again of this in a paper "Pour le pensée artistique au XVIIIᵉ siècle d'après les procès-verbaux de l'académie d'architecture" in *Bulletin de la Société de l'histoire de l'art français*, 1935, 275-288. The novelty and modernity demanded in subject and treatment in the prize competitions of 1738 and 1739 do not, however, imply any hospitality to the *genre pittoresque*.
[225] July, 1736, 1692.

Controller-general Orry, notoriously incompetent in artistic matters, who occupied himself almost exclusively with the financial aspects of his post.

As Premier Architecte, De Cotte had been succeeded on his retirement in December, 1734, by Jacques Gabriel, already sixty-seven years of age, as he, in turn, was to be succeeded, in 1742, by his vastly more gifted son. Ange-Jacques Gabriel (1698-1782) had his training wholly in France. Made Contrôleur des Bâtiments and admitted to the second class of the Academy on his marriage in 1728, Contrôleur de Versailles in 1734, he succeeded on De Cotte's death in 1735 to the vacancy in the first class of the Academy. In 1741 he was named "Architecte ordinaire du Roi," before his accession to the highest place. Unlike his father he was an exceedingly facile designer and draughtsman, whom it must have been a pleasure to watch. The Marquis d'Argenson noted in 1739: "Le Roi fait continuellement dessiner devant lui le jeune Gabriel de ses Bâtiments."[226] From many touches in his early work which are similar to those in the works on which Aubert collaborated with his father, we may well suppose he had learned much from that gifted designer. His biographer assumes, no doubt rightly, that the works of the elder Gabriel in his later years were from the hand of the son.[227] Hundreds of drawings, in the utmost detail, survive from his own hand at the Archives Nationales. Indeed, during his tenure, at least in its earlier years, subordinate draughtsmen played a rôle of complete unimportance in design, for the first time since the advent of Mansart.

The deaths of Dugoullons, Le Goupil and Taupin between 1731 and 1734 left as the leading executant Jacques Verberckt (1704-1771), born in Antwerp but from 1725 in Paris, where he is mentioned in their atelier, as we have seen, from 1730. Unlike Vassé, whose death had followed in 1736, Verberckt, for the royal work, did not make his own designs, but followed closely the extremely detailed indications of the younger Gabriel.

A first taste of the new administration came from the decision to panel the Chambre de la Reine. Two fine rendered drawings from the hand of Ange-Jacques Gabriel are preserved, of which one, with the royal approval, bears the inscription "Elevation du côte de la cheminée de la Chambre de la Reine, comme elle est résolue de faire lambrissé en 1735."[228] It shows the main piers of Vassé which were already in place, with new tall panels richly ornamented (Figure 175). Verberckt had nearly 50,000 livres for carving here in 1735 and 1736. The panels, which are much more delicate than the monumental frames of 1730, bear a close general resemblance to those of Dugoullons in the salon of the Hôtel de Lassay, having medallions with figural reliefs at top and bottom as well as at the center. In their details, however, they are less free, more conservative, more conventional: the main mouldings, squared out with *mosaïque*, have C-scrolls instead of S-scrolls, the outlines of the medallions themselves are simpler, the interlaces less delicate and naturalistic.

In the mid-'thirties were created the first rooms of the Petits Appartements du Roi, in the roofs to the right of the Cour de Marbre, above the Cabinets du Roi. These rooms are often loosely spoken of as the Appartement des Maîtresses, but this is a misnomer for the period prior to Madame Du Barry — Mesdames de Nesle and Madame de Pompadour hav-

---

[226] *Journal du marquis d'Argenson*, ed. Rathery, II, 192.
[227] E. de Fels: *Ange-Jacques Gabriel*.
[228] O¹ 1774, one reproduced in colour in Fels, *op. cit.*, as pls. XXXIX-XL.

ing occupied apartments distinct from but connected with them. At first the Petits Appartements du Roi comported a dining room (soon known as the Cabinet Vert) with a curved recess, and a gallery ending in a hemicycle. Both had dormers deeply recessed. As described by La Martinière in 1741, the carving, in which Verberckt participated, was of a delicacy proportioned to the low-ceilinged rooms; the woodwork, except for the mirror frames, was not gilded, but painted *au vernis* in tender colors. In the Cabinet Vert some remains of these colors, green and cream, survive, but the rooms have been so often remodelled[229] that we cannot be certain even that the delicate tracery of the window recesses is of the earliest period. Already by 1737 the total expenses in the Petits Cabinets, including this suite, had mounted since 1722 to 580,000 livres.[230]

At this period, before 1738, the inner cabinets in the main story of the King's apartment had undergone some first modifications,[231] by walling up the openings between the Cabinets des Tableaux to make two rooms, of which the Cabinet d'Angle, supplied with a corner fireplace, assumed the form and name of Cabinet à Pans.[232] Here the walls were then still covered with damask and hung with paintings. The doors were in shallow curved recesses, of the type initiated by Oppenord and popularized by Pineau. On the two mirror frames occupying the diagonal faces Verberckt lavished all his virtuosity. The inner moulding, beaded and wreathed with flowers, is accompanied by an outer band, reminiscent of the tapered gaine which Pineau had lately employed at the Hôtel de Rouillé, but here hung, above mid-height, with playful trophies. It is an interruption less pronounced than that in Meissonnier's frame for the King's portrait, which may well have been the first of all features of this kind. On the crossettes are winged cherubs, seated or floating; before the glass hang garlands of flowers as already at Bonn, at the Hôtel de Soubise and at Rambouillet, contemporary with the Cabinet à Pans.

The ceiling (Figure 231),[233] necessarily new, had a cove without an upper moulding, with winged cartouches at the corners and a fringe of scrollwork in which broad ribbed surfaces, as at the Hôtel de Lassay, are to be noted. As an indication of sources, however, we may mention also the profile heads in the medallions, so exceptional at the time, which we have seen in Pineau's work at the Hôtel de Rouillé and in the Grand Cabinet of the Hôtel de Soubise. The winged cartouche with rim of shell is conspicuous here as elsewhere in the apartment. In Gabriel's drawing, the field of the cartouche is modelled plastically, but in all surviving executed examples of the sort at Versailles the field airily continues the plane of the surrounding surface.

---

[229] The varnish was refreshed in 1756, and carving of some importance was executed in 1767, according to documents cited by Nolhac: *Le Château sous Louis XV*, 1898, 182.

[230] Memoir by Gabriel cited *ibid.*, 175, where on following pages other documents are assembled. The paintings of De Troy and Lancret for the dining room are of 1735.

[231] The detailed history of the transformations of the Arrière Cabinets, the Petits Cabinets and the Petits Appartements du Roi may be disentangled from the mass of drawings in the cartons o¹ 1771 and 1773. These show that all the work so far mentioned preceded the changes of 1738.

[232] Cf. Ch. Hirschauer: "Le Cabinet d'Angle et sa décoration" in *Revue de l'histoire de Versailles*, Années 1917-1918, 273-284. The drawings of 1753 in the Bibliothèque de Versailles clearly show the doorways as well as the mirror frame of the 'thirties, the latter moved in 1760 and still surviving.

[233] This drawing, mislaid in the carton for the Appartement de la Reine (o¹ 1773), corresponds exactly in dimensions with the Cabinet à Pans; the indication it bears of the adjoining room (not reproduced), transformed in 1738, correspond to the state before that date.

Evolution

It was in 1738 that the King, while retaining the great Chambre de Louis XIV — "extrêmement froid" — for the ceremonies of the *lever* and *coucher*, created a "petite chambre" in the Aile Droite, the Chambre de Louis XV, replacing the old Cabinet du Billard. Space was gained for the alcove at the expense of the Cours des Cerfs. The door casings are still those of 1685; the doors may also be the old ones, with slight modifications and with the addition of an inner, decorated band. The surviving work of 1738 comprises primarily the long vertical panels and the mirror frames (Figure 232). The panels are of the same general type, with figural central medallions, as those of the Chambre de la Reine, but they have a slight touch of Pineau's asymmetry in the sprays of the finials, not found in the Chambre de la Reine. The mirror frames, of reverse curvature, have busts *en espagnolette* like those of Oppenord in the Hôtel d'Assy a score of years before. The scroll clamped over the side of their mouldings at half their height is a feature found in an engraving of Pineau in Mariette's *Architecture française*.[234] The alcove as then made was not entirely as we see it now. In 1741 it was described by La Martinière as "ouverte entre deux pilastres, aux angles du flanc desquels on remarque des palmiers qui s'élèvent et se recourbent en cintre, en s'étendant le long de la traverse d'en haut; cette traverse est chatournée et les armes du Roi sont sculptées dans son milieu,"[235] thus more suggestive of Vassé's motifs, meanwhile taken up by Pineau. The cornice likewise has been modified, having originally had medallions also at the centers of the sides.

Beyond the new bedroom, the two existing cabinets — one of which, formerly containing the staircase, had always lacked a fireplace — were thrown together in 1738 to create the Grand Cabinet, called the Cabinet Ovale from its curved termination toward the Cabinet d'Angle. Here Verberckt's woodwork of the time (Figure 233) has survived the change of 1760 which squared this end of the room, under the injunction "d'employer tout le vieux." Its general effect is conservative, though there are certain features of more "picturesque" character. The tone is given by the major panels, which have figural medallions at the base, but centres merely of rosettes with interlaces relatively quiet in outline. The narrow panels, very close in style to those of the Chambre, again have free sprays in the finials. Above the mirror heads are radiating naturalistic sprays suggestive of some at the Hôtel de Roquelaure. It is the cornice, however, which — as in the Cabinet à Pans — surprises us by its freedom. There is no upper moulding; even the lower moulding is scrolled upward at the cardinal points. The swirling curves of tendril are more pronounced than even in the Grand Cabinet of the Hôtel de Soubise; birds do not merely perch on the sprays but fly off on the ceiling nearby.

It has not been appreciated that the Cabinet en Niche or Cabinet à Niche de la Reine (Grand Cabinet, or Cabinet Particulier) so scantly treated by De Cotte, was redecorated by Gabriel at this general period, though retaining the window wall of 1699, and, with modifications, the full entablature of that time. There survive hasty measured sketches which show the niche, still with oval head, flanked by large wall panels with rosettes closely related in design to those of the Cabinet Ovale of 1738.[236] There is indeed a second set of sketches with

---

[234] Plate 503 of the Hautecoeur edition.

[235] This and the other relevant documents are assembled by Nolhac in *Le château sous Louis XIV*, 1898, and summarized in *Versailles au XVIIIᵉ siècle*, 1926.

[236] O¹ 1773.

the inner wall and niche modified and enriched. The flowers of the mouldings, according to La Martinière's description of 1741, were "peintes en coloris au naturel." Later, the niche was replaced by a mirror, but the other walls remained untouched, or received duplicate panels, and are so shown in handsome drawings made for that transformation (Figure 234).[237] The room in this state was thus still in the style of 1738, of which it adds one other fine example, without more specific individuality.

At the same period, between 1737 and 1740, extensive renovations were undertaken at Fontainebleau, in the Antichambre du Roi (Cabinet du Conseil), in the Cabinet de la Reine and in the Galerie d'Ulysse,[238] although the present aspect of the first of these rooms dates from its further embellishments of 1752-1754 (Figure 267).[239] In the drawing of Gabriel reproduced by Fels,[240] these embellishments are sketched on what seems to be the design of the 'thirties, including a simple scalloped mirror frame of which all but the winged cartouche has been destroyed, and the lunette of the doorway, with its great cartouche recalling those of 1735 in the ceiling of the Chambre de la Reine at Versailles.

Reviewing the early work of the Bâtiments under the Gabriels, we find it was actually far from unmoved by what was going on outside. The talented Ange-Jacques, the gifted Verberckt, both still only in their 'thirties, did not fail to observe the brilliant innovations just made by Pineau, and to adopt a number of them. In the cornices, but only there, the designers even went to the full extreme of contemporary practise.

Private Works

The artistic creation of the *genre pittoresque* was early influential in the work of other architects, even when they did not adopt it wholeheartedly. The number of important surviving decorations of just this time in private buildings, aside from those we have previously discussed, is not great, but it includes two of extreme elaboration and beauty.

Among the most important were the decorations of the Hôtel de Soubise, which followed by some years the marriage of the Prince de Soubise in 1732. They adorned the rooms, now partly dismantled, constituting the apartments of the Prince in the ground story and those of the Princess in the principal story, these apartments terminating in the two famous oval salons. The work would seem to have been begun in 1735 or 1736,[241] when Boffrand was sixty-nine. The dates of execution of the several rooms are best established by those of the sculptured and painted overdoors, which can, in many cases, be determined exactly.[242] Thus, in the Prince's apartment, the medallions of the Chambre and other features by the sculptors Adam may apparently be placed in 1735 and 1736. The great Boucher tapestry of the Chambre du Prince, now in the Philadelphia Museum of Art, is dated 1736. The overdoors

[237] One of this set of drawings was reproduced by Nolhac in *Le Château sous Louis XV*, 1908, 125, under the supposition that the room first received this panelling shortly before the campaign of 1746-1747.

[238] *Op. cit.*, 182, 18, citing a letter to Ange-Jacques Gabriel concerning work in the Galerie d'Ulysse during 1739-1740, "sous vos ordres et ceux de Monsieur Gabriel pere."

[239] O¹ 1424.

[240] Pl. XLIII. At least the mirror frame with winged cartouche seems to be of the period of 1738.

[241] Delamair, in a memoir of 1737, quoted by Langlois, *op. cit.*, 160, speaks of the decorations as begun since the publication of his "Mémoire d'anecdotes," of the year before.

[242] Langlois, *op. cit.*, 175 ff. Cf. H. Thirion, *Les Adam et Clodion*, 1885, 85.

of the Grand Cabinet by Restout and Trémolières are of 1737. The paintings of the oval salon of the Princess were completed in 1739 or 1740.[243] The designs of the rooms were published in 1742 by Boffrand's *Livre d'architecture*, the elevations of the Appartement du Prince engraved by Lucas, the plan of its ceiling and the elevations of the Appartement de la Princesse by Babel.[244]

In the square rooms preceding the salons the ornament is very rich, but it offers us little that is new after previous examples with which we are now familiar.

There are indeed various features related to Pineau's work, although the freedom of movement is not carried to an equal extreme. The painted over-panel, on the lines of an overdoor, in the Chambre du Prince (Figure 235),[245] is like one in the 1738 edition of Daviler. The bat's-wing at top and bottom of the panels in the Chambre de la Princesse (Figure 236), appears both in Daviler and at the Hôtel de Rouillé. The double mirror head there is also used in both of those.

The cornices, executed by the sculptors Adam, are mostly of the more conservative types employed by Pineau, with the upper moulding parallel to the wall, but turning into scrolls at the central and corner motifs. In the Grand Cabinet du Prince, however, this moulding is entirely omitted; the ornaments profile freely upward from cove to ceiling, without any marked boundary — a treatment more advanced than any in Pineau's work, though paralleled at the same moment, as we have seen, in the Cabinet à Pans at Versailles of 1738.

The oval salons (Figures 237 and 238) are justly counted among the masterpieces of the style in France. Their shape, the high quality of their sculpture and painting, and the dazzling multiplication of features in the upper room, has blinded observers to the familiarity of their basic system, which is that of so many rooms from the Petit-Luxembourg and the Hôtel d'Assy onwards: with spreading, undivided spandrels between arches. This is readily appreciable in the lower room, where there is little new except that spandrels and cove are merged, the upper moulding being waved out slightly over each pier. Large figural reliefs in the spandrels and fine reliefs of heaped martial trophies in the lunettes give the room a more monumental air than is customary.

In the upper salon, a scheme basically similar is given an enrichment far beyond that of any other room of the French rococo, yet it is still ordered, disciplined, coherent. In one regard the treatment is significantly in advance of that of the room below: there the recesses are square in plan; here they are curved at the back, like some of Oppenord's and so many of Pineau's. Instead of reliefs, the spandrels have paintings, in which Natoire gave the story of Psyche an embodiment not unworthy of mention, as decoration, with the more noble span-

---

[243] The pavilion of Amalienburg at Nymphenberg, built by Cuvilliés from 1734 onward, where the decoration of the salon was so obviously based on Boffrand's Salon de la Princesse, was completed by 1739 according to Laran, *Cuvilliés*, cited above.

[244] A later reissue of what must be the same ten plates was announced in the *Mercure* for July, 1756, "chez P. Patte, architecte et graveur . . . dix planches *dessinées* et gravées par M. Babel." This later and casual expression would give but faint support to any thought that Babel might have been the actual designer of the interiors, especially as they show no relation to his independent engraved compositions.

[245] Reproduced from the drawing for the engraver in the De Cloux collection at the Cooper Union, New York. De Cloux supposed it to be from the hand of Boffrand, and as such unique, but we can scarcely assume the celebrated architect, then over seventy-five years old, would not have delegated to assistants the preparation of drawings merely for engraving. It shows the initial form of the mirror head, garbled in restoration.

drels of Psyche by Raphael at the Farnesina. Cherubs in relief perch on the crossettes of the piers, and rest on the cornice above the cartouches which here surmount the arches. Other cartouches rise above the spandrels and are embraced by the paired scrolls of cornice which here, as in the room below, wave forward at each pier. A genial invention, wholly new, is that of the open bands of scrollwork which rise thence to divide the vault and to unite in the central rosette. Rarely, at any period, does one find so perfect an artistic entity — supremely embodying, in this instance, a spirit of gaiety and of grace.

Another room of most delightful character was the Cabinet Vert, of which the surviving woodwork is now remounted at the Hôtel de Rohan. This room was in the principal story, where it was mentioned in an inventory of the Hôtel de Soubise in 1745. Here the chief ornaments are the carved medallions of fables, which have been supposed to be fables of La Fontaine. Actually they are fables of Aesop, translated into relief from the engravings of Sir Roger L'Estrange's edition of Aesop after the drawings of the English animal painter Francis Barlow,[246] a work which had gone through eight editions by 1738. The frames of these medallions and of the other panels are wholly coherent with those of the princely apartments, with rims of shell, with beads and stems of palm wound with sprays of flowers, and with no other asymmetry than that of the ultimate tendrils.

It is interesting, in relation to the Hôtel de Soubise, to read what Boffrand himself wrote in 1742 of the tyranny of fashion in art, "accompagné de la folle nouveauté qui plaît."[247] After condemning the ornaments of the baroque both in France and in Italy, he continued:

> D'autres ornaments ont pris leur place, qui n'ont autre mérite qu'un travail délicat à la vérité, mais sec et sans liaison au reste de la décoration: ils peuvent convenir dans de petites pièces; mais on a mis par tout, le crayon les trace en courant. En quelque maison que l'on aille, on les trouve toujours les mêmes. Ces ornements ont passés des décorations intérieures des maisons & des ouvrages en bois, auxquelles un travail plus délicat peut convenir, aux ouvrages extérieurs & en pierre qui exigent un travail plus moëleux & plus mâle. La mode les a poussés si avant dans le monde qu'on pourroit conjecturer sur sa variation, qu'ils ne dureront pas longtemps.

Of panelling he writes specifically:

> Lorsque les lambris de menuiseries sont ornés de sculpture, il faut que les masses de sculpture y soient bien distribuées, & sans confusion; qu'elles soient bien dessinées & bien travaillées, il y faut éviter les saillies trop fortes qui font paroître les lieux petits, & éviter pareillement les ornemens trop plats & trop déliés qui deviennent secs & mesquins, imitants les grotesques de peinture qui ne conviennent même qu'a des lieux de moyenne grandeur, ces ornements doivent être liés ensemble pour que leur forme & leurs contours ne fassent qu'un tout avec les compartiments de la menuiserie, & contribuent à faire paroître les lieux élevés: il faut rejetter les ornements de travers qui sont contre la régularité, qui ne peuvent être admis que lorsque des enfants, ou des genies portent des cartouches, ou quelques attributs.

[246] F. Kimball and E. Donnell: "Les boiseries du cabinet vert de l'hôtel de Soubise, in *Gazette des beaux-arts,* Ve pér., XVII, 1928, 183-186.
[247] *Livre d'architecture,* 1745, 42-43.

Evolution

His condemnation of "ornements de travers" is echoed also in Dargenville's account of his life:

> Voyant un fameux artiste [Boucher] qui peignoit avec beaucoup de soin des ornemens bizarres & de travers, *comment,* s'écria t-il, *un habile homme comme vous peut il s'appliquer à peindre de pareilles extravagances!* Il faut avouer néanmoins que malgré l'austerité de ses principes, il a quelque fois payé le tribut au mauvais goût du siècle, comme à l'hôtel de Soubise, la décoration de ses appartemens tient de ce goût de rocailles, & de cartouches informes qui n'appartiennent qu'au colifichet.

The rooms of the Hôtel de Soubise were Boffrand's last important interior designs. On their completion he was well over seventy. He turned to the publication of his works in the *Livre d'architecture,* with a text in French and Latin based on the *Ars Poetica* of Horace. The approbation is dated November 29, 1742, although the imprint is of 1745. From 1748 onwards, though past the age of eighty, he was yet to participate in the competition for designs of a Place Louis XV, three of which were submitted under his name,[249] and though he was attacked by paralysis in 1749,[250] he returned to frequent the Academy almost to the day of his death. In the *Correspondance littéraire*[251] we find him placed very high among French architects, though strangely bracketed: "les deux seuls sous Louis XV sont Boffrand et Cartaut; encore le premier, étant fort âgé, est autant du régne précédent que de celui-ci." That he was a most gifted architect and draughtsman is certain. One may wonder nevertheless whether he was solely responsible for the decorative design in his later works, or whether they were due in part to collaborators. Speculator, entrepreneur, official, author of comedies in his youth, he seems too protean in his occupations to have been personally responsible for every detail.

The wonderful decorations of the Appartements d'Assemblée at Rambouillet (Figures 239-242), on which we have no decisive documents, present a nice problem in dating and attribution. The architectural history of the château in general is well enough established.[252] Some time after a first remodelling of 1707-1708, the western wing was doubled by a second enfilade, constructed in two separate campaigns, one comprising the present antichambre and two salons, the other the three Cabinets de la Comtesse. The woodwork of the Premier Salon already bears the cypher MVS for Marie-Victoire-Sophie de Noailles, whose marriage to the Comte de Toulouse took place in 1723. In June, 1736, a year before the Count's death, more than three hundred workmen were still occupied, some of them on "un bâtiment attenant au château"—possibly the Communs, as Lorin believed; possibly, as Longon surmised, the end of the wing, containing the Cabinets. When, between these dates, were the decorations of the suite executed, and who were the designer and executants?

[248] Dargenville: *Vies des fameux architectes,* 1787.
[249] Patte figures three of them in *Monuments erigés à la gloire de Louis XV,* 1767.
[250] *Procès-verbaux,* November 17, 1749, VI, 130.
[251] Tourneux ed., I, 1877, 362.
[252] The early works of Seguin, 1834, of Moutié 1850, and of Maillard 1891, are of less value for this period than F. Lorin: *Histoire de Rambouillet. La ville, le château, ses hôtes,* 1907, and H. Longnon: *Le Château de Rambouillet* (Petites monographies des grands édifices), n.d. Although Piganiol de la Force, as Lorin states, was preceptor of the pages at Rambouillet from 1698 to 1737, his account of Rambouillet (1742 ed., VIII, 244-249) does not mention the date and authorship of the woodwork.

The Creation of the Rococo

Effort has been made to deduce the date from the favour and visits of Louis XV, attracted by the chase and by the wit and charm of the Countess, so much his senior, and the amusements — at first innocent — of the intimate circle she assembled. In 1726 the King, then but seventeen, began to hunt at Rambouillet; in 1727, the year of his marriage, he came two or three times a week.[253] Then and in the years following he frequently stayed three or four days, doubtless occupying the royal suite in the main body of the château, which Louis XIV had used during his visit of 1713. These stays totalled forty-one days in 1731, twenty-seven in 1732, when the Queen also came on March 17. The King was now thrown there increasingly with Madame de Mailly, and in 1733 the first infidelities began. Only presumptions, nothing more, can be inferred from these visits as to the completion of the Appartements d'Assemblée.

The carvings of all the rooms of the apartment are homogeneous, from a single hand, although those of the cabinets were doubtless executed last, after those of the salons. It has been easy to suppose, as did Lorin, that they were due to Vassé, who had so brilliantly adorned the Hôtel de Toulouse for the Count in 1719. We have seen that Vassé was ill for five years before his death in 1736, and the completion of the Salon d'Hercule in those years must have taken all his strength. Even in the Chambre de la Reine, where he must be responsible for the design of the bold ornaments executed by Dugoullons, Le Goupil and Verberckt in 1730, he was not called on for the delicate, carved panels added from Gabriel's design of 1735, which, as we have seen, were entrusted to Verberckt. Obviously the work at Rambouillet is far too attenuated to be from the same brain and hand as the masculine designs of Vassé.

It is to Verberckt, as Longnon surmised without venturing to decide the question, that we must refer the carvings at Rambouillet.

Notable in the so-called Boudoir de la Comtesse (Figure 242) is the reeded half-round moulding of the mirror frame and of the major frames, appearing already in the rosettes of the Premier Salon. Such a reed moulding, much bolder in scale, was first used in the overdoors of the Chambre de la Reine at Versailles, doubtless still from Vassé's sketches. Nowhere in private work do we find it so early. It recurs at smaller scale in the mirror moulding of the panelling which Verberckt added to the Chambre de la Reine in 1735 and 1736, and notably as the main moulding of the cartouches of the coved ceiling at that time. It again appears at Versailles in Verberckt's mirror frames of the Cabinet d'Angle before 1738, and of the Chambre and Cabinet du Roi, 1738. All these rooms, retaining certain elements of earlier date and form, were also subjected to the conservatism of the Bâtiments du Roi. Making allowance for these factors we have no difficulty in concluding that the woodwork at Rambouillet was executed primarily by Verberckt. In the salons he may still have been associated with the atelier of Dugoullons (died about 1731), Le Goupil (died in 1733) and Taupin (died in 1734). The "boudoir" may possibly have been his earliest independent commission, on which he demonstrated his virtuosity in an almost overladen richness, never to be repeated, or more probably may have been just subsequent to his first independent work of the mid-'thirties at Versailles — in either case just before or just after 1735.

[253] Lorin citing Barbier's *Journal.*
[254] Nolhac: *Louis XV et Marie Leczinska*, 1928, 157.

Evolution

The doorways of the apartment are all square headed, the casings of those of the salons perhaps being survivals of pre-existing woodwork. They have the small receding crown often used since the late 'twenties. The overdoor frames offer little which is really unusual. The same is true in the mirror frames proper, one moulded, the other of slender palm, both twined with sprays, as with Vassé and then with Pineau.

In the Premier Salon the major panels still have moulded central rosettes, rich examples of the traditional type. The mouldings of these panels, as well as of the main panels of the doors, are richly contoured, as frequently elsewhere toward 1730. The traverses of the doors have a scalloped inner moulding not found in other buildings, though recalling touches both of Aubert and of Pineau. The panel above the mirror is exceptional in having its scalloped moulding itself twined with sprays. What is really most remarkable, both in this and the following rooms, is the extreme wealth of the minor ornaments of the panels: the interlaces with their complexity of spray and tendril.

In the Second Salon the mouldings are less articulated. At the mid-point of the stiles they are interrupted by scrolls almost suggesting cupid's bows, not irrelated to the features which were to appear at the same point in the mirror frames of the Chambre du Roi in 1738. The central rosettes are scalloped and become part of the ornaments of the field. Above and below are superb trophies of the chase, of music and husbandry, of the type familiar since Pierre Lepautre, with many features — such as the Indian feather headdress — characteristic of Oppenord,[255] and also found in the overdoors of the Chambre de la Reine, 1730. The most striking features in this room are the frames over the mirrors. The field is flat, without any plastic suggestion, the frame however — the first on such a scale we know in this position — is of characteristic cartouche outline with flaming crown. The heavy upper shell has scroll leafage suggesting wings.

In the cabinets the general form is one which became a favorite at Versailles at the same moment, as in the Cabinet Vert of 1735, the Cabinet Ovale of 1738 — with a curved recess containing the fireplace. That is literally the case in the first of the Cabinets; the "boudoir" has all four corners similarly curved.

The first cabinet has tiers of square panels with traverses between, a treatment we shall find in the Salle à Manger du Roi at Versailles, the panelling of which as we shall see, may well go back in part of the Bains du Roi of the 1730's. Indeed there is a further similarity between the rooms, in the panels above the mirrors, with their reeded beads twined with sprays, their trophies of music. The room at Rambouillet is by far the richer and doubtless the later of the two, its interlaces very complex, with radiating sprays recalling those of Pineau, its traverses unbounded by any rectangular moulding.

It is the "boudoir" which is most fantastically ornate. The great panels, reeded and wreathed, are inscribed not with an inner moulding but with a wandering, scalloped border of turned reeds in C-scrolls and S-scrolls, with fragments of shell-rim and meandering sprays. The pilaster strips between are overlaid with a floral mosaic of incredible lace-like delicacy. The mirror is doubly outlined by twined beads large and small. The doors are set

---

[255] I pray I may be forgiven for the suggestion, in my early publication on Oppenord, that these trophies were actually from designs by him. They could well be so, like designs of Oppenord which other artists followed as their own, but we need not assume this of an artist of the ability of Verberckt.

in a unique square-headed recess, with splays curved and mitered, its jambs with arabesques of rococo interlace, its head with opposite fanciful motifs like those of a cornice, its corners and center with ethereal oval rosettes and cartouche. The panelling, without major assymetry, was the culmination and apotheosis of the traditional scheme which had hitherto prevailed.[256]

At Rambouillet it is as if Verberckt had sought to celebrate his independence by outrivalling the new works of Pineau. He did indeed exceed all those in France in elaboration and delicacy, with many original and personal touches. As compared with Pineau's masterpieces, however, the fundamental schemes at Rambouillet are more conventional. Any asymmetry even in the "boudoir" is confined to the delicate sprays of the finials alone. The innovations are more of detail, in which Verberckt was unsurpassed.

The cornices of the salons are of simple type, probably antedating the remodelling of their woodwork. Both have continuous upper mouldings, one purely rectilinear, the other but slightly curved over corner cartouches with a slight fringe of ornaments on the ceiling. The cornice of the first cabinet is also of great simplicity. In the "boudoir" on the contrary, the upper moulding is omitted; there is the wildest and boldest use of free sculpture with central as well as corner cartouches.

The apartment at the Arsenal miscalled that of the Duchesse du Maine long passed as a work of Boffrand in the period 1725-1728. Boffrand, however, built only the shell of the building, when funds were exhausted before there were doors, windows or any interior decoration whatever. In 1741 an architect named Dauphin, of whom we know nothing further, solicited the grant of five rooms, which he decorated at his own expense, and which are those now surviving.[257] The similarity with the work of Boffrand at the Hôtel de Soubise is indeed striking, but we appreciate today that the rooms at the Arsenal are the later ones, derivative from Boffrand's, which Dauphin could have had carried out by any competent executants. There is nothing in them either original or superior.

Without attempting a history of French architecture of the period, we must at least discuss briefly its major plastic forms on the exterior, to see how far they may have participated in the movements in interior design. It is a commonplace that in the France of Louis XV, where academism was so strongly entrenched, there was little modification in exterior ordonnance.

In the metropolis at this period there were few major undertakings. They included the façades of Saint-Roch, by Jules Robert de Cotte, about 1735, and of Saint-Sulpice.

For that of Saint-Sulpice, according to Blondel,[258] a competition was instituted in which Servadoni carried off the prize. We have seen that he succeeded Oppenord as architect of the

[256] Just because of this conventionality of the general scheme (which might render unnecessary the intervention of an architect), and of the elaboration of the carving for its own sake (which an architect might have restrained), we do not assume that Gabriel must have furnished designs for the panelling, as surmised by M.-J. Ballot: *Le décor intérieur au XVIIIᵉ siècle*, 1930, 67.

[257] L. Battifol: "L'architecte German Boffrand et l'Arsenal," in *Bulletin de la Société de histoire de l'art français*, Année 1930, 7-9. As noted by Lady Dilke — who drew correct conclusions from this as to the date, while still presuming Boffrand's authorship — the overdoors in grisaille reproduce the reliefs of Bouchardon, exhibited at the Salon of 1741, for the Fontaine de Grenelle.

[258] *Cours d'architecture*, III, 1772, 343, 349.

church in 1732. An early form of his design[259] shows that, while incomparably less baroque than Meissonnier's design of 1726, and substantially less so than Oppenord's designs, it was far from the executed work with which we are familiar, and which has led Servadoni to be regarded, wrongly, as a pioneer of classicism. So far as I know, no one has pointed out the relation between this design and the façade of Saint Paul's—which Servadoni had known in London and of which engravings were readily available—with its academic portico of superposed orders and pediment of four bays, detached from the flanking towers with their free crowns. In 1742 Servadoni modified this design to give the portico and pediment six bays, overlapping the towers, still with a break in the entablature at this point. From 1745 the execution was left to Oudot de Maclaurin, who erected the north tower in 1749. We do not have positive knowledge whether it was before or after Maclaurin's employment that the entablature was made unbroken, as it is shown in Blondel's *Architecture française* in 1752.[260]

In spite of the championship of Servadoni by Caylus "comme l'homme à opposer à nos architectes qu'il avait prit en grippe," as Mariette wrote, Servadoni was no rigid classicist. This is illustrated by his other architectural works, such as the baldaquin of Saint-Bruno des Chartreux at Lyons, executed in the early 'forties by Soufflot, to which we shall recur, and his baldaquin at Sens. In England, to which he returned in 1748 to do the illuminations for the Peace of Aix-la-Chapelle, he designed the gallery in the house of Thomas Wyndham on the Thames near Hammersmith, a house which had been built by Robert Morris for Lord Melcombe. An engraving of this gallery, "Servadoni Arch" appearing in the continuation of the *Vitruvius Britannicus*,[261] shows a range of Ionic pilasters, with columns flanking a recess, and a low coffered vault. It was a design conventional enough in England at that time, but which would then have been very revolutionary in France.

Two minor Paris churches, indeed, went further in a free direction. Jean-François Blondel, uncle of Jacques-François, built in 1733 the chapel of the Communion at Saint-Jean-en Grève, with the very unusual feature (anticipated only in Oppenord's cabinets at the Palais-Royal) of a wooden monitor instead of a clerestory. Treatment of the coves above and below this, as well as of the arched window heads, recalls the ornament of domestic interiors, while the altar represents an extreme of the rococo in France. May we not suppose that Pineau, who had designed for the same architect at the same moment the decorations of the Hôtel de Rouillé, was also largely responsible here? Saint-Louis du Louvre, 1738-1744, was designed by the famous goldsmith Thomas Germain (1673-1748) with a single nave of subtle spatial rhythms and with a convex front and concave wings, distantly recalling Santa Croce in Gerusalemme in Rome. We cannot agree that these works were not exceptional in the metropolis, where academism lost its hold on the exterior of buildings only for the briefest moment.

The work among all others which attracted the admiration of contemporaries there was one of a quite different character. This was the Fontaine de Grenelle, designed and executed

[259] Drawing reproduced by Brinckmann, *op. cit.*, fig. 305. His text, pp. 188, 282, gives the fullest account of the vicissitudes of the design.

[260] An engraving of 1750 published in England is cited by Bataille, *loc. cit.*

[261] IV, 1767, pls. 28-29. The house, later called Brandenburgh House, was destroyed in 1882, according to Blomfield: *History of Renaissance Architecture in England*, 1897, II, 259. It is not included in the volume of the *Survey of London* on Hammersmith, and I am unable to confirm its exact date.

in 1739-1745, at the very height of the *genre pittoresque* in interiors, by the sculptor Bouchardon. The Ionic order has capitals of the antique type, rather than the Scamozzian type with a necking, employed even at Saint-Sulpice.[262] We may indeed see in the shallow pilaster strips, without capital or base, which divide the wall, an echo of the similar pilaster strips of interiors, but there is no further transfer of interior motifs and effects. Such a transfer is found in France only in provincial works like the Fontaine de la Grosse Horloge at Rouen.

The Mid-century

The Bâtiments under Tournehem, 1745-1751

A new force was felt in the Bâtiments, as in so many other departments, on the advent of Madame de Pompadour, in the spring of 1745, to the position of *maîtresse en titre*, which she was to retain until her death in 1764. The rococo has often, both early and late, been loosely thought by writers of general literature to owe its origin to her taste and stimulus. We are already in a position to see how little truth there is in this supposition. Whether one considers that the rococo began with Oppenord, with Meissonnier, or with Pineau, their decisive works — to say nothing of the prophetic ones of Pierre Lepautre — were created long before the advent of the favorite. One could scarcely attribute to her, at twenty-four, a true artistic initiative.

Her rôle lay in patronage, in her passion for building and decoration. Her indefatigable effort to divert the King by constant change was responsible for many enterprises in the royal châteaux, as well as in her own houses. This patronage came at a time when the rococo was already in its fullest flower. We shall see that the work executed for her involved, for all its luxury, no fundamentally new artistic character. It is only in the rhetoric of the Goncourts that she could be called the godmother or even the queen of the rococo.

She lost no time in replacing Orry as Directeur des Bâtiments, installing her uncle, Lenormant de Tournehem in December of 1745. He served until his death in 1751. Without artistic prejudices, he was a man of ability, honesty and simplicity, who devoted himself to efficient administration. In January, 1747, he revived the post of Premier Peintre for Charles Coypel (1694-1752), on whom he leaned much. A facile eclectic, Coypel himself was influenced by two men behind the scenes, the Comte de Caylus and the Abbé Leblanc.

Caylus (1692-1765), a truly extraordinary figure, had turned from a brilliant youthful career, before his majority, in the army and at Court, to indulge his passion for the arts and for antiquity. After the Peace of Rastatt in 1713 he spent a year in Italy, then went to Constantinople with Bonnac, ambassador to the Porte, exploring Greece and the Troad. Back in Paris in 1717, he had lessons in drawing from Watteau, taught himself engraving, and flung himself passionately into reproduction of the drawings of the old masters, the coins and gems of the Cabinet du Roi. In 1722 he was in Holland and England, visiting the great collections. Named in 1731 honorary counsellor of the Academy of Painting, in 1742 member of the Academy of Inscriptions, he exercised during the ministry of his cousin, Maurepas, disgraced in 1749, and the directorship of Orry a great influence in the Bâtiments. This continued under Tournehem through the agency of Coypel. Caylus' patronage of younger artists

---

[262] The Academy of Architecture had occupied itself with both these types of Ionic capital in the years 1737-1739. *Procès-verbaux*, V, 206, 230, 265.

was exercised notably in the case of Bouchardon. The greatest service of Caylus was as the founder of archaeology as a conscious science, to whom Winckelmann was to acknowledge his indebtedness. His own collections of antiquities, begun in 1729, furnished the basis for his vast *Receuil d'antiquités egyptiennes, étrusques, grecques et romaines,* of which the first volume was to appear in 1752.

In intimate relation with Caylus was the connoisseur Pierre-Jean Mariette (1694-1774). He joined in admiration of Bouchardon, to which he testified in a *Lettre sur la fontaine de la rue de Grenelle,* dated March 1, 1746.[263] How far this admiration yet was from what we mean by neo-classicism is shown by what Mariette says of Bouchardon in the *Abededario:* he had for his models, during his study in Rome, Algardi and François Duquesnoy, "Personne n'a senti comme lui le prix d'une noble simplicité, ni n'a marché de plus près sur les traces du célèbre François Flamand." This, which was sufficient to render Bouchardon the idol of the forces of conservatism, shows that its ideal as yet was merely that of academism.

The position of the Abbé Leblanc (1707-1781) as a sort of *éminence grise* of the administration of Tournehem and Coypel has been recognized,[264] but not his precedence of all others in critical hostility to the rococo. Already in his *Lettres d'un françois,* 1745, following a visit to England, he closed the one on English architecture addressed to Caylus with these lines: "Celui (le goût) d'aujourdhui, Monsieur est si dépravé que je ne pense pas qu'il puisse durer encore longtemps, & si quelque chose peut en accélérer la chute, c'est l'attention & l'encouragement que vous donnez aux arts."[265] Leblanc, too, like Mariette, preceded Winckelmann in urging a noble simplicity, from which the French of his time had departed. "Le plus médiocre Dessinateur invente des Ornemens de toutes formes, & les entasse les uns sur les autres; un homme comme Bouchardon, n'en imagine que de noble, & les distribue avec intelligence. Les Goths en ont été aussi prodigues que les Grecs en ont été avare."

> On affecte déjà de s'éloigner du goût du Siécle de Louis XIV, l'âge d'or des Lettres & des beaux Arts en France. Rein n'est plus monstrueux, comme le remarque Horace, que de marier ensemble des Êtres d'une nature opposée; c'est cependant ce que grand nombre de nos Artistes se font aujourd'hui gloire de pratiquer. Ils contrastent un Amour avec un Dragon, & un Coquillage avec une aile de Chauve-Souris. Ils ne suivent plus aucun ordre, aucune vraisemblance dans leurs Productions. Ils entassent avec confusion des Corniches, des Bases, des Colonnes, des Cascades, des Joncs, des Rochers; dans quelque coin de ce Cahos, ils placeront un Amour épouvanté, & sur le tout, ils feront regner une Guirlande de fleurs. Voilà ce qu'on appelle des Desseins d'un nouveau Goût. Ainsi pour avoir passé le terme, nous sommes revenus à la barbarie des Goths. Peut-être est-il des choses où trop de symmétrie est un défaut... Mais qu'en fait d'ornemens nous sommes aujourd'hui loin de ce défaut! nous ne voulons plus rien de symmétrique. Si l'on orne le Frontispice d'un Hôtel des Armes de celui qui le fait bâtir, on pose l'Ecu en ligne diagonale, & la Couronne sur l'un des côtés, de façon qu'elle paroisse prête à tomber. On s'éloigne le plus qu'on peut de la ligne perpendiculaire & de l'horisontale: on ne met plus rien à plomb, ni de niveau...
>
> Ceux de nos Artistes qui ont quelque sens rougissent souvent des choses qu'ils sont obligés de faire, mais le torrent les entraine; il faut, pour être employés, qu'ils fassent

---

[263] Published as an appendix to Caylus' *Vie de Bouchardon,* 1762, and reprinted in the *Abecedario,* VI, 102.
[264] J. Locquin: *La peinture d'histoire en France de 1747 à 1785,* 1912, 5.
[265] Cited from *Lettres de M. l'Abbé Le Blanc,* II, 1751, 49-56.

comme les autres. On leur demande du goût nouveau, de ces Formes qui ne ressemblent à rien, & ils en donnent.

A qui ressemblent ces Pendules devenues si à la mode, qui n'ont ni base ni console, & qui paroissent sortir du Lambris où elles sont appliquées! Ces Cerfs, ces Chiens & ces Piqueurs, ou ces Figures Chinoises qu'on distribue d'une façon si bizarre autour d'un Cadran, en sont'ils les ornemens naturels? Ces Cartouches qui soit en haut, soit en bas, soit dans les côtés, n'ont aucunes Parties qui se répondent, sont'ils en effet de bon goût?

In his *Lettre sur les tableaux exposés au Louvre en 1747* Leblanc again inveighed against the "extravagances" of Meissonnier, of Boffrand and of Thomas Germain.

It was doubtless partly due to the influence of these men that the official architects of the Crown now leaned further to the conservative faction. Cochin in 1754 specifically makes the partisans of *contraste* say: "Les bâtimens du Roy nous ont donné une exculsion totale; tout ce qui s'y fait sent le vieille architecture."

Gabriel continued, as Premier Architecte, to design all the royal interiors, in the more important of which the carvings were by Verberckt.

In the work at Versailles during the sway of Madame de Pompadour we cannot always presume an initiative or intervention of the favorite. It would have been characteristic, however, of her diplomacy of consideration for the Queen[266] to have taken the lead in securing for Marie Leczinska more commodious installation, at the same time she herself was refurnishing the great apartment in the attic, along the gardens, where she had succeeded Madame de Châteauroux. Thus it may well have been on her initiative that there was undertaken almost at once, in 1746-1747, an enlargement and remodelling of the Cabinets de la Reine.[267] This carried with it an enlargement of the rooms of the Dauphin, just below, prior to his remarriage. These objects were achieved by widening the small rooms along the south side of the Cour de Monseigneur at the expense of that court. This space and the southern part of the wing dividing the courts were now rearranged. While the decoration was again changed for Marie Antoinette, the dated drawings of Gabriel for the rooms at this period survive substantially complete, so that we can fully envisage their treatment.

The Petite Pièce à Pans (the future Cabinet de la Méridienne) assumed at this time its octagonal form, with a niche, with wavy head, opposite the window (Figure 243). Here the extremely small wall surfaces were subdivided by horizontal traverses lining with the friezes above the doors. The four diagonal faces, one of them containing the chimney piece, had paintings in plain oval frames over the mirrors and doors, quite as they might have had a generation or more before. The adjoining rectangular Cabinet (Figure 244), slightly larger, was likewise very conservative in style. Both were of varnished oak.

In 1749[268] was first fitted up, beyond the Grand Cabinet de là Reine, in the very narrow space between it and the wall of the Premier Antichambre du Roi, the Petit Cabinet which later, in the inventory of 1768 after the death of Marie Leczinska, was listed as the "Boudoir" (Figures 245-246).[269] It was less than six feet in width and eleven in depth, with a window

[266] Cf. E. and J. de Goncourt: *Les Maîtresses de Louis XV*, 1860, I, 203.

[267] They may be traced in the plans and drawings in carton o¹ 1773, which show at least three major changes during her occupancy.

[268] Nolhac: *Versailles au XVIIIᵉ siecle*, 1926, 198n, where the contemporary sources are quoted.

[269] This is the first use I have encountered, in the documents, as its use by Cochin in the *Mercure* of 1755 is the first I know in literature, of this word, so much abused by popular writers on the eighteenth century.

close to the wall at one end and a door from the Grand Cabinet in the center of a long side. At first it was to have five paintings by Pierre, replaced in November by the "Five Senses" of Oudry. Later, at just what date we do not know, these were replaced by panels with carved trophies in delicate cartouches above, panels much freer in outline than the surviving central panel of the original wainscot. Alone of all the private rooms of the Queen, this one survived the transformations of Louis XVI and still exists, though injured under Louis Philippe.

From the remodelling of the apartment of the Dauphin at this time certain rooms still survive. Here the treatment of the mirror frames was much freer, their sides being interrupted at half their height — Pineau-like — by scrolls with dolphins, of which the sculptural and symbolic character were doubtless thought to excuse the asymmetry.

A favorite resort of the Court under Madame de Pompadour was the château of Choisy, which had been acquired by the Crown on the death of the Princesse de Conti in 1739. It was repeatedly remodelled and enlarged both before and after the advent of the favorite. Alas, the château itself has been swept away, and we have no designs of interiors executed there during the administration of Tournehem.[270]

At Compiègne, where remodellings of the old château had been begun in 1738, extensive projects made in 1747 were not followed in execution. In the modest apartment of Madame de Pompadour, blanketed by later constructions, a few elements still survive from those described in a memoir of 1749,[271] which speaks of "les lambris vert clair du cabinet relevés de moulures et d'ornements sculptés peints en blanc." Several sketches preserved at the Archives Nationales[272] show a discreet and sober version of the rococo.

Near the Ménagerie at Trianon was built in 1749-1750 the ravishing Pavillon Octogone or Pavillon de Jeux in the small formal garden later to be dominated by the château of the Petit Trianon. Its central circular room, here suggested less by classical models than by relation of the building to its site, was the first of this form since the Salon Rond of the Grand Trianon. As there, the cornice is supported by columns, equally a novelty in the mid-century. In general, however, the decorations, while conservative, are characteristic of Gabriel's work at this moment.

Men who first gained official importance in ornament at this period were the brothers Slodtz, sculptors, who were to follow Meissonnier, one after another, in his post at the Menus-Plaisirs: Sebastien-Antoine, 1750-1754, Paul-Ambroise, 1754-1758, and René-Michel, called Michel-Ange, 1758-1764. Among what appear to be their designs[273] is one for the famous commode with bronzes by Jacques Caffieri, made in 1738 for the Chambre du Roi at Versailles, in the height of rococo fire. Even before the death of Meissonnier they were otherwise active for the Crown as designers, for instance of the medal cabinet formerly at Versailles, now at the Bibliothèque Nationale. Most of their surviving drawings are from

[270] B. Chamchine: *Le Château de Choisy*, 1910, devoted pp. 138-156 to the decoration of the interior, citing many texts about craftsmen from Verberckt onward, but not producing any drawings. The paper by R.-A. Weigert, "Le Château de Choisy" in *Larousse Mensuel Illustré*, no. 335, September, 1936, 494-496, is based chiefly on Chamchine.

[271] Cited by J. Robiquet: *Le Palais de Compiègne*, 1938, 27.

[272] O¹ 1410, Nos. 20-34.

[273] Cf. E. Molinier: *Le Mobilier au XVIIᵉ et au XVIIIᵉ siècle*, n.d., 123-124; A. de Champeaux: *Portefeuille des arts-décoratifs*, 1888 ff., pls. 10, 52, 96, 103, 134, 472, 603; E. de Salverte: *Les Ébenistes du XVIIIᵉ siècle*, and *Le Meuble français*.

the earlier period of their work, often tormented, rarely unsymmetrical. This did not prevent René-Michel from becoming, in the sequel, the favorite sculptor of Cochin, who was to press his claims against Caylus' championship of Bouchardon.

Independent Designers

In the middle years of the century, with Versailles and the other palaces once more preempting the attention of the Court, artists outside the Bâtiments du Roi had less opportunity. Building in Paris was less active; very few new houses of importance were undertaken there in just these years. Accordingly the adherents of the *genre pittoresque*, mostly outside the charmed official circle, did not find equally brilliant opportunities. The academicians, when they did not themselves — like Jacques-Hardouin Mansart — use the services of these decorators, employed some of their forms in less extreme fashion.

We know little of Meissonnier's life and works after 1735, except that he was married without children, and was, in 1736, godfather of a child of Boucher. He died in 1750, at fifty-five, with a well-furnished house and comfortable means.

The ceremonial decorations of the years of his later tenure of the post of Dessinateur de la Chambre and du Cabinet should normally have been of his design, yet we nowhere hear them attributed to him. Mariette states, à propos of a design of Meissonnier's for fireworks, apparently for the celebration of the birth of the Dauphin in 1729, "on ne demanda plus à Meissonnier rien de semblable." [274] In Meissonnier's engraved works is a design for fireworks for the marriage of the Infanta in 1739, but we are not sure that it was executed, the designs for the festivities on that occasion having been given in general by Cochin, as we shall see.

Aside from this design for illuminations, only one of his works from the last fifteen years of his life can be dated. This one, however, comes presumably from his very last years, the "Projet d'un Sallon de la Princesse Sartorinski [Czartoriska] en Pologne," illustrated by his figures 84 to 86, for which he had received payment of 11,500 livres on account of work in his studio at his death. [275] The room (Figure 247) has a rounded central portion with rectangular alcoves at either end. The architectural membering is of substantial weight — in the window casings, in the cornice, broken at each bay, and in the vault — so that the effect of the salon proper is dominantly baroque. This is particularly true of the wall with the chimney pieces, where not only the doorway but also the mirrors are crowned by segmental fragments of the cornice, joined by concave arcs, and accented with large plastic cartouches and shells. The treatment of minor panels is more in consonance with French taste, but the whole work is unthinkable for execution for France at any period.

Likewise late in Meissonnier's career, to judge by equivalence of style and detail, was doubtless the "grand cabinet fait pour le Portugal," represented in Figures 92 and 93 of his works.

In general, after 1735, however, Meissonnier "ne s'est plus appliqué le reste de sa vie," says the author of his obituary in the *Mercure*, [276] "qu'à dessiner des projets d'Eglises de Palais

[274] MS. "Notice sur Meissonnier, orfèvre," Cabinet des Estampes, Deloyne Collection, IV, article 45 quoted in Dimier, *Les peintres français*, II, 368.

[275] Inventory after decease cited by Carsix: *op. cit.*, 396.

[276] October, 1750, 138-141.

& de Monumens publiques, qu'il n'achevoit seulement pas." [277] With due allowance for the journalist's hostility to Meissonnier, we see that indeed "les differens talens ausquels il s'étoit exercé favorisoient trop son inconstance naturelle." It is again this lack of constancy which the writer particularly emphasizes in concluding "Son génie auroit été capable de le rendre un très-grand homme, & il n'a été presque qu'un dessinateur ingénieux."

Pineau continued to be fully occupied in the decoration of interiors until his death in 1754. His manuscript drawings published by Deshairs permit many of these later works to be identified. With certain exceptions which we shall discuss more at length, these works do not seem to have been of magnificence equal to those of the brilliant period 1730-1735. The patrons included a M. de Fontenay, for designs sent to Dresden, 1743; the Prince d'Isenghien, in 1744, for a house at Suresnes, of which we know nothing further, designed by Briseux, who also employed Pineau at the Hôtel Daugny (Mairie du IXe arrondissement, where all has been changed internally); Michel-Étienne Bouret for his house in the Rue de la Grange-Batelière, 1744, as well as his château of Croix-Fontaine, both by the architect Le Carpentier, for whom Pineau also carved in 1749 a salon at the Hôtel de Luxembourg in the Rue Saint-Marc; the Comte de Middelbourg at Suresnes, 1747; and the Marquis Le Voyer d'Argenson for his château at Asnières, 1750-1751, by Jacques-Hardouin Mansart de Sagonne, grandson of the Premier Architecte. Asnières survives with some charming minor rooms, but was stripped in 1879 of the panelling of the grand salon. So far as we know these works, they embodied little of innovation beyond Pineau's previous designs, to which their character was similar. We note only, among the drawings for Bouret,[278] in 1744, a pilaster-head in which spreading vertical scrolls freely approximate an Ionic capital (Figure 250). It was an invention taken up later by Gabriel and Verberckt in remodellings of the Chambre du Roi and elsewhere. When we consider how difficult it is to develop a new columnar order, we admire all the more this perfect adaptation to the Ionic of the basic motifs of the rococo.

Pineau was not wholly devoid of royal employment. At La Muette, under the sway of Madame de Pompadour, he had his only commission for the royal interiors. In the latter half of 1747 he executed there "ouvrages en plâtre et en bois à la sacristie, salle à manger, salon, cabinet de compagnié, celui des jeux, garde robe du Roy, appartement du Dauphin, celui de Mme. de Pompadour et Mme. d'Estrades" [279]—to a total of 15,316 livres,[280] which does not suggest great elaboration. Nothing survived to the day of photography which can be identified with this work, of which we have no drawings. In the same year Pineau carved the frames of two portraits, of the Dauphin and of Madame de Pompadour. His design of this latter [281] is in the height of picturesque contrast. These were, however, but small exceptions to the general rule of private patronage of the masters of the *genre pittoresque*.

[277] Even Madame de Pompadour's Théâtre des Cabinets, from 1747 onwards, which would normally have fallen under the Menus-Plaisirs and thus in the sphere of Meissonnier as Dessinateur de la Chambre et du Cabinet, was installed and conducted by the Bâtiments, then directed by her uncle Le Normant de Tournehem. Cf. Nolhac: *Versailles au XVIIIe siècle*, 1926, 50.

[278] Deshairs: *Pineau*, fig. 98. The scheme goes back to a much earlier drawing of Pineau (Figure 249), with its genial transformation of the Ionic capital by C-scrolls and hawk's-bills.

[279] o¹ 1583.

[280] o¹ 2248, p. 183.

[281] Preserved at the Musée Stieglitz, Leningrad. Reproduced by Biais, *op. cit.*, facing p. 165, where both drawings are catalogued, pp. 160 and 165.

Pineau was also concerned in the 'forties with problems of decoration in religious buildings. We find designs of his dated 1742 and 1744[282] for features at the cathedral of Saint-Louis de Versailles, of which the architect was Jacques-Hardouin Mansart. That for an altarpiece for the Chapel of the Virgin, unexecuted or modified in execution, involves little more than a typical panel and overdoor-frame. From 1743 and 1745 came designs[283] for features at the Chartreuse de Lugny (Côte d'Or), destroyed after the Revolution. The tabernacles for these churches are freely composed but not of great significance. A design for stalls with a throne[284] takes suggestions from those of Notre Dame, and revises them in line with Pineau's domestic woodwork, with slight touches of asymmetry. Mariette's *Architecture française* includes an engraved suite of *Nouveaux desseins d'autels et baldaquins inventés par le Sieur Pineau*.[285] The baldaquins are free versions of the familiar type with consoles uniting above; the retables do not present any great novelty, which appears only in a four-sided altar with a central leafy obelisk. Clearly Pineau's religious works were secondary to his domestic designs.

More important historically, it would seem, than any of those discussed was the oval salon added to the Hôtel Desmares when it was bought by the Duc de Villeroy about 1746.[286] The house survives as the Ministry of Agriculture, but the interiors, in general, have been renovated out of recognition. Mariette's *Architecture française* includes a plate of the salon (Figure 248) "sur les desseins de M. Le Roux, Architecte," who died in that year. From the previous relations of Leroux and Pineau, as well as from the character of the room itself we cannot doubt that Pineau was the actual designer — indeed Biais[287] lists among Pineau's manuscript drawings several for various parts of the house. At either side of the chimney piece the heads of the large panels are oppositely curved in bold outlines, while all other panels also include unsymmetrical elements.

The Hôtel de Maisons, built by Lassurance I in 1708, passed to the Marquis de Soyecourt, who, as Blondel wrote in 1752, "vient d'y faire de très grandes augmentations sur les desseins de Mr. Mouret, architecte."[288] It was typical of the effort toward elevation that, to secure it in the ground story, even the façade was changed, giving a height there, as Blondel remarks, of twenty-one feet. Blondel's text and plans show that the rooms on that floor, as well as the staircase, were wholly new. Champeaux, though not always happily inspired in his attributions, rightly remarks "il y a des rapports trop étroits entre les sculptures de l'hôtel de Roquelaure et celles de l'hôtel de Soyecourt pour que le même crayon ne les ait pas tracées."[289] That hand at the Hôtel de Roquelaure, as the drawings for it show, was Pineau's; we believe he did indeed design also the decorations of the Hôtel de Soyecourt.

The great surviving room is the Salle de Compagnie (Figures 251-252). Its most significant feature is the hollowing of recesses in the two end walls, not only for the pairs of doorways but for the central pier glasses. This treatment — found also in the doorway under the stairs — is of course very typical of Pineau, though it had also been taken up by others, as we

[282] Deshairs, figs. 30 and 188, and no. 31.
[283] *Ibid.*, fig. 189, and nos. 113bis-114bis, with others cited by Biais, *op. cit.*, 162.
[284] Deshairs, fig. 187.
[285] Pls. 428-433 of the Hautecoeur edition.
[286] Blondel, I, 212.
[287] *Op. cit.*, 167.
[288] *Architecture française*, I, 257-260, and pls. 86-89 of the Guadet edition.
[289] *Op. cit.*, 108.

have seen. On the inner wall with the chimney piece, the mirrors are indeed very close to Pineau's sketch for Roquelaure which we have reproduced (Figure 219) likewise with "festons" as noted there, wreathing the mouldings or, in the central mirror, with fronds of palm. The mouldings of the side mirrors are interrupted by scrolls, oppositely inclined, at half their height. Over these mirrors are meandering sprays, little more firmly joined than those of the Salon Rouge at the Hôtel de Roquelaure. The larger wall panels have trophies, the whole treatment of the panels of the end walls being very like that of some in the Salon of the Hôtel de Roquelaure. The narrow strip-panels have, at the base, the unsymmetrical scrolls familiar to us in Pineau's handling of such features from the Hôtel de Rouillé onwards. Their central medallions show a sign-manual of his, the bust in profile. Again, as in one of the rooms at the Hôtel de Soubise, and in two at Versailles, there is no upper moulding to the cornice; the scrollwork of the cove profiles freely on the ceiling. As Blondel well said in 1752, before reaction set in, "la décoration ne peut que satisfaire."

In the 'forties two other ornamental designers gained importance, Babel and Peyrotte.

Babel was much occupied as an engraver for the books of others, the earliest being Jeurat's *Traité de perspective*, 1738. He also engraved Boffrand's designs for the Hôtel de Soubise, issued in 1745, and numerous plates of Meissonnier's work, including the salon for the Princess Czartoriska, designed as we have seen, about 1750. His own plates of engraved ornament, undated, are numerous, among others being the suite with the significant title *Cartouches pitoresques*. With ample personal character, he follows the general initiative of Meissonnier both in asymmetric cartouches of plastic type and in the use of cartouche elements to frame naturalistic scenes, in forms later influential in Germany. We may remark also a very individual spiral motif (Figure 255) which we have nowhere met before. This reappears in the plates of the volume entitled *L'art de bâtir des maisons de campagne*, 1743, by the architect Briseux (1680-1754), who employed Pineau at the Hôtel Daugny and elsewhere, and suffices to establish that these plates (Figure 253)—*Briseux inv. Babel sc.*—are really of Babel's design.

In the house built before 1713[290] at 142, Rue de Grenelle for the Abbé de Pompadour, with decorations of many periods, one delightful small room[291] (Figure 254) shows the same individual character, with inclined palmettes and flaming, undulant lines. We may thus assume that this extreme example of the "picturesque" was from designs by Babel, executed doubtless for the Duchesse de Boufflers who was occupying the house in 1742.[292]

Regarding Peyrotte (d. 1769), whose work was closely related to that of Mondon, we may remark only the titles of two of his suites, the *Vases Rocaille* of 1743 and the *Cartouches rocaille*.

In the engravings of Cuvilliès a new series extends from 1745 to 1755, a series issued in Munich but distributed also with a Paris imprint. The suites begin with *Morceaux de caprice* in the style of the Parisian masters Lajoue and Boucher. Others, of chimney pieces and gueridons (11e Livre M) are derivative from Blondel's *Masions de plaisance* of 1737-1738. Certain tall arabesque panels, very richly charged with ornaments (3e Livre C), seem to be

---

[290] Brice in his edition of that year already mentions it, in substantially the same words as in later editions.
[291] *Vieux hôtels*, III, pls. 10-14.
[292] Piganiol de la Force, 1742 ed., VII, 119.

more personal to Cuvilliès, as are certainly the *Plafonds en voussure* (17e Livre R) and the cartouche, the *agrafes* and the picture frames of the eighteenth and twentieth books (Figure 256), where the rocailles are given a tattered character which is the extreme of the rococo. In spite of the extravagance of these ultimate designs, which are scarcely thinkable in France, we concur in the conclusion of Berliner[293] that the style of Cuvilliès is rather individual than characteristic of Germany.

Jean Cailleteau, called Lassurance like his father, gains a special interest through having been the personal architect of Madame de Pompadour, from the beginning of her favour, in her very extensive private enterprises in building. We do not know the date of his birth. In 1723, the year before his father's death, he was admitted to the second class of the Academy; in 1734, to the first. Controller at Marly, then at Fontainebleau, he achieved the high rank of Architecte Ordinaire du Roi. As designs by him we know only his numerous works for the Marquise.

The Château of Crécy, near Dreux, was among her earlier acquisitions, in 1746. Lassurance was employed for a remodelling of the house, Garnier d'Isle for the gardens, and 700,000 livres were spent in two years without an end to the changes.[294] The building was demolished in 1830, but there survive eight panels painted by Boucher about 1751, now preserved in the Frick Collection in New York.[295] Neither the carved nor the painted frames of these delightful little compositions are of exceptional character or importance for the purpose of our study.

Another early acquisition was the Château of Champs in Brie, built by Bullet de Chamblin before 1717 and bought by the Marquise in 1747.[296] Her will states that she spent there 200,000 livres in three years. Her chief work surviving there, the Chambre à Coucher, has unbroken tall panels of very rich and delicate carving. Both inner and outer beads are twined with sprays, which break out naturalistically at half the height. The mirror is outlined with palm, reverse curves of which also frame the space above, ornamented with the motif of a peacock. The cornice is defined by an upper moulding, beyond which several sprays escape, and which surrounds the old projecting chimney breast in sweeping curves. In this earliest surviving work for the Marquise we see, more than in any other, traces of the *genre pittoresque*. Within a few years, on the building of Bellevue, Champs was rented to the Duc de Lavallière.

It is to Christophe Huet that Dargenville attributes the chinoiseries of Champs. These were executed on the simple panelling of the first period of the château; the inner painted frames, unlike Huet's earlier work at Chantilly, now show the freest disregard of symmetry.

We need not say much of the "Petit Château" of La Celle on the road toward Marly, rebuilt in 1747 by the Marquise, or of her three Hermitages, at Versailles,[297] at Fontaine-

---

[293] *Op. cit.*, 170-171.

[294] E. and J. de Goncourt: *Madame de Pompadour*, 1878, 112.

[295] Illustrated in *Duveen Pictures in Public Collections in America*, 1941, pls. 244 ff. Cf. Nolhac: *François Boucher*, 1907.

[296] Not in 1757 as frequently stated. Biver, in his volume on Bellevue, p. 7n, cites the date as August 4, 1747, from the Étude de Me. Laueffer, Paris notary, CVII, 447.

[297] A plan by Fichu in the Topographie at the Cabinet des Estampes is cited by Dussieux: *Le Château de Versailles*, 1885, II, 436n.

bleau,[298] both of 1749, and at Compiègne, of 1753-1754.[299] That of Compiègne — where Verberckt carved the wainscot which by 1767 Gabriel could speak of as "bien chargée" — has vanished by the same enchantment which evoked them, and, although those of Versailles and Fontainebleau survive in private hands, I know of no publication showing their interiors.

Vanished also is Bellevue, chief of the personal creations of the Marquise, but here we fortunately have drawings in abundance.[300] Ground was broken June 30, 1748, and the work was pushed with such magical celerity that the King could be entertained there on November 25, 1750, though the expenses of building listed by Lassurance continued to July 31, 1754. Many of the painted and sculptured features were not in place before 1752 and 1753. The payments included large sums for carving by Verberckt and Rousseau, to whom Biver supposes was left a considerable initiative. The drawings show, however, that Lassurance and his draughtsman Jeanson were fully responsible for the general form of the interiors and the disposition of the ornaments. Their designs, which preceded the departure of the brother of Madame de Pompadour on his famous Italian journey, present a sober version of the rococo, depending less on lavish ornament than on the high quality of the execution and of the paintings for the overdoors.

In such principal rooms as the Salle à Manger and the Chambre du Roi, the fields of the panels are rectangular, with trophies and garlands, the mirror heads, while scalloped and garlanded, conform closely to an arched outline. That this was not due to any severity of principles, however, is shown by the design for the Cabinet de Compagnie, where the panels, the overdoors, the medallions, are very richly curved and ornamented, the major mirror heads are flanked with herms, as at this moment at Versailles.

In the town house of Madame de Pompadour at Versailles (Hôtel des Reservoirs) on land ceded in 1752, some of the original decorations remain, but the woodwork offers nothing of novelty.

In 1753 Madame de Pompadour acquired the Hôtel d'Évreux (Élysée), where she expended in a single year over 95,000 livres in enlargements and remodellings. Blondel wrote of his visit in September, 1753:[301] "[elle] y fait faire actuellement quelques changemens sur les desseins de M. Lassurance." He describes the intended changes, with a note they might possibly not be carried out, and in fact no work of this period exists in the ground story, the only executed portions surviving being in the private apartments of the first story. Later Blondel recommended a visit to his students: "Ils seroient bien dédommagés ... par l'examen de quelques belles parties que contiennent les dedans, & qu'une dame de la Cour, protectrice des Beaux-Arts y a fait faire ... Ces parties de détails ... sont bien capables de leur faire naître le vrai goût de la décoration intérieure des appartements."[302] These words, from Blondel's pen, indicate that the decorations were of reasonably conservative character.

In sum, the work of Lassurance for Madame de Pompadour, rich as it was, can only be said to be of great conventionality. The legendary charm of these houses lay not in any novelty

[298] A first plan, "du dessein de M. Lassurance, was included by Lerouge in his *Jardins anglo-chinois*, 1788. A plan and elevation showing slight additions by Gabriel is reproduced by Fels, *op. cit.*, pls. XXX-XXL.

[299] Robiquet, *op. cit.*, 27, and Fels, *op. cit.*, 152-153.

[300] Reproduced by Biver: *Histoire du château de Bellevue*, 1933.

[301] *Architecture françoise*, IV, 1754, 149. He promised plates of this new work for his sixth volume, never issued.

[302] *Cours d'architecture*, III, 1772, 120-121.

of effects of space or surface, but in the wealth of painting and sculpture by the finest living masters, in the luxury of contents, the variety of accessories, the novelty of entertainment, endlessly fertile in imaginings.

By an oversight which emphasizes the confused ideas of style and chronology hitherto prevailing, the interiors of the Hôtel de Seignelay, built by Boffrand in 1713-1718, have passed for work of his at that time. Clearly, by their style (Figure 259), they date from the period after the death of the Marquis de Seignelay in 1746, and very probably after 1752.[303] Although doorways and central pier glass are recessed, we do not consider the work to be from designs of Pineau; the whole character of the outlines and of the carving is smoother, fatter, less piquant. The mouldings of overdoors and door panels tend to flow more continuously. Striking features are the palm stems rising the full height of the walls at the corners and at either side of the central recess, also the double wall-panels, themselves unbalanced, united into a singled balanced motif by outer mouldings and by a central painting at the top. Minor panels are wholly symmetrical. The cornice is quieter, with medallions only at the corners, into the frames of which the straight upper moulding is scrolled. There is an appreciable diminution of "contraste."

In much the same style were the interiors of the "maison de M. Dodun executé sur les desseins de Mr. de Chamblin," to which Mariette give six plates (Figure 260).[304] This, too, has passed as a work of the first part of the century, under the supposition that the architect was Bullet de Chamblin, who died in 1726. The 1752 edition of Brice, however, states (L, 360) that "Dodun . . . a fait bâtir depuis peu d'années sous la conduite de Champlain, une maison . . . dont les dedans sont décorés avec magnificence." This would fix the date as shortly before 1750, making the work among the latest of all those illustrated by Mariette. That is indeed the suggestion of the character of the work itself, in which, as in the Hôtel de Seignelay, double wall-panels are united by medallions above. The doors have oval transoms, as in some other works of this time.

A new campaign of decoration at the Hôtel de Rohan, from which certain elements survive, is fixed by Langlois[305] as dating from 1749-1752, between the advent of the Cardinal de Rohan and the publication of Blondel's *Architecture françoise*, which speaks of his having "décoré à neuf tous les appartemens du premier étage avec une magnificence extraordinaire . . . dans le goût le plus moderne."[306] The work in the Salon de Compagnie is related to Contant's at the Palais-Royal at the same period, as are the mouldings of the Cabinet des Singes (Figure 261), "enrichis d'Arabesques," says Blondel, "embellis de sujets Chinois, le tout peint par M. Huet, Peintre fort habile dans ce genre." Here, surrounding large naturalistic compositions, though scarcely fused with them, are light painted borders, once again symmetrical.

---

[303] There is as yet no mention of this remodelling in the first volume of Blondel's *Architecture françoise*, which appeared in that year.

[304] *Architecture françoise*, pls. 493-498 of the Hautecoeur edition. According to Champeaux, *op. cit.*, 272, this was the house at 21, Rue de Richelieu. He states that certain of the boiseries were sold to Baron Ferdinand de Rothschild, others to the Marquis de Breteuil for his house in the Avenue du Bois de Boulogne. The decorations of the stair hall, in stucco, remain in place.

[305] *Op. cit.*, 219.

[306] *Architecture françoise*, II, 1761. These decorations were executed, says Blondel, "sur les desseins et sous la conduite de M. de Saint-Martin, architecte."

Evolution

Some interiors of the time deserving mention, not only for their own simple elegance but because they have been placed so far from their true date as to upset any rational sequence, are those of the Hôtel Delisle-Mansart at 22, Rue Saint-Gilles. This house was indeed transformed by Delisle-Mansart before his death in 1720, but the surviving rooms must surely come from the period after 1750, when it was acquired by the Marquis de Castelnau. The charming small oval salon has recessed doorways, with heads smoothly rounded like the overdoor frames and the tall panels of the walls, and with the heavier mouldings characteristic of that period. The rectangular Grand Salon shows related forms and spirit.

Certain remodellings of the Hôtel Lambert, doubtless after its occupation by the financier Marin de la Haye in 1746, or its purchase by him, 1750, are important only for the unusual spatial forms of the library,[307] groined on strange Ionic corbels, with a central dome opening laterally into curved recesses. It is a very sober reality beside the wild dream of Lajoue, with some of the elements of his painted panels for Bonnier de la Mosson. All these are worthy works of the rank and file, with no great novelty or personal character.

Representative of the more conservative group was the architect Contant d'Ivry, admitted to the Academy in 1728, who was responsible at this time for remodelling the houses of the heirs of Crozat in the Place Vendôme.

The two houses at Nos. 17 and 19 there, built by Bullet for Antoine Crozat for himself and for his daughter, who had married the Comte d'Évreux, were occupied in the mid-century, after Crozat's death in 1738, by his sons, the Seigneur de Tugny (spelled Tunis by Blondel) and the Baron de Thiers. Both were extensively modified for them by Contant in 1747[308] and in 1741-1744,[309] respectively. Little of the finish of the period remains at the former; the latter, now the seat of the Crédit Foncier, preserves some fine interiors of this time or a little later, and we have also certain manuscript drawings for the work. In general effect the Grand Salon (Figure 264) presents a striking contrast with Pineau's work, being membered uniformly with pilasters, bearing a full entablature and framing, in most bays, semicircular arches of academic detail. Contant, however, was not averse to adopting, within the architectonic framework, suggestions from Pineau, as appears in the pairs of central doors, with their richly curved rails. These pairs of doors lack any dividing mouldings; the unbalanced leaves are united in a single symmetrical whole. Though the inner corners of the room are slightly curved, the cornice is uninterrupted by any medallions, and the ornaments, while free in line, are restrained in quantity.

At the Palais-Royal, Contant's new constructions of 1750-1752[310] were extensive, but, aside from the handsome staircase with an oval cage, little remains today beside a few fine doors. Fortunately the encyclopedia of Diderot and D'Alembert[311] includes seven engraved designs for interiors, some of which were published also in Blondel's *Cours d'architecture* (Figure 265).[312] Again we see an academic framework, a fondness for arches framed by orders, a

[307] *Vieux hôtels*, VIII, pl. 11.

[308] Blondel: *Architecture françoise*, III, 108.

[309] T.-H. Lunsingh-Schuerleer: "Deux projets pour l'hôtel de Thiers, attribués à Contant d'Ivry," in *Bulletin de la Société de l'histoire de l'art français*, 1934, 291-298.

[310] Champier and Sandoz, *op. cit.*, 36n.

[311] *Encyclopédie ou dictionnaire raisonné des sciences, des arts et des métiers*, 28 vols., 1751-1772. Blondel contributed the section "Architecture," as he states in his *Cours*, IV, 121n.

[312] VII, 1777, pls. L, LI.

quieting of the lines of the ornaments. The surviving doors are not unlike those of the Hôtel d'Évreux (de Thiers), with leaves sometimes unbalanced, sometimes self-contained, alike with rich curvature of the rails. They have some free ornaments such as dragons in the crosettes, contrasted with tall plain surfaces and with mouldings of considerable weight.

The *genre pittoresque* continued to find some literary support, notably from the architect Briseux, who, as we have seen, had himself employed Pineau and Babel. In his *Maisons de campagne* of 1743, after urging careful study of the general design of rooms and their panelling, so that they may please "par les seules formes," even prior to the placing of carving, he adds:

> Le ciseau & le pinceau, tous deux imitateurs de la Nature, qui diversifie ses productions à l'infini, mais qui les assortit à chaque Elément & à chaque Saison, peuvent aussi comme elle, faire voir des feuilles, des fleurs, des fruits, des palmes, des roseaux, des coquilles, des cartels, des oiseaux, des dragons, &c. sans crainte d'encourir de mépris qui est dû si justement aux décorations Gothiques, pourvû qu'ils n'en fassent point un assemblage monstreux; que ces différents objets ne soient point opposés à la destination de la piéce où on les place, & qu'au contraire, ils y soient ménagés avec prudence & avec art; autrement, si l'on vouloit priver l'imagination du secours de toutes ces productions naturelles, elle ne pourroit plus que présenter des fantômes, ou travailler sur le néant.
>
> Le maniére dont quelques Génies distingués ont traité pepuis peu ces ornemens, a soulevé d'abord ceux qui plus envieux de la réputation d'autrui, que jaloux de l'accroissement de leur Art, suivoient servilement les stériles desseins de leurs prédécesseurs; mais tandis qu'il se sont récriés que cette sculpture moderne ne ressembloit aucunement à celle d'autrefois, ceux d'entre eux qui sont les plus versés dans le dessein, n'ont pas laissé que de s'évertuer, jusqu'à tâcher de l'imiter, & les Censeurs mêmes de ces compositions ingénieuses, n'ont pû s'empêcher d'en faire usage.

As with every style, the question arises with the rococo whether its creative impulse became exhausted, or whether it was still capable of creative renewal but was cut off from without. We see that, down to the death of Pineau at least, there was no falling off in the creative brilliance of individual works. Where, however, the style was confined so closely as the rococo was in France to domestic interiors and ornament, it presented henceforth no fundamentally new problems to stimulate fresh achievement.

Later Years of Louis XV

Beginnings of Reaction

The Bâtiments under Marigny, from 1751

The successor of Tournehem as Directeur des Bâtiments was the own brother of Madame de Pompadour, the Marquis de Vandières, later Marquis de Marigny, for whom she had secured the reversion in 1746, and who now took office in November, 1751, at the age of twenty-four. With excellent natural endowments, he had been carefully prepared for his post, above all by a trip to Italy lasting from December, 1749, to September, 1751.[313] The

[313] Cf. H. Roujon: "Le voyage du marquis de Marigny en Italie," communication read at the séance of the Academie des Beaux-Arts, November, 1898. His sister's letters to him during the trip are published by A. P.-Malassis: *Correspondance de Mme. de Pompadour*, 1878.

men selected as his guides and mentors—"ses yeux," as he said[314]—were the Abbé Leblanc, the architect Soufflot, and the draughtsman and engraver Cochin the younger.

Jacques-Germain Soufflot[315] (1713-1780) had gone to Rome at eighteen without formal training except as an apprentice in Lyons. By intervention of the ambassador he was admitted to the Academy in 1734 and remained until 1738. Returning to Lyons in 1738 he was received at the local academy in 1739, where he presented several papers: on proportions; in 1741, on the Gothic, of which he admired the structural boldness; in 1744 on rules and taste, in which he allowed some liberties to genius, distinguishing this from "ce prétendu goût du siècle," which regards as cold and tiresome "cette sage et riche simplicité . . . des Grecs, des Romains." This did not prevent him from executing in these years, at Saint-Bruno des Chartreux, the baldaquin from Servadoni's bold and free design and from designing the frames for Trémolières' paintings, with the very height of rococo freedom.[316] The panelling of the Episcopal Palace, completed in 1749, also shows forms of the rococo typical of that moment. From 1741 he was occupied with the design of the Hôtel Dieu with its long cool academic front. It was apparently the diffusion of Soufflot's designs by engraving which enabled this architect of the provinces to keep himself in the mind of persons of influence in the capital. Already by 1739 he had published "les plans et description de l'église Saint-Pierre de Rome et de la colonnade de la place antérieure." In 1745, it was a design for a triumphal arch in honour of Fontenoy.[317] Plates of the design for the Hôtel Dieu were also available; indeed Soufflot's biographer attributes to these the choice of Soufflot by Madame de Pompadour to accompany her brother to Italy. At best it is hard to understand this choice of one who was still a provincial architect. November 17, 1749, Soufflot, as a result of this choice, was elected a member of the second class of the Academy in Paris; November 23 he attended there, a month before his departure.

Charles-Nicolas Cochin, the younger (1715-1790),[318] brought up in a family milieu of artists, showed precocious abilities in drawing and engraving which secured him employment in those lines, at twenty-four, in the Menus-Plaisirs. Here he made himself the graphic chronicler of the great ceremonies of 1745 and 1747. The same gift brought him early into contact with Madame de Pompadour through work for her Théâtre des Petits Cabinets at Versailles, inaugurated in the winter of 1747. The arrangements, to be sure, were not entrusted as usual to the Menus-Plaisirs, but to the Bâtiments under Tournehem. To Cochin, however, fell the task of illustrating the performances, as in his drawing of the favorite in the rôle of Galatea presented in 1748 and 1749.[319] It was Cochin who was later to teach and assist Madame de Pompadour in engraving, but her activities in that line did not themselves begin before the Italian journey. His allegory of her as Minerva, protectress of the arts, appeared, at the head of the dedication of the edition of Metastasio, only in 1750. His own dec-

[314] Cochin: "Notice nécrologique du Marquis de Marigny," *Journal de Paris*, June 1, 1781.

[315] Cf. J. Mondain-Monval: *Soufflot*, 1918, and *Correspondance de Soufflot avec les directeurs des bâtiments (1756-80)*, 1918.

[316] R. Le Naïl: *Lyon*, n.d., iii, cites the archives of the monastery. Cf. Forest: *L'Église Saint-Bruno des Chartreux de Lyon*, 1900.

[317] Preserved by the Musée des Arts-décoratifs. Cf. Chennevières in *l'Artiste*, 1885.

[318] E. and J. de Goncourt: *L'art du dixhuitième siècle*, II, 1874, 46-104; S. Rocheblave, *Les Cochin*, 1893; P. Mantz in *Gazette des beaux-arts*, Ire pér., XI, 1861, 251 ff.

[319] Goncourt: *Pompadour*, 68-70.

orative designs and vignettes prior to that are of a free character, often unsymmetrical and including rocaille elements, not unlike some of the compositions of his friend Boucher which he had engraved early in his career. His marvelous facility as a draughtsman well fitted him to illustrate the journey, while his agreeable personality, which was to render him constantly welcome in the salons of Madame Geoffrin and Madame du Deffand, fitted him to be a delightful travelling companion. The patent of nobility of Cochin the younger,[320] in 1757, after saying that his father "a éte choisi . . . pour exécuter . . . toutes les parties relatives à notre sacre, ainsi que différentes Fêtes et Pompes funèbres," adds that the son seconded his father in these works with ability equally in design and in execution, and that the ceremonies of marriage of the Infanta, 1739, of the two marriages of the Dauphin, 1745-1747, and of the birth of the Duc de Bourgogne were testimonies of his success in both lines. In general these decorations followed the tradition established by Berain. In the baldaquin for the funeral of the first Dauphine in 1746, as we see it in the younger Cochin's engraving, while its oval arches are unbroken, he surrounds them, like an Oppenord mirror head, with a comb of rugous scroll, supported on masks with a fringe of bats'-wings. Clearly, before Cochin went to Italy, he was none too severe in his principles.

It has been easy, too easy, to attribute the choice of these men to a desire on the part of Madame de Pompadour to effect a reform of the prevailing style.[321] We must hold with the Goncourts, in their very judicious statement,[322] against any such idea on her part. To the excellent reasons they give, which retain all their force, we may now add the character of the decorations at Bellevue, built for the favorite without intervention of the Bâtiments, in the very years of the journey. These, as we shall see, show no trace of impulse to reaction. At the close of her life, a little belatedly, she patronized the fashion of reaction, as she had earlier patronized the established fashion of the rococo itself.

Actually, we may surmise, the selection of companions was made or instigated by the Abbé Leblanc himself, intimate, as we have seen, in the councils of Tournehem, and the only man in France who had written strongly against the rococo. To him, unlike Madame de Pompadour, we may indeed attribute more than an *arrière-pensée* of reform in the arrangements for the journey.

Cochin has left a record of the Italian travels in his *Voyage d'Italie*, published in 1758. The form it assumed[323] gave little space to architecture, although at the beginning, in the notes on Turin, there are hostile, rationalistic criticisms of the Piedmontese baroque, particularly of the works "quelquefois ingénieux, plus souvent extravagant, du Père Guarini, qui étoit ennemi des lignes droites"—"la raison n'y trouve pas toujours son compte . . . Guarini . . . semble ne l'avoir jamais connue." Such academic distaste for Guarini, however, was nothing new; we have seen it in France even before 1700. As this journey has been thought to have prepared in France the second return to antiquity, it is important for us to note that so far from admiring the recently discovered works from Herculaneum, shown in the palace at Portici, Cochin treats them most severely. This is true especially of the paintings: "composition froide," "tableau médiocrement dessiné," "faire pesant et froid . . . couleur mauvaise,"

[320] Published by Rocheblave, *op. cit.*, 209-210.
[321] So Manz, Rocheblave (p. 82) and Monval (p. 22) in the works just cited, and many secondary writers.
[322] *Pompadour*, 1878, 419n.
[323] *Voyage d'Italie, ou Recueil des notes sur les ouvrages de peinture et de sculpture, qu'on voit dans les principales villes d'Italie.*

"architecture de mauvais goût — gothique par anticipation." While he has praise for the small decorative subjects, the sculpture, and the bronze utensils, he certainly has no unqualified admiration for the new discoveries. Similar judgments had already been expressed in a book by Cochin and Bellicard, appearing in 1754, *Observations sur les antiquités de la ville d'Herculaneum avec quelques réflexions sur la peinture et la sculpture des anciens*.

There can be no question that, after their return from Italy, Cochin and Soufflot set themselves definitely to reform the extravagances of the rococo. In the effort they had the support of Vandières, who, although his personal tastes were for trifles of Boucher, Vanloo and Natoire, as Directeur officially recalled the artists to the academic tradition of the sixteenth and seventeenth century. Certainly he was no friend of "antiquomania." He wrote to Natoire in 1762, after Leroy's presentation of his drawings of Athenian buildings:

> Les dessins du Sr Le Roy et du Sr Chalgrin sont assez bien. Je voudrais que nos architectes s'ocupassent plus qu'ils ne font des choses relatives à nos moeurs et nos usages que des temples de la Grèce. Ils s'eloignent de leur objet en se livrant à ce genre d'architecture.

With the eternal eclecticism of the layman he wrote to Soufflot, as late as 1760, of the character he wished in his house in the Faubourg du Roule: "Je ne veux point de la chicorée moderne, je ne veux point de l'austère ancien."[324]

The staff of Vandières,[325] on his accession to power in the Bâtiments, remained at first the same, with Charles Coypel, as Premier Peintre, continuing in a position of power. On Coypel's death in 1752 the post was left vacant for a decade, its administrative functions being lodged in the hands of the Secretary of the Academy, Bernard Lépicié, with the added title "Chargé du détail des Arts." Eclectic like Coypel, he was of feeble character and authority. On his death at the beginning of 1755, Cochin succeeded him in both offices. In the same year Soufflot, who had meanwhile worked again in Lyons, was named Contrôleur des Bâtiments du Roi au Département de Paris. The friends thus attained positions of much authority, though by no means all-powerful, as Gabriel remained entrenched as Premier Architecte, and as Contrôleur at Versailles.

Cochin's own account of the beginnings of reaction[326] has been little regarded. He writes: "On peut donner pour premier époque du retour d'un meilleur goust, l'arivée de Legeay architecte." Jean-Laurent Legeay had won the Prix de Rome in 1732, but was not sent until 1737; he left Rome for Paris in January, 1742.[327] In spite of the meglomania which prevented execution of his projects, says Cochin, "le goust de Legeay étoit excellent, il ouvrit les yeux de beaucoup de gens. Les jeunes architectes le saisirent autant qu'ils purent . . . On vit changer sensiblement l'école d'architecture au grand étonnement de tous les architectes anciens de l'Académie." In 1745 Legeay seems to have gone to Berlin, where he published views of the Hedwigskirche, begun in that year but not finished until 1773. Although we cannot be certain of his precise connection with its design, that design itself — with its Roman Pantheon dome, its pedimented frontispiece of six engaged columns rising from a stylobate

---

[324] Passages cited by Locquin, *op. cit.*, 16n.

[325] *Ibid.*, 18 ff.

[326] In his manuscript "Anecdotes," written some time after 1781, doubtless toward the end of his life in 1790. Published by Charles Henry as *Mémoires inédits de C.-N. Cochin*, 1880, where the passages quoted appear on pp. 140 ff.

[327] *Correspondance des directeurs*, X, 1, 11.

The Creation of the Rococo

—is of such an advanced character for its date that we must indeed assume that he was primarily responsible. Only in England could anything of the kind be found before this time.

"Depuis," wrote Cochin, "la véritable époque décisive, ç'à été le retour de M. de Marigny d'Italy et da sa compagnie. Nous avions vu et vu avec réflection. Le ridicule nous parut à tous bien sensible et nous ne nous en tûmes point. Nous cris gagnèrent dans la suite que Soufflot prêcha d'example. Il fut suivi de Potain et de plusieurs autres bons élèves architectes qui revinrent de Rome. J'y aiday aussi comme la mouche du cloche. J'écrivis dans le *Mercure* contre les folies anciennes et les couvris d'un assez bon dose de ridicule."

After the early strictures of the Abbé Leblanc, one of the first antagonistic expressions was the obituary of Meissonnier in the *Mercure* for October, 1750,[328] of which, as Cochin was still in Italy, we may surmise Mariette to have been the author. Even in praising the great beauty of his models for silverwork, it says:

> Cet éloge, tombe plutôt sur l'exécution que sur la composition qui étoit outrée, parce qu'il vouloit trouver du nouveau, paroître singulier, produire du piquant, en un mot devenir original, & sur tout ne ressembler à personne.
>
> Il est arrivé de cette erreur, qui aura toujours des mêmes suites, que le veritable goût s'est alteré, & que notre Artiste a eu des imitateurs, d'autant plus aisément, que les choses bizarres & irrégulieres sont mille fois plus faciles à produire que celles qui sont sages & conséquentes; on peut les regarder comme de fausses facilités, toujours ennemies du bon goût, & d'autant plus à redouter, qu'elles séduisent les ignorans & trouvent des admirateurs.
>
> M. Messonier évitoit toute espéce de symmétrie jusques dans l'ornement, & pour donner un exemple de l'abus auquel cette imitation a pû conduire, nous avons vû ses copistes décorer & placer de côté des consoles & des clefs de voutes, quoique ces corps exigent nécessairement par leur essence l'aplomb le plus exact: ils n'ont imité que ses défauts, & ils les ont répandus dans toute l'Europe.
>
> On voit par ce que nous venons de dire, que dégoûté de l'orfêvrerie, M. Messonier s'entêta de l'Architecture qu'il traita dans le même esprit. Il avoit été séduit par le goût du Boromini, qui dans la composition & le mouvement des parties de ce grand Art, a cependant été toujours plus conséquent, & n'a pas admis autant de véritables bizarreries que M. Messonier . . .
>
> (Il) a eu trop d'imitateurs; ils commencent à rougir, & par conséquent à se refroidir. C'est une chose à désirer pour les parties de l'Art, qui regardent l'ornement . . .

The most devastating attack on the *genre pittoresque* was indeed that of Cochin himself, in his two famous letters in the *Mercure*, in 1754 and 1755, already cited with reference to the origin of the movement. From the "Supplication aux Orfèvres, Ciseleurs, Sculpteurs en bois pour les appartemens & autres,"[329] well known as it is, we may quote some of the less familiar passages:

> Sont priés Messieurs les Sculpteurs des appartements d'avoir agréable dans les trophées qu'ils exécutent, de ne pas faire une faux plus petite qu'un horloge de sable . . .une tête d'homme plus petite qu'une rose . . . Nous ne voulons pas même leur demander un peu de retenue dans l'usage des palmiers qu'ils font croître si abondamment dans nos appartemens . . . Mais de moins pourrions-nous esperer d'obtenir que lorsque les choses pour-

[328] Pp. 138-141. Meissonnier had died July 31. Mariette's notes on Meissonnier, which we have cited, closely coincide in expression with the articles in the *Mercure*.

[329] December, 1754, 178-187.

ront être quarrées, ils veuillent bien ne les pas torturer ; que lorsque les couronnemens
pourront être de plein cintre, ils veuillent ne les pas corrompre par ces contours en S . . .
Nous consentons cependant qu'ils servent de cette marchandise tortue à tous Provinciaux
ou Étrangers qui seront assez mauvais connoisseurs pour préférer notre goût moderne
a celui du siècle passé . . . Les Sculpteurs sont donc priés de vouloir bien ajouter foi aux
assurances que nous leur donnons . . . que les formes droites, quarrées, rondes & ovales
régulières, decorent aussi richement que toutes leurs inventions . . .

In the pretended answer on behalf of partisans of the style, Cochin continued to pursue
them with delicate irony. Beyond the passages we have already given in our analysis of the
work of Meissonnier and Pineau, we need only quote the one in which, after citing the opposition of the Bâtiments and the Academy, he hints the growth of opposition among the architects: "quelques-uns que nous avons crû longtemps des nôtres"—we think of Blondel—"à la
première occasion qu'ils ont eu de faire quleque chose de remarquable, nous ont laissée là, &
se sont jettés dans l'ancien goût."[330]

What Cochin ultimately thought of the *genre pittoresque*, all diplomacy aside, he entrusted
to the privacy of the manuscript *Anecdotes* which he buried, by his will, in the Bibliothèque
du Roi:[331]

> Il y eut dan ce temps-là quantité de mauvais inventeurs d'ornemens qui jouirent de la
> plus brillante réputation, un Pineau qui estropia de sa sculpture touttes l'architecture qui
> se fit alors. La Joue même peintre d'architecture assés médiocre, fit des desseins d'orne-
> ments assés misérables, qui se vendirent avec la plus grande rapidité. Tout étoit livré à
> une esprit de vertige.
>
> Meissonier, homme qui avoit véritablement du génie, mais un génie sans règle et de
> plus gâté en Italie par son admiration pour le Borromini, achéva d'amener le désorde
> dans touttes les têtes . . .
>
> C'étoit M. Openor architecte, qui avoit commencé à sortir du bon goust du siècle de
> Louis XIV . . . d'excès en excès les choses arrivèrent au comble du ridicule oû nous les
> avons vües.

The teaching of the Academy of Architecture in the eighteenth century, as from its foundation, had steadily stressed the doctrine of the orders, of integral proportions, and of purity
of classical forms, with little reference to what was going on in interiors.

The most influential personage in instruction and criticism was Jacques-François Blondel
(1705-1774) who in 1743[332] had founded his own school in Paris, with a more systematic
and comprehensive course of study.[333] This rivalship with the official school perhaps occasioned the delay in his election to the Academy (1755), where he ultimately became Professor in 1762. In the beginning he had been far from hostile to the new forms, indeed we know
him as one of the first, in 1737, to publish designs by Pineau. In 1752-1756 appeared the
volumes of his *Architecture françoise*, in which, for the publisher Jombert (who had bought
Mariette's stock of plates) he provided an introduction and critical text to accompany the

---

[330] February, 1755, 148-171. Both these pieces were reprinted in the first volume of Cochin's *Oeuvres diverses*,
1771.

[331] *Memoires inédits*, 140.

[332] *Cours d'architecture*, III, 1772, lxxxij; *Procès-verbaux*, V, 314, 343.

[333] One may compare the course of Desgodetz, as recorded by Jean Pinard and described by Mademoiselle
Duportal, *loc. cit.*, with that of Blondel: *Cours d'Architecture*, III, lxxxj, where he describes in detail the curri-
culum of his school.

engravings of French buildings. His admiration was given primarily to works of the classical period of Louis XIV, above all to François Mansart, François Blondel, and Claude Perrault. For him the Château of Maisons, the Porte Saint-Denis and the Louvre colonnade were the supreme masterpieces of French architecture, unsurpassed in Italy, and quite worthy of mention with buildings of antiquity. Indeed, by contrast with earlier ones, his course of instruction was not based on antiquity itself, but on the study of the French works of academic character.

In the *Architecture françoise*, Blondel, as we have had many occasions to see, still has kind words for interiors in houses where these were of the freest character. His first volume of 1752, after speaking of the "décoration extérieure" where he recommended "de la convenance et de la modération dans les ornemens," devotes a general section to the "décoration intérieure"—"qui, quoique moins sévère dans son ordonnance, exige cependant de la retenue dans les formes, et du choix dans les parties que la compose." This counsel of discretion in ornaments is repeated more than once —"l'on doit éviter avec soin leur profusion;" "il faut de la prudence, affecter des parties lisses, afin de faire valoir celles qui sont ornées, et ne pas confondre indistinctement les attributs." It did not prevent him, however, from reprinting many plates of the freest character from his work of 1737 in his *Livre nouveau* of 1752, and from promising to include, in a projected final volume of the *Architecture françoise* which the publisher did not reach,[334] plates of such extreme interiors as the oval drawing room of the Hôtel de Villeroy.[335]

What the onslaughts of Cochin, the reserves of Blondel, demanded was an expurgation of the extravagances and extremes of the rococo. They were far from proposing a direct imitation of antiquity, which was not called for before the next decade. They suggested, as Cochin said later, and as other critics urged, "de se remettre sur la voye du bon goût du siècle précédent,"[336] that is to return to academism, which still admitted, as it had done in the last years of Louis XIV, many of the motifs and forms which the *genre pittoresque* had meanwhile so playfully contorted.

Thus we are not surprised to find no sharp break in the character of the interiors executed by the Bâtiments during the 'fifties. Gabriel continued to furnish the designs; Verberckt to lead in the execution. Beside him after 1755 appeared the carver Antoine Rousseau.

It is in the long series of decorations at Versailles at this period that we can best study the character and transformations of official style in the mid-century.

Nothing significant is left, alas, of the decorations of the quarters of Madame de Pompadour on the ground floor, where in 1750 she succeeded the Comtesse de Toulouse in occupancy of the former Appartement des Bains.

The Salle à Manger du Roi — created in 1751-1752, enlarged in 1754-1755 — in the building between the northern courts, has woodwork of extreme simplicity. Tiers of square panels alternate with traverses, as in the Cabinet de la Comtesse at Rambouillet — a treatment doubtless proportioned to the small size which the room had at first, some of the panels being perhaps re-used from the Bains du Roi which previously occupied this area.

In 1752-1753 the destruction of the old Escalier du Roi or des Ambassadeurs and of the

[334] Cf. Blondel's note in the *Cours d'architecture*, disclaiming responsibilty for the abandonment of the enterprise.

[335] I, 212.   [336] *Memoires inédits*, 143.

Evolution

Petite Galerie gave place for an apartment for Madame Adelaïde, the daughter who held this place of honour, adjoining the King's, until 1769. A room of the apartment surviving from this period is the Cabinet (Salon de Musique) which itself was enlarged by a recess in 1767 (Figure 266). The work of 1752-1753 here has simple panels with oval medallions at the top. The chimney piece with its mirror is set in a shallow curved recess of the type inaugurated by Pineau. The ceiling, preserving the high cove of the salon of the Petite Galerie, has this covered with a floral network or mosaic, with large corner cartouches, below the central circular field.

While the room at the eastern corner of the apartment was again transformed in 1769 to serve as the Grande Salle à Manger des Cabinets du Roi (Salon des Porcelaines) one cannot doubt that most of its decoration is work of the period 1752-1753 or matches that — indeed the window casings, where half-length figures are perched *en espagnolette* on the oval heads, are identical with those of the Cabinet de Madame Adelaïde.

A moment later, in 1753-1754, the Cabinet à Pans du Roi received panels carved by Verberckt, of which the major units survived a rearrangement of 1760 (Figure 268). It is interesting to compare these with the panels of 1738 in the Chambre du Roi and the Cabinet Ovale. The figural medallions still have a rim of shell, but it is suaver, less serrated; they are surrounded, no longer by interlaces descended from Lepautre, but by sprays of naturalistic flowers tied with ribbons. Even in the floral finials there is now scarcely a trace of asymmetry. Clearly Gabriel, as he had grown older, had already grown more conservative in his relation to the *genre pittoresque*.

The Bibliothèque du Dauphin, executed in 1755, of which some panelling is preserved, was also of conservative character. Its ceiling, still in place, no longer abandons the upper moulding of the cove, but corresponds closely with examples in private work before 1735.[337]

The great task of 1755-1756 was an enlargement of the Cabinet du Conseil (Figure 64) by the area of the Cabinet des Perruques. Many elements of the finish of 1701 were left in place, re-employed, duplicated, or extended: the window casings, the doors, the mirrors with their circular arches, the cornice, and parts of the dado. What was new was the panels with medallions crowned with trophies, carved by a new artist of the Crown, Antoine Rousseau. The two great panels flanking the fireplace are among the most magnificent single works of the sort. Their major elements are of much weight, proportioned to the enlarged scale of the room, with heavy garlands and large concentrated areas of gilding. The main medallions or cartouches are uniformly symmetrical, dominating the free groupings of elements in the trophies above. Here and elsewhere in the room the shellwork is reduced to narrow borders, slightly lobed and fluted.

In 1760 the elimination of the curved end of the Cabinet Ovale (Cabinet de la Pendule), involved changes in the Cabinet d'Angle, where at the same time a recess replaced the diagonal faces which had given it the name of Cabinet à Pans (Figure 268). Only a few minor panels had to be added, and these merely matched those of 1753. The overdoors, newly carved by Rousseau, had smoothly moulded oval medallions inscribed in rectangles with hawk's-bill crossettes, recurring very nearly to the type of treatment used by Pierre Lepautre, long ago, in dados and in the doors of the Chapel. The cornice had to be made over entirely

[337] Bibliothèque de la ville de Versailles, published by Ch. Hirschauer, *loc. cit.*

to fit the new shape. In this change the free forms of the 'thirties were abandoned for a uniform repetition of balanced olive branches, crowns and cyphers, confined within a continuous upper moulding.

For the similar recess added to the Cabinet de Madame Adelaïde in 1767, Verberckt carved four great panels with trophies of music and of peace. Unlike Rousseau in the Cabinet de Conseil, the older artist here preserved a diagonal placing of the main cartouches — as usual in examples since those of Ladoireau — and even made their winged cartouches unsymmetrical in themselves.

In the transformation, in 1769, of the last room of the apartment of Madame Adelaïde into the Grande Salle à Manger des Cabinets du Roi, the existing woodwork of 1752-1753, as we have seen, was preserved and repeated.

Even at this late time, when the first work in a new manner was already just completed at the Petit Trianon, Gabriel and the King were content to retain the style of the rococo in modifications of these important rooms at Versailles.

Naturally there were also works of the mid-century at the other palaces, but these do not modify greatly the idea we have derived from the rooms at Versailles.

At Fontainebleau the ultimate decoration of the Cabinet du Conseil and of the Chambre du Roi was executed in 1752-1754. The panels of the Cabinet (Figure 269) were adorned by Vanloo, Pierre, and Boucher with compositions in which the medallions of allegorical figures are almost secondary to the rich double frames of painted ornament.

For the Chambre du Roi (Figure 267) Gabriel designed a panelling where the pilaster-strips suggest those of 1735 in the Chambre de la Reine at Versailles, but where the great fields with their scroll tops and their trophies foreshadow those of 1755 in the Cabinet de Conseil there. The most striking features, however, are the doorways and overdoors. The doors are unique in the whole period of Louis XV in being of but a single valve and in having consoles and scrolled pediments of heavy plastic effect — features which we must imagine were survivals, like the main ceiling, from a much earlier treatment of the room. Above them, flanking an oval medallion, are heaped rich trophies of arms. Above the alcove, now replaced by the Napoleonic throne, a new ceiling with deep coffers carried on the character, but not the detail, of the old one.

As regards this new ceiling Marigny wrote to Moransel the Controller: "Observez surtout de ne pas tomber dans le goût moderne dont les Panneaux se ressentent beaucoup."[338] It is interesting to note that whereas the marble chimney piece of the Chambre du Roi has its central shell violently unbalanced, that of the Cabinet du Conseil, otherwise similar, is brought into rigid symmetry.

In the gardens at Trianon was built in 1751-1753[339] the Salon Frais, now demolished, from which some panelling, carved by Rousseau, has been installed in the Petit Trianon. Handsome as it was, this room, with its reverse-curved panel heads, was purely conventional for its date and need not detain us.

Of interiors at Choisy from this time we have only a section by Gabriel,[340] dated 1754, of

[338] Fels, *op. cit.*, 184.

[339] *Ibid.*, 155, where three of his drawings for the interior, preserved in the Archives Nationales o¹ 1887, are reproduced as pls. XXXV-XXXVII.

[340] From the Destailleur collection, *ibid.*, pl. XXIX.

the circular Salon and Vestibule of the Pavillon Particulier du Roi, or Petit Château. It shows a sober character analogous to the work in the Appartement de Madame Adelaïde at Versailles at just this time. One mirror head of scroll outline is subsumed within a semicircular arch. The overdoor is an unbroken oval crowned with shellwork and scrolls, but draped, for the first time I know in the Royal works, with the newly fashionable garland of husks.

At Compiègne constructions of this period provided the apartments of the Dauphin and the Dauphine carved from Gabriel's drawings by Verberckt, whose memoir is dated in July, 1755,[341] an enlarged apartment for Madame de Pompadour, and the Appartements des Mesdames, occupied in 1755, transformed in 1770 to receive the new Dauphin and his bride Marie-Antoinette.[342] Madame du Barry, whose entry at Compiègne came in 1769, had but an entresol which required slight change. Little remains of all these decorations after the drastic remodellings of the reigns of Louis XVI, Napoleon, and Louis Napoleon which gave the château its present internal character.

While we have noted many recessions from any extreme of freedom, we see how far the Bâtiments were, even as late as 1767 and 1769 at Versailles, from leading a consistent return to classicism. Indeed as they had been conservative in taking up the new forms of 1730, they were conservative in retaining them, by comparison with such a private designer as Contant.

Private Work

In private building the *genre pittoresque*, as we have seen, continued in Pineau's work down to his death in 1754. At least in the designs of Contant, however, we have seen in Paris a diminution of the fire of the rocaille.

It is somewhat surprising that we know so few private interiors of the later 'fifties and early 'sixties. The explanation must be that the Seven Years War (1756-1763), with its great disasters for France, brought practically an interruption of private building, as it brought suspension even to the major royal works.

Though the *genre pittoresque* thus effectively came to an end with the death of Pineau and with the attacks of Cochin at just that vulnerable moment, we see that this did not bring an end to the rococo as a whole. The revulsion was only against the extremes and extravagances — of curvature, of dissolution, and of shellwork. What had been demanded and achieved had been a return toward academism, toward the style of Louis XIV, still admitting, as it had first admitted in the later years of his reign, a gracious use of the elements employed by Pierre Lepautre. Like all such reactions, this effort was fundamentally negative and sterile. It expurgated without being creative. It did not, in itself, contain the seeds of artistic renewal, or determine the character of the following movement, which we shall have now to examine.

The Advent of Classicism and the End of the Rococo in France

It was not the return to academism but the advent of classicism which everywhere ultimately brought the rococo to a close, supplying it with new problems and — in spite of its retrospective character — with a new creative impulse.

This artistic classicism was the fruit of a renewed enthusiasm for antiquity, more informed,

[341] Robiquet, *op. cit.*, 31, which cites the drawings in o¹ 1410.
[342] o¹ 1411, Nos. 37, 38.

more literal, than that of the Renaissance, or of the intervening centuries.[343] In 1719 Montfaucon had published his *Antiquité expliquée*, foreshadowing archaeology; in 1730 the Earl of Burlington brought out a volume of Palladio's manuscript drawings of the Roman baths. Paintings of Roman ruins were made popular by Panini. Piranesi began in 1748 the issue of his engraved series the *Antichità Romane* and the *Varie Vedute*, followed in 1754 by the *Magnificenze di Roma*. Systematic excavation had begun at Herculaneum in 1738, at Pompeii in 1748; publication of the finds began with Cochin and Bellicard in 1754, followed, from 1757, by the official volumes of the Accademia Ercolanese. Caylus' *Receuil d'antiquités* appeared in six volumes from 1752 to 1755, establishing the new classical discipline of archaeology.

Scarcely later came the revelation of Greek buildings hitherto known only by the accounts of a few travellers. In 1750 Soufflot was measuring and drawing at Paestum.[344] In 1751 Stuart and Revett, as well as Leroy, were at Athens. In a few years publications regarding them began to pour forth: Leroy's *Ruines des plus beaux monuments de la Grèce* in 1758,[345] the first volume of Stuart and Revett's *Antiquities of Athens* in 1762, Major's *Paestum*, using Soufflot's measurements, in 1768. In 1764 appeared Winckelmann's *Geschichte der Kunst*, asserting for the first time the superiority of Greek architecture and sculpture.

It is as easy and superficial as it has been customary to suppose that the movement of classicism in creative art issued directly from the new discoveries and publications. In the actual course of events in France, however, it is extremely difficult to find any direct connection between them and the initiation of a classical movement in creative art there, which was merely favoured rather than evoked by archaeological discovery and classical dilletantism. France had participated richly in the second discovery of the antique. Down past 1760, however, no one had built in France even a temple portico, to say nothing of a whole building on the model of a classic temple.[346]

The artistic impulse of classicism has generally been thought to have been a spontaneous movement felt independently in every country. All our study, however, points to the conclusion that, like other artistic movements, it had a single point of origin, spreading thence to other countries. We have previously sought to demonstrate that the stricter classical phase, appearing in France at the very end of the reign of Louis XV and coming to flower there under his successor, was preceded and strongly influenced by works in England.[347] The

---

[343] Cf. L. Hautecoeur: *Rome et la renaissance de l'antiquité à la fin du XVIIIe siècle*, 1912.

[344] Blomfield: *History of French Architecture, 1661-1774*, II, 136n, states that he published in 1764 "*Suite de plans, coupes, etc. de trois temples antiques tels qu'ils existaient à Pestum en 1750*, Paris, 1764, which I am unable to verify elsewhere.

[345] It was presented to the Academy of Architecture by Blondel, with a laudatory notice, at the session of November 13 of that year, Gabriel presiding as Director. At the following session of November 20 the Academy petitioned Marigny to obtain royal consent to the election of Leroy to the second class. We need scarcely assume, with Fels, that this action is a proof of the interest and support of Gabriel; he was frequently at odds with Marigny over appointments to the Academy.

[346] The first such projects in France seem to have been those published by M.-J. Peyre: *Oeuvres d'Architecture*, 1765, and by Neufforge in his *Receuil élémentaire de l'architecture*, VII, cahier 69, 1765, the latter with full peristyles having fronts of six to ten columns.

[347] Kimball: "Les influences anglaises dans la formation du style Louis XVI," in *Gazette des beaux-arts*, VIe pér., V, 1931, 29-44, 231-255.

crucial question here is whether this was already true in the earlier phase of the classical movement.

The deep historical tide of the eighteenth century was the rise of England. Victorious with Marlborough at the end of the reign of Louis XIV, the British steadily advanced in political, economic, and cultural importance. The War of Austrian Succession, 1740-1748, with its injuries to French prestige, was to be followed by the Seven Years War, when in the "great year" of 1759 France was to lose both Canada and India. The English philosophers, critics,[348] and political thinkers, from Locke and Shaftesbury onward, had taken a lead which was to be deeply influential both in the Illuminism of France and, later of Germany. Addison and Pope in their essays had laid the foundation of the cult of nature; even Rousseau was to write of his youthful reading "le Spectateur surtout me plût beaucoup, et me fit du bien."

It is less appreciated that in art also England was taking an artistic leadership — not, to be sure, in the realms of painting and sculpture, but in those of gardening and architecture.[349] The landscape garden, the *jardin anglais*, was coming into being from the 'twenties onward. Features of the English romantic garden, which early imitated the painted "Italian" landscape of Poussin and Salvator, were classic temples and ruins, and even Gothic towers. Temples and towers were both already built by Vanbrugh, whose designs for Eastbury, 1718, included a prostyle garden temple of six columns, and who built a monopteros at Stowe. His baroque made a large use of tall porticoes of isolated columns, one of which had early been prefixed by Jones to old Saint Paul's and which henceforth were used in English houses having no parallel in contemporary France. The neo-Palladianism of Colen Campbell, who had published in 1717 a project for a church in temple form, "Prostile, Hexastile, Eustyle," was taken up powerfully by the Earl of Burlington. In the façade of Burlington House (1717), in the semicircular colonnade there (before 1725) and in his *villa rotonda* at Chiswick (1727-1736) he sought to expurgate Palladio of baroque liberties. It was he who first went beyond academism by his building of the York Assembly Rooms (1730-1736) with their "Egyptian hall" of Vitruvius, their sequence of rooms suggested by those of the Roman baths. His protége, William Kent, in gardens at Stowe, built temples in all the basic Roman forms, both rectangular and circular, including the monopteros. Under Burlington's leadership a veritable classicism was thus firmly established in England well before 1750.

Their treatment of interiors was likewise of a more classical character than had hitherto prevailed since the Renaissance. They made a large use of the vault. In his villa at Chiswick, Burlington domed not only the rotonda but also the circular and octagonal rooms at the end of the gallery. The great niches which terminate the gallery have coffered semi-domes and subordinate niches. At Kensington Palace, 1724, and in the smoking-room at Rousham (before 1741) Kent decorated the ceilings with mannerist-classical arabesques with central medallions of mythological figure subjects.

This British movement, recorded in publications which the patronage of Burlington and other noblemen assured a magnificent format, sought a hearing even beyond the bounds of England. Campbell's engraved folio, the *Vitruvius Britannicus*, of which the first two volumes

---

[348] For the influence of English aesthetic thought on the Continent at this time, cf. K. Borinski: *Die Antike in Poetik und Kunsttheorie*, II, 1924, 127.

[349] Kimball: "Burlington Architectus," in *Journal of the Royal Institute of British Architects*, 1927, XXXIV, 675-693, XXXV, 14-16.

appeared in 1715 and 1717, had title-pages and legends in French as well as English, the third volume, 1725, had also text in French, as did Leoni's fine translation of Palladio (1715). Campbell's first two volumes included Wren's Saint Paul's, many works of Inigo Jones, and others with free-standing porticoes, as well as with the "colossal order," rising from the ground. In the third volume were Vanbrugh's temple for Eastbury and many of the *villa rotondas* and casinos then rising in England, under Palladian influence. Others were included in Kent's *Designs of Inigo Jones*, 1727, which illustrated the villa at Chiswick and other buildings of Roman cast. A suite of fifteen plates of the buildings and temples at Stowe was engraved in 1739 by Rigaud with titles in English and French.

An impressive folio appearing at a decisive moment, in 1759, was *A Treatise on Civil Architecture* by William Chambers, afterwards to be knighted, and already architect of the Prince of Wales. Chambers had returned from Italy in 1755; his work, while not affected by the Roman domestic interiors which were to influence Robert Adam, has a markedly classical cast. Beside the orders and other details, the book illustrates several casinos and temples, rectangular and circular, designed by Chambers for various noblemen. It is worth our notice that the subscribers included four in France: Blondel, Barreau—"de Chef de Ville, Architect," Leroy of the Academy of Architecture, and the sculptor Pajou.

In England, where thus classicism was so strongly entrenched, the fire of the French rococo made but small inroads, chiefly in furniture. Matthew Lock, from 1740, his partner Copland from 1746, engraved designs of freely French character, then taken up more powerfully by Chippendale and others.[350] Other noblemen than Burlington essayed to rival him as patrons of other movements: Horace Walpole of the Gothic, the Earl of Chesterfield of the French. It was only under protest, however, that the Palladian architect Isaac Ware executed French ceilings at Chesterfield House,[351] and classicism was soon to rise again like a phoenix in the work of Robert Adam, on his return to England in 1759.

The French of the eighteenth century, in sharp contrast with those of the seventeenth, had soon taken account of the current English advance. Voltaire was in England from 1726 to 1729, consorting with Bolingbroke and Pope; Montesquieu was there in the winter of 1729-1730, having made the crossing with Chesterfield. Books on the English had poured forth from French presses: Muralt's *Lettres sur les anglais et les français* appeared in 1725, Voltaire's *Lettre sur les anglais* in 1731.[352] At first they were none too friendly, though Voltaire's praise of English institutions, like that of Montesquieu's *Esprit des lois* in 1748, led to the suppression of these books. Montesquieu, about 1750, had a garden at La Brède in the first style of Kent. In 1726 George Selwyn, back from Paris, told Horace Walpole "our passion for everything French is nothing to theirs for everything English. There is a book published called the *anglomanie*."[353]

Voltaire and Montesquieu said nothing of British art, but others soon began to speak of it.

[350] Kimball and E. Donnell: "The Creators of the Chippendale Style," in *Metropolitan Museum Studies*, I, 1929, 115-154.

[351] Cf. Ware's *Complete Body of Architecture*, 1756, 521, 545.

[352] It is perhaps not fanciful to suppose that Voltaire's *Temple du Goût*, published in 1733, was influenced by Pope's *Epistle to the Earl of Burlington*, first printed in 1731, likewise with satire on the architectural follies of the "wealthy fool," and praise of classical simplicity: "You taught us Rome was glorious, not profuse."

[353] Walpole to George Montague, December 20, 1762. *Letters*, Toynbee ed., V, 280.

Evolution

Most of the comparisons drawn by the Abbé Leblanc, aside from those in agriculture and commerce, were very unfavourable to the English. In remarking on the landscape gardens of England, however, he grants them some advantages, though he demands only minor reforms in the French gardens. He attacks English architecture, either as a barbarous piling up of stone, as at Blenheim, or as an unwise copying of the Italian under a different climate.

Nicolas Rouquet in his *État des Arts en Angleterre*, 1755, while remarking on the extreme severity of Leblanc, is himself scarcely less severe. He does praise Saint Paul's as being "comme le plupart des grands edifices modernes, une compilation des plus belles parties de l'architecture ancienne," and the portico of Saint Martin-in-the-Fields, that of "un ancien temple grec sans changement," as a proof of the taste and judgment of the architect.

It is significant that Cochin in 1755 mentions English classicism, as a citadel even itself then invaded by ornaments of gallican picturesqueness. The French critics of the *genre pittoresque* were evidently already seeking moral support, in their irony, from across the Channel.

Later, Blondel was likewise to cite English example. In 1772,[354] contrasting her work with the singularity and bizarrerie of the other, "Peuples du Nord," he wrote:

> L'Angleterre, nous osons l'avouer, est peut-être la seule qui ait suivi de plus près le bon genre des Anciens: moins jaloux de créer de neuf, que d'imiter les excellentes productions des Grecs, & les beaux monuments de l'ancienne Rome, les Anglois se sont garantis de cet esprit national qui a gagné toutes les Cours; quelle différence en effet entre le Vitruve Britannique & le Vitruve Danois!

Blondel's *Cours d'architecture* did not begin to appear in print until 1771, when the classical movement was well advanced, and was only completed after his death, by Patte, in 1778, but doubtless embodies views he had professed for some years. In the plates of the last volume were included Oppenord's hemicycle of the Palais-Royal and Vassé's gallery of the Hôtel de Toulouse, along with more conservative interiors by Contant, but none by Pineau. Blondel condemns "les ouvrages des Meissonnier, des Oppenor, des Cuvillier" (I, 384 ff.) as a "genre frivole . . . une singularité, une bizarrerie, permise tout au plus dans les ameublements, les porcelaines, les bronzes, etc." (III, 419). We have seen that in his dialogue *Les Amours rivaux* of 1774 he obviously favoured the views of the amateur who ridiculed the interiors of a generation before—"temps où le plupart de nos architectes avaient la tête tournée."

To reinforce these views came a rationalistic or moralistic criticism of monumental architecture. Here a beginning had earlier been made by the Abbé de Cordemoy in his *Nouveau traité de l'art de l'architecture* (1706, 1714), which had used criteria of relation to material, technique and use for a condemnation of the baroque, and even of the giving of bases to columns. This found fertile soil in the thought of Lodoli in Venice, whence it was brought back to be reincarnated by the Abbé Laugier in his *Essai sur l'architecture* (1753, 1755). Like Cordemoy, he seeks in nature the origin of architectural forms, such as those of the orders. Thus

---

[354] *Cours d'Architecture*, III, 1772, 423. In the sixth volume issued in 1777, after his death, by Patte, he praises Wren—"Aussi est-ce un de ces hommes, que l'Angleterre ne se glorifie pas moins d'avoir produit que les Locke et les Newton." He mentions Saint Paul's and Greenwich Hospital, both illustrated in the *Vitruvius Britannicus*, and quotes Steele's praise of Wren in the *Spectator* of 1709.

there must be no engaged columns, no pedestals; the gable must appear only as the ending of a roof. We may remark that these demands, which were a reproach to French academic practise, could be found fulfilled in the English classicism of Burlington,[355] which had tacitly embodied the same criticism.

Our problem here will be to establish to what degree the end of the rococo, the advent of classical design in France, came about independently within France itself, to what degree they were stimulated from without.

The major personnel of the Bâtiments in France underwent little change down to the end of the reign of Louis XV. Marigny retired as Directeur in 1773, the year before the King's death. Gabriel retired, at the age of seventy-seven, in 1775. Cochin and Soufflot continued to hold their high offices some years into the following reign.

A little-known figure who may have had greater importance than has been realized was Nicolas-Marie Potain (1718?-1791) who became Gabriel's intimate collaborator in later years. He had won the Grand Prix in 1738, and had been in Rome from 1739 to 1744. He was named to the second class of the Academy in 1755, to the first in 1762, when he presented a treatise on construction, followed by numerous other communications. We have seen that Cochin names Potain as one of those followed the example of Soufflot toward a more classical style; he was to be the master and father-in-law of Pierre Rousseau,[356] designer of the Hôtel de Salm.

Richard Mique (1728-1794)[357] who had worked under Héré at Nancy and had succeeded him as Director-general of the buildings there, was appointed, on the death of Stanislas in 1766, Intendant and Controller-general of Buildings and Gardens to the Queen. Though her death followed in 1768, he was to utilize his opportunities so well as to become the successor of Gabriel in 1775.

In other offices under the Bâtiments progressive younger men began to take office before the end of the reign. Thus Jacques Gondouin, later to be designer of the coolly classical École de Chirugie (1777), was appointed in 1772 Dessinateur du Mobilier de la Couronne. Born in 1737, he was in Rome from 1761 to 1763, and had travelled in Holland and England before his establishment in France.[358]

In contrast to the conservatism of the Premier Architecte relative to the newer movements was the attitude prevailing in the Menus Plaisirs. The Duc d'Aumont, as Premier Gentilhomme de la Chambre, was a leader in patronage of advanced craftsmen like Gouthière. Here the amateur Papillon de la Ferté, one of the three Intendants in 1756, was left sole Intendant after 1762. In 1767, to second Michel-Ange Challe, Dessinateur de la Chambre since the death of the last of the Slodtz in 1764, François-Joseph Belanger[359] was appointed Dessinateur des Menus. Born in 1744, he had received the encouragement of Caylus to study in the Academy of Architecture under Leroy and Contant, where in June, 1764, he won the Prix d'Émulation with a design for a colossal column in the court of the Louvre. Missing the Prix de Rome in 1765, he went instead to England — itself a step of revolutionary significance

[355] Kimball: "Burlington Architectus," *loc. cit., passim.*

[356] Sent to Rome without winning the prize, he was at the Academy from 1773-1775, visiting the cities of north Italy on his return journey.

[357] M.-P. Morey: *R. Mique,* 1865.

[358] E. de Salverte: *Le meuble français,* 1930, 45-46.   [359] J. Stern: *Belanger,* 2 vols., 1930.

cance. An album preserved at the École des Beaux-Arts (120 D 20), is filled with his sketches and observations there, of temples and gardens at Bowood, Wilton, and other great estates, the influence of which we shall see in his work. In 1770 he was named Dessinateur du Cabinet of the Comte de Provence; in 1777, Premier Architecte of the Comte d'Artois, the brothers of Louis XVI.

Of architects outside the royal employ, Contant remained the most important, receiving the commission for the new Madeleine in 1765, when he was approaching the age of seventy. Newer figures were Peyre, born in 1730, who won the Prix de Rome in 1751 and De Wailly, born in 1729, prize-winner of the following year. Peyre's published ideal designs of 1765 adopt the monumental character of the Roman imperial baths. Antoine, born in 1733, rising from the ranks of the masons and contractors, was to achieve importance just at the end of the reign; Victor Louis, born 1735, not until after the advent of Louis XVI.

It was even younger men than these who were to take the lead in the ultimate reform of French architecture. Claude-Nicolas Ledoux,[360] born in 1736, never was in Italy. He studied under Blondel and began with minor restoration work before his Paris houses of 1765-1770 drew him to the attention of Madame du Barry. Of Goudouin and Belanger we have spoken above.

One figure requires special mention, as high claims have been made for his importance in the classical movement in France and, like Piranesi, as a supposed master of Robert Adam; Charles-Louis Clérisseau, born in 1722. He had been a pensioner of the Academy from 1749 to 1753, when he was expelled for non-conformity to the religious requirements, but remained in Rome, drawing and painting the monuments, for many years longer.

Robert Adam came to Rome in 1754, at twenty-six, having already a full Palladian training under his father and a passionate devotion to the antique. Piranesi wrote, in dedicating to Adam in 1762 his superb folio of the Campus Martius: "Imperrocchè ben mi sovviene allora che alcuni anni sono ci ritrovavamo insieme in Roma, sol qual impegno da Voi si recercava ciascheduno di que'tanti monumenti, e fra Voi stesso ne contemplavate la magnificenza, et la forma, massimo quando venimmo nel Campo Marzio, facendomi Voi spesso anche premura di disegnare ed incidere gli avanzi degli edifizj . . . Qualcunque poi sia per essere il vostro giudizio interno a questa piccola opera io saro contento di avervi obbedito, e che resti alla posterità qualche attestato della nostra amicizia." These are not the words of a master to his pupil. Piranesi's own architectural designs, still tinged with the baroque, are of a character very different from those of Adam.[361]

So, too, with Clérisseau, of whom Adam was not the pupil but the employer. In 1757 Adam engaged him as a draughtsman to accompany him to Spalatro. Clérisseau's only known architectural work in Italy, the decoration of a room at the Villa Albani in 1764, was commissioned long after Robert Adam had returned to England and had executed his decisive works in which his style is fully formed. Clérisseau returned to Paris in 1768, and was elected in 1769 to the Academy of Painting, in which year his pupil the sculptor Lhuillier followed him back from Italy. His designs for works in Russia, the sale of his drawings to Catherine II, were in the years from 1773 onward.

[360] G. Levallet-Haug: *Ledoux*, 1934.

[361] W. Körte: "Giovanni Battista Piranesi als practischer Architekt," in *Zeitschrift für Kunstgeschichte*, II, 1933, 16-33.

The Creation of the Rococo

It will be noted that the advent of the new men came very late in the reign: of Belanger in 1770, of Goudouin in 1772; the return of Clérisseau in 1768, of Lhuillier in 1769 — all ten years or so after the decisive English works of Robert Adam, which these men had meanwhile come to know.

Just as the free tendency had begun in interiors, and only gradually influenced the exterior, so the classical tendency was felt first on the exterior, and subsequently penetrated the interiors. We must accordingly review developments in external architecture to this point.

To Gabriel fell several great undertakings which followed the Peace of Aix-la-Chapelle in 1748. One initiated by Madame de Pompadour was the École Royale Militaire, first proposed in 1748., and commissioned to Gabriel in 1751 with injunction for a "belle et noble simplicité." The first project, preserved in an engraving dedicated by Lerouge to Marigny as Director-General, shows the façade of the main building with central and end pavilions alike of academic form, with an order through two stories above a high basement and below a windowed attic. These designs must soon have been changed, for, in spite of delays and suspensions, the central pavilion and right wing, of different form, were provisionally occupied in July, 1756. The basement had been abandoned for a colossal Corinthian order rising from the ground. On each façade there was a pedimented frontispiece of columns, detached but without the projection of a portico — the pavilion toward the Seine being extended by columns flanking an additional bay. This final design, in which the influence of English Palladianism has been observed,[362] was but half-heartedly classical, preserving as it did the grouping of supports and also the high domical roof of earlier days.

While thus on the exterior the classical movement began to make itself felt, on the interior[363] the first decorations executed from Gabriel's designs in 1755 and 1756 by Verberckt — which remain in some rooms of the principal story and in the Bibliothèque de l'École de Guerre — were not more advanced than the Cabinet du Conseil at Versailles. In the Salle du Conseil (Salon des Maréchaux) Verberckt carved a large frame for the King's portrait on the chimney breast and Caffieri the bronzes of the mantel, but it is impossible to recognize these in the surviving decoration of the room, which must have been radically changed in 1775, when Antoine Boulanger carved the mirror frame opposite the windows.

The competitions for the design for a Place Louis XV (now the Place de la Concorde) began in 1748 and were renewed in 1750 and 1753.[364] The designs published by Patte[365] and others are without exceptions of academic character and employ the academic scheme of an order (now sometimes with open colonades) above a high basement or a pedestal. The final design of Gabriel was made in 1755, the façades of the buildings were begun in 1757, and though the square was dedicated in 1763, construction continued until 1772.

In 1749 Gabriel first prepared his designs for the "Grand Projet" of rebuilding the façades of the château of Versailles toward the court, offered again with slight modifications in 1759, but executed, in small part, only beginning in 1771. The ordonnance was again a

[362] H. Willich in Thieme-Becker, *Künstler-Lexikon*, article "Gabriel," 1920.

[363] Fels, *op. cit.*, 80, 82.

[364] The literature is assembled by E. Lambert, "Un projet de Place Royale à Paris en honneur de Louis XV" in *Bulletin de la Société de l'histoire de l'art français*, 1938, 85-97.

[365] *Monuments érigés à la gloire de Louis XV*, 1765.

Corinthian order of two stories raised on a basement story; the number of breaks and transitional elements was somewhat diminished, but at most the effect was Palladian, not classical.

The major remodelling of Compiègne follows a design by Gabriel of 1753, establishing the form of the façades gradually executed over a long period. "J'espère," Gabriel wrote, "que Sa Majesté se contente de la simplicité et de la noblesse de l'architecture."[366] Essentially the scheme was again the typical one with the high basement, although this was replaced along the park by an elevated terrace which left the order on that side, when executed in 1781, rising from the ground. Thus nowhere in Gabriel's exteriors does the membering abandon a gracious academism.

An initiative new in French architecture was taken by Soufflot in building the church of Sainte-Geneviève. The first designs were of 1755; an accepted one was engraved in 1757. This shows but a small dome, of hemispherical form without ribs, its drum buttressed by pairs of projecting columns with broken entablatures. The novel feature[367] was the portico, with a front of six free-standing Corinthian columns over seventy feet in height.[368] In 1764, at the laying of the cornerstone, this portico, simulated in canvas at full size, must have made a profound effect of novelty and monumental quality. The portal was not completed and cleared of scaffolding until 1775. The question of structural adequacy of the supports of the dome, which Patte attacked, caused long delays in determining its final design. Soufflot wrote of Patte to Marigny in 1769: "C'est après avoir diné chez moi pour conférer sur les dômes qu'il est allé à Londres étudier Saint-Paul."[369] As late as 1777 Soufflot hesitated between an octagonal dome with an octagonal colonnade and a circular dome with projecting masses. By 1778 he had determined on a circular dome with circular colonnade, as executed after his death in 1780. The final design of this dome bears the very closest resemblance to the great English model of Saint Paul's.

We need not follow the classical movement further in monumental buildings, such as Contant's design of 1763 for the Madeleine, since at this moment we encounter the decisive work in domestic design, the Petit Trianon. Begun in 1762 on the initiative of Madame de Pompadour, whose death followed in 1764, it found on its internal completion in 1768 a new mistress just coming into favour in the person of Madame du Barry. It was intended essentially as a garden pavilion or casino, in relation to the recently created botanical garden. Though Gabriel's gentle, refined, and somewhat facile academism appears in the external treatment, both the basic mass and the interior design break sharply with the style hitherto prevailing under Louis XV.[370]

We must seek to follow the genesis of the design for any clue as to its sources, and thus to

---

[366] Cited by Robiquet, *Compiègne*, 33.

[367] Patte, in the *Mercure* for 1755, mooted a portico of such columns for Saint-Sulpice.

[368] "Vue perspective du portail de la nouvelle église de Sainte-Geneviève . . . tel qu'il a été exécuté en décoration d'après les desseins de M. Soufflot . . . lorsque Sa Majesté a posé la première pierre le 6 septembre 1764," from the Collection J.-Ch. Moreux, included in the exhibition of 1938, *Quatre siècles du Service des Bâtiments*, no. 197. A painting of the event by De Machy, from the Collection David-Weill, showing the same model, is reproduced by Réau, *Histoire de la peinture française au XVIII⁰ siècle*, II, pl. XLIII.

[369] Monval, *Soufflot*, 450.

[370] Fels, *op. cit.*, 22-23, in inaugurating with the Petit Trianon the third phase of Gabriel's style, sees in it the result of Gabriel's reflections on Leroy's drawings of Greek monuments. We shall see there were influences both more closely related and nearer at hand.

the influences under which the change in interior style took place. Incredible as it may seem, the preliminary elevations for the exterior at the Archives Nationales[371] have remained unpublished (Figures 270-271). They show a building which, like the executed one, is an exact square, but is some ten feet less on each side. The four façades are varied in much the same manner as we see them today — one with engaged columns, two with pilasters, and one without any ordonnance. Instead of the columns or pilasters being equally spaced, however, they are grouped with the spacing of a triumphal arch, a grouping unexampled in eighteenth-century France, but found in Palladio's church fronts and in a number of English buildings of which engraved designs were available. The number of windows is inevitably less — only three on the sides with an order, four on the other side, instead of five on each side, as executed. The crystalline square or cubical form, in this respect like that of Marly a century before, goes back ultimately to the scheme of the Palladian villas, a basic type out of character with the spatial conceptions of the rococo, and meanwhile wholly neglected in France.

The only country in which small Palladian villas or casinos, likewise square in mass with columnar frontispieces, had been built in the intervening century was England. There, so far from being exceptional, they were numerous and programmatic. Burlington's villa at Chiswick — "too small to inhabit and too large to hang to one's watch" — had set the fashion. It preserved the central salon and dome of the Palladian *villa rotonda*, as did Campbell's Mereworth Castle, 1723, and Goodwood, 1725, and Gibbs' Foot's Cray. Many other houses merely had their rooms fitted at convenience into the square, porticoed mass.[372] We may cite Campbell's Stourhead in Wiltshire, and Newby in Yorkshire, 1721, both illustrated in the third volume of the *Vitruvius Britannicus*. Both of these have the five bays ultimately adopted at Trianon. The resemblance at Stourhead extends somewhat to the plan, where, as at Trianon, the balanced steps lead to a square room flanked by narrower rooms with the stairs behind.

The most significant relationship of the Trianon designs, however, would seem to have been with the works of Robert Morris. He had built Marble Hill, Twickenham, for the Countess of Suffolk in 1723-1727, with pilasters above a rustic basement flanked by L-shaped wing-walls, suggestive of the entrance front of Trianon. Among his published volumes, *Select Architecture*,[373] which appeared before 1757,[374] shows numerous villas of cubical mass, a number of his designs having frontispieces with side bays narrower than the central one, with medallions and tablets. On the title-page, is an elevation (Figure 272) very suggestive of the final design for Trianon, even to the scheme of proportions, though it has a pediment and some other divergent features.

[371] F²¹. Two of these drawings were exhibited 1938, *Quatre siècles du Service des Bâtiments*, nos. 146 bis and 146 ter.

[372] The Hermitage of Madame de Pompadour at Fontainebleau, as built by Gabriel in 1749 was originally a square of forty feet, prior to the addition of wings, disguised by treillage, in 1756, but the contrast between its treatment and that of Trianon only brings out more clearly the novel and foreign character of the latter. The Hermitage at Compiègne, likewise square, of which no elevation survives, was merely a garden pavilion with accommodations on the order of those of the Pavillon Octogone at Trianon. Cf. Fels, *op. cit.*, 151.

[373] The book was most widely influential, even in faraway America, where John Hawks used it in designing Tryon's Palace at Newbern, and Jefferson, at Monticello.

[374] This is the date of the 2d edition; I know of no copy of the 1st.

In execution, the spacing of the order was made uniform, with three openings in the pavilions. The principal front was slightly recessed to make the central columns stand free. In some other regards the executed design was less academic than the initial one, in that it introduced transitional breaks on either side of the pavilions. In minor respects, to be sure, the number of such transitional elements, surviving from the baroque, was decreased in execution —as in the counter-casings and friezes of the windows.

One would not expect so facile and experienced a designer as Gabriel to follow slavishly any single model; mere suggestions would suffice for him. In exterior detail, Trianon is wholly coherent with his other designs at this time.

Even more than the general mass, the interiors at Trianon represent a great novelty in France. All the major rooms are rectangular, without any easing of the corners; all the ceilings are flat, without even a cove cornice, except one only, in the salon. Elsewhere the membering of the wall is strictly academic, with full entablatures. The main outlines of the panellings are entirely geometrical, rectilinear except for the unbroken semicircular arches of certain central doorways and mirrors, and for the segments, like those of doorways at Versailles in 1680, in the wall panels of the Salon. The profiles of architraves, and even of panels, in sharp contrast to those in Gabriel's earlier work, are strictly classical; the bolection moulding disappears. The principal chimney pieces resume rectangular forms, with gaines or consoles on the supports. The chief motifs of ornament are the acanthus, the swag, the rosette, the wreath. In the arched tympanums of the Salle à Manger are pairs of Roman griffins, unexampled in France, though long employed in England, as at Holkham, and shown in the plates of Chambers' *Civil Architecture*, 1759. Nowhere is there any rocaille shellwork; the unbroken scallop-shell itself survives only in a few minor instances. There are still, to be sure, some remains of rococo motifs: the inner bands of the great panels in the Salle à Manger, and those of the principal bedroom, are rounded with paired scrolls; the minor mantels are of earlier Louis XV types. There is no gilding or japanning; only a slight modulation of pale tones.

Thus the design of Trianon both without and within, has, in spite of its novelty in France, the character of a derivative work, making compromise between old and new—not of a programmatic manifesto of a self-confident innovator, as Robert Adam was at the same moment in England. The "uncertainty" of the French work at this time and in the following period, which has been remarked more than once,[375] was due not to a general loss of the sense of unity of form but to this derivative character of French classicism. If similar analysis of form were to be made in England, the home of eighteenth-century classicism, no such uncertainty or compromise would be found.

It was in 1768 that the decision was taken to devote the eastern building of the Place Louis XV to the Garde-Meuble de la Couronne, when Gabriel, as we have just seen, submitted the designs for its woodwork, completed under Potain's conduct about 1772. The narrow Galerie Dorée is notable for its monumental doorways with their octagonal, cofferlike panels, though there is still an echo of earlier grace in the garlands of the mirrors and the wreaths of the ceiling against backgrounds of *mosaïque*. In the Salon Diplomatique we

[375] P. Frankl: *Die Entwicklungsphasen der neueren Baukunst*, 1914, e.g., pp. 98, 124, 142, and Brinckmann, *op. cit.*, 280-281.

might almost think ourselves back in the Chambre de Conseil of 1701 at Versailles, with its arched mirrors, its oval-headed embrasures, its spandrels with their hawk's-bills, if again the doors were not so Roman in their effect and the ceiling were less heavily moulded. Only in the Grand Salon and the Salon Rouge, among the major rooms, are all motifs of the rococo abandoned. Indeed the so-called Chambre de Marie Antoinette might almost pass for a work of around 1720, so largely did Gabriel draw his inspiration from the earlier works of the century.

The construction of the long-envisaged Salle des Ballets, or Opéra, at Versailles had been authorized and begun on plans drawn by Gabriel in November, 1748, but work was suspended during the Seven Years War. Projects of 1763 included not only details of the exterior, completed by 1766, but designs for the interior. The prospective marriage of the Dauphin led to their rapid execution between 1768 and 1770. The auditorium, with its monumental columnar elements, its abandonment of all flowing framework and its gracious mythological reliefs, is matched in character by the foyer, designed in 1768-1769, where the academic architectural elements, devoid of all rococo ornaments, are given a more classical tinge by the sculptured Olympian divinities of Pajou.

The central feature of Gabriel's "Grand Projet" at Versailles was a new Cabinet du Conseil. The design for this,[376] from 1771 or 1772, shows an ordonnance of the greatest sobriety: Corinthian pilasters frame square-headed openings; the ornaments are acanthus scrolls and trophies; the effect is here not that of 1720 but more that of 1685 — of the mature style of Louis XIV, expurgated, however, of any of its lingering baroque elements.

The new trend was embodied also in certain changes of the Chambre de la Reine to receive the new Dauphine Marie Antoinette in 1770. The ceiling was given a more classical character, with coffers and with corner trophies by Rousseau — though without destroying the medallions of 1735 by Boucher in their rocaille cartouches.

Few other surviving French interiors designed before 1770 share the character of those of the Petit Trianon, although Grimm wrote in May, 1763, "que tout à Paris est à la grecque." How little this yet implied, how belated it seemed to an English observer, is witnessed by a letter of Walpole to Mann, April 9, 1764: "They (the French) . . . believe they make discoveries, when they adopt what we have had these twenty years. For instance, they begin to see beauties in the antique — everything must be à la grecque. Monsieur de Guerchy, seeing a Doric fret on a fender at Woburn, which was common before I went abroad (i.e., about 1740, in the style of Burlington), said to the Duchess of Bedford, 'Comment, Madame, vous avez là du grec, sans le savoir.' " He wrote again to Ann Pitt in 1766: "Their rooms are just surprised with the *soupçon* of a Doric fret." The mode was still subject to caricature some years later, as in Petitot's *Mascarade a la Grecque* of 1771.

Cochin also speaks of this craze, still as being a return to the style of Louis XIV:[377]

> Enfin tout le monde se remit, ou tacha de se remettre sur la voye du bon goust du siècle précédent. Et comme il faut tout soit tourné en soubriquet à Paris, on apella cela de l'architecture à la grecque et bientôt en fit jusqu'à des galons et des rubans à la

[376] Reproduced by Fels, *op. cit.*, pl. XX.
[377] *Memoires inédits*, 142-143.

Evolution

grecque; il ne resta bon goust qu'entre les mains d'un petit nombre de personnes et devint une folie entre les mains des autres.

Nos architectes anciens qui n'avoient pas sorti de Paris voulurent faire voir qu'ils feroient bien aussi dans ce goust grec; il en fut de meme des commençans et meme des maitres macons. Tous ces honnêtes gens déplacerent les ornemens antiques, les dénaturèrent, decovèrent de guillochis bien lourds les appuis des croisées et commirent mille autres bévuës.

Cochin goes on to mention as one of the first decorations "à la grecque" the apartment of the financier and collector, La Live de Jully,[378] for which "Le Lorrain, peintre, donna des dessins bien lourds pour tous les ornemens. Ils firent d'autant plus de bruit," added Cochin, "que M. de Caylus les loua avec enthusiasme; de la nous virent les guirlands en forme de corde à puits,[379] vases devenus pendules, belles inventions qui furent imitèes par tous les ignorans et qui inondèrent Paris de drogues à la grecque." The praise of Caylus places these decorations before the date of his death in 1765.

In 1765 Contant was executing further interiors at the Palais-Royal, including the Salle à Manger (Conseil d'État). A rich Composite order, of engaged columns as well as pilasters, frames bays of loosely academic treatment, but rococo elements survive in the woodwork of the doors.

Ledoux' first independent work, the Hôtel Hallweil, 1765-1766, was followed by the Hôtel d'Usès, the château of Benouville, 1768-1777, and the Hôtel de Montmorency, 1770. These, which made a rich use on the exterior of porticoes and colonnades, have interiors coolly academic, with pilasters and even columns in the more elaborate rooms.

The first work of Belanger as an architect was a pavilion for the Comte de Lauraguais at the Hôtel de Brancas, commissioned in 1769.[380] Its cubical mass was fronted by a tall projecting portico rising from the ground; its circular salon was surrounded by coupled columns — a monumental character already being abandoned in domestic English interiors under the attacks of Adam.[381]

The English landscape garden, the *jardin anglais,* was popularized in 1764 by the *Essai sur les jardins* of Watelet, whose own *ferme ornée* evoked the ridicule of Walpole, and the style was praised by Grimm in 1765. In 1771 followed the translation of the English manual of the style, Whately's *Observations on Modern Gardening.*

The style of Robert Adam in English decoration, inaugurating a literal revival of Roman domestic ornament, including the classical arabesque,[382] was fully formed at Shardeloes

---

[378] Clément de Ris devotes a chapter to La Live de Jully in his *Amateurs d'autrefois,* 1877, but does not mention these decorations.

[379] Cochin himself occasionally used these in engravings about 1755-1762.

[380] The designs are cited and reproduced by Stern, *op. cit.,* 21 ff.

[381] We can by no means assume, as Stern does by implication, that the character of the chimney pieces at the Pavillon de Brancas had the character of those included in the album of chimney pieces by Belanger preserved at the Cabinet des Estampes, Ha 58 f., stated by Stern to illustrate, among others, works for the Comte d'Artois, which would place them after 1777. Their derivation is far less from Piransi's *Diverse maniere d'adornare i cammini* of 1769, as Stern supposed, than from Adam's published works, which began to appear in 1773.

[382] The claims which have been made for Piranesi as the creator of this style, based on two or three plates only of his *Diverse maniere d'adornare i cammini,* 1769, I have dealt with in my paper on the *style Louis XVI,* already cited.

The Creation of the Rococo

(1759-1761), at Bowood (1763), at Syon (1763-1765), and at Harewood (1765). Toward the end of the 'sixties such designs were incorporated in publications accessible to the French, the first being Matthew Lock's *New Book of Pier Frames* and *New Book of Foliage* in 1769, and his *Principles of Ornament*. After other books by imitators, Adam's own *Works in Architecture* was to follow in parts from 1773 to 1778. In the '60's also, he inaugurated his reform of furniture design on classic lines, with straight square or turned and fluted legs, with acanthus leaves and husks. Of the curtain cornices at Luton, with their palmettes and urns, designed in 1768, he wrote specifically that they "were intended as an attempt to banish the absurd French compositions of this kind, hitherto so servilely imitated."

Their influence appeared first in furniture, in forms derived specifically from the earliest of these publications. The Bureau du Roi, begun by Oeben in 1760 and finished by Riesener in 1769, still has all its lines and surfaces curved and swelling, though it is ornamented with classical garlands and medallions. That it was not considered out of fashion on its completion is shown by the similar, though simpler, desk at Hertford House with the date 1769. Many other pieces have this character as late as 1770. The new forms were adopted first in that year in the jewel cabinet designed by Belanger for the marriage of Marie Antoinette to the Dauphin. In 1768 Neufforge took them up in his engraved designs; in 1771, Riesener, in the little table at the Petit Trianon, which has been called the first affirmation of a change of style in his work. Such a character appears in the chairs made about 1772 by Delanois for the salon of Madame du Barry at Louveciennes.

It was, indeed, at Louveciennes that began the real inundation of English influence in architecture and decoration. The pavilion built for her by Ledoux was, like Trianon, an isolated cubical casino, but now with a true recessed portico. The interior was still quite monumental, the vestibule having marble pilasters and a coffered ceiling. Its landscape garden had not merely one monopteros, but two, the first to be built in France.[383] Although a design of this classic type was readily available in Perrault's *Vitruvius*, one has far more detailed similarity to the rotunda at Stowe, shown in Rigaud's engraving of 1739. The other follows closely a design of Chambers for the Temple of Aeolus, built in 1760 in the royal garden at Kew and published in his *Views of the Gardens and Buildings at Kew*, 1763.

It was not until after the first transformation, in 1769, of rooms of the apartment of Madame Adelaïde for the King that a classical style was first adopted in the domestic rooms of the château at Versailles. For the Salle des Bains subsequently created there, Gabriel supplied the plan and specifications in June, 1770. The carving is entirely by Antoine Rousseau, with a ravishing development of aquatic motives. The major outlines are entirely rectilinear, but the inner beads of the panels are still handled with playful reminiscences of the rococo.

Any more extensive and consistent embodiment of classical ideas at Versailles had to await the new reign, when the Bibliothèque du Roi, in June, 1774, was at once given a new severity of line. The transformation of the Cabinets of Marie Antoinette[384] began only in 1779.

[383] Soufflot had spoken of his rotunda or "Temple toscan" of 1768 for Marigny at Menars as giving the idea of a monopteros, but in spite of its domed central feature, this was rather a rectangular building with wings and a circular central portico.

[384] Sketches dated August 29, 1770, survive in o¹ 1773.

Evolution

Meanwhile, at Bellevue, within one year of his death, Louis XV undertook extensive changes for which numerous designs of Gabriel survive.[385] While in the Salon Neuf certain panels of 1750, bearing trophies within scrolled mouldings, were re-used, the mirror heads were now made semicircular, the medallions circular or oval. The Salle à Manger was wholly redesigned, with considerable severity and weight, and very rich sculpture by Pajou, of figures both in relief and in the round.

This was not just the turn which French decoration was now to take; henceforth it was to follow the line, already long established in England, of a lighter, more domestic classicism. The first instance I know of painted classical arabesques in France is offered by the small Salon Ovale surviving in the third story of the house on the Quai Voltaire rented to the Marquis de Villette in 1766 and redecorated before 1774, when a description speaks of various "sculptures antiques," and specifically, in this room, of "ornemens arabesques coloriés."[386]

Among the most advanced decorations during the last years of the reign were those of the Petits Appartements of the Palais Bourbon, a new structure to the west of the gardens, built in 1771 and 1772. Its sculpture was of 1772-1775, its decorative painting of 1774-1776 by Dussaulx, whose later work with Lhuillier, on the classical arabesques at Bagatelle, the lost ones at the Palais Bourbon must have resembled and anticipated.[387] It will be noted that these decorations themselves extended beyond the death of the old king in 1774 and well into the first years of his successor.

The ornamentalist characteristic of the early phase of French classicism was Jean-Charles Delafosse. Some of his plates, like the *Suite de cartels et de trophées*, are still unsymmetrical, and he occasionally offers an alternative between the *goût pittoresque* and the *goût antique*. His immense *Nouvelle iconologie historique*, with a title-page of 1768, however, is mainly *à la grecque* in precisely the sense described by Cochin. Neufforge, in his *Receuil élémentaire d'architecture*, 1757-1772, showed heavily academic interiors as early as 1761, others approaching the Petit Trianon in 1767, and furniture of related character in 1768 ff. That there were not more engraved works in this manner is due, no doubt, to the relative brevity of the period of transition. Even after the Petit Trianon, as we have seen, the rococo continued in the remodellings of Versailles. By 1769 the first English plates of classical arabesques and furniture began to appear; in 1773-1778 those of Adam himself, on which followed the full tide of the ornamentalists of Louis XVI.

The reign of Louis XVI lies beyond our scope, as the new tendencies in France, if not yet fully established, followed directions already determined.[388] Leadership lay with the artists who served the extravagance and passion for luxury of Marie Antoinette and of her brother-in-law, the Comte d'Artois. For the queen a *jardin anglais* at the Petit Trianon was projected in 1774 and realized in 1778 by Mique and Hubert Robert, with a monopteros and, in 1781, with the Belvedere based on Chambers' Temple of Solitude at Kew. For Artois, Belanger,

---

[385] Cf. Biver, *Meudon*, where they are reproduced on plates 25-29.

[386] Commission du Vieux Paris — Annexes de 10 novembre, 1904, quoted by M.-J. Ballot, *le Décor interieur*, 1930, 92-93.

[387] Memoir of Dussaulx, quoted by Macon, *Les arts dans la maison de Condé*, 1903, 133.

[388] For details of the subsequent steps, see my paper on the formation of the style of Louis XVI, previously cited.

The Creation of the Rococo

Lhuillier,[389] and the Scottish gardener, Thomas Blaikie, transformed Maisons after 1777, and magically created Bagatelle with its classical arabesques. The decoration of the royal palaces henceforth followed similar lines, which everywhere prevailed also in private work.[390]

Thus, with the reign of Louis XV, ended the rococo at the Court of France.

[389] Whereas Stern, *op. cit.*, 21, attributed the style of Lhuillier to the influence of Clérisseau and Piranesi, it is amusing to note that his medallion at the principal doorway of Maisons derives from an English source, a composition of Angelica Kauffman engraved by Wynne Rowland, May 1, 1776. L. Deshair's "Notes sur le sculpteur Lhuillier," *Bulletin de la Société de l'histoire de l'art français*, 1907, 66-71.

[390] The salon with arabesques designed by Clérisseau for Grimod de la Reynière has been attributed by L. Réau ("La decoration de l'hotel Grimod de la Reynière d'après les dessins de l'architecte polonais Kamsetzer," in *Bulletin de la Société de l'histoire de l'art français*, 1937, 7-17) to 1678 or 1769, the time of Clérisseau's first return and of the first building of the hôtel. These decorations, however, were obviously the greatest novelty in 1782, when they were not only drawn by Kamsetzer but shown to the Comte du Nord, son of the Empress Catherine, on his visit to Paris, as Grimm wrote her. Even had these decorations been of 1769, that is ten years after Adam's related designs at Shardeloes.

Conclusions[1]

THE background for the development of the rococo was furnished by French architecture and decoration of the reign of Louis XIV to the end of the seventeenth century. Italian baroque influence was felt most strongly during his minority and early personal rule, when, in 1639-1650, Stefano della Bella and, in 1644-1658, Romanelli were working in Paris and when, in the years between 1642 and 1656, Le Brun, Puget, Michel Anguier, Girardon, and Mignard returned from years in Rome, where they had been keenly alive to the contemporary high-baroque, especially in the work of Pietro da Cortona. In their work the whole repertory of high-baroque forms, heavily plastic, was naturalized in France, but without evoking the rococo. The visit of Bernini in 1665 marks the apogee of Italian prestige; its disappointing outcome marks the downfall of Italian supremacy and the end of French artistic subjection.

The founding of the Academy at Rome in 1666, of the Academy of Architecture in 1670, represented a reaction against the height of baroque tendency in France. During the central period of Louis XIV's reign there followed, in artistic theory, a triumph of academism, in actual practise, a progressive enfranchisement of French creative effort. While in the architecture of interiors the plastic baroque forms were subordinated to a tectonic treatment of panelling, almost purely geometric and with multiplied superposition of elements, in painted surface ornament a new development, purely French, was going forward, above all in the arabesque, which abandoned both the mannerist type of Vouet and the Raphaelesque adaptations of Errard. Bandwork, mingled with acanthus foliage in the patterns of embroiderers and of *parterres en broderie* by gardeners like Mollet and Boyceau, was taken up into painted arabesque by Le Brun, in the characteristic form of C-scrolls connected by short straight bars, with palmettes radiating from the junction of opposite scrolls. This innovation was given an immense and fertile exploitation in the arabesque of Jean Berain, a French product of a man who had never been in Italy. His architectural forms remained massive, his arabesque remained a surface ornament confined strictly within the geometric outline of the panels.

The essential creative act in the genesis of the rococo was performed by Pierre Lepautre (*c.* 1648-1716), on his appointment in 1699 as Dessinateur in the Bâtiments, in designing changes at Marly. Taking elements of the painted arabesque of Berain, he transposed it from the flat to relief, from a panel-filling to a frame, superseding the rigid geometry of assemblage. This frame of delicate plastic arabesque elements replaced any massive architectural treatment. The monumental academism of Mansart and Le Brun's Grand Galerie, the complex and broken architectural mannerism of Berain, the tectonic articulation and superposition of Lassurance, alike gave place to a delicate linear organism, with unified verticality, attenuated proportions and slight relief. Contrary to received opinion, spatial impulses were not determining factors in this genesis, which took place chiefly within the pre-

---

[1] These were embodied in a paper presented at the Fifteenth International Congress of the History of Art in London, July, 1939, and published in the *Journal of the Warburg and Courtauld Institutes*, IV, 1940-1941, 119-123, here revised in accordance with further researches.

existing walls of rooms of simple and indifferent form. Although certain Italian baroque motifs (already so long domesticated in France) survived, transformed, in Lepautre's work, the decisive factor in the genesis of the Louis XV style was thus not Italian influence but a purely French initiative. The derivative elements, French and Italian alike, were fused in a new creation, essentially distinct from either.

Lepautre was the actual designer of a long series of genial decorative works which gave lustre to the last years of Louis XIV. These furnished the inspiration for the works of the following reign, and thus initiated the whole evolution of the rococo.

In this period 1699-1715, which was decisive for the subsequent development, none of the other architectural designers played a rôle at all comparable in importance with that of Pierre Lepautre. To Boffrand has been given an undue degree of credit; his surviving interiors from this time follow the lead of Lepautre with only minor contributions of his own. Oppenord's early works are of pronounced Italian high-baroque character. Little employed at first, he fell meanwhile under the influence of Berain and Lepautre. From 1712, Vassé began to take a position of leadership.

From the accession of Louis XV, coincident with the death of Lepautre, the lead was held by Oppenord, appointed architect of the Regent, and by Vassé, henceforth the right-hand man of Robert de Cotte. They pursued the line struck out by Lepautre, as may well be seen by the general dependence on the Salon d'Hercule of Oppenord's hemicycle at the Palais-Royal, 1717, and of Vassé Galerie Dorée at the Hôtel de Toulouse, 1718-1719. In the work of both men there was richer use of sculptural and figural motives, a progressive enfranchisement from geometry in favour of flowing line. The greater survival of undigested baroque elements of plastic character in their work, disappearing in the sequel, is typical of a moment of "transition after the fact," universal in the process of artistic creation and evolution.

A new phase of the movement, the "genre pittoresque," characterized by asymmetry, was inaugurated in interiors by the sculptor Nicolas Pineau after his return from Russia. While his work there had followed essentially Lepautre's creative initiative before Pineau's departure in 1716, on his return (some time after 1727) he soon assumed the leadership. In the introduction of asymmetry in French decorative art he was preceded by Meissonnier, who had adopted it in designs for silversmith's work as early as 1728, but the earliest datable designs for interiors by Meissonnier are later than the decisive works of Pineau in the Hôtel de Rouillé, c. 1732, in the gallery of the Hôtel de Villars, 1732-1733, and in the Hôtel de Roquelaure, 1733 ff. The latest work we can authenticate as Pineau's was in the Hôtel de Villeroy (Desmares) as remodelled in 1746; the last masterpiece of the *genre pittoresque* in French interiors was the remodelling of the Hôtel de Maisons (de Soyecourt) completed about 1750.

No fundamentally new impulse in this direction was felt in French decoration after this time. The work of Gabriel and Verberckt in the royal châteaux to after 1760 merely continued the conservative phase of the movement. In the work of Contant at the Palais-Royal and elsewhere during the early 'fifties, reaction was already beginning, before Cochin published his attack and ironic defense in 1754 and 1755. No sharp break occurred, however, before the sudden turn in Gabriel's work at the Petit Trianon (1762-1768) which we attribute even more to the influence of English Palladian models than to the growing direct

Conclusions

interest in the antique. The English classical revivalism of Robert Adam, from 1759, which began to be followed in France about 1770, was to give the rococo its *coup de grace*.

The art of the rococo, one of the freshest artistic creations since the Gothic, was, like the Gothic, a product of French creative genius. We have seen that the creative leadership was held in successive artistic generations of nearly equal duration by Jean Berain and Lassurance from 1684 to 1699, by Pierre Lepautre from 1699 to 1712, by François-Antoine Vassé and Oppenord from 1712 to 1730, by Meissonnier and Nicolas Pineau from 1730 to 1745 or 1750. Then came the beginnings of reaction, with the negative ideal of academism, a reaction first led, under Tournehem, from 1745, by laymen and amateurs like Caylus, Mariette, and Leblanc, then under Marigny, after 1750, by Cochin and Soufflot. From about 1760 came the influence of English classicism, which triumphed around 1774 on the accession of Louis XVI.

Epilogue

TO discuss the expansion of the rococo, which swept the western world and its colonies, with isolated penetrations of the Orient,[1] is beyond our province here. We shall speak of this expansion only so far as it throws light on the nature of the rococo itself, and on the ideas which have been held of its nature.

We do not even enlarge on the diffusion of the rococo in provincial France, where the initiative of the Court and of Paris, center of its creation, was naturally everywhere followed in the attempt to conform to the fashionable mode as closely as possible. From the time of Louis XIV, the effort toward centralization in France was so successful that local initiative, local variety were largely destroyed. French work of the eighteenth century not directly from designs of artists of the Crown and of the metropolis can only be regarded as provincial in greater or less degree, provincial not, as earlier, in the sense of being racily regional, but of being imitative — more or less happily, more or less haltingly. This is often true also of work executed by local craftsmen on designs sent from Paris, with an effect, at best, of inferiority, at worst, of caricature. Only in the South does the work depart sufficiently from the reigning style to gain, occasionally, a distinct artistic character of its own. On the other hand, in Lorraine, with its fiction of independence, its real advantage of having a monarch, a capital and a Court, a monarch passionately devoted to building, it is hard to see more, in the proud effort to rival Parisian work, than an imitative provincial version, exceptionally accomplished and successful. Revisiting the squares of Nancy, loved and admired since student days, I could not overcome a feeling that, by contrast with the magisterial self-confidence of Versailles and the Parisian monuments, the buildings of Héré have a touch of ingenuous timidity, which even the virtuosity of Jean Lamour cannot efface.

In Germany, in Italy, to a less degree in Spain and England and Russia, it was otherwise. Here the rococo, on its adoption from France, took on a national character, which indeed was differentiated in many minor local variants.

Immense study has been given to the rococo of Germany, less to that of Spain and Italy, very little to that of England,[2] where the style had small vogue except in furniture. This study has included two aspects. One, constituting the history of taste, has defined the propagation of French influence by designs sent from Paris, by French artists working abroad, by foreign artists visiting or studying in France, and by engraved publications of French designs. The other, constituting the history of art, has analysed the individual character of single monuments, and the generic character of the bodies of monuments, in other countries, establishing their right to independent consideration as authentic creative works, having an existence and a validity independent of their derivation.

A new history of the rococo outside of France could take into account the clearer understanding we have gained of the nature of the French rococo, and of its successive phases in

---

[1] A room from Damascus shown in 1913 at the Victoria and Albert Museum, and lately offered in the New York art market as of 1550 A.D., is actually derivative from French work of the early eighteenth century.

[2] F. Kimball and Edna Donnell: "The Creators of the Chippendale Style" in *Metropolitan Museum Studies*, I, 1929, 115-154. The inspiration of Matthias Lock and H. Copland, the English pioneers, from 1740 onward, seems to have come partly from the engraved plates of Cuvilliès.

The Creation of the Rococo

France, each of which started a new wave of influence abroad. One could now distinguish more precisely the effects of these waves of influence, felt with varying degrees of retardation: first the foreign embodiment of the inventions of the last years of Louis XIV as reflected in the designs of De Cotte and of Boffrand for Spain and Germany, and in the work of such native artists as Balthasar Neumann — where there is also so much that is of Italian baroque derivation, fused in a union which is native and his own. Then, the advent of the *genre pittoresque*, as with Cuvilliès in Germany, its adoption and transformation by a hundred gifted native artists in different countries. Such gains in comprehension of the foreign work, however, would be relatively small. The fact is that — as in the case of other great original styles, the French Gothic, the Italian Renaissance — foreign work missed the essential character of its models while gaining, happily, a different character of its own, a character which, in Germany at least, has been much more fully studied and better understood there than has been the nature of the French work itself.

It is not the foreign work which has failed of comprehension by foreign scholars, but the French work, to which they have been all too ready to transfer and apply deductions as to the essential character of the rococo based on its transformations in their own countries.

Everyone realizes that in Germany the new French forms had a particularly sympathetic reception and enjoyed a fruitful native development, beginning some time after their genesis and extending long after their abandonment in France; that these forms found in Germany application on the exterior of buildings and more extensive use in religious architecture; that their use there exceeded that in France in fantasy if not in discipline. We may remark, however, that in the work of native German artists the superficial linear forms of the French Louis XV were crossed with a highly vital, baroque art, having all the baroque interest in spatial and plastic variety. This was done with such success that, in spite of the fundamental disparity of the parents, the resulting new hybrids are true and living works of art, which we see with ever growing delight. It is these German works, with their baroque heritage, which have misled many scholars into supposing that the rococo issued directly from the baroque — as a necessary "last phase,"[3] and that its character can be analysed on that basis. We have seen, genetically, the fallacy of this supposition.

We are now in a position to review more intelligently the various ideas which have thus been advanced in the past as to the essential character of the rococo.

As a corollary of the functional theory of the mid-nineteenth century, Gottfried Semper inaugurated the attempt to interpret the rococo as *Stoffstil*[4] with the plastic character of its ornament closely related to the genesis of European porcelain. The actual course of events belies this view. Böttger's discovery, at Meissen about 1710, of the way to make porcelain was wholly irrelated to the beginning of the rococo, which had its genesis in France a decade earlier. Von Zahn, recognizing this irrelation, emphasized the adaptation of the forms to execution in stucco. Again the idea was unhistorical. The ornaments of the rococo — in their first use in the panelling of walls, preceding their application in cornices and ceilings — were carved in the hardest oak, as they always continued to be at the French Court.

[3] Brinckmann in his *Baukunst des 17. u. 18 Jahrhunderts*, 239, is a notable exception. In his edition of *Die Kunst des Rokoko*, 1940, 146, however, he writes "Rokoko ist die organische Entfaltung des Barock."

[4] Cf. A. von Zahn: "Barock, Rococo, und Zopf," in *Zeitschrift für Bildende Kunst*, 1873.

Epilogue

A first attempt to analyse the formal character of the rococo was also made by Semper.[5] Concentrating his attention (rightly, as we now see) on the treatment of surface, he found "the true idea of the Rococo," in that the framework becomes "organic," in the biological sense. "The frame," he said, "embraces the field plant-like, twines about it like a living organism . . . The constructive framework dissolves in flowing elements . . . resisting regulations." The frame certainly ceased to be tectonic and became fanciful. Its ultimate resemblance, in some instances, to vegetal growth was a superficial one, not rooted in the genesis of the style. It is cruel but not unjustified to compare Semper's idea with the old belief that the suggestion of Gothic architecture had come to the the northern barbarians from their forest aisles, to which only the later, not the initial phases of Gothic had any great similarity.

Jessen[6] and Geymüller[7] found the characteristics of the style not only in flowing lines but in naturalism — a property likewise inadequate as a differentia. Schmarsow[8] sought to generalize the contrast of baroque and rococo as plastic and painterly, and interpreted the rococo as "malerisch gewordene Kunst im eminenten Sinn," its organization as a unity of the plastic and the spatial. "Im Augenschein verfliesst die Organizasion wie die Krystallisation zu einem gememsamen Eindruck, in dem wir allein des Zusammenhanges alle Dinge als solche inne werden . . . Jede Eigenschaft des Materie verschwindet, jede Form verschwimmt, jede Farbe verduftet in der Region, wo über alle Zeugnisse unsrer Sinne sonst der Augenschien als Bild sein Recht verlangt." It is a marvellous characterization not of the French work Schmarsow was discussing, but of the German rococo. He admirably analysed, indeed, the spatial characteristics of the French hôtels, to which they held almost uniformly from a period before the genesis of the rococo to a period after its disappearance. He missed only the essential, the linear organization of surface through the transformation of the frame on the suggestion of the arabesque — a linear organization rejecting plasticity and largely indifferent to spatial or painterly effects.

Schmarsow illustrates, in a dozen instances, the fallacies of superficial theorizing. The rococo, for him, was the creation of Watteau, a Fleming, of Meissonnier, an Italian, and of Op den Oordt, a Dutchman. First and foremost, of course, of a painter, whose indebtedness was primarily to the great baroque Fleming, Rubens, and whose activity preceded the full development of the architectural rococo. For Schmarsow, the Frenchmen Berain and Audran, Pierre Lepautre and Vassé, none of whom had ever crossed the Alps or the Sambre, might never have existed; he does not so much as mention them. The altar and ornaments of the Chapel and the Salon d'Hercule at Versailles, the stalls and thrones of Notre Dame, he likewise passes over in silence. By thus presuming the onset of the rococo to have occurred as late as 1715 or 1720, and by equating it in architecture and decoration with the two men whose work was least fully characteristic of France, Schmarsow readily established his views, which are still widely repeated.

Brinckman[9] operated, in the rococo as in the baroque, entirely with spatial and plastic con-

---

[5] Der Stil, II, 1863, 333.

[6] Das Ornament des Rococo, 1894, 12-17.

[7] Op. cit., 261 ff.

[8] Barock und Rokoko, 1897, 341 ff.

[9] Baukunst des 17. und 18. Jahrhunderts in den romanischen Ländern, 1919, 246-247, 256; Kunst des Rokoko, 149-150. Of his Geist der Nationen: Italiener, Franzosen, Deutsche, 1939, reviewed in the Burlington

cepts. In his analysis of the "plastic mass" of the French rococo, he was applying criteria really foreign to the style. That he had to go as far as Lyons for a pier to illustrate his conception of the hollowing of the mass shows, indeed, how far from central to the style this conception was. Thus he was led to reduce to little more than a single paragraph the discussion of "decoration and ornament," with the linear organization of the flat surface which we find so important. He abandoned even the effort to follow the development of these elements and to correct previous discussion of it by writers who, he said, were led astray by the numerous ornamentalists into thinking that the essence of the rococo is to be found in the evolution of such forms.

Rather than consider that the essence of the rococo must include all the characteristics found in work of the period in Germany, we consider that—just as Gothic elements are there mingled with Italian elements in the early Renaissance—baroque elements are there united with the new French forms of the rococo.

Certain other supposed contrasts between the rococo in France and in Germany are to be explained, not so much by difference in national traits, as in part by the belated adoption in Germany of features from earlier times in France, and, in part by the accident of survival of monuments in Germany when the French monuments have suffered so much greater destruction. Thus the building of great stair halls in the German palaces of the rococo was stimulated not only by Italian examples—closer to them in basic form—but by the Escalier du Roi at Versailles, so soon destroyed. Whereas it had the tempered classicism of 1675, they were brought up to date with the ornaments of 1725 or later. So too, the cabinets of mirrors, which we today associate with the German and Italian rococo, are the belated descendants, with later finery, of those in France which ceased to multiply there, indeed began to be remodelled, after 1700, and had mostly disappeared by 1755.

The relatively late adoption of the style in Germany and elsewhere was also responsible for the larger influence there of Meissonnier and Oppenord, and thus likewise for the supposition by modern scholars that they were the true creators and most characteristic artists of the rococo. Although Oppenord's chief creative period was from 1715 to 1730 and Meissonnier's was but little later, their engraved works, issued belatedly, or even (in the case of Oppenord) posthumously, scarcely became influential before the 'fifties. This was the very moment when Germany was most receptive. Such handsome folios, just issued, were naturally supposed to represent the latest French fashion. Actually their publication represented not the *dernier cri* but the last gasp of the *genre pittoresque*. Their reception was all the more eager precisely because of the baroque, Italianate admixture which renders the architectural works of these two masters actually exceptional in the French rococo, and even, in the case of Meissonnier, uncharacteristic of it. One may thus readily understand how a false conception of their position, and of the style itself, should have grown up.

Hans Rose[10] attempted to equate "late baroque" with the phase of European style under French dominance, from the time of Colbert onward, achieving in Germany, like the Gothic,

---

Magazine, October, 1939, I was unable to secure any copy in America until after this manuscript had gone to press. His attempt to relate the history of forms with abiding national characteristics suffers, like other such attempts, both from the fallacy of positive instances and from confusion of supposed national factors with the temporal factor of delay in the adoption of new forms developed elsewhere.

[10] *Spätbarock*, 1922, especially p. ix.

Epilogue

a last, unconditional greatness. The rococo he regarded merely as a subordinate aspect of this late baroque, "die private Adelskunst im Gegensatz zür höfisch-souvränen Kunst," marked by cosmopolitan elegance, acquiring the upper hand in the eighteenth century. This overlooks, on the one hand, the antithesis of formal characteristics of baroque and rococo, on the other, the essential coherence of French royal and private work, and the precedence of royal initiative in the earlier phases of the creation of the rococo.

Rose attempted[11] to draw a contrast between personal, individual values characteristic of the art of the high-baroque and values merely representative of social rank, which he considers characteristic of the late baroque and rococo. He regarded as inherent in the nature of this contrast a supposed inability to establish in these later periods, under absolutism, even the most important relations of master and pupil, and the attribution of works to individual artistic personalities. We have seen that, as formerly in the case of the art of the Middle Ages, the supposed lack of individuality of the artist is apt to be often merely a reflection of our ignorance of his identity, due to inadequate preservation and study of the monuments and documents.

In quite another manner the influence of absolutism is indeed to be observed under Louis XIV and in the earlier years of Louis XV—namely, in the successive placing of creative individual artists in official positions where substantially all the important work of a certain span of years was from a single hand. We have observed, however, that the crucial position was not, per se, as has been supposed, that of Surintendant or Director, but of Dessinateur. The true creative artist, as in other periods, was the designer whose hand actually held the pencil.

Confusion has likewise attended the end of the rococo. Giedion,[12] basing his discussion primarily on the German monuments, distinguished a late-baroque classicism ("Rokokoklassizismus, Zopf, Louis XVI") and a romantic classicism, the latter appearing shortly before 1800 with such men as Gilly and Schinkel. Actually "baroque classicism" was again a provincial hybrid of old and new, appearing peripherally to a new movement, just as had appeared what might be called the "baroque rococo" of Germany. If we examine neo-classicism at its center, in England, and above all in the work of its creators themselves, such as Burlington and Adam, we find the true transition very brief, the enfranchisement from the baroque very early and complete. Then follows the so-called transition—the mingling of old and new, or compromise after the fact—in the work of French leaders taking up the foreign initiative (late Louis XV), and of designers in Germany influenced partly from England but more largely, at second hand, from France. Later both French and German classicism achieved independence, co-ordinate with later English classicism.

Our own view, as illustrated in this book, is that the history of art at this or at any period should not be forcibly subjected to chronological, sociological or systematic concepts, but should be so ordered as to follow out the lines of purely artistic movements in their actual initiation and development. As always in artistic creation, these movements were initiated by individuals, the subsequent development of their fruitful ideas was made by other individual artists. The baroque was one such creative movement of great sweep, embracing sculpture, architecture, and painting, initiated chiefly by Michelangelo, developed by artists of the

---

[11] E.g., pp. 1, 231.
[12] *Spätbarocker und romantischer Klassizimus*, 1922.

The Creation of the Rococo

stature of Tintoretto and Rubens, Bernini and Borromini. The rococo was another, of less scope and duration, primarily in the field of decoration though with parallels in the other arts, initiated by Pierre Lepautre, developed most fruitfully by Vassé and Oppenord, by Meissonnier and Pineau. Classicism, which brought it to an end, was a third, initiated in architecture and decoration by Burlington and Adam. All these movements, in their expansion and diffusion, encountered survivals of other artistic movements, and, according to the creative power of individual artists, evoked merely provincial imitations of no true value, variants with valid artistic qualities, or hybrids having their own deep originality.

Index

References to figures are given in italics.

Index

Index

Index

Index

[239]

Index

Index

Illustrations

Figure 2. Louvre: Galerie d'Apollon, 1661–1677.

Figure 1. Vaux-le-Vicomte: Salle à Manger, about 1660.

Figure 3. Versailles: Cabinet des Bains, 1672.

Figure 4. Versailles: Escalier du Roi, 1674-1678.

Figure 8. Arabesque design by Le Brun.

Figure 6. Embroidered border drawn by Georges Boissonet, 1610.

Figure 7. Marble intarsia of Santa Maria del Carmine, Naples.

Figure 5. Plan for a parterre by Boyceau, 1638.

Figure 10. Ceiling panel of the Galerie d'Apollon, about 1670.
Engraved by Berain.

Figure 9. Wall panel of the Galerie d'Apollon, about 1670.
Engraved by Berain.

Figure 11. Clagny: Section of the gallery, 1674-1678.

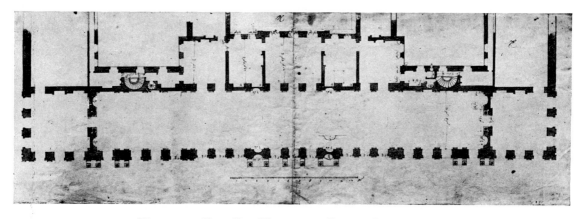

Figure 12. Versailles: Plan for the Grande Galerie, 1678.

Figure 13. Versailles: Half-elevation of the gallery, 1679. Atelier of Le Brun.

Figure 15. Versailles: Elevation of the Salon de la Guerre.
Atelier of Le Brun.

Figure 14. Detail of Figure 13.

Figure 16. Versailles: Chambre and Cabinet du Roi, 1679.

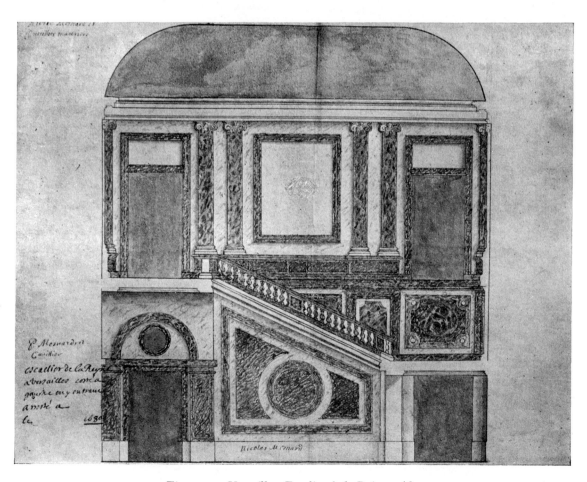

Figure 17. Versailles: Escalier de la Reine, 1680.

Figure 18. Versailles: Escalier de la Reine, 1680.

Figure 19. Versailles: Salles des Gardes de la Reine, 1679-1681.

Figure 20. Versailles: Chambre du Roi, 1684.

Figure 21. Versailles: Cabinet du Billard, 1684.
Engraved by Pierre Lepautre.

Figure 22. Versailles: Cabinet du Conseil,
1684.

Figure 23. Versailles: Project for the Petite Galerie, 1685. Designed by Lassurance.

Figure 24. Versailles: Floor of the Petite Galerie, 1685.

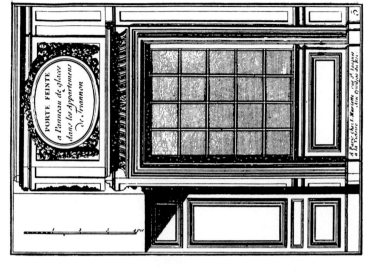

Figures 25–27. Trianon: Interiors of 1686–1688. Engraved by Pierre Lepautre.

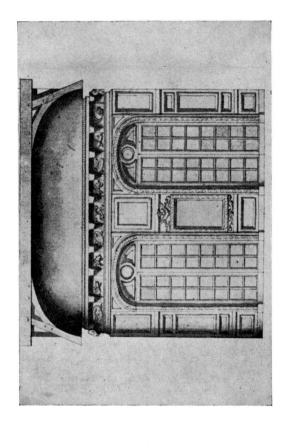
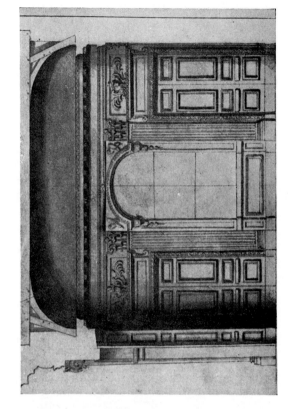
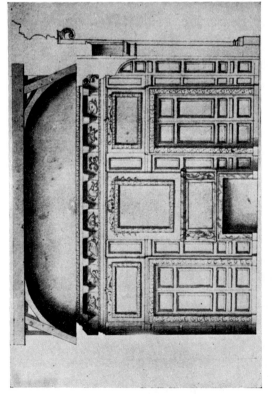

Figures 28–31. Trianon: Appartement du Roi, Aile Gauche, 1692. Designs by Lassurance.

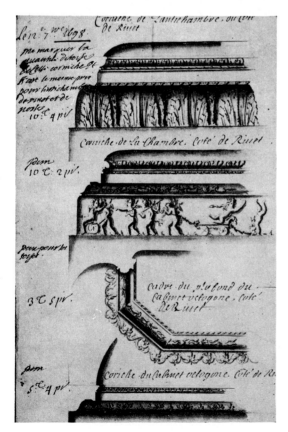

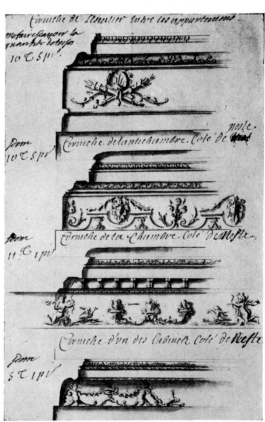

Figure 32. Versailles: Salon Ovale, 1692. Design by Lassurance.
Figure 33. Trianon: Chambre de la Duchesse de Bourgogne, 1698. Design by Lassurance.
Figures 34–36. Versailles: Château de la Ménagerie. Interiors and details. Designs by Lassurance.

Figures 37–38. Versailles: Château de la Ménagerie. Appartement d'Été, 1698-1699.
Designs by Lassurance.

Figures 39–41. Hôtel de Mailly: Ceilings and arabesques designed by Berain.

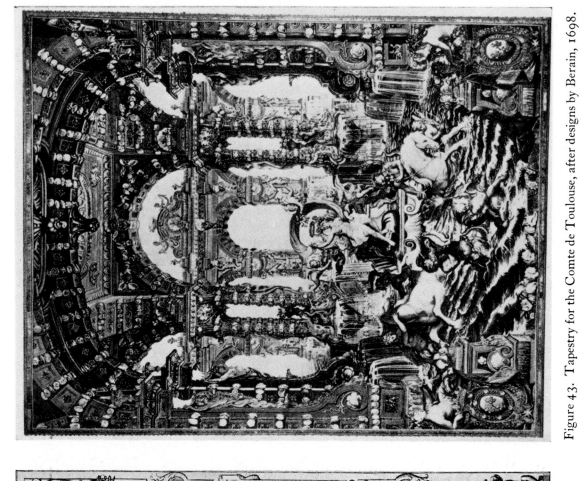

Figure 43. Tapestry for the Comte de Toulouse, after designs by Berain, 1698.

Figure 42. Berain arabesque engraved before 1693.

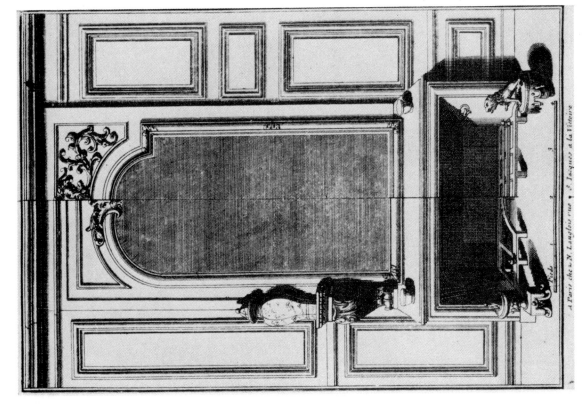

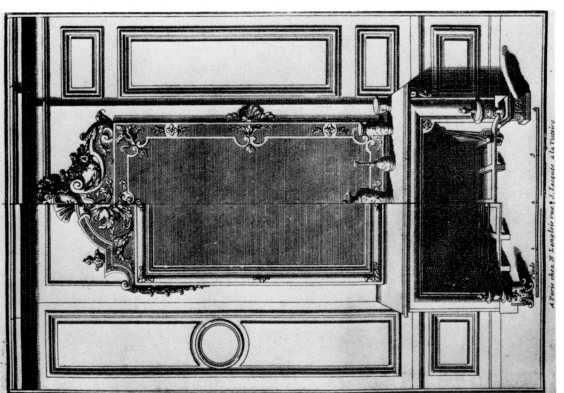

Figures 44–45. *Cheminées à la royalle.* Engraved by Pierre Lepautre, about 1698.

Figure 46. Meudon: Cabinet du Dauphin, March-June, 1699. Designed by Berain.

Figure 47. Marly: Grand Salon, as remodelled 1699 ff.

Figures 48–49. Marly: Chambre du Roi, 1699. Designs by Pierre Lepautre.

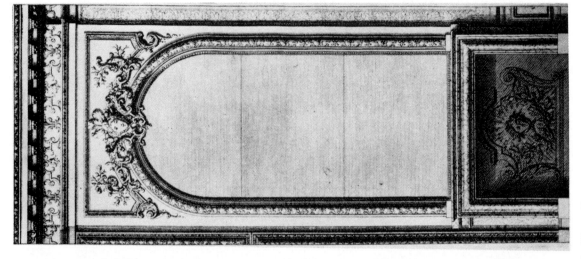

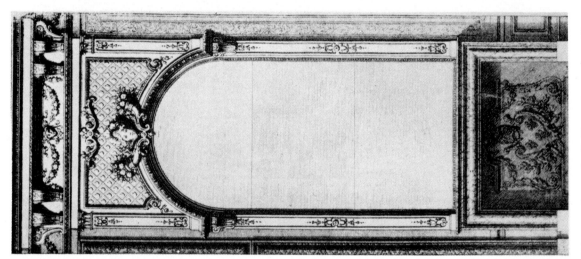

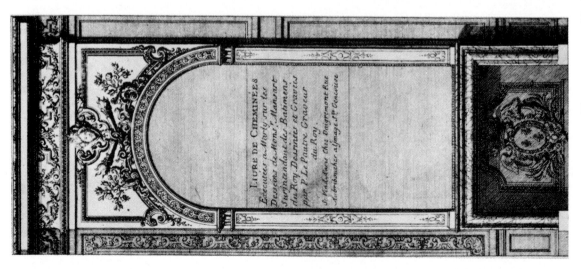

LIURE DE CHEMINÉES
Executée a Marly sur les
Desseins de Mons.ʳ Mansart
Surintendant des Batiments
du Roy. Desinée et Gravés
par P. Le Pautre Graveur
du Roy.
A Paris chez Duqrement rue
S.ᵗ Jaques a l'image S.ᵗ Geneuieue

Figures 50–52. Marly: Chimney pieces, April–December, 1699. Engraved by Pierre Lepautre.

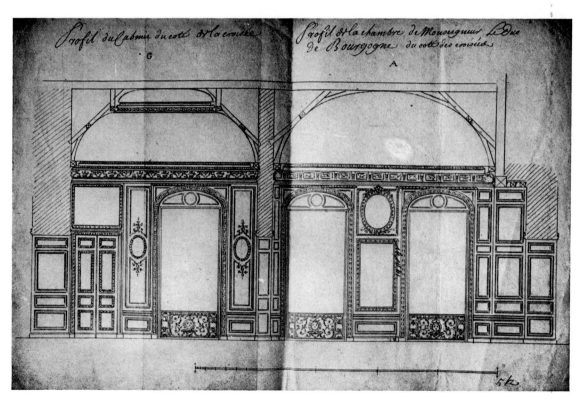

Figures 53–54. Versailles: Appartement de Nuit of the Duc de Bourgogne, 1699.

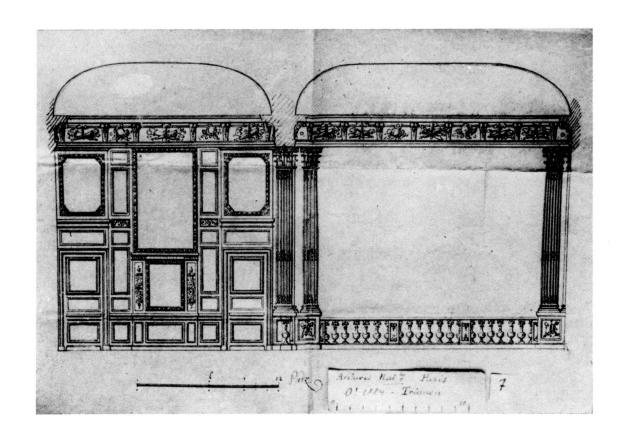

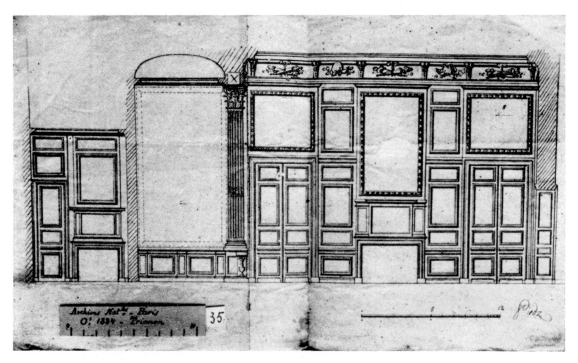

Figures 55–56. Trianon: Chambre du Roi, Aile Gauche, February, 1700. Designs of Carlier.

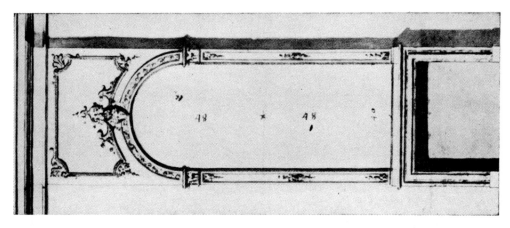

Figures 58–59. Versailles: Chimney pieces, 1700.

Figure 57. Versailles: Chimney pieces, 1699–1700.
Engraved by Pierre Lepautre.

Figures 60–61. Versailles: Chambre du Roi, 1701. Designs by Pierre Lepautre.

Figure 62. Versailles: Chambre du Roi, 1701.

Figure 63. Versailles: Antichambre de l'Oeil-de-Boeuf, 1701.

Figure 64. Versailles: Cabinet du Conseil, 1701, remodelled 1755-1756.

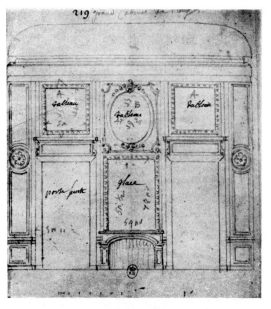

Figure 65. Grand Cabinet, first study.

Figure 66. Grand Cabinet, final design.

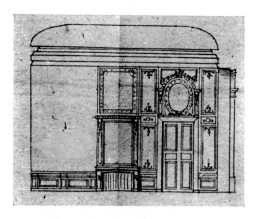

Figure 67. Chambre du Roi.

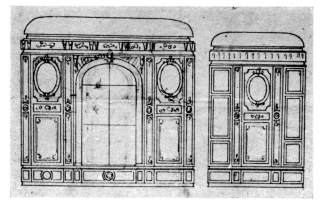

Figure 68. Cabinets. Inner walls.

Figure 69. Window walls of the apartment.

Figures 65–69. Trianon: Appartement du Roi, 1703. Atelier of De Cotte.

Figures 70–72. Trianon: Cornices, 1703-1706. Engraved by Pierre Lepautre.

Figure 73. Trianon: Salon de la Chapelle, 1706. Engraved by Pierre Lepautre.

Figure 74. Trianon: Cabinet des Glaces, 1706. Engraved by Pierre Lepautre.

Figure 75. Project for the altar of Notre Dame, 1699. Design by Pierre Lepautre.

Figure 76. Medal of the altar of Notre Dame, 1699.

Figures 77–79. Projects for the Choir of Notre Dame, 1703.
Designs by Pierre Lepautre.

Figure 80. Orléans: Stalls of the Cathedral, 1702-1706.

Figure 81. Detail of a salon. Engraved by Pierre Lepautre.

Figure 82. Versailles: Project for the high altar of the Chapel, 1707-1708. Design by Pierre Lepautre.

Figure 83. Versailles: Altar of the Chapel
of the Virgin, 1707-1708.
Design by Pierre Lepautre.

Figure 84. Versailles: Oratories,
about 1710.
Drawing by A.-J. Gabriel.

Figure 85. Versailles: Details of a door of the Chapel, 1710.

Figure 87. Versailles: Organ of the Chapel, 1709–1710.

Figure 86. Versailles: Aisle of the Chapel.

Figure 89. Versailles: Project for the pavement of the Chapel.
Design by Pierre Lepautre.

Figure 88. Versailles: Pulpit of the Chapel.

Figure 91. Notre Dame: Jubé, before 1712. Design by Pierre Lepautre.

Figure 90. Notre Dame: Choir, before 1712. Design by Pierre Lepautre.

Figure 92. Notre Dame: Altar, 1712. Design by François-Antoine Vassé.

Figure 93. Notre Dame: Throne, 1711-1712.

Figure 95. Versailles: Salon d'Hercule, 1711 ff.

Figure 94. Notre Dame: Stalls, 1710-1711.
Design by Pierre Lepautre.

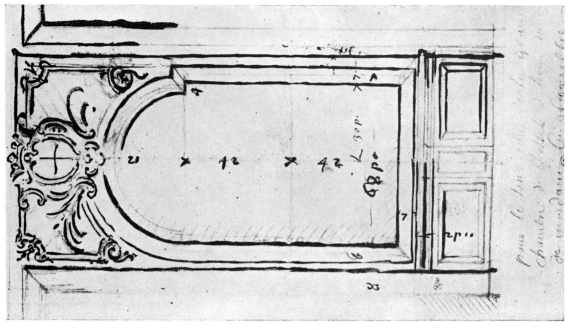

Figures 96–97. Hôtel de Pontchartrain (Chancellerie), 1703. Designs by Pierre Lepautre.

Figure 99. Bercy: Library, 1712.

Figure 98. Bercy: Grand Salon, 1712.

Figure 100. Petit-Luxembourg: Salon, 1710.

Figure 101. Petit-Luxembourg: Chambre d'Apparat, 1710.

Figure 102. Project for Salon of La Malgrange, by Boffrand, 1711.

Figure 103. Chimney pieces from Le Blond's edition, *Cours d'architecture*, 1710.

Figure 104. Project for the altar of Notre Dame,
1699. Design by Oppenord.

Figure 105. Altar of Saint-Germain-des-Prés,
1704. Design by Oppenord.

Figure 106. Amiens: Altar of Saint John,
1709.

Figure 107. Project for the altar of Saint-
Jacques de la Boucherie, 1712.

Figure 110. Design by Oppenord.

Figures 108–109. Hôtel de Pomponne: Wainscot, 1714.

Figure 111. Hôtel de Toulouse: Stairway, 1714-1715.

Figure 112. Besançon. Hôtel de Grammont: Chambre, 1714. Atelier of De Cotte.

Figure 116. Berain arabesque of the late period.

Figure 115. Berain arabesque, 1699.

Figures 113–114. Meudon: Ceilings, 1699.

Figure 118. *Mois grotesques*, 1708-1709.
Drawings after designs by Audran.

Figure 117. Versailles: Château de la Ménagerie, ceiling, 1700.
Design by Audran.

Figure 119. Palais-Royal: Chambre du Régent, 1716. Design by Oppenord.

Figure 120. Palais-Royal: Hemicycle of the gallery, 1717.

Figures 121–123. Palais-Royal: Projects for the Salon à l'Italienne, 1717.

Figures 124–125. Hôtel de Toulouse: Projects for the gallery, 1718. Designs by Vassé.

Figures 126–127. Hôtel de Toulouse: Gallery, 1718–1719.

Figures 131–132. Palais-Royal: Grands Appartements, 1720.

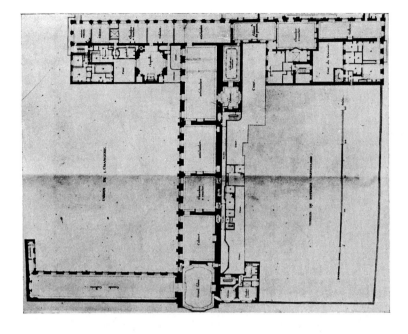

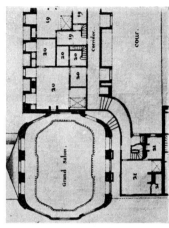

Figures 134–135. Palais-Royal: Plans.

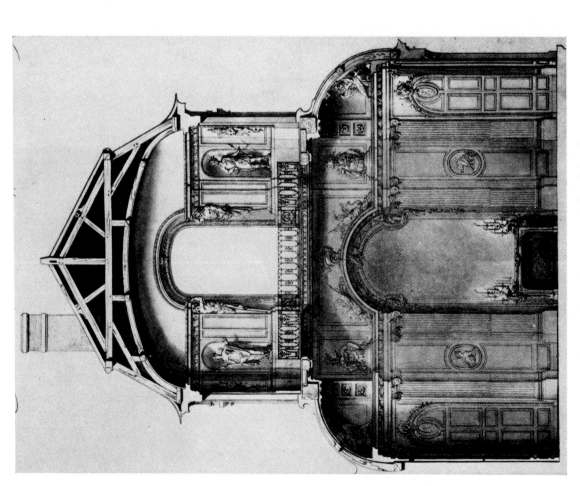

Figure 133. Palais-Royal: Project for the Salon d'Angle, 1719–1720.
Design by Oppenord.

Figures 136–137. Hôtel d'Assy: Salon, 1719.

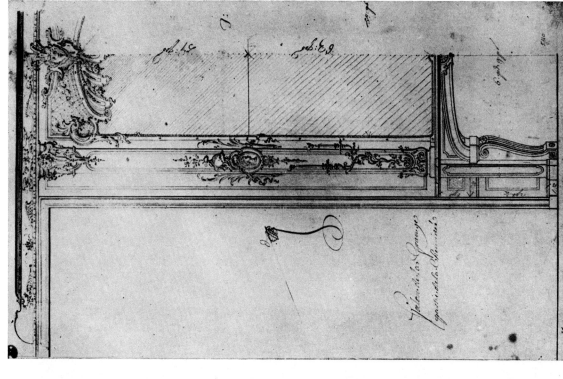

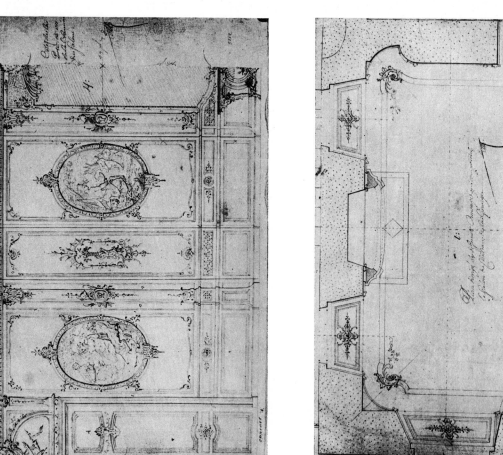

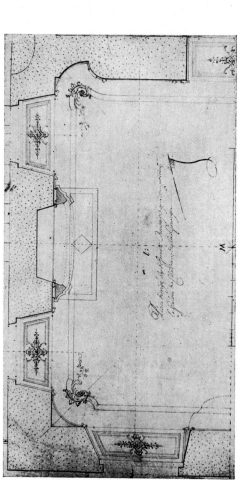

Figures 138–140. La Granja(?): Salon, about 1720. Designs by Oppenord.

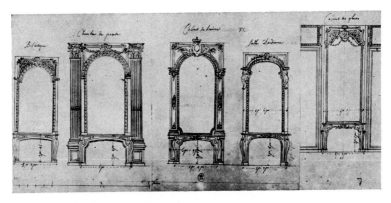

Figure 141. Bonn: Electoral Palace. Chimney pieces, 1716-1717.
Atelier of De Cotte.

Figures 142–147. Bonn: Buen Retiro, 1717. Atelier of De Cotte.

Figure 148. Hôtel de Bourvallais: Grand Salon, about 1717.

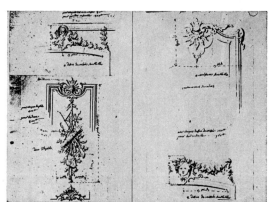

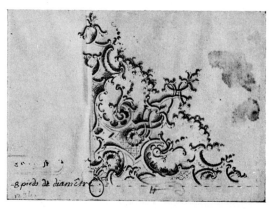

Figure 149. Versailles: Chambre du Régent, 1722.
Atelier of De Cotte.

Figures 150–151. Saverne: Appartement de Parade,
1721-1722. Atelier of De Cotte.

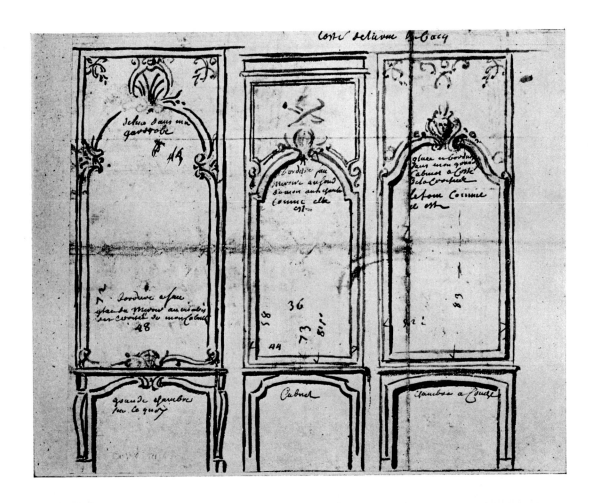

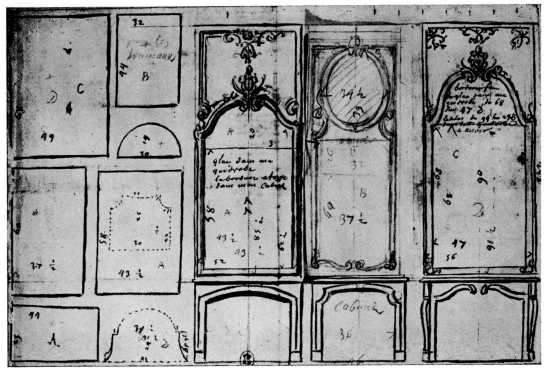

Figures 152–153. Hôtel de Cotte, 1721-1722. Designs by Robert de Cotte.

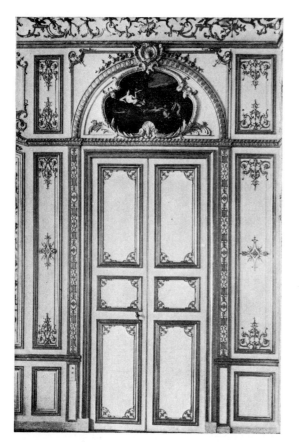

Figures 154–155. Hôtel de Villars: Salon, about 1716.

Figure 156. Hôtel de Parabère, 1718-1720.

Figure 157. Chantilly: Chambre de M. le Prince, 1722.

Figure 158. Chantilly: Salon de Musique, 1722.

Figures 159–161. Hôtel d'Évreux (Élysée) : Interiors, 1720.

Figure 163. Pier glass by A. Le Blond.

Figure 162. Peterhof: Cabinet of Peter the Great, about 1720.

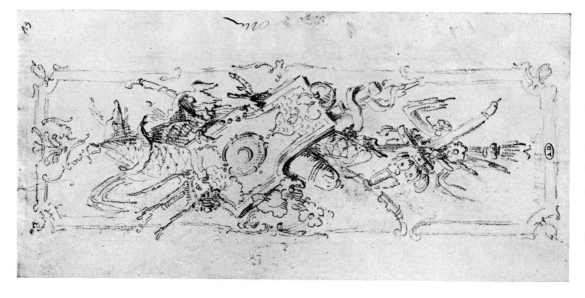

Figure 165. Design by Pineau.

Figure 164. Peterhof: Cabinet of Peter the Great.

Figures 166–169. Peterhof: Cabinet of Peter the Great. Details.

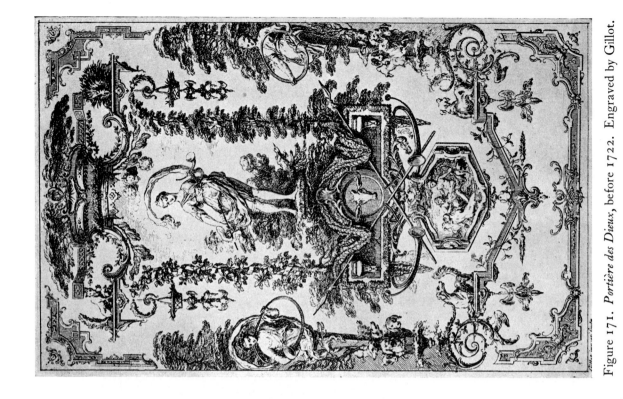

Figure 171. *Portière des Dieux*, before 1722. Engraved by Gillot.

Figure 170. Cartouche by Toro.

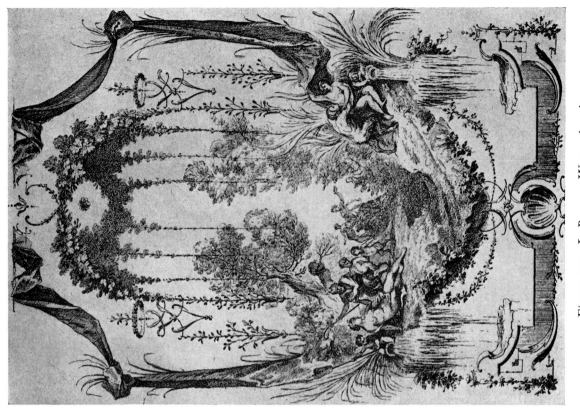

Figure 173. *Le Berceau. Watteau invenit.*

Figure 172. Arabesque. Design by Oppenord.

Figures 174–175. Versailles: Chambre de la Reine, 1730, 1735.

Figure 177. Clock, about 1735. Design by Vassé.

Figure 176. Versailles: Salon d'Hercule, 1711, 1729-1736.

Figure 178. Versailles: Cabinet en Niche de la Reine, about 1725. Atelier of De Cotte.

Figure 179. Bibliothèque Nationale: Cabinet du Roi, 1735-1741.

Figures 182–183. Sketches by Oppenord.

Figures 180–181. Hôtel d'Évreux (Élysée) : Grand Cabinet.

Figure 185. Hôtel d'Évreux: Grand Cabinet.

Figure 186. Sketches by Oppenord.

Figure 184. Hôtel d'Évreux (Élysée): Grand Salon.

Figure 187. Hôtel de Lassay: Grand Salon, after 1725.

Figures 188–189. Hôtel de Lassay: Ceilings, after 1725.

Figure 190. Chancellerie d'Orléans: Salon, about 1725.

Figure 191. Würzburg: Project for the Bishop's apartment, 1724.
Design by Boffrand and Castelli.

Antichambre.

Chambre à Coucher and Petit Cabinet.

"Antichambre où est la Chapelle"

Chambre à Coucher.

Figures 192–195. Hôtel de Roquelaure: Interiors, 1724-1726.

Figure 197. Hôtel de la Fare: Cabinet.

Figure 196. Hôtel de Roquelaure: Petit Cabinet, 1724–1726.

Figure 200. Monstrance for Notre Dame, 1708.

Figure 198. Weathervane for the Duc de Mortemart by Meissonnier, 1724.

Figure 199. Monstrance for the Carmelites of Poitiers by Meissonnier, 1727.

Figure 201. Candlestick by Meissonnier, 1728.

Figure 202. Surtout and Terrines by Meissonnier, 1735.

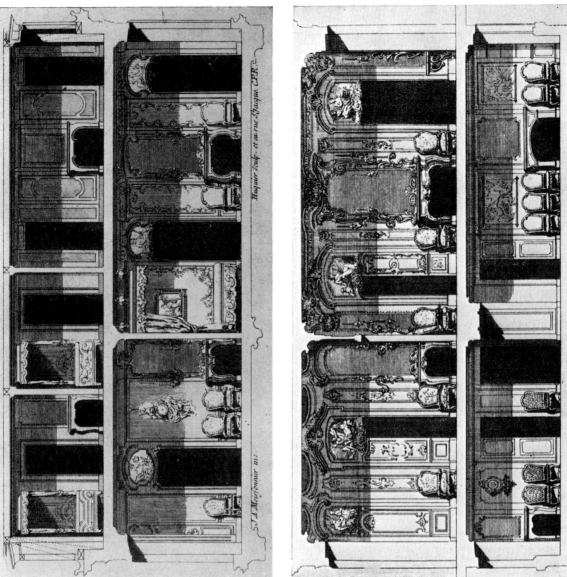

Figures 204–205. Bayonne: Maison du Sieur Brethous, 1733.

Figure 203. Saint-Sulpice: Project for a chapel by Meissonnier, 1727.

Figure 207. Apartment for the Baronne de Besenval, after 1736.

Figure 206. Cabinet of M. Bielenski, 1734.

Figures 208-210. Ornaments by Meissonnier, 1734.

Figure 212. Hôtel de Matignon:
Ceiling rosette of Salle à Manger,
about 1731.

Figure 211. Hôtel de Matignon: Antichambre, about 1731.

Figures 213–216. Hôtel de Rouillé: Interiors, about 1732.

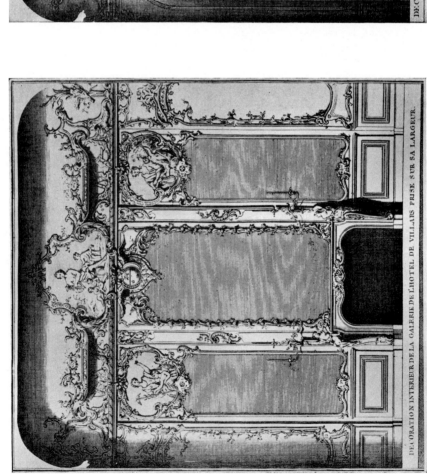

DÉCORATION INTÉRIEUR DE LA GALERIE DE L'HOTEL DE VILLARS PRISE SUR SA LARGEUR.

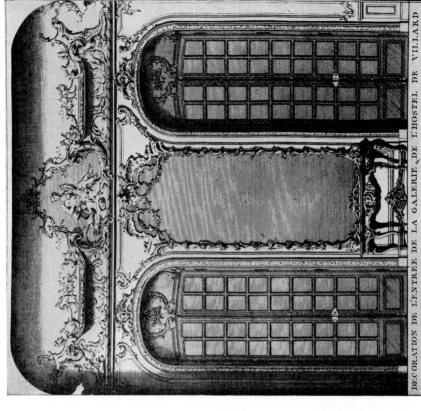

DÉCORATION DE L'ENTRÉE DE LA GALERIE DE L'HOSTEL DE VILLARD

Figures 217–218. Hôtel de Villars: Gallery, 1733.

Figure 219. Hôtel de Roquelaure: Mirror.
Design by Pineau.

Figure 220. Hôtel de Roquelaure:
Grand Salon, 1733.

Figure 221. Hôtel de Roquelaure: Salon Rouge, 1733.

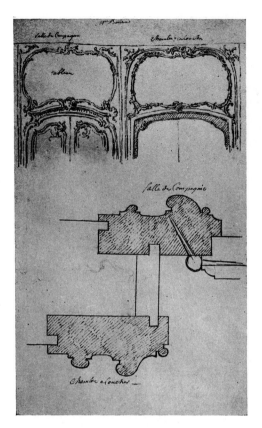

Figure 222. House of M. Boutin:
Salle de Compagnie, 1738.
Design by Pineau.

Figure 223. Chimney piece from
Blondel's *Maisons de Plaisance*,
1738.

Figure 224. Hôtel de Soubise: Project for a Salle de Compagnie, about 1732.

Figure 225. Chimney piece from Mariette's edition, *Cours d'architecture*, 1738.

Figure 226. *Morceau de fantaisie* by Lajoue, 1736.

Figure 227. Hôtel Bonnier de la Mosson: Overdoor of Cabinet, 1734. Painting by Lajoue.

Figure 228. *Forme rocquaille* by Mondon, 1736.

Figure 229. Cartouche by Cuvilliès, 1738.

Figure 230. Wainscot from Cuvilliès' *Livre de lambris*, about 1740.

Figure 232. Versailles: Chambre de Louis XV, 1738.

Figure 231. Versailles: Cabinet à Pans. Ceiling, before 1738. Design by Gabriel.

Figure 234. Versailles: Grand Cabinet de la Reine, 1738 ff. Design by Gabriel.

Figure 233. Versailles: Cabinet Ovale (de la Pendule), 1738.

Figure 235. Hôtel de Soubise: Chambre du Prince, 1736. Drawing after Boffrand.

Figure 236. Hôtel de Soubise: Chambre de la Princesse, about 1737.

Figure 237. Hôtel de Soubise: Salon du Prince, about 1737.

Figure 238. Hôtel de Soubise: Salon de la Princesse, 1738-1740.

Figures 239–240. Rambouillet: Salons, about 1735.

Figures 241–242. Rambouillet: Boudoir of the Comtesse de Toulouse, about 1735.

Figure 243. Versailles: Pièce à Pans de la Reine, 1746-1747. Design by Gabriel.

Figure 244. Versailles: Petit Cabinet de la Reine, 1746-1747. Design by Gabriel.

Figures 245–246. Versailles: Boudoir de la Reine, 1738, 1746-1747. Designs by Gabriel.

Figure 247. Salon de la Princesse Czartorinska, before 1750.

Figure 248. Hôtel de Villeroy: Salon, about 1746.

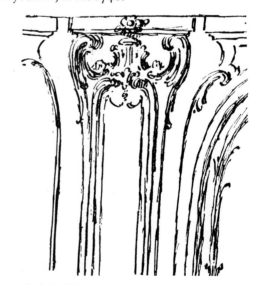

Figures 249–250. Ionic capitals by Pineau.

Figures 251–252. Hôtel de Maisons: Salle de Compagnie, about 1750.

Figure 253. Panels from Briseux' *Maisons de Campagne*, 1743. Engraved by Babel.

Figure 254. Hôtel Chanac de Pompadour: Petite Chambre à Coucher, about 1743.

Figure 255. Cartouche by Babel, about 1743.

Figure 256. Ornaments by Cuvilliès about 1753.

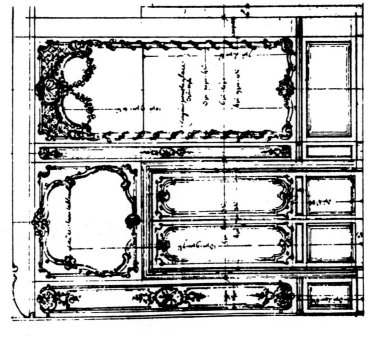

Figure 258. Bellevue. 1750-1752.
Design by Lassurance II.

Figure 257. Champs: Chambre à Coucher, 1747 ff.

Figure 259. Hôtel de Seignelay: Grand Salon, about 1752.

Plan du Lambris

Figure 260. House of M. Dodun: Grand Cabinet, about 1750.

Figure 261. Hôtel de Rohan: Cabinet des Singes, 1749-1752.

Figures 262–263. Hôtel Delisle-Mansart: Interiors, about 1750.

Figure 264. Hôtel d'Évreux: Grand Salon, about 1750.

Figure 265. Palais-Royal: Chambre de Parade, 1750-1752.

Figure 267. Fontainebleau: Chambre du Roi, 1752-1754.

Figure 266. Versailles: Cabinet de Madame Adelaïde, 1753, 1767.

Figure 268. Versailles: Cabinet d'Angle, 1754, 1760.

Figure 269. Fontainebleau: Antichambre du Roi, 1752-1754.

Figures 270–271. Petit Trianon: Early project, 1762. Designs by Gabriel.

Figure 272. Design from Robert Morris' *Select Architecture*,
before 1757.

Figure 273. Petit Trianon: Salle à Manger, 1768.

Figure 274. Petit Trianon: Salon, 1768.